Welfare States
in Transition

UNITED NATIONS RESEARCH INSTITUTE FOR SOCIAL DEVELOPMENT

The United Nations Research Institute for Social Development (UNRISD) is an autonomous agency that engages in multi-disciplinary research on the social dimensions of contemporary problems affecting development. Its work is guided by the conviction that, for effective development policies to be formulated, an understanding of the social and political context is crucial. The Institute attempts to provide governments, development agencies, grassroots organizations and scholars with a better understanding of how development policies and processes of economic, social and environmental change affect different social groups. Working through an extensive network of national research centres, UNRISD aims to promote original research and strengthen research capacity in developing countries.

Its research themes include Crisis, Adjustment and Social Change; Socio-Economic and Political Consequences of the International Trade in Illicit Drugs; Environment, Sustainable Development and Social Change; Ethnic Conflict and Development; Integrating Gender into Development Policy; Participation and Changes in Property Relations in Communist and Post-Communist Societies; Refugees, Returnees and Local Society; and Political Violence and Social Movements. UNRISD research projects focused on the 1995 World Summit for Social Development included Rethinking Social Development in the 1990s; Economic Restructuring and New Social Policies; Ethnic Diversity and Public Policies; and the War-Torn Societies Project.

A list of the Institute's free and priced publications can be obtained by writing to: UNRISD, Reference Centre, Palais des Nations, CH-1211, Geneva 10, Switzerland.

WELFARE STATES IN TRANSITION

National Adaptations in Global Economies

edited by
Gøsta Esping-Andersen

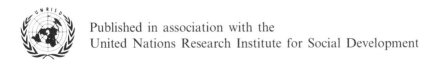

Published in association with the
United Nations Research Institute for Social Development

SAGE Publications
London • Thousand Oaks • New Delhi

© UNRISD 1996

First published 1996 Reprinted 1997

 SAGE Publications Ltd
6 Bonhill Street
London EC2A 4PU

SAGE Publications Inc
2455 Teller Road
Thousand Oaks, California 91320

SAGE Publications India Pvt Ltd
32, M-Block Market
Greater Kailash – I
New Delhi 110 048

British Library Cataloguing in Publication data

A catalogue record for this book is
available from the British Library

ISBN 0 7619 5047 8
ISBN 0 7619 5048 6 (pbk)

Library of Congress catalog card number 96–68418

Typeset by Mayhew Typesetting, Rhayader, Powys
Printed in Great Britain by The Cromwell Press Ltd,
Broughton Gifford, Melksham, Wiltshire

Contents

Foreword

The future of the welfare state, the theme of this book, is one of the most important social issues of our times. The publication of this book could not therefore be more timely as social policy everywhere is in a state of flux and is hence a subject of intense and passionate debate. The great virtue of this book is that it looks at the welfare state in a historical and comparative perspective, analysing its recent evolution and likely trends in the light of startling changes in recent years in economic policy, social structures and political configurations. The result is an admirable survey of the key forces shaping the welfare state in different regions of the world and an insightful exploration of alternative responses and options in an increasingly integrated global economy.

The welfare state is the culmination of a centuries-old struggle for social protection and security in the industrialized countries. It may justly be regarded as one of their proudest achievements in the post-war period. It set a model and a standard for aspiration for the newly industrializing and transitional countries as also for the poorer countries. All too often the welfare state is treated as a homogeneous entity and as an economic project. This book brings out clearly the rich diversity of the welfare state not only across different regions of the world but among the advanced industrialized countries themselves.

At the same time the book reveals the multifaceted character of the welfare state. It is at one and the same time a manifestation of a political community, an expression of social solidarity, and an attempt to eliminate destitution, reduce class differences and forge cohesive and stable communities. It has served as a defining element in national identity and citizenship. Now that the welfare state is under threat from powerful forces and interests, it is important to recall its encompassing mission and solid achievements in promoting economic security and well-being, human dignity and social solidarity, political participation and empowerment.

Almost everywhere the welfare state is under siege and is being recast in new directions. A number of forces have come together to question its viability, efficacy and utility. These forces include ageing of the population, changes in family structures, slowdown in economic growth, high levels of unemployment, soaring budget deficits, growing resistance to high taxes, ascendancy of market forces, privatization of economic and social activities, increasing national and international competition, accelerated globalization and technological change. The pressures exerted by these forces are being reinforced by new ideologies and powerful interests stressing the harmful economic, social and psychological effects of the operation of the welfare state. The result is that an increasing number of countries are dismantling key programmes, reducing the scope and diluting the level and range of benefits.

What can be done in this situation? There appears to be a need for action on several fronts to preserve the major achievements of the welfare state. First, there must be reform of the welfare state to eliminate or reduce its abuses and adverse effects. For instance, if welfare provisions discourage the search for work and the acquisition of skills, or give incentives to unjustified absenteeism, their reform is needed for both efficiency and equity. Efficiency may also be promoted through greater decentralization and community participation in the planning and implementation of social security and welfare. Likewise beyond a certain point, high rates of taxation can exert strong adverse effects on work, investment and risk taking and reward efforts to evade taxes.

Second, policies which promote growth and employment are also likely to be beneficial for preservation and strengthening of the welfare system. By the same token, sustained economic crisis and stagnation are likely to erode the support and viability of comprehensive welfare schemes. Third, a certain measure of coordination of social policy of countries at similar stages of development may be necessary to resist pressures to improve competitive positions through progressive dismantling or dilution of the welfare state. Fourth, efforts must be stepped up at national and international levels to promote growth, employment and provision of a core set of entitlements in poor countries. In the long run, the surest guarantee for the preservation of the welfare state in the advanced countries must lie in a steady reduction of international income inequalities and a gradual extension of social protection and welfare to the disadvantaged population of the world.

Dharam Ghai
Director
United Nations Research Institute
for Social Development

Editor's Preface

This book is the result of a study commissioned by UNRISD in preparation for the United Nations World Summit in Copenhagen, March 1995. The idea was to assess the future of the beleaguered welfare states of Western Europe, North America and the Antipodes and, at the same time, the prospects for welfare state construction in the newly democratized nations in East Asia, Latin America, and East-Central Europe. The latter group includes countries with existing, if perhaps rudimentary, social security systems and some, like the ex-communist nations, which once boasted genuine and comprehensive 'Soviet' welfare models, now rapidly being undone. Some Latin American nations, like Argentina and Chile, have a long tradition of social insurance, but now espouse liberalization. The East Asian countries now match Europe in economic development, but their social security systems remain, so far, much less comprehensive.

Trends in the 'new' industrial democracies, in fact, fit badly with conventional modernization theory, which claimed that economic development breeds institutional convergence. Our study will examine one group of countries – led by Chile – which has adopted a neo-liberal course; another, exemplified by Costa Rica, which exhibits embryonic social democratic traits; and a third, more hybrid path, characteristic of the East Asian nations.

It is clearly not the case that all developing nations will follow the Western welfare state trajectory. But then it is now obvious that the advanced Western democracies built highly diverse social security systems. Moreover, their response to the contemporary crisis is as diverse as are social policy developments in the 'new' nations. In brief, the neo-liberal deregulatory thrust is present in advanced welfare states such as the United States, Great Britain and the Antipodes, and also in new industrial democracies. Other new and old industrial democracies pursue radically different approaches. In this regard, our study could not escape the necessity of omission. Within the group of advanced nations, the omission of Britain may seem curious, both because it was a welfare state pioneer, and because it is the only notable case of radical change in Europe so far. We shall discuss this case in passing, but it proved too difficult to include it under any of the region headings. In any case, the literature on the British case is voluminous. Likewise, it proved logistically impossible to include major countries such as India or the People's Republic of China, and the entire African continent.

The study is structured as a double-layered comparison. We compare global 'welfare state regions', and select nations within each region. One criterion for our selection of regions has to do with their respective position in the new global order. Many of the difficulties facing the Western welfare states are linked to the new competition from East Asia, East Europe, and Latin America; in turn, as the latter become successful industrializers, their traditional forms of social protection become untenable if not outright incompatible with sustained growth and democracy. The regions we examine are, additionally, quite distinct in terms of cultural and political legacies, economic development, and shared social policy traditions.

Nonetheless, in each region we discover sharply different and, in most cases, opposite policy choices. The Anglo-Saxon nations have favoured deregulation, but with varying degrees of commitment to equality. Europe is bifurcating into a vaguely distinguishable renovation of the Nordic social democratic welfare state amidst crisis, and essentially 'frozen' continental European welfare states. Likewise, we see the contours of two distinct Latin American and East-Central European trajectories, one with a strong neo-liberal bias, another more 'social democratic'.

Gøsta Esping-Andersen

Notes on the Contributors

Francis G. Castles is Coordinator of the Reshaping Australian Institutions project in the Research School of Social Sciences at the Australian National University, having formerly been Professor of Public Policy and Head of the Graduate Program in Public Policy at the same university. He is a specialist in social policy development in both Scandinavia and Australasia and has been editor of a number of influential books in the area of comparative public policy, including *The Impact of Parties* (Sage, 1982), *The Comparative History of Public Policy* (Polity Press, 1989) and *Families of Nations* (Dartmouth Press, 1993).

Gøsta Esping-Andersen is currently Professor of Comparative Social Systems at the University of Trento, Italy. He has previously taught at Harvard University and at the European University in Florence. His research has concentrated on social democracy, comparative social policy, welfare states, and labour markets. He is the author of *Politics against Markets* (Princeton University Press, 1985) and *The Three Worlds of Welfare Capitalism* (Polity Press and Princeton University Press, 1990), and co-author and editor of *Changing Classes* (Sage, 1993).

Roger Goodman is a Fellow of St Antony's College and Lecturer in the Social Anthropology of Japan at the University of Oxford. He is the author of *Japan's 'International Youth'* (Oxford University Press, 1990) and *Kikokushijo* (Iwanami Shoten, 1992); and co-editor and author of *Ideology and Practice in Modern Japan* (Routledge, 1992) and *Case Studies on Human Rights in Japan* (Japan Library, 1996).

Evelyne Huber is Morehead Alumni Professor of Political Science and Director of the Institute of Latin American Studies at the University of North Carolina. Her research interests are in the areas of democratic politics and social policy, comparing Latin America, Europe and the Caribbean. Among her publications are *The Politics of Workers' Participation: the Peruvian Approach in Comparative Perspective* (Academic Press, 1980); *Democratic Socialism in Jamaica* (with John D. Stephens, Princeton University Press, 1986) and *Capitalist Development and Democracy* (with Dietrich Rueschemeyer and John D. Stephens, Polity Press and University of Chicago Press, 1992).

John Myles, previously Professor of Sociology at Carleton University, Ottawa, is currently Professor of Sociology at Florida State University. He has published widely on the welfare state, labour markets, and contemporary class structures. His most recent book is *Relations of Ruling* (with Wallace Clements, McGill–Queens University Press, 1994).

Ito Peng, born in Taiwan, was educated in Japan and Canada and obtained her PhD from the London School of Economics. At the time of writing, she was Post-Doctoral Fellow associated with the Suntory and Toyota International Centre for Economics and Related Disciplines (STICERD) at LSE, and was undertaking further research on East Asian welfare regimes at the Institute of Social Science, University of Tokyo. She is now a Lecturer at Hokusei Gakuen University in Sapporo, Japan. She has worked at policy level with the Ministry of Health and Welfare in Japan and with the Ontario Provincial Government in Canada.

Guy Standing is Director of Labour Market Polities in the International Labour Organization. From 1992 to 1994, he was Director of the ILO's Central and Eastern European Team, based in Budapest, responsible for the ILO's technical and advisory work. He has a doctorate in economics from the University of Cambridge, and among his most recent publications are *Reviving Dead Souls: Enterprise Restructuring and Mass Unemployment in Russia* (Macmillan, 1996) and *Minimum Wages in Central and Eastern Europe: From Protection to Destitution* (edited with Daniel Vaughan-Whitehead, Central European University Press, 1995). He is co-chairman of the Basic Income European Network.

John D. Stephens is Professor of Political Science and Sociology at the University of North Carolina at Chapel Hill. He is the author of *The Transition from Capitalism to Socialism* (Macmillan, 1979), and the co-author of *Democratic Socialism in Jamaica* (with Evelyne Huber Stephens, Princeton University Press, 1986) and of *Capitalist Development and Democracy* (with Dietrich Rueschemeyer and Evelyne Huber Stephens, Polity Press and University of Chicago Press, 1992). He is currently working on a comparative historical and quantitative study of the social origins and outcomes of welfare states, and on the current impasse of social democracy.

1

After the Golden Age? Welfare State Dilemmas in a Global Economy

Gøsta Esping-Andersen

According to T.H. Marshall (1950), modern citizenship is the fruition of a democratization that spans three centuries. In the eighteenth century the foundations were laid with the principle of legal-civil rights; political rights emerged in the nineteenth century; and, as a preliminary culmination of the democratic ideal, we see the consolidation of social citizenship in the twentieth century.

On the threshold of yet another century, legal and political rights appear firmly entrenched in most parts of the advanced, industrialized world. The same, however, cannot be said for social rights. Many believe that the welfare state has become incompatible with other cherished goals, such as economic development, full employment, and even personal liberties – that it is at odds with the fabric of advanced postindustrial capitalism.

The case for the inevitability of a third historical stage of social citizenship also seems circumspect when we broaden our analysis beyond the old, mature democracies. Despite what modernization theory believed some decades ago, the new emerging industrial democracies do not appear set to converge along the Western welfare state path. Was T.H. Marshall, then, wrong to assume that modern civilization is cumulative and irreversible? Or, put differently, what kind of welfare state is likely to emerge in the future?

The modern welfare state became an intrinsic part of capitalism's postwar 'Golden Age', an era in which prosperity, equality, and full employment seemed in perfect harmony. It cannot be for lack of prosperity that welfare states are in crisis. The dizzying levels of postwar economic growth are long gone, but nevertheless real gross national product in the rich OECD countries has increased by a respectable 45 per cent since the oil crisis in the mid 1970s. Public (and private) social outlays, of course, grew even faster but this trend was generally arrested in the 1980s. It is in the equality/full-employment nexus that the essence of the crisis must be found.

There seem to be as many diagnoses of the welfare state crisis as there are experts. Most can, nonetheless, be conveniently subsumed under three main headings. There is, firstly, the 'market-distortion' view which argues that the welfare state stifles the market and erodes incentives to work, save and invest. A second popular diagnosis focuses on the cataclysmic long-term effects of population ageing. And a third group of arguments focuses on the consequences of the new global economy, which mercilessly punishes profligate governments and uncompetitive economies.

Our study will not reject these arguments. We basically agree that a new, and quite fundamental, trade-off does exist between egalitarianism and employment; that global competition does narrow the field of domestic policy choice; and that ageing is a problem. At the same time, we feel that these standard accounts are exaggerated and risk being misleading. In part, the diversity of welfare state types speaks against too much generalization. In part, we must be very careful to distinguish what are chiefly exogenous and endogenous sources of the crisis. On the one hand, many of the difficulties that welfare states today face are caused by *market* failure: that is, badly functioning labour markets produce an overload on existing social programmes. Some, of course, insist that this is the fault of the welfare state itself. Thus, on the other hand, there is possibly also *welfare state* failure: that is, the edifice of social protection in many countries is 'frozen' in a past socio-economic order that no longer obtains, rendering it incapable of responding adequately to new risks and needs.

The malaise that now afflicts the advanced welfare states influences also strategic thinking on social security development within the emerging industrial democracies. Most pointedly, there no longer seems to be a Swedish 'middle way'. The neo-liberals suggest that the road to growth and prosperity is paved with flexibility and deregulation. Their recommendation for Latin America and East-Central Europe is therefore to emulate Chilean privatization rather than Swedish welfare statism. Critics hold that such a choice causes too much polarization and needless impoverishment, and that it may prove counter-productive for modernization. Comprehensive social security, they hold, is necessary because traditional familial, communal, or private market welfare arrangements are wholly inadequate. It is also necessary because stable democracy demands a level of social integration that only genuine social citizenship can inculcate.

Indeed, these were the very same issues that dominated in postwar Europe. Then, welfare state construction implied much more than a mere upgrading of existing social policies. In economic terms, the extension of income and employment security as a citizen's right meant a deliberate departure from the orthodoxies of the pure market. In moral terms, the welfare state promised a more universal, classless justice and solidarity of 'the people'; it was presented as a ray of hope to those who were asked to sacrifice for the common good in the war effort. The welfare state was therefore also a political project of nation-building: the affirmation of liberal democracy against the twin perils of fascism and bolshevism. Many countries became self-proclaimed welfare states, not so much to give a label to their social policies as to foster national social integration.

Such issues are of pressing concern in contemporary Asia, South America, and East Europe precisely because economic modernization tears apart the old institutions of social integration. Yet, policy makers in these nations also fear that such moral and political aims might jeopardize their comparative economic advantage (cheaper labour), traditional elite privileges (non-taxation of the rich in Latin America), or social culture (Confucianism in East Asia).

The advanced Western nations' welfare states were built to cater to an economy dominated by industrial mass production. In the era of the 'Keynesian consensus' there was no perceived trade-off between social security and economic growth, between equality and efficiency. This consensus has disappeared because the underlying assumptions no longer obtain. Non-inflationary demand-led growth within one country appears impossible; full employment today must be attained via services, given industrial decline; the conventional male breadwinner family is eroding, fertility is falling, and the life course is increasingly 'non-standard'.

Such structural shifts challenge traditional social policy thinking. In many respects the symptoms of crisis are similar across all nations. In others, there is notable divergence. Europe's single largest problem is chronically high unemployment, while in North America it is rising inequality and poverty. Both symptomize what many believe is a basic trade-off between employment growth and generous egalitarian social protection. Heavy social contributions and taxes, high and rigid wages, and extensive job rights make the hiring of additional workers prohibitively costly and the labour market too inflexible. The case in favour of deregulation seems validated in the North American 'job miracle' of the 1980s even if this occurred against the backdrop of greater inequalities.

Critics insist that the associated social costs of the American route are too high in terms of polarization and poverty. They suggest a 'social investment' strategy as an alternative. Rather than draconian roll-backs, the idea is to redirect social policy from its current bias in favour of passive income maintenance towards active labour market programmes that 'put people back to work', help households harmonize work and family obligations, and train the population in the kinds of skills that postindustrial society demands. The stress on human capital investment has, in the guise of 'productivist social policy', been official dogma in the Swedish model for decades. It is now also a leading theme in the Clinton administration, in the European Community, and also in East Asian countries (see European Community, 1993b; Freeman, 1993).

The debate within the 'emerging' economies is quite parallel. Since their perceived advantage lies in competitive labour costs, there is a natural reluctance to build costly welfare state programmes. Many of these nations – particularly Japan – also face unusually rapid population ageing and the spectre of unpayable future pension burdens. They recognize, however, that as their wage cost advantage evaporates (there is always a cheaper economy waiting on the horizon), they will have to shift towards higher value-added production: hence, the East Asian governments' phenomenal stress on education.

What, then, are the prospects for the welfare state as we step into the twenty-first century? Will the advanced nations be forced to sacrifice some, or even most, of their welfare state principles? Will the new industrializing nations opt for a model without a welfare state or, alternatively, adopt some variant of Western style welfare states?

Overall trends, alas, give little comfort to those who adhere to the ideals of the welfare state, at least as it was traditionally conceived. The new conflict between equality and employment that the advanced nations confront is increasingly difficult to harmonize. The conditions that made the welfare state an essential part of economic development in the postwar Western nations may not apply to, say, contemporary Argentina, Poland, or South Korea. The causes of such pessimism are to be found in both international and domestic change.

The changing international environment

The harmonious coexistence of full employment and income equalization that defined the postwar epoch appears no longer possible. Many believe that North America's positive employment performance could only be achieved by deregulation and freed markets which, in turn, reward the winners and punish the losers: hence, rising wage and household income inequalities, growing poverty rates, and maybe even the re-emergence of an 'underclass' (Gottschalk, 1993; OECD, 1993; Jencks and Peterson, 1991; Room, 1990). Western Europe, with its much more comprehensive industrial relations systems, welfare states, and also powerful trade unions, has maintained equality and avoided growing poverty, but at the price of heavy (especially youth and long-term) unemployment, and swelling armies of welfare dependants, the combination of which overburdens social security finances. Demand-led, reflationary strategies are no longer an option, partly because unemployment is not merely cyclical, and partly because income growth leaks out of the economy to purchase imported goods.[1]

The case for convergence: global integration

Integration in the world today almost automatically implies open economies. Sweden, Australia and New Zealand, Chile, and the ex-communist countries in Europe, are all shedding the protectionist measures that once upheld their respective welfare state arrangements.

Openness is said to sharply restrict nations' capacity to autonomously design their own political economy. Both Australia and Sweden illustrate the erosion of national options. As Castles shows in Chapter 4, Australia could pursue what he calls the 'wage earners' welfare state' model of job security, full employment and high wages only as long as it adhered to protectionist measures. The price that Australia paid was lagging growth. Sweden, as Stephens shows in Chapter 2, could balance (over-) full employment with the world's most generous and egalitarian welfare state only as long as governments could control domestic credit and investments, and as long as the labour market partners could guarantee wage moderation consensually. Following liberalization in the early 1980s, the Swedish economy suffered heavy capital leakage abroad, thus undercutting domestic investment and job generation. At the same time, Sweden's tradition of centralized national social pacts eroded. Enhanced openness in both countries has compelled governments (both left and right) to cut back social expenditure. Is it, then, the case that openness inexorably drives welfare states towards a lowest common welfare denominator?

Much of Latin America and East-Central Europe is presently undergoing harsh liberal adjustment strategies. In the short run this tends to cause heavy unemployment, an often dramatic fall in incomes, and more inequalities. In the longer run – as the case of Chile since the mid 1980s suggests – it can improve nations' competitiveness, growth, and thus employment.[2] The problem with radical liberalization is that its costs are unequally distributed and thus easily provoke organized resistance. The Chilean case is illustrative. Huber shows in Chapter 6 that Chile's poverty rate rose from 17 per cent in 1970 to 38 per cent in 1986. In 1983, the unemployment rate reached a third of the labour force.[3] In authoritarian Chile, organized resistance was effectively crushed. In liberal democracies, policy makers will have to rely on either persuasion or compensatory social guarantees. Persuasion assumes broad consensus, while compensation may strain governments' already fragile finances. In Latin America, as in East and Central Europe, the gap between social need and financial means is deepened by rising 'informalization' of employment. Employers and workers exit from the formal employment relationship to dodge taxation and job regulations.

If global wage competition is a major source of welfare state crisis in the advanced nations, convergence may paradoxically emerge from two opposite responses. Lowering wage costs in Europe and America may, at least in the interim, safeguard otherwise uncompetitive domestic firms. The offshoot, of course, is an implicit sanctioning of poor productivity performance. The other source of convergence would come from rising labour costs among the main global competitors, such as Japan, Korea or Taiwan. Their relative labour costs *have* been rising, and will do so even more if, as our study believes, these countries are hard put to stall major social security reforms in coming years.

The case for divergence: the role of institutions

There are additional reasons why we should not exaggerate the degree to which global forces overdetermine the fate of national welfare states.

One of the most powerful conclusions in comparative research is that political and institutional mechanisms of interest representation and political consensus-building matter tremendously in terms of managing welfare, employment and growth objectives.[4] The postwar European economies were able to maximize *both* welfare and efficiency owing to the capacity of encompassing interest organizations to promise wage restraint in return for full employment. For these reasons, a strong social safety net had no major negative effects on economies' adjustment capacities or, more generally, on growth (Calmfors and Driffill, 1988; Atkinson and Mogensen, 1993; Blank, 1993; 1994; Buechtemann, 1993).

But, countries with fragmented institutions will lack the capacity to negotiate binding agreements between contending interests. Opposed welfare, employment and efficiency goals more easily turn into zero-sum trade-offs, causing inflation and possibly an inferior capacity to adapt to change. Hence, a favourable institutional environment may be as capable as free markets of nurturing flexibility and efficiency. Thus, citing Ronald Dore, de Neubourg (1995: 6) points to the fallacy of wondering why, despite her rigid institutions, Japan manages to perform so well. Instead, the real question should be: 'which features make the Japanese institutional arrangements successful?' Strong consensus-building institutions in Sweden, as in Japan, helped avoid negative trade-offs for decades. It is arguably their erosion in the 1980s that best explains Sweden's dramatic recent slide.

These issues are clearly relevant for the new industrial democracies. For the ex-communist nations there is of course little doubt that the market transition requires sweeping privatization and institutional reconstruction. It is equally clear that Latin America's protectionist institutions have stifled growth. It may also be that the quite 'rigid' regulatory mechanisms that launched full employment growth in East Asia will erode. Japan's life-time employment guarantee, for example, is now threatened (Freeman, 1993; Freeman and Katz, 1994).

Our study documents the continued dominance of national institutional traditions. This comes out in two important respects. Firstly, while the postwar Western welfare states addressed fairly similar objectives, they differed both in terms of ambition and in terms of *how* they did it. Secondly, as these same welfare states today seek to adapt, they do so very differently. A major reason has to do with institutional legacies, inherited system characteristics, and the vested interests that these cultivate.[5]

Challenges to Western welfare states

The contemporary advanced welfare state faces two sets of challenges, one specific to the welfare state itself, the other provoked by exogenous forces. In the former case, there is a growing disjuncture between existing social protection schemes and evolving needs and risks. This is due to changes in family structure (the rise of single-parent households, for example), in occupational structure (increased professionalization and differentiation), and in the life cycle (which is becoming less linear and standard). Hence, there is growing dissatisfaction with the welfare state's capacity to address emerging new demands.

In the second case, the welfare state crisis is spurred by changing economic conditions (slower growth and 'deindustrialization', for example) and demographic trends (especially population ageing), both of which threaten the future viability of present welfare state commitments.

The demographic and economic problems have received most attention. The former are caused by the combination of low fertility and longer life expectancy which will engender burdensome dependency ratios and, without strong economic growth, severe fiscal strain. In the EEC, the age-dependency ratio will increase by 50 per cent between now and 2020; with existing rules and benefits, this will absorb an estimated additional 5–7 per cent of GDP (European Community, 1993a: 24). OECD (1988) projections until 2040 indicate that ageing alone will double or triple health and pension expenditures, especially in countries, like Japan, which experience unusually rapid ageing.

Still, population ageing does not automatically imply crisis. In part, the cost of ageing depends on long-run productivity growth. The OECD (1988: 70) estimates that real earnings growth at an annual average rate of 0.5–1.2 per cent (depending on nation) will suffice to finance the additional pension expenditures.[6] More to the point, the demographic burden is subject to political management. Many countries are today reversing a decades-long policy of lowering retirement age. Also, maximizing employment will automatically lower dependency rates. It makes a huge difference when, as in Scandinavia today, the overall activity rate is 10 or even 15 per cent higher than in continental Europe. Here, again, it is decisive whether social policy encourages low female employment and early retirement (as in the EEC nations), or maximum participation (as in Scandinavia).[7] It is also decisive whether, as in Southern Europe and Latin America, the incidence of informal, black market employment is high and growing. The spread of irregular work in countries like Italy is very much part of an inbuilt negative spiral: the heavy social contribution burdens incurred by over-loaded income maintenance programmes stimulate informal employment which, in turn, further erodes the tax base.

The ageing problem depends mainly on births. It is often feared that female employment will jeopardize fertility, and thus aggravate the ageing crisis. The facts, however, tell a different story. High fertility may accompany low female employment (as in Ireland), but then it may not (Italy and Spain have, today, Europe's lowest fertility levels). Female employment *and* fertility are record-high in Scandinavia. The welfare state makes a decisive difference because female employment *with* fertility is possible if social services and liberal provisions for leave are available. They are in Sweden, but not in most of continental Europe. To the extent that women's economic independence is a defining element of postindustrial society, the contemporary family needs the welfare state in order to harmonize work and family objectives; likewise, the welfare state needs children.

The *economic* problems that confront the Western welfare states are typically identified in terms of the unemployment problem. The combination of high wage costs (due to mandatory social contributions) and rigidities (such as job tenure, costly termination payments, or generous social benefits) is widely regarded as a main impediment to job growth. Generous social benefits are also held to reduce the work incentive.

There is evidence that high marginal labour costs and stringent job rights prohibit job growth. However, privatization of social security may not offer a real solution. Firstly, as we know from the United States and, more recently, Chile, private plans depend on favourable tax concessions, that is on public subsidization. Secondly, experience from the United States shows that defined-benefit type occupational welfare plans may incur the exact same kinds of rigidities and cost burdens as social insurance. They tend to inhibit labour mobility because workers fear to lose benefits, and because of vesting requirements (the norm in the US is a five-year minimum); like social security, private plans also impose high fixed labour costs.[8] Hence, public sector efforts to trim social security are paralleled in the private sector. In the United States, coverage under occupational plans has declined dramatically in the past decade: medical care coverage by 14 per cent, defined-benefit retirement coverage by 25 per cent. In its place have grown individual contribution plans.

Postindustrial employment trends are also potentially problematic. Since they favour professional and skilled occupations, demand for unqualified labour will depend mainly on low wages. They also seem to foster 'atypical', precarious jobs, such as in contingent work, involuntary part-time work, homework, or self-employment; the consequence may be greater polarization between a core and a periphery workforce (European Community, 1993b; OECD, 1993). The United States enjoys comparatively low unemployment, but a disturbing rise in jobs that pay below-poverty wages. The level of many social benefits has followed suit, producing unprecedented levels of poverty.

Indeed, as we see in the United States, wage decline may easily produce a vicious downward spiral of social benefits too, since adequate social transfers in a low-wage environment are likely to nurture poverty traps. Hence, both unemployment insurance and social welfare have eroded noticeably. Poverty and polarization, in turn, may threaten the social order and thus burden the public sector on alternative expenditure accounts. The American male prison population is above one million (and is rising), pushing up spending on prisons, law and order. Security guards and law enforcement personnel are among the fastest growing occupations; the annual per-inmate cost of incarceration is almost twice that of tuition costs at Harvard University.[9]

The 'endogenous' problems of the welfare state lie in the growing discrepancy between existing programme design and social demands. The contemporary welfare state addresses a past social order; its ideals of universalism and equality emerged with reference to a relatively homogeneous industrial working class. The much greater occupational and life cycle differentiation that characterizes 'postindustrial' society implies also more heterogeneous needs and expectations. With greater career uncertainty, demands for more flexible adjustment, and changing family arrangements, not to forget female employment, citizens also face more diverse risks.

Also the welfare state's erstwhile 'model family' is no longer pre-eminent. On the one hand, we see the rise of the two-earner, double-career unit; on the other, the rise of divorced, single-person, and single-parent households. The former are often privileged, but it is also clear that wives' labour supply is becoming the only means by which lower-income households can escape poverty or maintain accustomed living standards today. This is evident in the American case (Mishel and Bernstein, 1993). 'Atypical' families constitute a rapidly growing high-risk poverty clientele.[10]

Welfare regime challenges in other regions

The ageing problem is, with the notable exception of Japan, less acute in other regions. However, an equally severe demographic problem is massive migration into urban industrial centres, a process which undermines traditional forms of social protection. In East Asia, this poses a dilemma between welfare state construction (in Japan and South Korea combined with corporate plans) and the Confucian tradition of familialism with its care obligations.[11]

The main *economic* problems of the 'non-welfare states' depend on their position in the world economy. In Eastern Europe, the old communist welfare regime was characterized by three basic pillars: full and quasi-obligatory employment; broad and universalistic social insurance; and a highly developed, typically company-based, system of services and fringe benefits. In fact, very much as in Scandinavia, its employment-maximization strategy was the *sine qua non* of system equilibrium since it assured minimal social dependencies. The post-democracy reforms have eroded the first and third of these pillars. Instead of full employment has emerged mass unemployment; the collapsing (or privatized) state enterprises are decreasingly capable of furnishing accustomed services. As the viability of both is destroyed, existing income maintenance programmes face under-financing and over-burdening. The consequence, as Standing shows in Chapter 8, is an alarming rise in poverty and mortality.

Where countries define their competitive edge in terms of favourable labour costs, they will be wary of major welfare state advances. This is, however, only partially the case. Following Japan, East Asia in general, and South Korea in particular, see their economic future in terms of an educated workforce – very much like Sweden did with her 'productivistic' welfare state design. This obviously implies growing commitments to education, health, and social services.[12] A strong income maintenance system will probably be difficult to avoid in this scenario to the extent that (1) an increasingly educated, urbane, and professionalized labour force is likely to distance itself from the traditionalist principles of the Confucian culture; and (2) occupational company schemes are highly uneven in coverage, being rarely present or even viable in small or medium firms.

In contrast, Latin American development is to a much greater extent based on natural resources. As these countries abandon protectionist, import-substition policies they clearly face the labour cost problem more acutely. It is in this light that Chile's vanguard attempt to shift social security from state to market must be understood.

Welfare state adaptation in the past decade

Simmering symptoms of crisis became increasingly evident in the past decade. Popular perceptions notwithstanding, the degree of welfare state roll-back, let alone significant change, has so far been modest. This is clear from the essentially stable levels of social expenditure (see Table 1.1–1.3). Most nations, with the notable exception of Britain and New Zealand, have limited intervention to marginal adjustments, such as delayed benefit indexation, diminished income replacement rates and, most recently, a return to contribution-based (rather than earnings-based) pension benefit calculation. Still, marginal cuts today may have long-term cumulative effects of a quite radical nature. If social benefits gradually fall behind earnings, those who can seek compensation in private insurance will do so, thus weakening broad support for the welfare state. Among the 'new nations' the signs of system change are more evident: on the one hand, active privatization in Latin America and East-Central Europe; on the other hand, embryonic welfare state construction in East Asia.

Since the early 1970s, we can identify three distinct welfare state responses to economic and social change. Scandinavia followed until recently a strategy of welfare state employment expansion. The Anglo-Saxon countries, in particular North America, New Zealand, and Britain, have favoured a strategy of deregulating wages and the labour market, combined with a certain degree of welfare state erosion. And the continental European nations, like Germany, France and Italy, have induced labour supply reduction while basically maintaining existing social security standards. All three strategies were intimately related to the nature of their welfare states.

The Scandinavian route

By the late 1960s, the Scandinavian welfare states had largely achieved their aims as far as income maintenance programmes are concerned. Albeit more comprehensive, universalistic, and generous, at this point the 'social democratic model' was not radically different from, say, the Dutch or

Table 1.1 *Public social security and health expenditures as a percentage of gross domestic product in selected countries, 1980–1990*

OECD countries[1]	1980	1990
Canada[2]	17.3	18.8
Denmark	26.0	27.8
France	23.9	26.5
Germany	25.4	23.5
Netherlands	27.2	28.8
Norway	21.4	28.7
Sweden	32.4	33.1
United Kingdom	21.3	22.3
United States	14.1	14.6
Other countries[3]	*1975*	*1986*
Czechoslovakia	17.2	21.5
Hungary	14.9	16.2
Ukraine	13.8	17.3
USSR	13.6	15.5
Australia	10.3	9.2
New Zealand	14.5	17.9
Japan	8.9	12.2
Argentina	6.8	6.1
Brazil	5.2	5.0
Chile	11.0	13.1
Costa Rica	5.1	7.3

[1] These figures are based on OECD definitions which are not comparable with the ILO's.

[2] Data for Canada refer to 1982 and 1990.

[3] ILO-based data. For the ex-communist nations, spending is calculated in terms of net material product.

Sources: OECD, *Employment Outlook*, Paris, 1994, Table 4.7; ILO, *The Cost of Social Security*, Geneva, 1991

German. A truly distinct Nordic – and especially Swedish – model came into being with the shift towards active labour market policies, social service expansion, and gender equalization in the 1970s and 1980s. The move heralded an explicit second stage to consolidate both equality and a productivistic social policy by maximizing employment and equalizing the status of women. It was, however, also motivated by growing employment problems.

With a steady decline in manufacturing employment, and given Scandinavia's unusually egalitarian wage policies, it was from the start clear that sustained full employment, let alone the rise in women's employment, would have to rely on public sector service jobs. Indeed, until the mid 1980s when its expansion came to a halt, this sector accounted for roughly 80 per cent of total net job growth in Denmark and Sweden (with Norway as a laggard), and public employment now constitutes about 30 per cent of the total. From the point of view of women's economic emancipation, the policy succeeded. With public day care covering about 50 per cent of small

Table 1.2 *Social investment policies:*[1] *(a) percentage of labour force involved in public training and employment measures, averaged 1990–1993; (b) percentage of 18-year-olds attending full-time education and training, 1990–1991*

	(a)	(b)
Denmark	12.8	69
Sweden	6.3	56
France	9.9	78
Germany	4.9	81
Italy	4.8	na
Netherlands	3.0	74
Australia	4.9	52
Canada	3.3	58
United Kingdom	2.0	25
United States	2.6	55
Japan	0.1	na
Czech Republic	1.7	na
Hungary (1992–3)	3.0	na
Poland (1992–3)	3.6	na

[1] These figures exclude general education and private training programmes

Source: OECD, *Employment Outlook*, Paris, 1994, Table 1.18 and Table 1.B.3

Table 1.3 *Population share of the elderly (aged 60-plus) in 1990*

	Share of aged (%)
Europe	
Czech Republic	16.6
France	18.9
Germany	20.9
Hungary	19.0
Italy	19.9
Norway	21.2
Poland	14.8
Russia	15.3
Sweden	23.4
The Americas	
Argentina	13.1
Brazil	7.1
Canada	15.7
Chile	8.9
Costa Rica	6.4
United States	16.9
Asia and Pacific	
Australia	15.3
Japan	17.2
Korea (South)	7.4
New Zealand	15.1

Source: United Nations, *Demographic Yearbook*, New York, 1993

children, and with generous provisions for paid maternity and parental leave, women's participation rates (also with small children) in Denmark and Sweden, at around 80 per cent, are higher than those of prime-aged males in the rest of Europe.

The consequences of this strategy, intended or not, are both positive and negative. On the positive side, it permits women to harmonize careers and fertility. It has helped absorb unskilled workers in well-paid employment. And, it has also generated equality: the difference in men's and women's earnings and life cycle behaviour is rapidly eroding; the two-earner, double-career household is now the norm; and in comparison with everywhere else, the poverty rate among female-headed families is insignificant. And, with maximum employment levels, the welfare state is assured of higher tax revenue and lower dependency levels.[13]

On the negative side, the most dramatic result is an extremely high degree of gender segregation, with women concentrated in (typically part-time) public sector jobs, and males in the private sector. Although this may partly reflect women's preference for the more flexible conditions of public employment, the high social costs, absenteeism rates, and disruptions to production that are connected with women's employment lead private employers to prefer male workers. Work absenteeism rates in Sweden are in fact extremely high.[14] Another, less noticeable, consequence is the very high proportion of low-skilled (albeit well-paid) jobs that a social-services-led strategy produces. In fact, the overall share of unskilled service jobs is higher in Denmark and Sweden than in the notorious case of the United States (Esping-Andersen, 1993). This, again, suggests an unpleasant trade-off between either mass joblessness or mass suboptimal employment in services, be they driven by the private sector (as in America) or the public sector. Of course, it makes a huge difference from a welfare point of view that Scandinavian public employment offers good pay and security, but here we also arrive at the increasingly evident Achilles heel of the system: the growing tax burden that a huge public sector labour market incurs. With high rates of productivity growth the system can be sustained; when productivity or private investments are sluggish, severe cost problems emerge. This is exactly the situation that especially Sweden faces today: declining fiscal capacity combined with rising pressures on public job creation and/or income maintenance. Only Norway, with her oil revenues, has so far avoided the problem. Swedish policy makers and unionists can no longer avoid wage flexibility and major social benefit cuts.[15]

Still, Nordic social policy trends hardly point in an 'American' direction. True, wage differentials have grown and adjustments of the marginal tax rate and social entitlements have aimed to reduce negative work incentives and high absenteeism. Thus waiting days for sickness benefits have been re-introduced, replacement rates for sickness, parental leave, and unemployment benefits have been trimmed and, in Sweden, the second-tier pension programme (the second-tier earnings-related pensions) has been radically overhauled: pension contribution years have been extended and, more importantly, benefits are now more closely related to contributions. This marks a move away from Sweden's tradition of allocating benefits as a matter of rights relatively independent of contributions.

There is also a visibly stronger accent on 'workfare' (despite rising unemployment). Thus, work and training requirements have been strengthened substantially in Swedish unemployment insurance, and Denmark introduced a job guarantee for young workers with one year's unemployment. Also, to combat informal employment and negative work incentives, the marginal tax rates have been drastically reduced – as with the Reagan reform, particularly so for higher-income earners. Finally, there is a drift towards decentralization and privatization of service delivery, particularly in Sweden. It would, however, be a mistake to see this as a neo-liberal strategy of marketization. All providers remain subject to centrally defined, stringent norms and the move appears much more motivated in terms of efficiency criteria and in terms of allowing services to vary more in accordance with differentiated client demands. Here we see an example of how the more heterogeneous 'postindustrial' need structure compels social democracy to depart from its traditional universalism. Regardless, as Stephens argues in Chapter 2, the drift of these reforms is marginal adjustment, not a paradigmatic shift away from the basic principles of the welfare state.

Perhaps the most remarkable trend in Scandinavian social policy is the shift of priorities in favour of the young and adults – groups that in the traditional full employment setting were assumed to require only marginal welfare state intervention. In a sense what is emerging is a new life cycle definition of social policy with the recognition that contemporary family and employment transformation poses new risks and needs over the active, adult phase of people's life courses. This is reflected in the surge of adult retraining policies and lifelong learning, in the schemes to facilitate geographical and job mobility, and in the joint parental leave provisions. It is also reflected in the attempts to secure the economic well-being of new family types, such as single-parent households. Scandinavia, indeed, is the only group of European countries in which social expenditure trends favour the young over the old.

Here, then, is one manifestation of an emerging 'social investment' approach. However, its longer-term viability is doubly uncertain. There is, firstly, the conflict between the principle of universalist egalitarianism and the growing heterogeneity of the population structure. There *are* indications that the more privileged social strata are exiting from the welfare state, be it in terms of private (mainly individual) pension plans or services. Thus, failures to constantly upgrade welfare programmes may, in the long run, provoke an exodus of the elites which, in turn, will undermine the solidity of the welfare state foundations. The dilemma, of course, is that the fiscal capacity to effect such an upgrading does not exist.

A second, and more serious, threat comes from the collapse of full employment. The limits to public employment growth have been reached, which means that any employment strategy must rely mainly on services in the private sector. This, in turn, poses the question of investment incentives and wage differentials. A low-wage strategy of the American type might generate more jobs but would, in effect, seriously weaken the welfare state edifice.

Regardless, presently very high unemployment rates seem to contradict the validity of an active 'social investment' approach. In other words, does the presently severe crisis of the Swedish model affirm the neo-liberal position that large welfare states in whatever guise are to be dismantled? The answer will ultimately depend on one's diagnosis of the present crisis. Some, like the Swedish economist Assar Lindbeck (1994), diagnose it as a one-way causal street: a crisis induced primarily by the welfare state's negative effects on work, savings, and investment. This analysis is, however, hotly contested. The main negative effect seems to derive from the very egalitarian wage structure and marginal taxes which give disincentives to work more hours and to invest in additional skills. Otherwise, evidence of any major work-disincentive effect is scarce (Atkinson and Mogensen, 1993); moreover, Swedish long-term productivity performance has not been appreciably inferior to the European or OECD average (Korpi, 1992). In fact, the slowdown in growth, productivity and employment over the past 5–8 years may easily be attributed to transitory factors (especially the sudden haemorrhage of capital to the EEC in anticipation of the single market in 1992) or cyclical factors (the recent recession). As Sweden is now a full EEC member, investors' fears of being left out should subside. In the final analysis, the viability of the Swedish model will depend a lot on whether Sweden's once so celebrated consensus-building infrastructure is capable of overcoming its present fragmentation. The real issue may then have more to do with rebuilding institutions rather than dismantling the welfare state.

The neo-liberal route

A group of nations deliberately adopted deregulatory, market-driven strategies during the 1980s, notably the United States, Britain, and New Zealand; to a lesser degree, also Canada and Australia. Since Britain and New Zealand were once pioneer welfare states with strong full employment commitments, this exemplifies a radical regime shift. This cannot be said for the United States.

The policy shift has been far from uniform. It accompanied the curtailment of protectionism in New Zealand and Australia; it meant a noticeable weakening of trade unions in the US and UK, while in contrast Australia's liberalization policies were actually implemented with trade union cooperation. In either case the gist of the policy was to manage economic decline and domestic unemployment with greater labour market and wage flexibility. This has involved social policies, primarily in terms of reducing the social wage and legislated or *de facto* minimum wages. Except for New Zealand's active programme dismantling, the most favoured approach combines a move towards greater selectivity, gradual erosion of benefits and/or coverage through failure to adjust social programmes in line with economic change, and 'workfare'. This style of more 'passive' alteration will, as Myles argues in Chapter 5, have only marginal effects in the immediate term, but possibly far-reaching consequences in the longer run.

The failure-to-adjust approach typifies American social policy. The minimum wage dropped to only 38 per cent of average earnings, and the value of social assistance benefits (aid to families with dependent children: AFDC) to 24 per cent by 1989 (Moffitt, 1990: 210). Similarly, the percentage of the unemployed receiving insurance benefits declined steadily from about 70 per cent in the mid 1970s to 33 per cent in 1989. Thus, with the principal exception of pensions, the already quite weak American social safety net was allowed to further erode.

A basic assumption in the American model is that the market should supplement the basic public safety net. In the postwar era this meant primarily negotiated occupational plans. In this sense, however, welfare state decay is accompanied by market decay: private coverage in health and pensions has declined steadily during the 1980s, particularly among young and low-wage workers. The reasons are quite clear: on the one hand, employers seek to cut down on high (and growing) fixed labour costs; on the other hand, an increasing share of the labour force is employed in firms and sectors with traditionally low coverage. Yet, while conventional occupational plans decline, there is a noticeable growth in more individualized employee financed (and tax advantaged) programmes, such as the 401K plans.

A common feature in the neo-liberal route is rising inequality and poverty. During the 1980s, the lowest-decile earners lost ground, relative to the median, by 11 per cent in the US, 14 per cent in the UK, 9 per cent in Canada, and 5 per cent in Australia (OECD, 1993). In contrast, most European countries exhibit essentially stable earnings differentials, and a very modest rise in poverty.

The underlying cause is wage deregulation. The 'low-wage' phenomenon in these countries is especially acute among unskilled, non-unionized workers, and among young entering cohorts. However, as we have seen there are substantial national variations in the incidence of poverty and income polarization. Both Castles's (Chapter 4) and Myles's (Chapter 5) studies suggest that this can be explained by welfare state differences. Compared with the United States, Canada's unemployment coverage did not erode. Both Australian and Canadian welfare policies have become less universalistic and much more targeted. The methods of targeting, however, differ appreciably from classical means-testing: eligibility is decided on the basis of income or tax returns, and the principles of selectivity are meant to preclude the rich rather than to include only the demonstrably poor. Take-up rates appear high, and the approach seems quite effective in protecting high-risk groups. Indeed, Australia actually raised benefits for especially vulnerable groups, such as families with many children. It is primarily this which accounts for Australia's substantially lower incidence of poverty.

There is some evidence in favour of the positive employment effect of wage flexibilization. Employment growth in the 1980s has been two to three times higher in these countries than in the rest of the OECD. This is also quite consistent with the 'Baumol cost-disease' thesis, since much of the job growth appears related to lower wages in services (see Baumol, 1967; Blackburn et al., 1990: 72ff). The question, however, is whether the employment outcome is desirable. Low-end jobs may be unattractive, but they do provide a large pool of easily accessible first-entry jobs. This helps integrate youth, women, and immigrants into the labour market. On this count, the American scenario contrasts very favourably with the European. The burning issue, of course, is whether these jobs become dead-end traps; that is, whether the low-wage strategy fosters a new kind of chronically impoverished postindustrial proletariat. Research on this issue is still fairly rudimentary, but much suggests that mobility chances are substantial, *conditional upon adequate skills* (Esping-Andersen, 1993). Unskilled workers have a high risk of remaining trapped. Hence, an active social investment strategy seems to be paramount if we wish to avoid the emergence of a proletariat of the working poor.

The low-wage strategy nurtures employment growth in low-productivity 'lousy jobs' where even full-time, all-year employment results in below-poverty income (Burtless, 1990). Hence, a low-wage labour market entails a double-jeopardy: it necessitates higher income maintenance transfers (such as social assistance) and, at the same time, produces poverty traps (since low wages create a disincentive to work). The wage flexibility scenario brings with it additional problematic consequences. There is a worrying erosion of the traditional fringe benefit packages of corporate welfare. Disappearing jobs tend to be in industries with developed welfare plans; a large part of the new jobs is concentrated in companies with little or no occupational benefits. Despite the fact that the United States spends almost 13 per cent of GDP on health care, the number of persons without adequate protection is very high (an estimated 30–40 million) and growing. In other words, an American style lean welfare state that assumes company provided supplements is likely to face a growing crisis of adequate social protection.

The gap in social protection is most acute in younger child families. This is due to the low earnings capacity of single mothers combined with a real decline in social benefits. But also married women's ability to supplement the incomes of low-earner husbands is often impaired by the lack of affordable child care. In both types of cases, we see an alarming rise of child poverty in Canada, the UK and in the USA.[16]

The poverty problem associated with the 'low-wage' strategy is clearly concentrated among particularly vulnerable clienteles such as the unskilled and single-parent households. In the short run the risk can be reduced by upholding the standards of income maintenance programmes, but if low wages remain the only option to welfare dependency, this clearly nurtures poverty traps. Political conflict in today's America is heavily flavoured by two opposed solutions to this: the right's strategy of essentially abolishing welfare; and the Clinton administration's active social investment strategy which favours subsidized training. A strategy of wage flexibility would be potentially much less harmful were it systematically connected to an active training programme (Lynch, 1993).[17]

The labour reduction route

The jobless growth scenario is especially acute in EEC Europe. If we go back to the late 1960s, overall employment ratios were basically identical in Scandinavia, North America, and contintental Europe (an average of 65 per cent of the working-age population). Since then, the *employed-*population rate has risen to 76 per cent for males and 60 per cent for women in the United States, and to 83 per cent for males and 76 per cent for women in Sweden; meanwhile, the EEC average has fallen to 57 per cent. Besides unemployment, the main difference lies in married women's and older males' activity rates.[18]

While the Scandinavians have managed the surplus of 'deindustrialized', largely unskilled, masses with retraining and job creation, and the Americans with wage erosion, the continental European nations have opted to subsidize their exit, especially through early retirement. This has arguably produced an 'insider–outsider' divide, with a small, predominantly male, 'insider' workforce enjoying high wages, expensive social rights, and strong job security, combined with a swelling population of 'outsiders' depending either on the male breadwinner's pay or on welfare state transfers.

The roots of this strategy lie in the continental European welfare states' combination of highly (if not overly) developed social insurance (inordinately biased towards pensions) and underdeveloped social services.[19] Social insurance means that entitlements are related to one's employment record, implying the necessity of a long unbroken career. The underlying assumption is that family members can depend on the full-time male breadwinner, and that wives are generally responsible for social care within the household. Hence, tax policies typically punish working wives, and the welfare state is extremely underdeveloped in terms of social services to families. Public child care coverage in Germany, the Netherlands, and Italy is below 5 per cent. Similarly, the percentage of elderly living with their children is about 40 per cent in Italy and Spain, but under 10 per cent in Scandinavia and 15 per cent in the US (OECD, 1994a: Table 13).[20] The continental European welfare state is thus essentially a familialistic transfer state.

This helps explain its preference for early retirement (or disability pensions) as the principal policy for managing 'deindustrialization'. As a derived consequence, it also explains the high labour cost problem, employment inflexibilities, and the catastrophic levels of long-term youth unemployment. The productivity gains that may come from labour reductions are easily outweighed by the associated costs. Social insurance finances are increasingly in deficit because contributions fall short of benefit payments. This problem is augmented by fragmented insurance funds: deficits are sometimes alarming in funds covering declining occupations (such as miners' or general workers' insurance), while the funds for growing occupations tend to be financially healthy.

The rising financial requirements that come from mass retirement and mass unemployment mean growing social contributions and thus fixed labour costs. This is especially true in Italy and France where labour supply reduction has been most intense. The indirect effect is that employers will prefer to regulate their labour needs via an adjustment of hours rather than assume extra workers; it also means that the marginal cost of part-time workers tends to be prohibitively high, thus additionally disfavouring female employment. And, high labour costs with rigidity in the context of mass unemployment mean that both employers and job seekers have a strong incentive to exit from formal employment relationships. This can be seen in the very large black economy, and in the rise of self-employment, neither of which of course broaden the welfare state's tax base.

This kind of system has an inbuilt tendency to augment labour market rigidities. If we consider that most families depend on the male earner's pay and social rights, and when we add to this the declining number of active years due to later entry and early exit, the result is that the typical worker can ill afford any risks or employment breaks across his active career. The consequence is that voters and trade unions will defend the existing rights of the 'insiders' as forcefully as possible. There is an implicit conspiracy to safeguard the prime-age male worker even when this harms his wife's, sons' and daughters' employment prospects.

The problem has obviously not gone unnoticed, but owing to trade union, employee and even employer resistance, major efforts at flexibilization are easily blocked or neutralized. Italy's liberalization of part-time employment in the 1980s has had virtually no practical effect. Many countries have implemented temporary hiring provisions, but except for Spain and, to a lesser degree, France there has been no visible rise in temporary workers – and,in these two countries the reform has augmented the temporary worker share but not overall *net* job growth. Paradoxically, there is strong evidence that a growing workforce of flexible temporaries only enhances the rigidities and privileges of the insiders (Bentolila and Dolado, 1994).

There are two equally plausible explanations for why flexibility fails: (1) it is still too early to fully see the effects of flexibilization; (2) employers may avoid shifting to new labour practices in the interest of maintaining harmonious industrial relations.[21] A case in point is that, despite weakened worker dismissal provisions in Belgium, France and Germany, employers' lay-off behaviour has hardly changed (Blank, 1993: 166).

Most agree that these countries need to decrease labour market rigidities. The problem is twofold. The first aspect is that the welfare of individuals and families depends on precisely those elements that cause rigidities in the first place: job security, high wages and expensive social contributions. The second is that informal, atypical and often black market activity becomes the chief compensatory strategy for those seeking work. These have in common that they dodge burdensome social contributions and rigid dismissal regulations. It is symptomatic that self-employment is the only source of real job growth in economies like the Italian or Spanish.

From this perspective, it seems clear that the transfer-induced labour reduction strategy must be drastically reversed. In fact, on this there is widespread agreement. There is now a uniform move to raise retirement age, lengthen contribution requirements, and also diminish the burden of mandated social contributions. One strategy is to encourage the growth of employer plans, and a certain trend in this direction is visible. Still, it is unlikely to be a panacea precisely because – as in North America – this does not solve employers' labour cost problems. Privatization, then, more likely implies individual insurance plans and, thus, very uneven coverage.

More generally, to reduce rigidities it is clearly necessary to diminish families' dependence on the single male earner. The key, then, is to augment the supply of, and demand for, women workers. Thus, it is difficult to see how the continental European model can avoid breaking with its traditional familialist, income transfer bias. It is in fact on this issue that much of contemporary political conflict focuses: the left typically advocating a 'Scandinavian' social service expansion; the right (especially Christian democracy) proposing a 'welfare society' approach that would reinforce the family – for example by introducing a housewife salary – and local community voluntarism. Considering the fiscal strains of the present social insurance systems, neither strategy seems particularly viable.[22]

The emergence of new welfare states?

Are the nations of East-Central Europe, East Asia, or Latin America in the process of emulating the Western model, or are they following qualitatively new trajectories? If by 'new' we mean models that deviate markedly from existing welfare states, the answer is essentially no. Our survey suggests the makings of distinct trajectories that do not necessarily correspond to regional clusters.

One, comprising East-Central Europe, Chile, and Argentina, follows broadly a liberal strategy based on privatization of social insurance, a reduced public social safety net, a shift towards targeted means-tested assistance, and a free-market bias in labour market regulation. The market-driven strategy in Latin America must be seen against the backdrop of a highly status-segmented, quite clientelistic, and seriously underfunded social insurance tradition.

A second group of countries, exemplified by Brazil and Costa Rica, has so far shunned neo-liberalism and has in fact taken some steps towards strengthening their public social safety nets, in both cases adopting a fairly universalistic approach in terms of population coverage.

The third, East Asian, group is paradoxically both globally unique and a hybrid of existing welfare state characteristics. It shares with the continental European model an emphasis on familialism and an aversion to public social services. Its embryonic social insurance schemes tend to follow the European tradition of occupationally segmented plans, favouring in particular privileged groups such as the civil service, teachers or the military. In these countries, social security is far from comprehensive, nor does it aim to furnish income *maintenance*. By default more than design, the vacuum of social protection has spurred the rise of company sponsored occupational welfare, especially in Japan. As a consequence, a certain degree of 'Americanization' has evolved: the modesty of public welfare rests on the assumption that primary sector male workers will be covered under private plans.

When we evaluate the paths taken in these regions, we should first of all remember the stark contrast between the crisis-ridden economies of Latin America (and recently also East-Central Europe), and the amazingly dynamic economies of East Asia. Indeed, the general economic climate of the former two regions in the 1980s was much more similar than most believe: declining per capita GDP, inflationary pressures, huge debt problems, soaring unemployment, and the urgency to reform highly protected monopolistic industries.[23] Both regions embarked on more or less rigorous liberal stabilization and restructuration strategies in the 1980s.

A common trait in the ex-communist nations' transition is a first attempt to cushion the shock therapy with social security. Initially, virtually all introduced generous unemployment insurance, and industrial redundancies were countered with attrition and early retirement. The dramatic fall in revenues, coupled with unexpected levels of unemployment and income loss (real wages have fallen by 20–35 per cent, and in the CIS by as much as 50 per cent), led in many countries to virtual collapse of the existing social security system and a uniform shift towards targeted means-testing.

The region as a whole experienced a net job loss of 6 million (12 per cent of the labour force) between 1989 and 1993. Participation rates have declined while irregular unemployment and under-employment have risen (OECD, 1994b). Unemployment and poverty have been growing everywhere, but there is a clear difference between countries like Hungary and the Czech Republic on the one hand, and Poland and the CIS states on the other. As Burda (1993) and OECD (1994b) suggest, the former countries were more prone to negotiate the transition strategy, the social safety net remained stronger, and there were more active employment policies, particularly for youth and the unskilled.[24]

As Standing demonstrates in Chapter 8, the shock therapy – combined with social policy – has often added to already existing distortions. The policy of taxing wage growth (as a means to stem inflation) gives the stronger firms incentives to shift to non-money wages. Those outside this sector find their living standards dramatically reduced. An often sharp deterioration of the minimum wage has eroded both earnings and most social benefits (the latter, pegged to the minimum wage, have eroded to the point where they equal 20–30 per cent of average wage: OECD, 1994b). In the labour market, the drift is from protected, full-time jobs towards marginal, often black economy jobs, and the results are unemployment (the effect of which is to exacerbate the tax problem), an across-the-board fall in real wages, and the emergence of 'Third World' poverty rates (at present, 40 per cent in Poland; reputedly 80 per cent in the Ukraine).

In a nutshell, what has been privatized are individual risks rather than the means to confront them. The lack of functioning financial institutions makes private insurance difficult to establish. Hence, with the crumbling of the public social security system and the obstacles to a private alternative, the structure of social protection that remains resembles increasingly the kind of poor relief that the advanced nations successfully left behind.

A quite similar scenario is described for those Latin American countries which embarked on a neo-liberal restructuration strategy. Traditional social security in most Latin American nations can best be described as a patchwork of patronage insurance, typically favouring privileged workers. Hyper-inflation and tax avoidance have meant that these face serious fiscal problems, but also that more aggressive reform efforts are difficult to contemplate. For these, as well as for other reasons, the Chilean experiment with privatization holds considerable interest.

Huber's study indicates that privatization has so far been a mixed blessing. Chile's shift to a private individual retirement account system has necessitated huge public subsidies and, hence, the net effect is a *de facto* subsidization of private welfare. Also, operating costs appear to be prohibitively high. Genuine coverage under the programme appears also quite modest, perhaps because it is purely employee financed. The new private schemes are essentially inoperable for the large mass of low-paid, marginalized, or unemployed workers. In other words, privatization in Chile has largely meant a replication of many of the same faults that characterized public insurance. The principal advantage of the new system is that it is financially solvent, and that its huge savings help capital markets.

It is on the labour market front that Chile's liberalization strategy appears more positive, at least over the longer run. The short-run effects, as we have indicated earlier, were devastating in terms of industrial closures, mass unemployment, and immiseration, a trend we also see in Argentina. Clearly, Latin America's over-protected and monopolistic industries were hardly viable and primary sector labour markets, too, were extremely rigid. The Chilean shock therapy relied on the authoritarian regime's ability to crush the trade unions, and it may therefore not exemplify a viable strategy for other nations. In fact, the Argentine approach seems to favour accords with existing interest organizations.

As Pereira (1993: 60) suggests, the earlier the adjustment programme, the lower the long-run cost. The indicators for Chile, at any rate, are indeed positive. Unemployment levels have fallen from a catastrophic 30 per cent in 1983 to 5 per cent today, and investments, GDP and wages have all grown healthily. But this should be considered against past erosion: per capita income had fallen 26 per cent in 1974–5, and another 16 per cent in 1982. Real incomes in 1988 were no higher than before Pinochet, but they were much more unequally distributed (Pereira, 1993: 37–9).[25]

The alternative response, exemplified by Costa Rica and Brazil, has been to strengthen social policy in a clearly universalistic direction, especially in health care (although, as Huber notes in Chapter 6, universalism in Brazil is questionable owing to heavy political patronage). So far, these countries have experienced neither declining incomes, nor rising unemployment and poverty. But the long-run viability of this route is uncertain. It remained possible in Costa Rica until generous American aid dried up, and considering inflation (especially in Brazil), huge foreign debt, and stagnant or falling GDP, the future prospects for a Latin American style 'social democracy' seem in doubt.

Turning finally to the peculiarly hybrid East Asian welfare regimes, the first thing one notes in a comparative framework is that social security development lags behind their economic achievement. One argument has been that Confucian family welfare remains an effective functional equivalent to welfare statism. Critics hold that the survival of three-generation households is pretty much due to lack of any alternative.

Be that as it may, the issue of welfare state construction is now, for several reasons, intensely debated. In Korea and Taiwan, post-democratic nation-building efforts mean also a need to extend citizens' rights. Also, population ageing, urban mobility, and modernization are causing a growing crisis of elderly care. Moreover, the low-wage-based industrial miracle of Korea and Taiwan is rapidly being exhausted, implying the need for sweeping industrial restructuration and, in its wake, the likely emergence of unemployment and a host of new welfare problems. In much more advanced Japan, the system of lifelong employment and, with it, corporate welfare guarantees is weakening. The equilibrium of the Japanese combination of rather modest public benefits, private supplements, and virtual employment security (for the male labour force at any rate) rests not only on familial care, but also on the job guarantee.

So far, these fast growing economies have suffered labour shortages rather than unemployment, and this has helped minimize the income risks of the male breadwinner and has sustained families' caring capacity. But this is not likely to continue indefinitely. In response to the growing strains of the 'Confucian model', these countries have taken a series of cautious steps towards a more comprehensive social policy. However, exemplified by South Korea's reforms in the late 1980s, neither do they approach anything close to universal coverage, nor are benefit levels adequate to bring recipients much beyond subsistence level. Taiwan's recent national health care reform (September 1994), initially intended as universal and obligatory, is voluntary and gaps in coverage are thus likely to remain.

Policy makers' hesitation to commit themselves to a genuine income maintenance system is partly due to fears of unusually rapid population ageing in the coming decades. This is particularly the case in Japan where, indeed, the conservatives seek to reinvigorate Confucian familialism as a compensatory strategy. This closely parallels the Christian democratic policy in much of Europe, and for basically the same reasons it is unlikely to be effective. Women in Japan and South Korea, as in Germany and Italy, are having far fewer children (fertility rates are now far below replacement), and are increasingly entering the labour market. What is more, population ageing in Japan is, comparatively speaking, extremely skewed towards the very old, meaning those with particularly intense caring needs. The percentage of people aged 80-plus will triple by the year 2020 (OECD, 1994a: Table 15).

Another concern is with the possibly negative impact on savings. The Asian tigers' economic miracle was premised on high savings rather than Keynesianism: families save for lack of adequate social security coverage. A genuine welfare state, it is feared, will undermine this incentive. Since, moreover, these economies are characterized by sustained growth *and* quite egalitarian income distributions, there is some legitimacy to the assumption that most households have the capacity to save – at least if they are urban and based on a primary sector breadwinner. Nonetheless, as Japan already demonstrates, the suppression of consumption is not possible forever. The East Asian countries place much greater emphasis on education than on income maintenance, in large part in anticipation of structural unemployment and (partial) 'deindustrialization'. They are therefore potential vanguards in terms of stressing a 'social investment strategy'.

Conclusions: major trends and policy dilemmas

In most countries what we see is not radical change, but rather a 'frozen' welfare state landscape. Resistance to change is to be expected: long-established policies become institutionalized, and cultivate vested interests in their perpetuation; major interest groups define their interests in terms of how the welfare state works. Thus, social security systems that are backed by powerful interest aggregations are less amenable to radical reform and, when reform is undertaken, it tends to be negotiated and consensual. Continental Europe is the clearest case of impasse, while Australia and Scandinavia represent change via negotiation. At the other extreme, in Chile and the ex-communist nations, whole scale change occurred against the backdrop of the collapse or destruction of the existing organizational structure. In between these poles are countries, like the United States or Britain, in which a more gradual erosion occurred in tandem with weakened trade unionism.

The decay of comprehensive and centralized consensus-building mechanisms over the past decade is one of the primary reasons for the difficulties that now also beset the famed Swedish model. Its long-standing capacity to reconcile ambitious and egalitarian welfare goals with full employment has seriously decayed.

There is a seemingly universal trade-off between equality and employment. Its roots may lie primarily in the new global order, but our study identifies significantly different national responses. Within the group of advanced welfare states, only a few have undertaken radical steps to roll back or deregulate the existing system. All, however, have sought to trim benefits at the margin or to introduce cautious measures of flexibilization. As we have seen, those following a more radical liberalization strategy do better in terms of employment but suffer a high cost in terms of inequality and poverty. In contrast, those resilient to change pay the price of high unemployment – continental Europe in particular.

A similar perception of a trade-off between equality and efficiency has always dominated social policy debates. In the postwar era it was widely accepted that the Keynesian welfare state provided a positive-sum solution. Today, there are few that are optimistic with regard to a viable 'third way'. Still, many of the countries we have surveyed pursue strategies designed to mediate or soften the trade-off. One, represented by Australia and Canada, combines liberalization and a shift towards more selectivity and targeting with a concomitant rise in benefits to those most at risk. Their approach to selectivity is broad rather than narrow, aiming to guarantee against abject poverty and stark inequalities. Comparative income and poverty data suggest that the strategy is somewhat successful. These countries have enjoyed an employment performance that equals the American without alarming rates of impoverishment.

Another strategy, evident in Scandinavia, consists in shifting welfare state resources from passive income maintenance to employment and family promotion. The era of public employment growth has clearly ended and, instead, policy is directed to active labour market measures, such as training and mobility, and wage subsidies. Scandinavia appears now to have accepted that greater inequalities are unavoidable but seeks to build in guarantees against these being concentrated in any particular stratum, or becoming permanent across people's life courses. In this regard, the Nordic welfare states may be said to spearhead a 'social investment' strategy. They have clearly not escaped high unemployment, or the necessity for significant cuts in social benefit levels. Yet, their unemployment record must be gauged against the backdrop of record high activity rates and, contrary to continental Europe, very modest degrees of social marginalization, exclusion, and youth unemployment.

More generally, if a return to full employment will have to rely on greater earnings inequalities and a profusion of 'lousy' service jobs, active social investment policies should diminish the chance that certain groups become chronic losers. 'Lousy' jobs will constitute only a marginal welfare problem (and may even be beneficial) if they are merely stop-gap, or easy first-entry, jobs for school leavers or immigrant workers. They are a major problem if they become life cycle traps. We know that education and skills offer the best odds for people to move on to better jobs. Hence, a low-wage-based employment strategy can be reconciled with equality if there exist guarantees of mobility and improvement.

Privatization is one of the most commonly advocated strategies in the current welfare state crisis. In fact, it is promoted for two distinct reasons: one, to diminish public spending burdens and encourage self-reliance; the other, to respond to the more differentiated and individualistic demands of 'postindustrial' society. In practice, there have as yet been very few substantial privatization reforms and the case of Chile remains therefore quite unique. However, a process of 'creeping' privatization may be under way in many countries, mostly because of gradual erosion of benefit or service levels.

If privatization entails a shift of welfare responsibilities to companies, it is very unlikely to become a panacea since corporate plans similarly inhibit flexibility and incur heavy fixed labour costs. Indeed, they are being rolled back in tandem with public programmes. In addition, such plans are hardly viable in a service-dominated employment structure where firms are smaller and the labour force less unionized. The alternative is defined contribution plans or individual insurance schemes (like the Chilean model, or the rapidly growing IRA or 401K type plans in America).

Individual plans do have positive aspects. Besides encouraging savings, they permit individuals to tailor their welfare package. However, if they are meant to substitute for, rather than merely supplement, public schemes, their capacity to furnish social security in any universal way is highly dubious. Besides, the growth of such schemes has everywhere been nourished by public subsidies, such as favourable tax treatment.

Parallel to privatization is a certain shift away from defined-benefit to contribution-based entitlements, particularly in pensions. This means essentially that welfare states (or companies) are withdrawing their commitment to benefit *adequacy* – one of the major welfare reforms of the 1960s and 1970s. In the Swedish case, this is less likely to generate major inequalities owing to the high levels of income security guaranteed by the basic, universal 'people's pension'. But this is not the case in systems, such as the Chilean, where individual contribution-based plans are the sole source of income maintenance – short of means-tested public assistance.

In many welfare states, income transfer programmes were perverted over the past decades, becoming an inducement *not* to work. In the continental European countries, this strategy has exacerbated rather than eased the underlying employment problem: adding to the burden of labour costs for the shrinking 'insider' labour force and thus raising the cost of entry for the 'outsiders', youth especially. It increases the family's dependence on the sole (usually male) breadwinner's job stability and pay.

It is, then, clear that one of the greatest challenges for the future welfare state is how to harmonize women's employment with family formation.

Women demand employment and greater economic independence; the family is more likely to be flexible, and less likely to be poor, if it can rely on two earners; and the ageing burden will be lessened if fertility rises. The Scandinavian experience demonstrates that these demands can be harmonized with a comprehensive network of public services. However, the fiscal strains of contemporary welfare states generally prohibit such an expansion; high wage costs make it unlikely in the private sector.

To the extent that the trade-off between social security and jobs is induced by global wage competition, there is an alternative source of positive-sum outcomes since the main competitors to the advanced economies are likely to build more comprehensive social protection systems in the foreseeable future. It would, indeed, be a sad irony if the West engaged in welfare state dismantling in its drive to remain competitive if, at the same time, the main competition were to raise its labour costs.

On a final note, we should not forget that the initial impetus behind the postwar welfare state went beyond the narrower social policy concerns. As a mechanism for social integration, the eradication of class differences, and nation-building, the advanced welfare states have been hugely successful. Part of the welfare state crisis today may be simply a question of financial strain and rising unemployment. In part, it is clearly also related to less tangible needs for new modes of social integration, solidarity, and citizenship. The market may indeed be an efficient mechanism of allocation, but not of building solidarities. There is little doubt that these more intangible qualities constitute an important element in the embryonic welfare state evolution in the new industrial democracies of Asia, South America and Eastern Europe. The economic effects of the welfare state can certainly not be disregarded. Yet, we should not forget that the only credible rationale behind economic efficiency is that it will produce welfare. The idea of social citizenship may therefore extend also into the twenty-first century.

Notes

1 This argument, while prevalent in current debates, must be accepted with serious caution. To give an example, while the import share from the newly industrialized countries (NICs) has grown substantially, it remains the case that an estimated 80 per cent of total EC member state trade occurs *within* the EC.

2 A recent study of trade liberalization in Latin America suggests strong, positive effects in terms of productivity performance and growth (Edwards, 1994).

3 Poverty trends in the ex-communist states seem to correlate closely with the extent to which the new regimes apply radical 'shock therapies'. In a recent overview, Cornia (1994) presents figures for the 'ultra-poor', meaning households with income less than 25–35 per cent of the average wage. From 1989 to 1992, their share rose from 8 to 20 per cent in Poland; from 19 to 30 per cent in Romania; and from 3 to 27 per cent in Russia. In contrast, the rise was moderate in Hungary (from 3 to 6 per cent) and in the Czech Republic (from 1.5 to 7 per cent). Similarly, the Czech Republic and Hungary have experienced much lower unemployment rates (OECD, 1994b).

4 The literature on this topic is truly enormous. For a very recent comparative study, see Freeman (1993); for a general review of research, see Esping-Andersen (1994). Streeck (1992)

has recently argued that these very same conditions also facilitate economies' adaptation to new and more flexible production methods.

5 Two examples will suffice at this point. First, as Castles demonstrates in Chapter 4, the negotiated liberalization strategy that the Australian Labor government pursued with the unions scores more favourably in terms of both equality and growth than New Zealand's, which was pursued in conflict with existing interest associations. Secondly, decades of social security institutionalization cultivate vested interests. Thus, it is virtually impossible to amalgamate occupationally exclusive social insurance schemes.

6 An economy's productivity performance is thus vital. The earnings performance of many nations in the past decade suggests that such levels of growth may not be so easily attainable. In the United States, for example, real manufacturing earnings declined by an annual average of 0.2 per cent during the 1980s. In Europe, where labour shedding has been much more dramatic, productivity and thus wages have grown at higher rates (1.7 per cent in France, 0.9 per cent in Italy, and 2.4 per cent in Germany) (Mishel and Bernstein, 1993: Figure 9A).

7 Freeman (1993: 3) shows that the percentage aged 15–64 years working (adjusted for hours worked) was identical in Europe and the United States in 1973. By 1990, Europe's activity rate was about 12 per cent lower than the American. As Freeman concludes, Americans work the equivalent of one month per year more than the Europeans.

8 In the United States, the typical company pays 11 per cent of wages to legislated social contributions, and another 12 per cent towards fringe welfare benefits (Blank, 1993: 167). This compares with the EC average of 24 per cent to the former and 5 per cent to the latter. In heavy social contribution nations, like Italy, the former approximates 47 per cent, the latter 2 per cent (recalculations from European Community 1993a, Table 21).

9 I owe this point to Richard Freeman who, with considerable justification, sees the prison population as the American equivalent to Europe's long-term unemployed (personal communication).

10 Own calculations of Luxembourg Income Study (LIS) data for the mid 1980s show that single-parent (almost all female-headed) households face extraordinarily high poverty risks. Using the standard 50 per cent (adjusted) of median income as the poverty measure, the percentage of these households in poverty is 60 per cent in the US, 57 per cent in Canada, 27 per cent in Germany, and 19 per cent in both France and Italy. In contrast, the Swedish rate is 4.5 per cent. The impact of divorce may also be economically catastrophic, at least for wives. Burkhauser et al. (1991) show a 24 per cent income decline for American wives one year after divorce, and a full 44 per cent drop for German wives. The husbands' income loss is relatively inconsequential: 6 per cent in the US and 7 per cent in Germany.

11 Hashimoto (1992: 38) shows that 65 per cent of the elderly in Japan live with their children (down from 77 per cent in 1970). Choi's (1992: 151) data for South Korea show even higher rates (76 per cent). He also shows that 44 per cent of the aged are economically entirely dependent on their children. According to the official South Korean poverty line definition, more than 20 per cent of the aged are poor; about half have financial difficulties; and more than half of those who actually receive a pension find it difficult to live on it. A major reason cited for poverty among the aged is that their children avoid providing or are unable to provide, support for their parents (1992: 151).

12 The accent on education is already visible. According to Goodman and Peng's data in Chapter 7, the proportion of middle school (junior high school) graduates that continue to secondary-level education (senior high school) is 96 per cent in Japan and around 90 per cent in Taiwan and South Korea.

13 This discussion has focused on the gender angle of the policy, but it should rightly be generalized to the population at large, and to older workers in particular. Thus, combined with active labour market policies of retraining, rehabilitation, and job reinsertion, the strategy has succeeded – so far – in maintaining high employment levels also among youth and aged workers. The activity rate of males aged 60–64 is 64 per cent compared with 54 per cent in the US, 32 per cent in Germany, 25 per cent in France, and only 15 per cent in the Netherlands.

14 In the aggregate, Swedish absenteeism rates are about double those in Germany or the Netherlands. In 1985 the absenteeism rate on 'any given day' among Swedish women with a

child aged 0–2 was a whopping 47.5 per cent. Critics argue that the system is too generous and thus encourages abuse. This is partly true, but ignores also the Swedes' tremendous effort to move the disabled and hard-to-employ from passive income maintenance to active employment in the economy (Bjorklund and Freeman, 1994).

15 The high wage costs and taxes are widely believed to spur negative work incentives and hidden employment, although hard evidence is difficult to come by (see, however, Atkinson and Mogensen, 1993). Still, it is indicative that self-employment has been the fastest growing form of Swedish job growth in the 1980s.

16 Based on own calculations of LIS data, child poverty in two-parent families doubled in the United States during the 1980s (from 12 to 22 per cent) and tripled in the UK (from 5 to 15 per cent). Canada's rise was more modest (from 11 to 14 per cent). The rise in poverty among single-parent households was even more dramatic, except in the UK which registered a decline.

17 The presence of a more active training policy may, however, in itself not suffice if not coupled to a strong institutional framework. As Soskice (1991) suggests, the lack of this in the UK means that only a tiny proportion of those leaving school at age 16 receive any apprenticeship training.

18 Again, starting similarly in the 1960s, the activity rate of males, aged 60–64, has dropped to 25 per cent in France, 31 per cent in Germany, and 15 per cent in the Netherlands. The comparable rate is 64 per cent in Sweden and 54 per cent in the US. Note, however, that female employment rates, especially among the younger cohorts, have begun to rise since the mid 1980s in Germany and the Netherlands where part-time jobs have become more common.

19 In Italy, 60 per cent of total social expenditure goes to the aged; in Germany, about 45 per cent. This contrasts with 30 per cent in Sweden (which is equally 'aged') and 40 per cent in the US (OECD, 1994a: Chart 1).

20 As in East Asia, there is a clear declining trend. The problem of aged care is doubly acute since the only real alternative to family care is (extremely costly) hospitalization.

21 Several studies give credence to the former interpretation, suggesting that the shift to temporary workers will accelerate throughout the 1990s (Standing, 1993). On the other hand, Buechtemann's (1993) analysis of the German experience suggests that employers use temporary contracts as a screening device but subsequently extend permanent contracts in most cases.

22 In Italy, voluntary associations have grown tremendously over the past decade, particularly in areas such as care for the elderly and disabled or drug addicted. It is, however, evident that this has been helped by the availability of a huge pool of non-employed youth and women.

23 State ownership has been widespread in Latin America, accounting for 40 per cent of industrial output (compared with 80–90 per cent in East Europe) (Przeworksi, 1991: 143).

24 The Czech case is interesting since it combines low unemployment rates with a level of employment loss (at 10 percent) equal to others. In part, this is explained by retirement, in part by job creation schemes (250,000 jobs were created in 1992). It also seems that more drastic employment losses have been avoided by the strategy of privatizing prior to rationalizing firms (OECD, 1994b).

25 It is also unclear how liberal is this liberalization strategy. The encouragement of markets appears to require heavy public subsidies; in part, as we have seen with pensions; in part, subsidies to private enterprises which in the 1980s were around 4.3 per cent of GDP (Pereira, 1993: 37).

References

Atkinson, A.B. and Mogensen, G.V. (1993) *Welfare and Work Incentives.* Oxford: Clarendon Press.

Atkinson, A.B. and Rein, M. (1993) *Age, Work and Social Security.* New York: St Martin's Press.

Baumol, W. (1967) 'The macro-economics of unbalanced growth', *American Economic Review*, 57: 415–26.

Bentolila, S. and Dolado, J. (1994) 'Spanish labour markets', *Economic Policy*, April: 55–99.

Bjorklund, A. and Freeman, R. (1994) 'Generating equality and eliminating poverty, the Swedish way', National Bureau of Economic Research, Working Paper no. 4945.

Blackburn, L., Bloom, D. and Freeman, R. (1990) 'The declining economic position of the less skilled American men', in G. Burtless (ed.), *A Future of Lousy Jobs?* Washington, DC: Brookings Institution. pp. 178–204.

Blank, R. (1993) 'Does a larger safety net mean less economic flexibility?', in R. Freeman (ed.), *Working under Different Rules.* New York: Russell Sage.

Blank, R. (ed.) (1994) *Social Protection Versus Economic Flexibility.* Chicago: University of Chicago Press.

Buechtemann, C. (1993) *Employment Security and Labor Market Behavior.* Ithaca, NY: ILR Press.

Burda, M. (1993) 'Unemployment, labor markets and structural change in Eastern Europe', *Economic Policy*, 16.

Burkhauser, R., Duncan, G., Hauser, R. and Berntsen, R. (1991) 'Wife or Frau, women do worse', *Demography*, 28: 353–60.

Burtless, G. (1990) *A Future of Lousy Jobs?* Washington, DC: Brookings Institution.

Calmfors, L. and Driffill, J. (1988) 'Bargaining structure, corporatism, and macroeconomic performance', *Economic Policy*, 6: 14–61.

Choi, S. (1992) 'Ageing and social welfare in South Korea', in D. Phillips (ed.), *Ageing in East and South East Asia.* London: Edward Arnold. pp. 148–66.

Cornia, A. (1994) 'Poverty, food consumption and nutrition during the transition to the market economy in Eastern Europe', *American Economic Review*, May: 297–302.

de Neubourg, C. (1995) 'Switching to the policy mode: incentives by the OECD jobs study to change our mindset'. Unpublished paper, Faculty of Economics, University of Maastricht.

Edwards, S. (1994) 'Trade policies, exchange rates, and growth', National Bureau of Economic Research, Working Paper no. 4511.

Esping-Andersen, G. (1993) *Changing Classes.* London: Sage.

Esping-Andersen, G. (1994) 'Welfare states and the economy', in N. Smelser and R. Swedberg (eds), *Handbook of Economic Sociology.* Princeton: Princeton University Press.

European Community (1993a) *Social Protection in Europe.* Bruxelles: EC.

European Community (1993b) *Green Paper on European Social Policy.* Bruxelles: DG5 (communication by Mr Flynn).

Freeman, R. 1993. 'How labor fares in different countries', in R. Freeman (ed.), *Working under Different Rules.* New York: Russell Sage. pp. 1–28.

Freeman, R. and Katz, L. (eds) (1994) *Differences and Changes in Wage Structure.* Chicago: University of Chicago Press.

Gottschalk, P. (1993) 'Changes in inequality of family income in seven industrialized countries', *American Economic Review*, 2: 136–42.

Hashimoto, A. (1992) 'Ageing in Japan', in D. Phillips (ed.), *Ageing in East and South East Asia.* London: Edward Arnold. pp. 36–44.

Jencks, C. and Peterson, P. (1991) *The Urban Underclass.* Washington, DC: Brookings Institution.

Korpi, W. (1992) *Halkar Sverige Efter.* Stockholm: Carlssons.

Lindbeck, A. (1994) *Turning Sweden Around.* Cambridge, MA: MIT Press.

Lynch, L. (1993) 'Payoffs to alternative training strategies', in R. Freeman (ed.), *Working under Different Rules.* New York: Russell Sage. pp. 63–96.

Marshall, T.H. (1950) *Citizenship and Social Class.* Oxford: Oxford University Press.

Mishel, L. and Bernstein, J. (1993) *The State of Working America, 1992–1993.* Armon, NY: M.E. Sharpe.

Moffitt, R. (1990) 'The distribution of earnings and the welfare state', in G. Burtless (ed.), *A Future of Lousy Jobs?* Washington, DC: Brookings Institution. pp. 201–35.

OECD (1988) *Ageing Populations.* Paris: OECD.

OECD (1993) *Employment Outlook*. Paris: OECD.

OECD (1994a) *New Orientations for Social Policy*. Paris: OECD.

OECD (1994b) *Unemployment in Transition Countries: Transient or Persistent?* Paris: OECD.

Pereira, L. (1993) 'Economic reforms and economic growth: efficiency and politics in Latin America', in L. Pereira, J.M. Maravall and A. Przeworski (eds), *Economic Reforms in New Democracies*. Cambridge: Cambridge University Press.

Przeworski, A. (1991) *Democracy and the Market*. Cambridge: Cambridge University Press.

Room, G. (1990) *New Poverty in the European Community*. London: Macmillan.

Soskice, D. (1991) 'Wage determination: the changing role of institutions in advanced industrial countries', *Oxford Review of Economic Policy* no. 6: 36–61.

Standing, G. (1993) 'Labor regulation in an era of fragmented flexibility', in C. Buechtemann (ed.), *Employment Security and Labor Market Behavior*. Ithaca, NY: ILR Press. pp. 425–41.

Streeck, W. (1992) *Social Institutions and Economic Performance*. London: Sage.

PART ONE

DECLINE OR RENEWAL IN THE ADVANCED WELFARE STATES?

2

The Scandinavian Welfare States: Achievements, Crisis, and Prospects

John D. Stephens

The Scandinavian welfare states have enjoyed an international reputation for combining generous welfare state entitlements with rapid economic growth, low unemployment and very high levels of labour force participation, particularly among women. They appeared to have achieved the elusive combination of social equality and economic efficiency. As recently as 1988, Sweden, Norway, and Finland appeared as international exceptions, maintaining very low levels of unemployment while having actually expanded welfare state entitlements over the previous decade. Denmark, with a decade of high unemployment and attendant economic problems, seemed to be the outsider. Within five years, all three experienced historically unprecedented increases in unemployment. Indeed, in Sweden and Finland, the turn of economic events was widely termed a 'crisis' which equalled or exceeded that of the Great Depression.

Many analysts link the poor performance of the Nordic economies to their welfare states. The entitlements are expensive and, it is argued, make the Scandinavian economies uncompetitive. This has been accentuated by the economic internationalization and European integration which make international competitiveness all the more imperative. This critical view of the Nordic welfare states appears to have found some acceptance even among its principal architects, the social democrats and trade unions, as they have recently agreed to cuts in some entitlements, such as lowering replacement rates and introducing waiting days for benefits. Moreover, trade unionists and social democrats, in Scandinavia and elsewhere in

Europe, have expressed fears that the long term result of the 1992 initiative would be to reduce welfare state provisions to the lowest common denominator within the European Union.

In this chapter, I examine the development, achievements, and current crisis of the Scandinavian welfare states. My main focus is on social policy but this cannot be understood without considering also the complementary economic policies that produce growth and thus employment. My main argument will be that, taken as a whole, welfare state entitlements have made little if any direct contribution to the current economic problems of the Scandinavian countries. Arguably, many of them actually result in competitive advantages. Rather I argue that the Scandinavian growth and employment model, which was so successful up to the mid 1970s, is much less effective today. This, in turn, makes welfare state entitlements which were affordable in the past no longer affordable. Quite simply, as unemployment rises, more people draw on the social welfare system and fewer contribute to it, making precisely the same set of entitlements now excessively expensive.

I begin with a description of the Scandinavian welfare states and their supportive economic policies. I then analyse the current crisis, and conclude with some speculation on future trajectories of economic and social policy in the region. Throughout, I focus on Sweden, while the other three countries serve as comparisons and contrasts. I do this not only because treating all four cases in equal depth would make this chapter inordinately long but also because Sweden is frequently singled out as the paradigmatic example of social democracy. Moreover, actors in the other three countries frequently attempted to emulate (or avoid) Swedish policies.

Social policy patterns: commonalities and contrasts

Recent scholarship on the welfare state, inspired by Titmuss's (1974) tri-partite 'models of social policy', attempts to develop typologies of welfare states (e.g. see Esping-Andersen, 1990; Palme, 1990; van Kersbergen, 1991; Huber et al., 1993; Korpi and Palme, 1994). Following Esping-Andersen (1987; 1990), these typologies have generally distinguished three types of welfare states: the social democratic or institutional; the corporativist, Catholic or work merit, and the liberal or residualist (however, see Castles and Mitchell, 1990; Ragin, 1994; Kangas, 1994). Esping-Andersen and Kolberg (1992b) have argued that these social policy types are associated with patterns of labour market entry and exit and employment, characterizing the intersection of these two as 'welfare state regimes'. Moreover, in the case of Scandinavia, many analysts have connected the social policies to the policies promoting growth and employment to designate a 'Scandinavian model' of the full employment welfare state.[1]

A good starting point is Palme's (1990: 82ff) analysis of pensions. In Palme's classification the institutional pension model unites 'basic security'

Table 2.1 *Earnings replacement rates for an average production worker (per cent of working wage) and coverage (per cent) in major transfer programmes, 1985*

	Sweden	Norway	Finland	Denmark
Earnings replacement				
Pensions:				
Minimum	48	48	48	54
Full qualifications	77	67	69	56
Sick pay (26 week absence)	90	100	74	77
Maternity/parental leave				
(26 week absence)	92	83	77	83
Unemployment (26 weeks)	72	61	56	59
Coverage				
Pensions	100	100	100	100
Sick pay	87	85	92	81
Maternity/parental leave	100	100	100	81
Unemployment	75	90	63	80

Sources: most figures are from Hagen, 1992: 141, 147, 151, 154; the remainder are from Olli Kangas and Joakim Palme (personal correspondence)

and 'income security'. In practice, such a system combines a basic flat rate pension which is a right of citizenship (that is, all citizens receive it regardless of work history) and an earnings related pension with a relatively high income replacement rate. To extend this to the welfare state as a whole, we can say that the institutional model combines citizenship benefits equal for all citizens with income security for the working population in cases of temporary (illness, unemployment) or permanent (retirement, work injury) interruption of work. The major transfer programmes (pensions, sick pay, work injury, unemployment compensation, maternity/parental leave) are designed to provide income security. In addition, the flat rate citizenship pensions which form the first tier of all of the Scandinavian pension systems provide basic security, and some of these countries provide additional citizenship benefits such as sickness and unemployment allowances. Moreover, all four Scandinavian countries provide flat rate child allowances, and housing allowances which are generally related to need.

Replacement rates and coverage rates in the major transfer programmes for an average production worker are shown in Table 2.1. It is apparent from these figures that the Nordic welfare states do approximate the institutional model. Both the coverage rates and replacement rates are high. The effect of the basic citizenship pension can be seen from the figures for the minimum pension, that is, that which a single person without labour market experience would receive. The Luxembourg Income Study (LIS) clearly shows that the citizenship pensions have been effective in reducing poverty among the aged for the three Nordic countries for which there are LIS data: only 5 per cent of aged Norwegians, 4 per cent of aged Finns, and less than 0.5 per cent of aged Swedes live in poverty.[2]

The pension data in Table 2.1 show that the Danish model is somewhat less institutional. Its second-tier pensions provide only a modest supplement which is related to work experience but not to income level; thus the income replacement rate falls steeply as income rises. By contrast, in the other three countries, supplementary pensions are earnings related, rising with income to ceilings which are set at 7.5 or 8 times a 'base amount' in Sweden and Norway (approximately three times the wages of an average production worker) or without a ceiling in the case of Finland. Because the replacement rates in Table 2.1 for sick pay, parental leave, and unemployment insurance refer to the average production worker they do not reveal the extent to which replacement rates in Denmark for higher paid workers fall to a much greater extent than they do in the other three countries. Danish legislation generally provides for a replacement rate up to 90 per cent of the pay of an average industrial worker. Swedish and Norwegian replacement rates generally are 90–100 per cent and are paid up to the same ceilings as the public pensions, thus providing high replacement rates well up into the ranks of white collar workers. Finnish provisions vary but are closer to the Swedish and Norwegian with regard to income replacement rates for better paid employees.

The Finnish transfer system does differ from the other Scandinavian countries in one regard: even if legislated, a substantial portion of it is administered outside the state apparatus and does not appear in the public budget and in the figures in Table 2.1. This is true of the first week of sick pay and work injury insurance.

If the welfare state is conceived broadly to include also services such as education, day care, elderly care, public transit subsidies, housing subsidies, and active labour market expenditure, transfer payments make up less than half of total expenditure. The Scandinavian welfare states are service intensive in contrast to the Catholic welfare states (Huber et al., 1993). In Scandinavia, health care, education, and, to a lesser extent, day care are citizenship or residence rights, provided free or with a small co-payment. In all four countries, these three make up the bulk of service expenditure.

It is worth underlining how distinctive the Scandinavian welfare states are in terms of the expansion of public social services. Along with parental leave, these have been the main area of welfare state innovation in the last two decades. As Cusack and Rein (1991) show, in the mid 1980s, welfare state employment (i.e. public health, education, and welfare employment) accounted for an average of 15.4 per cent of the working age population in the four Scandinavian countries compared with 5.1 per cent in six continental European countries (roughly equivalent to the category of Christian democratic welfare states) and 6.1 per cent in the four Anglo-American countries (the liberal welfare states). From 1975 to 1985, the increase in welfare state employment as a percentage of the working age population was 5.6 per cent in Denmark, Norway, and Sweden compared with only 0.3 per cent for the other six countries for which comparable data are available.[3] The Nordic welfare states are also distinctive in their attention to youth and the working age population, relative to the aged. This holds for both public social services, most of which are directed at youth and the working age population (e.g. education, day care, labour market retraining), and transfers such as parental leave and child allowances.

Thus, broad, usually universal, coverage, high income replacement rates, the scope of citizenship rights, and service intensity are four of the basic institutional parameters of the Scandinavian welfare states. Additional dimensions are liberal qualifying conditions for benefits, comprehensiveness, and statism. As we pointed out above, basic pensions and most services are provided on the basis of citizenship or merely residence. In the case of other transfers, the qualifying conditions (e.g. number of waiting days before benefits begin, number of weeks or years worked to qualify for benefits or full benefits) are liberal compared with similar requirements elsewhere. Means, needs, or income testing for benefits is not frequent in the Nordic welfare states. Housing allowances, the special pension supplements for those with no or small earnings related pensions, and social assistance are the only programmes of importance where such tests are required.

By comprehensiveness, I mean that the social provisions in the Nordic welfare states cover virtually all areas in which the state provides services or benefits in any advanced industrial democracy. And by statism I mean that services are provided by the state rather than by subsidized non-profit institutions (e.g. religious organizations) or by subcontracted private firms. As pointed out above, Finland is a partial exception here. The result of all these characteristics is that public provisions crowd out private alternatives such as negotiated collective benefits or private insurance. These play a much smaller role in Scandinavia than in other advanced industrial countries.

For the social and political forces that shaped the Scandinavian welfare states, above all the socialist parties and manual worker unions but also the white collar unions and the agrarian parties,[4] the institutional parameters themselves were not a primary goal of legislation. The real aims were security, decommodification, labour training and mobilization, and redistribution. It is my contention that these welfare states achieved these goals to a degree unrecognized by even their supporters. In the case of security and decommodification, this is uncontroversial as it can be read off from the institutional characteristics themselves. High income replacement rates, citizenship benefits, liberal qualifying conditions, and comprehensiveness all contribute to security. As a result of universal coverage, high income replacement rates for most transfers, citizenship pensions and services, and liberal qualifying conditions, Scandinavian welfare states are 'decommodifying' in Esping-Andersen's terms, that is, citizenship rather than market participation and market position forms the basis for entitlement to income or publicly provided goods and services, and individuals suffer relatively small losses of income from exiting paid work temporarily or permanently.

As to training and labour mobilization, it would take us too far afield to provide a comprehensive assessment of the effectiveness of Scandinavian education and labour market training systems in providing a highly skilled workforce. Suffice it to say that labour quality is a major comparative advantage for these countries. In the case of labour mobilization the figures on labour force participation and, until the late 1980s, unemployment speak for themselves. It is important to point out here that this goal and decommodification can conflict with one another. It is those features that reduce the work incentive which have been under attack in recent years. It is, of course, a commonplace contention (and not only from the right) that high taxes and generous transfers produce work disincentives. But, as a comprehensive review of research on Denmark and Sweden (as well as on Germany and the United Kingdom) demonstrates, the empirical evidence is much more mixed than the commonplace view would assume (Atkinson and Mogensen, 1993). Some robust findings stand out: generous early retirement pensions do induce early exit from the labour force, and the array of policies aimed to facilitate women's labour force participation (parental leave, public day care, etc.) have had their intended effect. Otherwise the negative effects on labour supply are generally small or insignificant and positive effects are not infrequent for some subgroups such as prime age men. Moreover, variations across programmes are relatively great and findings for one country do not necessarily hold for another. For example, in the case of sickness insurance which has provoked heated debate in Scandinavia, Gustafsson and Klevmarken (1993: 95) suggest that increases in replacement rates (but not decreases in waiting days) are strongly associated with increases in absenteeism in Sweden. By contrast, in Kangas's (1991) cross-national study, fewer waiting days but not high replacement rates were associated with high absenteeism. Esping-Andersen and Kolberg (1992a) find that, though Sweden, Norway, and Denmark all have generous sick pay provisions, they vary greatly in rates of absenteeism.

Two points are worth underlining with regard to redistribution, both of which are of considerable importance for our concluding discussion on future directions for the Nordic welfare states. First, as Mitchell's (1991) work on the redistributive effect of direct taxes and transfers shows, the welfare state under social democratic auspices has been massively redistributive. Saunders's (1991) work, also based on LIS data, indicates that the inclusion of the distributive effect of public services strengthens the redistributive effect additionally.[5] Second, though the apparent effect of earnings related benefits would seem to lessen the redistributive impact of the welfare state, the opposite is the case. This counter-intuitive finding is explained by the fact that the institutional welfare state crowds out the even more inegalitarian private alternatives. This has been demonstrated conclusively for pensions (Kangas and Palme, 1993; Palme, 1993) and also for a broader range of welfare state benefits in the work of Korpi and Palme. Kangas and Palme (1993) present LIS data on ten countries showing that other sources of support for the elderly are vastly more unequally distributed than public pensions (with Ginis varying from 0.41 to 0.82 depending on source and country compared with 0.15 for the highest Gini for public pensions). They also show that generous public pensions greatly reduce reliance on these alternatives. And, though public pension income is more unequally distributed in countries with earnings related pensions, gross income (and final disposable income) is more equally distributed. For example, the Gini index for public pension income in Sweden is 0.15; in Australia, which has means tested pensions, it is –0.07.[6] Yet the Gini index for gross income (including all sources but before tax) and for final disposable income are considerably lower in Sweden (0.24 and 0.14 respectively) than in Australia (0.34 and 0.28 respectively). Palme (1993) presents yet more evidence of the egalitarian nature of institutional pension systems, showing that his measure of pension institutionalism (as defined above) is highly correlated with inequality of disposable income among the aged (–0.83). In their analysis of income distribution among the elderly in Finland at six points in time between 1966 and 1991, Jäntti et al. (1994) show that the maturation of the Finnish statutory earnings related schemes led to dramatic declines in income inequality (the squared coefficient of variation declined from 0.57 in 1966 to 0.16 in 1991). They conclude that 'despite their income-graduation, legislated universal programmes have equalizing effects by crowding out more regressive components of the income package of the elderly'.

The economic model: commonalities and contrasts

As Esping-Andersen and Kolberg (1992b) have argued, the Scandinavian welfare states have been associated with a distinct labour market regime. By the end of the 'Golden Age', all four countries were characterized by very low unemployment, high labour force participation among women, and comparatively high levels of public health, education, and welfare employment. It is useful to view the labour market regime as the inter-section of Scandinavian economic and social policy; all three are inter-linked in a more or less coherent model. With regard to the employment regime, one can make the following crude characterization as a baseline against which the actual experiences of the individual countries can be compared. By the mid 1960s, the employment/growth models had produced high rates of labour participation and very low unemployment among males. Unlike other European countries, Scandinavia limited the recruit-ment of non-Nordic foreign labour. This provided greater job opportunities for women in the private sector. More important for female employment, the Scandinavian welfare states became service intensive, thus providing employment opportunities for women in public health, education, and welfare. This was facilitated by the expansion of maternity/parental leave and day care, the latter, in turn, providing additional jobs. And, as female participation rose so did demands for a further expansion of such transfers and services.

Active labour market policy (public employment services, moving allowances, job training, temporary public employment, and subsidized employment in the public or private sectors) has often been viewed as an integral part of the Nordic welfare-state/labour-market regime. It is true that the Scandinavian countries all do have active labour market policies, and their concentration on active measures as opposed to passive measures (i.e. unemployment compensation) does distinguish them from the continental welfare states. However, there is great variation among the four countries which is directly related to the growth/employment policy. For reasons we outline below, Sweden is distinctive and has constituted a model for emulation by the other three countries.[7] In 1970, when all four countries enjoyed very low unemployment, Sweden spent three times more than the others on active labour market measures. In 1987, when unemployment rates were 5 per cent in Finland, 8 per cent in Denmark, and only 1.9 per cent in Sweden, Sweden, nevertheless, spent 1.9 per cent of GDP on active labour market measures compared with only 0.9 per cent and 1.1 per cent in Finland and Denmark respectively.

Though the policy goals of all four countries were broadly similar, the specific economic/employment policies of the Nordic countries vary more than their welfare state regimes. Nevertheless, one can identify a general Nordic type which fits all of the countries except Denmark.[8] They are small, open economies and thus depend on competitive exports. The export sector has traditionally been based on the countries' raw materials and has been closely linked to financial interests. These are economies with strong backward and forward integrated industrial complexes with a strong human capital base. This, combined with rising capital intensity, became increasingly important for international competitiveness as the countries moved beyond the export of raw and semi-processed materials.

Scandinavia boasts the highest union density rates of industrial societies, and unions are highly centralized. The employers are likewise well organized and highly centralized. The combination of strong unions and export dependency has necessitated wage restraint, which was possible due to centralized bargaining. The unions' 'side payment' for wage restraint has been full employment and the institutional welfare state. For this kind of trade-off to work, government cooperation was necessary. From a union point of view this was facilitated by the frequent government position of the Social Democratic party. Thus a pattern of tripartite bargaining ('neo-corporatism') over wages, economic, and social policy emerged in Scandinavia.

Given this balance of power, it is not surprising that economic policy prioritized full employment and economic growth based on rapid technological change. Fiscal policies were moderately counter-cyclical, backed up by occasional devaluations. However, and this cannot be overemphasized, the core of long term growth/employment policy was on the supply side. Supply side policies extended beyond general measures (such as education and job training, infrastructure, cheap credit policies, and generalized support for R&D) to include also selective measures (such as active labour market policy, credit policies favouring industrial borrowers over consumers and speculators, regional policies, and subsidies or subsidized credit to selected industries). Interest rates were kept low through credit rationing and through public sector surpluses. Accordingly, fiscal policy was generally austere, and these countries usually ran budget surpluses. Aggregate demand was mainly a question of world demand for Scandinavian exports.

The Nordic countries are also individually distinct in important respects. In Sweden it is the nature of business which is most distinctive. As in Finland and Norway, export manufacturing is highly concentrated. But it differs in that export industry has always been dominated by a small number of privately owned, internationalized and internationally competitive, oligopolistic firms. More quickly than the other two countries, Sweden turned from export of raw materials and semi-processed goods to export of capital goods and finished consumer products.

The nature of Sweden's business sector has encouraged the development of aggressive policies on the part of the employers' association, SAF. At first, it aimed to defeat the nascent union movement; then, when this failed, to limit its political influence; and, finally, when this failed, to preserve private ownership and employers' prerogatives in the workplace and private sector direction of the overall investment process.[9]

After the re-election of the Social Democrats in 1936, the employers' federation abandoned its attempt to defeat the labour movement and entered into negotiations with Landsorganisationen (the manual worker' unions' central organization) resulting in the Saltsjöbaden agreement of 1938. Korpi (1983: 47–8) characterizes the long term effects of this 'historic compromise' as an agreement by both parties to cooperate in creating economic growth: the labour movement would receive greater influence over the results of production; and employers would retain the right to control the productive process and the direction of investment. The cooperative arrangement paved the way for labour peace and later for the centralization of collective bargaining at the national level.

The postwar programme of the labour movement contained elements of more ambitious planning that would have moved Sweden closer to the more statist direction of investment characteristic of Norway and Finland. Such a move was cut short by the Social Democratic retreat in the postwar 'planning debate'. As a result the Swedish version of the Scandinavian supply side model came to focus on labour supply, and only indirectly on investment.

The contours of this policy emerged in the famous Rehn-Meidner model of equal pay for equal work across the economy (the so-called solidaristic wage policy). This would force labour intensive, low productivity enterprises to rationalize or go out of business. The displaced labour would then be moved to high productivity sectors through the active labour market policy. Wages in high productivity sectors would be restrained to facilitate international competition and encourage investment.[10] The active labour market policy, by reducing structural unemployment, would further facilitate wage restraint and thus reduce the trade-off between unemployment and inflation, moving the Phillips curve down and to the left.

Restrictive economic policy should be pursued in order to facilitate wage restraint. Full employment would be achieved through the active labour market policy and other selective measures, including loans at low interest rates from public savings such as pension funds. State controls in currency and credit markets facilitated macro-economic adjustment. Acceptable distributive outcomes for labour were achieved by tight fiscal policy which dampened domestic demand and thus profit levels[11] and by expansion of transfer payments and free or subsidized public goods and services. Given modest profit levels, levels of business investment adequate for economic growth were to be achieved through the low interest loans from public savings. The tax regime also favoured investment over distribution of profits.

The growth of the economy was, of course, essential for the expansion of the welfare state. At least as important was the pattern of employment generation. Low levels of unemployment and high levels of labour force participation meant more people supported the welfare state with taxes while relatively fewer drew on its benefits. Thus, generous entitlements were less costly than would have been the case if Scandinavia's participation rates had been as low (or unemployment levels as high) as in continental Europe.

Norway and Finland lacked the internationalized, large scale, corporate structure of Sweden. This may help explain why the conservative parties accepted state leadership in economic planning in Norway and even initiated it in Finland. This reflected the difficulty that Norwegian and Finnish business faced in mobilizing the capital necessary for an ambitious programme of industrialization, but also their weaker political ability to oppose such a programme had they wanted to.

The Norwegian model was characterized by an active industrial policy with low interest rates, a policy that was facilitated by extensive state ownership of industry and of banks. Mjøset (1986: 121) has characterized the Norwegian model as 'credit socialism'.

Active labour market policy was less central to the Norwegian model. One reason for this was the possibility of direct intervention to support employment in declining areas. Thus, in contrast to Sweden, Norwegian policy has always had a strong element of regional subsidization and, as a result, many industries suffer from greater micro-efficiency problems than in Sweden.

If anything, the state was even more active in the Finnish industrialization process, not only promoting and subsidizing industrial diversification but also directly owning and creating new industrial concerns. Like Norway and Sweden, the state used low interest rates and channelling of credit to industrial users. In order to create public savings the model was fiscally very conservative, running consistent surpluses. Unlike in Norway and Sweden, labour was ideologically divided and was largely excluded from the policy process. Finland fits Lehmbruch's (1984) notion of 'concertation without labour', bearing similarities to Japan and East Asian newly industralized countries (NICs) (Vartiainen, 1994).

The mid 1960s mark a system shift in Finnish policy, moving it in the direction of the Swedish and Norwegian models. The 1966 election ushered in a period of Social Democratic rule in cooperation with the Communists and/or Agrarians, divisions in the trade union movement were overcome, and union membership began to increase rapidly. As a result, Finland moved towards tripartite corporatism with the agreement on the comprehensive incomes policy in 1968, the first of its kind in Finland, symbolically marking the transition. Social policy followed a similar pattern: enabled by the new affluence, the centre-left political alignment carried out a series of social reforms over two decades, extending into the period of slowdown or retrenchment in the other three Scandinavian countries. Thus, the Finnish welfare state caught up with its neighbours.

The different nature of the Danish model can be traced to its industrial structure. Denmark's exports were dominated by agricultural products until the 1960s, and industry was traditionally small scale and craft oriented. Even after the 'second industrial revolution' beginning in the late 1950s, small scale manufacturing dominated the new niche oriented manufacturing export industries. Moreover Denmark lacked the kind of finance–industry linkages found in Sweden, Norway and Finland.

As a consequence, agrarian interests were stronger and the left weaker in Denmark, and the unions remained more decentralized. This prohibited strong central planning, and also a more modest Swedish style supply side policy (Esping-Andersen, 1985). Danish financial markets were strongly integrated in international credit markets, and thus interest rates were higher than in the other countries (Mjøset, 1986). With no long term supply side policies, government efforts to combat unemployment were predominantly short term Keynesian demand management measures which fuelled inflation, thus threatening the balance of payments and consequently leading to contractionary measures, the 'stop–go' cycle familiar to students of British political economy (Esping-Andersen, 1985: 207).[12]

These same economic and political characteristics strongly influenced social policy outcomes. Typically, the Social Democrats could not dispense with support from the agrarian Radicals. Thus, they failed in their efforts to pass earnings related supplementary pensions. And, similarly, the Danish trade union movement – especially the unskilled workers' unions – has favoured increasing the flat rate pension, rather than promoting a second-tier pension, and has generally been opposed to high income replacement rates for upper income earners in most transfer programmes. Hence, as we have seen, benefit levels in Denmark fall rapidly as one moves above the income level of the average production worker (Salminen, 1993: 275–6).

Denmark also stands out in an international context in terms of the very low rates of employer social contribution. The lion's share of welfare state financing is via general taxation. The main reason must be attributed to the small scale nature of Danish employers.

The crisis of the Scandinavian model

'Crisis' is perhaps the most overused word in studies of the advanced political economies. In the 1970s, it usually referred to the sudden advent of low economic growth. The advanced economies have gone through a sea change since the break-up of the Bretton Woods system of fixed but flexible exchange rates in 1971 and the OPEC oil price increase of 1973. These events have combined with long term secular changes such as increasing internationalization of trade, capital, and finance, currency instability, the decline of industry and the rise of the service sector. These trends have been held responsible for what truly is a crisis of the Scandinavian models. In this section, I will argue that they did have a major impact on the employment/growth and labour market models but only indirectly affected the welfare state via the resultant increase in unemployment.

Sweden

As in the other Scandinavian countries, Swedish governments initially treated the new economic era as if it were a temporary downturn.[13] Thus, the Social Democratic government reacted with counter-cyclical measures. As the difficulties wore on, the series of bourgeois coalition governments, which took power in 1976, introduced a combination of restrictive and expansive measures which Mjøset (1986) characterizes as 'fumbling'. These governments were eager to defend unemployment and welfare state entitlements to prove Social Democratic propaganda against them to be incorrect. While no major social policy innovations were passed, neither were there any significant rollbacks. To fight unemployment, the governments subsidized some industries and took over failing ones. As a result, budget deficits mounted. In part in reaction to the deficits, but also as a result of a neo-liberal turn on the part of the conservatives and the aggressive neo-liberal posture of SAF, the government began to introduce some very modest entitlement reductions in 1980, such as reducing compensation for part-time pensions and introducing one waiting day for sick pay (Marklund, 1988).

That the sick pay waiting day became a major issue in the 1982 election which brought the Social Democrats back to power indicates the widespread support for the welfare state in Sweden and also the policy mandate the new government had. The new government knew that the changed world required new policies. Before entering office, leading Social Democratic economists had come to the conclusion that it was impossible to expand public expenditure as a percentage of GDP. Thus, any new reforms would have to be financed by other budget cuts or by economic growth (Feldt, 1991). In office, the Social Democrats not only cut spending as a percentage of GDP (while, remarkably, actually introducing some new reforms), but also cut state intervention in the economy in other ways, notably deregulating financial markets in 1985–6, directing all state enterprises to make profitability their only goal, and partially privatizing some state enterprises.

There is no doubt that some of these policies followed the preferences of Finance Minister Feldt and his advisers whose neo-liberal (at least, neo-liberal within the context of Swedish Social Democracy) bent went further than many in the labour movement, above all the LO leadership and the LO economists, would have done had they controlled policy. However, with regard to the size of the welfare state, there was agreement. In 1986, a group of LO policy experts (who would hardly count among Feldt's allies) issued a report which argued that it was not necessary for the welfare state to grow additionally in order for it to guarantee the basic goals of social security and equality. In a way, the LO report confirmed that the Swedish welfare state was fully developed. Putting the LO report and the Feldt group's assessment together, one can say that the promoters of the Swedish welfare state were left with less to do but, then, they also had less to do it with.

While still in opposition, the Social Democrats supported a tax reform proposed by the Centre-Liberal government which lowered marginal rates in the middle and higher brackets. This prefigured the 1989–90 'tax reform of the century' in which the Social Democratic government in cooperation with the Liberals reduced the rates of marginal taxation to 50 per cent for those in higher income brackets. This implied less redistribution, and an acceptance that high marginal taxation reduces incentives to save and work.[14]

The new Social Democratic 'Third Road' (between Keynesian reflation and Thatcherite austerity policies) was a response to these developments. A currency devaluation of 16 per cent, on top of a devaluation of 10 per cent the previous year, created a substantial competitive edge for Swedish industry. They followed this up by securing wage restraint from the unions and deficit cuts, which restrained consumption, created a profits boom, and led to a redistribution of income from labour to capital. Aided by resumed international demand, the policy appeared very successful as the economy picked up and unemployment and deficits fell. Based on this performance, the Social Democrats won the 1985 election, and by the 1988 election the 'Third Road' seemed wildly successful: the budget deficits, which had been 8 per cent of GDP when the Social Democrats had come to office, had been eliminated; unemployment was under 2 per cent; the balance of trade was in surplus; and new social reforms had been passed. With these successes, the Social Democrats campaigned in 1988 on promises of a new round of social reforms: the introduction of a sixth week of vacation, extension of parental leave insurance from 9 to 15 months, and provision of public day care places for all pre-school children over the age of one and a half.

Within a year of their re-election, the bubble burst. Owing to the economic crisis that the government encountered during its period in office, it failed to deliver on any of these promises. The government introduced an austerity package in February 1990 which called for a pay freeze and a strike ban, reversing its commitment to non-interference in collective bargaining. Though the government fell owing to lack of parliamentary support for the package, it reconstituted itself and two months later, with Liberal support, passed a similar austerity package (though without the offensive labour market features). Among other things, it reduced the replacement rate for sick pay from 90 per cent to 65 per cent for the first three days and to 80 per cent for days 4 to 90. In the autumn of 1990, the Social Democrats reversed their stand on the EC, now favouring membership.

Given that Swedish Social Democracy's electoral success has been largely built on the public perception that it possessed a unique capacity to simultaneously institute social reforms and manage the economy effectively, it is not so surprising that their apparent failure to do either resulted in their worst election result since 1928 in the 1991 election. The economy continued to worsen under the Conservative-led minority coalition. Open unemployment increased from 1.6 per cent in 1990 to 7.7 per cent in 1993; counting those in active labour market measures the increase was from 2.1 per cent to 12.5 per cent (OECD, 1994: 36). GDP growth was negative in 1991, 1992 and 1993. During the European currency turbulence of 1992, the government and Social Democrats went to extraordinary lengths to defend the crown (krona), agreeing to two 'crisis packages' that included significant cuts in entitlements, such as reducing pensions and sick pay, and introducing one waiting day. In the end, the measures were unsuccessful and the crown was floated. Though the decision to float meant that the basis for the agreement was now absent, it was clear that all political actors regarded the economic situation as critical and thus warranting cuts in entitlements. Some of these have already been instituted. What made these cuts necessary is the widespread conviction that Sweden will not be able to return to anywhere near the 2 per cent open unemployment (with no more than an additional 1 per cent in labour market measures) in the foreseeable future. The fact that the new policy of self-financing of the unemployment insurance system assumes a normal rate of unemployment of 5 per cent shows that policy is already being made on this assumption.[15] Thus, though the budget was in surplus in 1989 before the recent modest cuts, it is assumed to be in structural (and not just cyclical) deficit now.

Before outlining the changes instituted in response to the crisis and likely future changes in the Swedish welfare state, it is important to point out that a number of reforms were already planned prior to the crisis. Three are worth mentioning here.[16] First, owing to the forecast demographic burdens, the earnings-related tier of the pension system ('ATP') faced a future crisis since it was only partially funded. Since any reform that emerged would have to hold far into the future, all parties in the parliamentary committee working on the plan committed themselves to working out a broad compromise. A quickly agreed-upon baseline was that, in the new system, each generation would have to pay for its own pensions. A full pension will now require 40 years of contributions with no special consideration for 'best earning years'; benefits are to be based on lifetime income. In a fundamental change of principle, the new system will be one of defined contribution not defined benefit. Also in contrast to the previous system which was financed by an employer tax, the new system will be funded by equal contributions of employers and employees of 9.25 per cent of the payroll each. As a consequence, the new design benefits full-time, full-career (read 'male') workers. It was immediately recognized that women and to a lesser extent workers with higher education would be disadvantaged by the system and that adjustments had to be made. Therefore, the bill agreed upon in 1994 by the governing parties and the Social Democrats provided for extra pension points for child care, studies, and compulsory military service. Some redistribution is built into the system as there is a benefits ceiling (indexed to real economic growth) but contributions would be paid above the ceiling albeit at half the rate as below.

Second, the rapidly rising costs of both sick pay and work injury insurance had already evoked considerable concern by the late 1980s. In the case of work injury, court decisions in the early 1980s liberalized qualifying conditions which led to rapid increases in the number of claims without compensating adjustments in financing. The abolition of the waiting day for sick pay in the early 1980s, and improved compensation, had led to increased absenteeism and thus costs. A reform of these programmes had been contemplated even before the employment crisis. The ideas that emerged from the Working Environment Commission of the late 1980s stressed the 'work line' as a possible way to economize while maintaining generous benefits. In this view, the costs of work injury insurance and early pensions and, by extension also sick pay, could be reduced by rehabilitation and other efforts to keep people in the workforce. One approach would be to provide workers and employers with the proper incentives to sustain employment rather than resort to social insurance. For instance, shifting the costs to employers with high incidence of work related injuries and sickness would provide an incentive for them to improve the working environment.

Third, in the course of the 1980s, the delivery of public services came under fire. First, consumers increasingly expressed dissatisfaction with the delivery of welfare state services in general. Specifically, citizens in their roles as clients, patients and parents felt that they had no choice as to types of service or where to obtain them. Hence, the providers of welfare state services were perceived as distant bureaucrats. Second, politicians became increasingly concerned with the cost of all public services, including welfare services.

The Conservative answer was to promote privatization and competition in order to improve the quality of delivery of services and reduce their cost, while the Centre Party promoted decentralization. The Social Democrats in general, and Olaf Palme in particular, attributed the electoral losses of the 1970s in part to the issue of an unresponsive and distant public bureaucracy (Feldt, 1991) and they had been eager to address the issue once they returned to office in 1982. After some false starts, the government settled on a programme which emphasized decentralization of authority in the delivery of services to lower levels of government combined with the introduction of market models in public services, such as payment by output (Olsson, 1990; Rothstein, 1992).

Initially, the Social Democrats resisted any movement toward privatization, especially welfare services. The bourgeois parties won a rare debate on basic principles of the future welfare state by arguing that private alternatives should in principle be allowed to compete with public providers of services.[17] Let us be clear here: Swedes favour allowing choice between public and private providers. They do not think that private providers would necessarily be better. On the contrary, in the case of every major service except child care, very large majorities believe 'state or local authorities' are 'best suited' to deliver the service in question; and even in the case of child care, a plurality thinks state and local authorities are best suited, followed by the family (Svalforss, 1991; 1992).

The Social Democrats have come to accept the idea of private competition with the state, albeit subject to state regulation and financing. The Conservatives for their part have backed off from their neo-liberal ideal of privatization and deregulation and have come to accept the need for continued state regulation. Nevertheless, subtle but important differences remain with regard to the goal of equality in service delivery. Many Conservatives favour allowing households to pay extra for services, whereas the Social Democrats are firmly opposed to this on the grounds that it would create a two class (or multi-class) system of services. Furthermore, the Social Democrats along with most Liberals insist that any private alternatives must avoid the problems of selectivity and social dumping. For instance, they oppose admissions tests by schools which could lead to a situation where private schools admit only good students, and students with any kind of learning or behavioural problems would be dumped on public schools.

Three important changes in service delivery have been introduced so far. First, in education, the bourgeois government introduced a voucher system under which parents can choose any public or private school. For those choosing a private school, the government will provide a voucher equivalent to 85 per cent of the cost of educating a student in a public school. Schools are allowed to charge fees beyond the amount provided by the vouchers. Second, the option for private providers to offer day care under the same conditions as public providers was also introduced. Third, a so-called 'house doctor' system was introduced which, by allowing individuals to freely choose their own doctor, expanded the possibilities for private practice. As yet, private providers have not become significant in any of these areas: they account for only 8 per cent of health care, 1.5 per cent of schooling, and 2 per cent of day care.[18]

The Conservative government elected in 1991 implemented a number of cuts in social benefits, most of them with Social Democratic support.[19] Early retirement pensions will no longer be given owing to slack labour markets. Sick pay was reduced to 80 per cent after 90 days, and the basic pension was reduced to 98 per cent of the base amount. Industrial injury insurance was coordinated with sick pay which entailed a reduction of the replacement rate, and qualifying conditions were sharpened for both benefits. Employers must now pay for the first two weeks of sick pay. Since this was accompanied by a corresponding decrease in employer contributions to the system (and thus no savings for the government), this move was primarily designed to reduce absenteeism by increasing employer surveillance of sickness claims. A five day waiting period for unemployment benefits, which was eliminated by the Social Democratic government of the 1980s, was reintroduced and replacement rates were lowered to 80 per cent. And, as with the new supplementary pension system, employees will now co-finance sick pay insurance. While the Social Democrats opposed the changes in the unemployment system and much of the changes in the work injury system, once in government they lowered the replacement rate for parental insurance from 90 per cent to 80 per cent to make it consistent with the unemployment compensation, sick pay, and work injury insurance and now plan to lower replacement rates to 75 per cent.

The cuts in benefits and the tightening of qualifying conditions were accompanied by increased spending on active labour market policies to increase employment. Thus, taken as a package, these reforms follow the Social Democrats' 'work line' policy. However, the emphasis has changed. Before, employees were to be provided with increased training and rehabilitation and other positive incentives to remain in the active workforce while employers were to be provided with both 'carrots' and 'sticks' to reduce absenteeism and work injury. The policies passed in the past few years contain a lot of 'sticks' along with a few 'carrots' for employees; they entail stronger incentives to remain employed and more disincentives to take up welfare benefits. This change in emphasis is clearly motivated by the need to reduce expenditures in response to the economic crisis, rising unemployment, and the resultant growing budget deficit.

The cuts have had some of the desired effects. Even before they were instituted, absenteeism began to decline substantially owing to the rise in unemployment. The reforms of the work injury and sick pay insurance schemes did result in the elimination of deficits in these two programmes. However, the unemployment insurance scheme is still in substantial deficit.

The sequencing of events offers compelling evidence that the recent rollbacks in the Swedish welfare state were a product of the rise in unemployment and the belief that unemployment will not return to its previous levels. The argument that entitlements *per se* make Swedish industry uncompetitive is untenable, particularly after the floating of the crown which reduced Swedish wage costs by one-quarter in a year. Yet, the high unemployment and thus pressure to cut entitlements remains.

This turns our attention to the causes of the problems in the Swedish model. As Pontusson (1992) has argued, many of the problems faced by Social Democracy were products of the structural changes in the advanced industrial economies. However, policy mistakes were made which interacted with these structural changes to produce the crisis, and it is important to disentangle these two to make some assessment of where the Swedish welfare state is going. I begin with the changes in the structural constraints.[20]

A number of parallel developments in both the international and the Swedish economy helped undermine the old distributive strategy. The world economy became increasingly internationalized as the volume of trade increased modestly, the multinationalization of enterprises greatly, and the volume of financial transactions dramatically. The collapse of Bretton Woods ended the regime of fixed but flexible exchange rates. OPEC ended the long term secular decline of energy costs which had served to subsidize postwar growth. In the post-1973 era, international interest rates increased dramatically, partly as a direct product of attempts of governments across the advanced industrial world to fight recession with deficit spending. The internationalization and deregulation of financial markets made it very difficult for governments to deviate from international interest rates. Only governments with large trade surpluses could pursue low interest rate policies without putting great pressure on the exchange rates. As Moses (1994) points out in his comparison of Norway and Sweden, the current era is one of financial *and* trade openness in contrast to the interwar period in which trade was regulated and the postwar era in which financial flows were regulated. Thus, neither capital controls nor trade regulations can be deployed to defend the external balance.

In the Swedish case, internationalization led to a successive deregulation of Swedish financial markets during the 1980s. This deprived the government of essential elements of its supply side policy that in the past had been used to secure full employment, price stability, growth, and redistributive aims. Active labour market policy became increasingly the sole remaining policy tool.

A number of special trends in Swedish industry aggravated this situation. Swedish industry became increasingly export oriented and, especially from the 1970s on, increasingly multinational (see especially Erixon, 1985: 45ff). Capital also became increasingly detached from its Swedish raw materials base. The international character of Swedish business dealings, the unstable exchange rates and the greater role of R&D in total investment made investment more risky. Therefore, investments came to depend on profit expectations to a much greater degree than assumed by the Rehn-Meidner model.

The development of Swedish industry had broader ramifications for the Swedish growth/employment model as it changed the interests of capital and the balance of power between labour and capital. Because of its reorientation, Swedish business became markedly less interested in a compromise with domestic labour. Instead, its main concerns became access to foreign markets, lower wage costs, and less competition for labour from the public sector. These concerns help explain the employers' new political offensive from the late 1970s onwards: their mounting criticism of the welfare state, and their advocacy of privatization, of deregulation and of EC membership (Pestoff, 1991; Pontusson, 1992). In addition, these very same trends (together with the growing strength of the bourgeois parties) also helped weaken the relative position of the trade unions.

The increasing strength of capital and the change in its interests contributed to the end of Swedish tripartism: its decline in the 1980s, the termination of centralized bargaining in 1990 and then, in 1991, the withdrawal of SAF representatives from the boards of all state agencies. As Pontusson and Swenson (1992) argue, and as our interviews with union and employer economists confirm, employers in the crucial engineering sector began to prioritize wage flexibility which meant opposition to centralized bargaining and the solidaristic wage policy. They were particularly opposed to LO's extension of the solidaristic wage policy from simply equal pay for equal work to the compression of wages between low and high paid work, because this made it difficult, in their view, to attract and reward skilled labour. In the 1980s we see a rise in wage dispersion (Hibbs, 1990), which helps account for the modest rise in income inequality in the decade, reversing a long postwar trend (Fritzell, 1993).

Pontusson and Swenson's argument for the end of Swedish centralized bargaining is incomplete. While it explains the reasons for the end of the wage policy of solidarity, Austria demonstrates that centralized bargaining is fully possible even without solidarity wage bargaining. While ending centralized bargaining did facilitate rising wage differentials, it also made wage restraint more difficult, an obvious cost for employers. Our interviews at SAF and LO indicate that an additional reason for employers to end centralized bargaining was to weaken LO *vis-à-vis* its constituents both politically and in wage bargaining. That is, employers perceived that the constituent unions making up LO were more flexible in the bargaining process. More important, the repeated resort of LO to legislation during the 1970s, first on industrial democracy and then on the wage earner funds, when negotiations with SAF failed to produce the result LO desired, made SAF see the political weakening of LO as highly desirable. It is mainly this which explains why SAF withdrew its representatives from all tripartite institutions in 1991: it had little to do with flexible wages and much with SAF's perception that these institutions coopted employers and strengthened the influence of labour and the left.[21]

To turn to policy errors, it is now clear that the 'Third Road' strategy was not successful in the long run. By 1989, the benefits of the devaluations had been eaten up by insufficient wage restraint and low productivity growth.[22] In addition, owing to sluggish GDP growth and the limits of welfare state growth, the government's room to compensate the unions for wage restraint with social policy innovations was limited.

But these structural changes did not determine the outcome. The high profits policy combined with a tight labour market in the 1980s encouraged employers to offer wages above the negotiated levels. The government's continued expansion of public sector employment in this context aggravated the situation. Above all, the deregulation of credit markets was poorly timed. This was done in 1985 when there were still generous tax deductions for consumer interest payments,[23] and it fuelled an unprecedented credit and consumer boom at a time when the economy was already overheated. This made wage restraint impossible.

The outcome was that Swedish exports became uncompetitive. Despite the failure of wage restraint, both Social Democratic and Conservative governments refused to let the crown devalue and, thereby, restore the cost competitiveness of export industry. Devaluation did not occur until the economy was in deep recession, causing failed businesses, lost markets, and lost jobs.

Both the Social Democratic and bourgeois governments continued to follow policies which inadvertently had strong procyclical effects on consumer behaviour, this time in the context of a deep recession. As the economy moved into recession in 1990, the tax reform significantly reduced the tax rate on capital income. With falling inflation and stable nominal interest rates, this meant a substantial upward shift in real after-tax interest rates. All this contributed to a rise in the household savings rate and a corresponding depressed level of personal consumption in the midst of a depression (OECD, 1994: 16–17).

On the side of the banks, this same set of circumstances – the asset boom and bust caused by speculation in the wake of financial deregulation – left many banks insolvent. The government bail out operation cost the public coffers 74 billion crowns (5 per cent of GDP) in 1991 and 1992 alone, thus adding to the already spiralling budget deficit (OECD, 1994: 129).

Had productivity growth been stronger, the burden on wage restraint to maintain international competitiveness could have been eased. But, on this count Sweden hardly differs from other advanced countries in the period (Moene and Wallerstein, 1993). Nonetheless, productivity growth was lower than earlier and one reason is that a key tool of the Swedish supply side model, the provision of cheap credit to industry and the favouring of industrial investors over other potential users of credit, was no longer available because of the deregulation of financial markets. Another reason for the low productivity growth was that Swedish business increasingly invested profits abroad, especially in EC countries following the Single European Act in 1985 (Pontusson, 1992: 322). Thus, the high profits policy failed to fuel domestic investment.

Norway

Owing to huge oil revenues, Norway has avoided a severe unemployment crisis, and thus has also escaped the need for welfare state rollbacks. On balance, the past decade has seen neither cutbacks nor innovation. On the one hand, maternal leave was upgraded in 1986, 1987, and 1993, providing for 52 weeks with an 80 per cent income replacement (or 42 weeks at full pay), a level of generosity second only to Sweden. In addition, since 1990, qualifying conditions for unemployment compensation have been liberalized. On the other hand, indexation of benefits has been modified; the replacement rate in the supplementary pension plan has been cut by 3 per cent; work requirements for unemployment compensation have been strengthened; the qualifying conditions for disability tightened; and the strictly medical criteria for disability pensions (re)introduced. While the Norwegian authorities are now also committed to a 'work line', this has only been manifested in the stricter qualifying conditions for unemployment, disability, and sickness benefits and greater efforts at rehabilitation. In contrast to the other Nordic countries, replacement rates have not been cut, nor have waiting days been increased. For instance, the replacement rate for sick pay is still 100 per cent and there are no waiting days.

Underlying this mixed picture are serious difficulties in the Norwegian economic policy model which are partially masked by revenues from the oil sector.[24] Government's capacity to direct credit and investment has been weakened, though the resources from the oil sector still give the state considerable leverage compared with Sweden. As in Sweden and Finland, deregulation of credit markets in the mid 1980s led to a consumer spending boom which was followed by a spate of bank failures and consumer retrenchment. As in Sweden, all governments pursued hard currency policies which certainly aggravated the competitiveness problems of industry until Norway was forced to float the crown (krone) in the autumn of 1992 (though with less dramatic consequences for the currency's value). Even the Labour government has prioritized fighting inflation over unemployment (Moene and Wallerstein, 1993).

Centralized bargaining has been weakened as local level bargaining accounts for a larger proportion of wage increases (Moene and Wallerstein, 1993). However, 'corporatism' has not broken down. After briefly considering withdrawing from public committees like its Swedish counterpart, the Norwegian employers' association joined an initiative of the Social Democratic government aimed at promoting industrial innovation which includes leaders of business, the government, and LO (Mjøset et al., 1994: 71). The contrast with Sweden is certainly partly related to the character of national capital in the two countries. Not only is Norwegian capital less multinational and more tied to domestic resources, but the state owns the most important natural resource, oil.

Unemployment began to rise in the mid 1980s, reaching 5.9 per cent in 1992 with an additional 3 per cent in active labour market measures.

Moreover, this was accompanied by a steep rise in the number of people receiving disability pensions for which medical certification was not required. The OECD estimates that unemployment would have been 2.2 per cent higher were these also counted. Thus, with the 'real' unemployment rate in excess of 11 per cent, it is not surprising that also Norway has turned to some of the economizing measures previously mentioned.

Finland

Finland's period of vigorous social reform extended well past the end of the Golden Age (Marklund, 1988: 35–8). This is not surprising given that Finland remained a welfare state laggard, and that economic growth remained strong. In fact, Finnish economic growth in the 1980s was second only to the Japanese (Korpi, 1992: 64). Finland did experience higher unemployment than Norway or Sweden in the 1970s and 1980s, and this helps explain why this period of welfare state expansion was punctuated by bouts of retrenchment. Nonetheless, things looked rosy as late as 1989 when, after the revaluation of the mark, statisticians of the industrialists' association announced that Finland had surpassed Sweden and Norway in terms of per capita income (Andersson et al., 1993: 30).

The crash was as catastrophic as it was rapid. GDP growth fell to 0.4 per cent in 1990 and turned negative in 1991 (–6.4 per cent) and 1992 (–3.6 per cent) (OECD, 1993: 14). Unemployment increased to 17 per cent of the labour force. Significant cuts in expenditure which will affect a wide range of transfers and social services have been instituted. Stricter qualifying conditions for unemployment benefits have been passed and the replacement rate cut by 3 per cent.[25] The replacement rate for sick pay has been reduced (from 80 per cent to 67 per cent), contributions have been increased and waiting days have been increased from seven to nine. Replacement rates for parental benefits have been cut similarly, and the benefit period has been cut from 275 to 263 days. Subsidies to prescription drugs have been significantly reduced. The replacement rates for the earnings related tier of public employee pensions has been cut from 66 per cent to 60 per cent and an employee contribution of 6 per cent of income introduced. Further cuts in the replacement rate for all employees to 55 per cent or even 50 per cent and a change in the calculation of the replacement rate on the basis of lifetime and not final income are planned. A number of new taxes and fees have been introduced.

Part of Finland's problem is idiosyncratic: the collapse of Soviet trade. Otherwise we see a familiar pattern. Deregulation of financial markets led to a (pro-cyclical) boom in consumer borrowing, inflation of asset prices, and overheating of the economy followed by banking collapse and consumer retrenchment. The banking crisis in Finland was the most severe of the three countries, costing the government and central bank the equivalent of 7 per cent of GDP. As in Sweden and to a lesser extent

Norway, the economic difficulties were further aggravated by the attempt to follow a hard currency policy, which ultimately failed as Finland was also forced to float. In Finland, the traditional pro-cyclical policies of the government added to the economic plight (Andersson et al., 1993).

These policy errors should not be allowed to obscure the influence of the basic long term changes in the domestic and international economy. Financial deregulation and high interest rates undermined important features of the supply side policies. On the demand side, the decline in demand for Finnish exports in the core capitalist countries was temporarily plugged with Soviet trade, which is no longer an option. Finnish business, like Swedish, became increasingly internationalized, especially in the second half of the 1980s as direct foreign investment increased substantially. Thus, even to the extent that government policy could encourage investment, it was less able to ensure that it occurred in Finland.

Denmark

Danish unemployment began to rise almost immediately after the first oil shock, from 0.9 per cent in 1973 to 5.1 per cent in 1975, continuing to a peak of 10.5 per cent, subsiding in the 1980s, only to increase to a new peak of 11.3 per cent in 1992 (Furåker et al., 1990: 148; Kosonen, 1993: 27). Denmark's liberal economic policies, its lack of an industrial policy and active labour market policy, as well as its concentration on consumer exports, all contributed to its greater international vulnerability and to the rise in unemployment. In fact, its period of full employment lasted only a decade and a half.

The economic difficulties and particularly unemployment made existing entitlements increasingly expensive. Successive Danish governments have responded with significant welfare state cuts which have nonetheless only prevented government expenditure from rising as fast as it otherwise would have done. The measures include more selectivity and income testing, modifications of indexing, temporary deindexation, increases in qualifying conditions, and introduction of waiting days. Unemployment compensation has fallen dramatically from 80.5 per cent in 1975 to 59.2 per cent in 1985 without actually lowering the nominal replacement rate for a worker with full qualifications (Hagen, 1992: 154; Marklund, 1988: 31–5; Nørby Johansen, 1986: 362–3). Some improvements of benefits have also been made but, outside the substantial increase in maternity leave (from 98 to 144 days), these too have been responses to the unemployment crisis: eased conditions for pre-retirement pensions, increased subsidies for industries employing new workers, increased severance pay, and introduction of active labour market measures (Hagen, 1992: 145; Nørby Johansen, 1986: 363). More recently, the Danish government has developed its version of a work or 'active line' (DNISR, 1994: 29). It features a combination of positive incentives (e.g. improved vocational and job training) and negative incentives for workers (ceilings on wages for public employment programmes) and employers (responsibility for the first two days of unemployment compensation). In a significant departure from past principles, the citizenship pension for those over 70 was subject to an income test beginning 1994.

Conclusion

There is no question that the Scandinavian model is under assault. In all four countries unemployment has increased to levels that would have been intolerable for any government before the mid 1970s. In Norway, Sweden, and Finland, a major cause has been high interest rates and financial deregulation which made it impossible to privilege borrowing by industry over other consumers, a key element of these countries' supply side management. Moreover, the decline of centralized bargaining has made the imposition of wage restraint, another important tool in macro-economic management, more difficult. In addition, international demand stagnated. Finally, for different reasons, the employment 'bridging strategies' had exhausted themselves by the end of the 1980s: in all four countries, the expansion of the public sector; in Norway, sheltered employment in public enterprises; and in Finland, expansion of Soviet trade (Huber and Stephens, 1995).

As Moene and Wallerstein (1993) point out, the welfare state has been the most resilient part of the Scandinavian model. While expansion of entitlements did slow down before the unemployment crisis in all four countries, economic difficulties were only one, and perhaps not the main, contributor to this. The Nordic welfare states had truly 'grown to limits', be it in terms of comprehensiveness, universalism, or benefit generosity. Even in social services, which were the main area of Nordic welfare state innovation in the 1970s and 1980s (outside Finland), there were no longer pressing needs except for expansion of day care. As a result, tax burdens had arguably reached saturation point. This is to argue not that there was nothing to be done but rather, as I have said, that there was less to do and less to do it with.

In all four countries, significant rollbacks were resisted until a severe and apparently long term employment crisis hit. This meant that demands on the welfare state rose while the intake of social security contributions and taxes fell, making prevailing entitlements unaffordable. Thus, replacement rates were cut, waiting days introduced, qualifying conditions increased, and services cut. Moreover, the degree of cutting reflects the depth and duration of the employment crisis, with Finland and Denmark cutting the most and Norway very little.

Does retrenchment represent a qualitative change in the Scandinavian welfare states? To answer this question, let us return to the institutional characteristics and goals outlined in the initial section of this chapter. In terms of institutional characteristics, qualifying conditions have been made more strict in a number of programmes in all four countries and all but Norway have experienced significant reductions in replacement rates in major transfer programmes. There has been some trend towards private service delivery, but within a framework of public financing. It would be difficult to claim that these amount to a fundamental change. Only in the case of Danish unemployment benefits are replacement rates in major transfer programmes below what they were in 1970. By contrast, coverage rates in unemployment insurance today are far higher than they were then in all four cases (Hagen, 1992). In the cases of parental leave and public services, the two main areas of innovation in the 1970s and 1980s, benefits are far more generous even after the recent cuts than they were two decades ago. And service privatization has been far too modest to call this a fundamental change, though it may be an area of significant future change.

One can say, however, that recent reforms represent an important change in emphasis on different goals: labour training and mobilization have been greatly strengthened at the expense of decommodification. We should note that, except in Denmark, this goal shift pre-dated the employment and budget crisis. Thus, even in the hypothetical (and unlikely) case of a return to low unemployment, this goal shift is likely to survive.

The Scandinavian welfare states are undergoing three additional institutional changes. First, the Swedish earnings related pension system has been altered from one of defined benefit to one of defined contribution. Second, in all of the Scandinavian countries, employee contributions have been (re)introduced. Third, a number of recent reforms aim to make transfer programmes self-financing. Together, these three changes represent a trend towards greater 'market conformity' in the transfer system.

Superficially, these changes might appear to entail a reduction in the emphasis on the goal of redistribution. I contend that their effect on redistribution is likely to be very modest. Although it seems counter-intuitive, I would contend that lower replacement rates or lower ceilings on earnings related benefits are more likely to lessen the redistributive effect of social provisions. My reasoning here is based on the data referred to in the initial section of this chapter as well as comparative and historical evidence I analyse elsewhere (Stephens, 1995; also see Korpi and Palme, 1994). First, making each programme financially sound does not necessarily mean there is no redistribution within the programme. Second, and more important, a significant reduction in earnings related benefits will probably mean that employers will provide additional benefits to their upper level employees but not to manual workers. This should result in greater inequality.

If the retrenchment to date hardly represents a fundamental change in the Scandinavian welfare states, the question is then: is this just the beginning? Will further cuts which do change the fundamental character of the Nordic welfare states be necessary? In order to provide a baseline for speculation on the future of the Scandinavian welfare states, it is useful first to explore why these very generous welfare states have been so resistant to rollback. First, contrary to conservative hopes and social democratic fears, there is little reason to believe that integration in the international economy *per se* would force national welfare states down to the lowest common denominator. Ultimately, maintaining a generous welfare state, like maintaining high wages,[26] depends on international competitiveness. A high social wage and a high market wage are dependent on labour productivity, on unit labour costs. The assumption that market integration will necessarily exert a strong downward pressure on social provisions is based on the assumption that the competitive advantage of low wages will be more important than the advantage of capital intensity and highly qualified labour. In the case of the EU, it assumes that the non-tariff barriers to trade existing up to the end of 1992 discriminate more against low wage countries than the other members of the European Economic Area. This is far from clear. On the contrary, the logic of the EU's structural funds was that the low wage areas would be hurt by the integration process.

Second, moving to the specifics of the Scandinavian cases, their welfare states are particularly resistant to changes induced by international competition because they were built so as to maximize the competitiveness of the domestic manufacturing export sector. Thus, unlike in Latin America and the Antipodes (see Chapter 6 by Huber and Chapter 4 by Castles, respectively) where primary sector exports essentially subsidized entitlements of workers in a protected urban sector, the end of tariff barriers represented no change for Scandinavia; the increasing internationalization of trade represents, likewise, only a quantitative change not a qualitative change.

Finally, the political coalitions supporting the welfare state both at the party level and at the level of public opinion are very broad. Thus it is not surprising that only a widespread perception of crisis can lead governing parties to institute rollbacks. The conservative parties and their supporters are the only groups that are ideologically in favour of welfare state rollbacks. A major attack on the welfare state edifice is therefore only likely if there are long term secular shifts in party support. Once instituted, support for the basic, and most expensive, welfare state programmes was and is very broad, extending far beyond the strata and parties that originally supported the reform (Pöntinen and Uusitalo, 1988; Svalforss, 1991; 1992). As can be seen from other countries as well, the politics of welfare state expansion are different from the politics of welfare state rollback (Pierson, 1994; Stephens et al., 1994). It is very difficult to roll back entitlements, especially the universal ones typical of Scandinavia, once they are instituted.

Future scenarios

What is the future of the Scandinavian welfare states: further rollback, stagnation, or even new innovations? If my analysis of the centrality of unemployment is correct, it would seem, on the surface of it, that prospects are not good. Denmark has passed through a decade and a half of high unemployment and recent developments in Sweden and particularly Finland are of crisis proportions. Only Norway with its oil revenue is a hold out and its oil wealth has masked, or better said enabled, the continuation of the least efficient manufacturing economy of the Nordic countries. Without oil, Norway would surely face wrenching economic restructuring that would rival the process that Finland is currently enduring.

Fortunately, this picture is too negative. Finland faces a number of difficult years, but this is primarily due to the collapse of trade with the Soviet bloc and the banking crisis, not to fundamental flaws in its international competitiveness or its welfare system. In Sweden, Norway, and Finland, we saw that the current crisis was not simply structurally determined but rather a product of the interaction of structural change with a series of policy decisions which greatly aggravated the current situation. On the other hand, the prospects for getting back to 2–3 per cent unemployment are not good. As a result of financial internationalization and deregulation, an essential element of the supply side of the old model cannot be restored; at best selective measures can be used to supply cheap credit and encourage investment on a much more modest scale. The demand side depends, as always, heavily on the economic health of other countries. An unemployment rate of 5 per cent seems the best achievable in the mid-term. If the government budgets are not in structural balance at that level of unemployment, and they now apparently are in Finland and Norway but not in Sweden, then further cuts will be forthcoming.

A prime reason that further reductions in unemployment seem unlikely is that it is not at all clear what sectors would produce the new jobs. Job growth in Scandinavia has been almost entirely a product of the expansion of public services in the past two decades and it is widely agreed that this pattern cannot continue. Manufacturing is not producing significant increases in employment in relative terms in any of the advanced industrial economies. The high wage structure of the Scandinavian countries has prevented the rapid growth of private sector services along American lines (Esping-Andersen, 1990). Recent legislation in Denmark attempts to encourage small business development by offering a two year subsidy to new businesses and to encourage the growth of private household services by subsidies. In Norway, individuals setting up independent businesses are now eligible for a six month extension of unemployment compensation (DNISR, 1994). More flexible wage schemes which would allow employers to hire youths at lower wages have been suggested in Norway and Sweden but have been met with scepticism by the unions. In all of these cases, the schemes are too new to assess whether they have significant promise.

There are too many unknowns to say what the longer run possibilities for employment creation are. One aspect of the future does seem relatively clear based on recent history. The Scandinavian countries had difficulties restraining wages to maintain competitiveness during the 1980s. The decline of centralized bargaining is bound to contribute to these difficulties. The negative experience all of these countries had with the attempt to follow a hard currency policy in the late 1980s and early 1990s argues that, until these countries find a sure method of controlling wage developments, they will need to be able to resort to devaluation and thus should stay out of the European monetary union (or, in the case of Norway, should not rigidly fix its currency to the ECU which is the functional equivalent of monetary union). Indeed, given asymmetric shocks in a recessionary period, countries in a monetary union must be able to *lower* wages when their economies are particularly hard hit.

Within these macro-economic parameters, we can speculate about the near to mid-term future of the Scandinavian welfare states. First, the support base for the welfare state is broad, but more diverse in its needs than in the past, thus requiring policy adjustments in some areas. Second, those programmes which positively support international competitiveness and/or are market conforming are most likely to survive the axe, and those which do not are likely to be restructured to do so. Let me illustrate these alignments and options using the current Swedish situation.

While the welfare state enjoys wide support among the Swedish public, there are divisions on the kinds of programmes and benefits which different social groups prioritize. The growth of public employment, services, white collar employment, and women's labour force participation, the decline of Fordist production and increase in skill differentiation, all have created a more differentiated constituency for the welfare state. This creates pressures for more service differentiation. The long term policy to enable women to enter the labour force and support dual income earning families is likely to be intensified in the future. The institution of day care, parental leave, flexible work schedules, and so on over the past two to three decades is likely to be deepened, resources permitting.

However, the old 'Fordist' constituency remains and this can create competitive and contradictory pressures for innovation in a situation of limited resources. The struggle within Social Democracy before the 1988 election (Feldt, 1991: 357ff) is an example of this: the women's movement pressed for an extension of parental leave while LO pressed for an extra week of vacation pay. In the end, the party included both in its electoral platform in a situation where it appeared unlikely that there would be resources to do either.

The introduction of alternative private providers of welfare state services (though retaining public financing) represents a significant change in philosophy. Though few citizens have opted for private alternatives, the change does make the welfare state potentially more responsive to increasingly diversified demands from its clientele, not only by making private alternatives possible but also by stimulating diversity and responsiveness in public sector services. However, as we have seen there are trade-offs, which depend, at least in part, on the design of the particular programme.

The Social Democrats prior to the 1994 election had called for the abolition of the school-voucher system which would have effectively ended private alternatives for all but the very wealthy. The Social Democrats were deeply concerned about the development of a dual class system of education. Once in office the party moderated its stand and apparently will only lower the value of the voucher to 75 per cent of the cost of educating students in public schools. In the case of day care, no reversal of policy is in sight if only because very few private providers appeared: they simply could not compete with the public sector. The effects of the bourgeois government's health care reforms illustrate another side of the cost problem. Costs increased, in part because the private doctors were compensated on a fee-for-service basis, which, as the experience of other countries had already shown, creates an incentive for the provision of unneeded services. As a result, the Social Democratic government has made the house doctor system optional for counties (who are the main providers of health care) and, if the cost problems continue, further reversals are likely, either at the county level or by central government mandate.

The recent Swedish experience suggests on the one hand that future directions will be determined by cost considerations. Part of the argument of the political right for privatization of services has been that it would be more cost effective. In the case of day care, this was apparently not true; and in the case of health care, privatization actually resulted in increases in costs. Given the severe budget constraints, privatization of services certainly will proceed where it can be demonstrated that it will result in savings. On the other hand, the case of schooling demonstrates that ideology, and thus political party alignments, are still of great importance where cost considerations are not overriding. Where privatization results in inequality in access to services, it is likely to be strongly resisted by the left.[27]

To the extent that macro-economic conditions make further cuts in transfer programmes necessary, they are likely to be targeted at those programmes that damage or, at least, do not support international competitiveness, which is to say, they will reflect the recent experience with cuts.[28] Even without cuts, restructuring of programmes in the direction of the 'work line' seems very likely. Further 'marketization' of transfer programmes to put them on a firm financial footing also seems likely. Not only would such programmes eliminate losses that would be transferred to the state budget, but if they follow the example of the Swedish pension system, they would actually create savings and thus a source of reinvestment, restoring one feature of the old supply side model.

Notes

I have accumulated a number of debts in the process of researching and writing this chapter. Research in Sweden in May 1992 was supported by a grant from the Swedish American Bicentennial Foundation. The Swedish Institute provided valuable help in arranging interviews and the Institute for Social Research, Stockholm University, provided a stimulating and supportive environment. Evelyne Huber collaborated with me in this research. The paper was redrafted while I was a fellow at the Swedish Collegium for Advanced Study in the Social Sciences. Joakim Palme and Olli Kangas provided valuable figures, and Francis Castles, Gøsta Esping-Andersen, Evelyne Huber, Jonathon Moses, Joakim Palme, Olli Kangas, and Bo Rothstein made useful comments on an earlier draft.

1 This is not to imply that welfare state regimes clearly cluster into three groups, particularly if one includes the employment regime and related economic and industrial policy. I have criticized this view elsewhere (Stephens, 1994b). However, the designation of three types can be defended as ideal types, with Sweden being the closest empirical example of the social democratic or institutional type. Moreover, of the three groups, the Scandinavian group shows the most empirical tendency to cluster (Ragin, 1994; Kangas, 1994).

2 The poverty level referred to in the text is 50 per cent of median income. The figures were kindly provided to me by Joakim Palme and Olli Kangas. For further analysis, see Palme (1993).

3 Recalculated from Cusack et al. (1989: 478).

4 The question of which social forces shaped the Scandinavian welfare states is still contested terrain (compare Baldwin, 1990; Immergut, 1992; Esping-Andersen, 1985; Korpi, 1983; Olsson 1990). The view expressed in the text is my own view and is the most common view. See Stephens (1979; 1994a) and Huber and Stephens (1995) for elaborations.

5 I realize that my claim of 'massive redistribution' is controversial and that the data I present here will not convince sceptics. For a more extensive analysis, see Stephens (1995).

6 Since these Ginis are calculated on the basis of final disposable income, it is possible to have a negative Gini. It indicates that lower income recipients get larger pensions than higher ones.

7 The description here follows Furåker et al. (1990). All the figures cited are from this source except the unemployment figure for Finland which is from OECD (1993).

8 This characterization leans heavily on Mjøset (1986), Mjøset (1987) and Andersson et al. (1993).

9 This is not to imply that such attitudes were absent among employers in Norway and Finland. They were simply less able to resist state initiative. Perhaps more important, it was much more difficult for them to claim that they could mobilize the capital necessary for rapid industrialization without state assistance or even direction.

10 For a formal analysis of how this policy simultaneously affects equality and efficiency, see Moene and Wallerstein (1994).

11 At least in theory. In fact, profits in the export sector could not be controlled by tight fiscal policy.

12 Denmark and Britain share characteristics which underpin this policy orientation: strong, decentralized unions, low concentration in industry, few links between banks and industry, and strong international integration of financial interests.

13 For an analysis of policy in this period, see Martin (1984; 1985).

14 Along with lowering marginal tax rates, the reform eliminated many deductions and thus tax loopholes and child allowances were increased at the same time. An independent simulation study (Schwarz and Gustafsson, 1991) confirmed government simulations that the reform as a whole was distributionally neutral. The public perception, though, particularly among the Social Democrats' supporters, was otherwise.

15 Interview with Willy Bergström, June 1993.

16 For more details on these reforms, see Huber and Stephens (1993) which is based on research in Sweden in June and November 1992 including interviews with politicians and interest group experts working on social policy questions.

17 For further discussion of this issue and its contribution to the Social Democrats' defeat in 1991, see Rothstein (1992).

18 These figures were provided to me by Bo Rothstein based on his ongoing research.

19 The changes mentioned here as well as a number of other changes of lesser import are outlined in DNISR (1994).

20 In addition to Pontusson (1992), I draw on Erixon (1985), Pestoff (1991), Pontusson and Swensson (1992), the memoirs of Feldt (1991), the Social Democratic Finance Minister from 1982 to 1990, and 25 interviews with politicians, academic economists, and economists for unions and employers conducted in Stockholm in May 1992, November 1992, and June 1993. These interviews are also the basis for much of my analysis of contemporary social policy development. I also draw on two excellent comparative analyses of parallel developments in Norway and Sweden by Moene and Wallerstein (1993) and Moses (1994).

21 See Martin (1991) on the political implications of the decentralization of collective bargaining.

22 Erixon (1991) contends that the large devaluation itself was partly at fault. He argues, and now many industry spokesmen admit, the devaluation of 1982 was too large. It was too easy to make money; there was no competitive pressure on industry to rationalize and upgrade productivity, which contributed to the decline in productivity growth in Sweden.

23 These were eliminated with the tax reform of 1990.

24 For a more indepth analysis of the recent development of the Norwegian political economy, see Moene and Wallerstein (1993), Moses (1994), and Mjøset et al. (1994).

25 The sources for these social policy changes are DNISR (1994) and Olli Kangas (personal communication).

26 This parallel between the social wage and the market wage is largely missed in the literature. At any rate, it is rarely argued that there will be a massive downward pressure on market wages as a result of European integration. For an exception, see Edling (1992).

27 Here I leave the merits of the particular case (educational reforms of the bourgeois government) aside. Arguably, a voucher system which did not allow additional fees and did not permit creaming off the best students would not have been inegalitarian. See Rothstein (1994) for a general discussion of this issue. Interestingly, the political left in Denmark has been a principal defender of private (read 'alternative') schools and more than 10 per cent of Danish children attend such schools.

28 Let me clarify here. The empirical evidence for adverse incentive effects of transfers and taxes in Scandinavia is thin even for programmes in which the arguments for such an effect have been most plausible, such as for the sick pay regimes in Sweden and Norway which provided for 90–100 per cent replacement rates, no waiting days, and no doctor's certification (see Atkinson and Mogensen, 1993). It is probably more accurate to say that when budget constraints make cuts necessary, provisions which have *plausible* work disincentives are likely to get the cut first.

References

Andersson, Jan Otto, Kosonen, Pekka and Vartiainen, Juhana (1993) *The Finnish Model of Economic and Social Policy: From Emulation to Crash*. Åbo: Nationalekonomiska Institutionen, Åbo Akademi.

Atkinson, A.B. and Mogensen, Gunnar Viby (1993) *Welfare and Work Incentives: a North European Perspective*. Oxford: Clarendon Press.

Baldwin, Peter (1990) *The Politics of Social Solidarity: Class Bases of the European Welfare State 1875–1975*. Cambridge: Cambridge University Press.

Castles, Francis G. and Mitchell, Deborah (1990) 'Three worlds of welfare capitalism or four?' Australian National University, Public Policy Program, Discussion Paper 21.

Cusack, Thomas R. and Rein, Martin (1991) 'Social policy and service employment'. Unpublished paper, Wißenschaftszentrum Berlin.

Cusack, Thomas R., Noterman, Ton and Rein, Martin (1989) 'Political-economic aspects of public employment', *European Journal of Political Research*, 17: 471–500.

DNISR (1994) *Recent Trends in Cash Benefits in Europe*. Copenhagen: Danish National Institute of Social Research.

Edling, Jan (1992) *Labour Cost and Social Protection: an International Comparison*. Stockholm: LO.

Erixon, Lennart (1985) *What's Wrong with the Swedish Model? An Analysis of its Effects and Changed Conditions 1974–1985*. Stockholm: Institutet för Social Forskning, Meddelande 12/1985.

Erixon, Lennart (1991) 'Omvandlingstryck och produktivitet', in *Konkurrens, Regleringar, och Produktivitet: Expertrapport nr. 7 till Produktivitetsdelegationen*. Stockholm: Norstedts.

Esping-Andersen, Gøsta (1985) *Politics against Markets*. Princeton: Princeton University Press.

Esping-Andersen, Gøsta (1987) 'State and market in the formation of social security regimes'. European University Institute, Florence, Working Paper 87/281.

Esping-Andersen, Gøsta (1990) *The Three Worlds of Welfare Capitalism*. Princeton: Princeton University Press.

Esping-Andersen, Gøsta and Kolberg, Jon Eivind (1992a) 'Decommodification and work absence in the welfare state', in Jon Eivind Kolberg (ed.), *Between Work and Citizenship*. Armonk, NY: M.E. Sharpe. pp. 77–111.

Esping-Andersen, Gøsta and Kolberg, Jon Eivind (1992b) 'Welfare states and employment regimes', in Jon Eivind Kolberg (ed.), *The Study of Welfare State Regimes*. Armonk, NY: M.E. Sharpe. pp. 3–36.

Feldt, Kjell-Olof (1991) *Alla Dessa Dagar . . . I Regeringen 1982–1990*. Stockholm: Norstedts.

Fritzell, Johan (1993) 'Income inequality trends in the 1980s: a five country comparison', *Acta Sociologica*, 36: 47–62.

Furåker, Bengt, Johansson, Leif and Lind, Jens (1990) 'Unemployment and labour market policies in the Scandinavian countries', *Acta Sociologica*, 33(2): 141–64.

Gustafsson, Björn and Klevmarken, N. Anders (1993) 'Taxes and transfers in Sweden: incentive effects on labour supply', in A.B. Atkinson and Gunnar Viby Mogensen (eds), *Welfare and Work Incentives: a North European Perspective*. Oxford: Clarendon Press. pp. 50–134.

Hagen, Kåre. (1992) 'The interaction of welfare states and labor markets: the institutional level', in Jon Eivind Kolberg (ed.), *The Study of Welfare State Regimes*. Armonk, NY: M.E. Sharpe. pp. 124–68.

Hibbs, Douglas A. Jr (1990) 'Wage compression under solidarity bargaining in Sweden'. FIEF, Stockholm: Economic Research Report no. 30.

Huber, Evelyne and Stephens, John D. (1993) 'The Swedish welfare state at the crossroads', *Current Sweden*, no. 394, January.

Huber, Evelyne and Stephens, John D. (1995) The social democratic welfare state: achievements, crisis, and options. Unpublished manuscript.

Huber, Evelyne, Ragin, Charles and Stephens, John D. (1993) 'Social democracy, Christian democracy, constitutional structure and the welfare state', *American Journal of Sociology*, 99(3): 711–49.

Immergut, Ellen (1992) *The Political Construction of Interests: National Health Insurance Politics in Switzerland, France and Sweden, 1930–1970*. New York: Cambridge University Press.

Jäntti, Markus, Kangas, Olli and Ritakallio, Veli-Matti (1994) 'From marginalism to institutionalism: distributional consequences of the transformation of the Finnish pension regime'. Paper delivered at the XIIIth World Congress of Sociology, Bielefeld, 18–23 July, 1994.

Kangas, Olli (1991) *The Politics of Social Rights: Studies on the Dimensions of Sickness Insurance in OECD Countries*. Stockholm: Swedish Institute for Social Research.

Kangas, Olli (1994) 'The politics of social security: on regressions, qualitative comparisons, and clusters', in Thomas Janoski and Alexander M. Hicks (eds), *The Comparative Political Economy of the Welfare State*. New York: Cambridge University Press. pp. 346–64.

Kangas, Olli and Palme, Joakim (1993) 'Statism eroded? Labor-market benefits and challenges to the Scandinavian welfare states', in Erik Jørgen Hansen, Robert Erikson, Stein Ringen and Hannu Uusitalo (eds), *Welfare Trends in the Scandinavian Countries*. Armonk, NY: M.E. Sharpe. pp. 3–24.

Korpi, Walter (1983) *The Democratic Class Struggle*. London: Routledge and Kegan Paul.

Korpi, Walter (1992) *Halker Sverige Efter?* Stockholm: Carlssons.

Korpi, Walter and Palme, Joakim (1994) 'The strategy of equality and the paradox of redistribution'. Paper delivered at the XIIIth World Congress of Sociology, Bielefeld, 18–23 July 1994.

Kosonen, Pekka (1993) 'Europeanization, globalization, and the lost stability of national welfare states'. Paper delivered at the Conference on Comparative Research on Welfare States in Transition, Oxford, 9–12 September 1993.

Lehmbruch, Gerhard (1984) 'Concertation and the structure of corporatist networks' in John H. Goldthorpe (ed.), *Order and Conflict in Contemporary Capitalism*. Oxford: Clarendon Press. pp. 60–80.

Marklund, Steffan (1988) *Paradise Lost? The Nordic Welfare States and the Recession 1975–1985*. Lund: Arkiv.

Martin, Andrew (1984) 'Trade unions in Sweden: strategic responses to change and crisis', in Peter Gourevitch et al. (eds), *Unions and Economic Crisis: Britain, West Germany, and Sweden*. London: Allen and Unwin. pp. 189–359.

Martin, Andrew (1985) 'Distributive conflict, inflation, and investment: the Swedish case', in Leon Lindberg and Charles Maier (eds), *The Politics of Inflation and Stagnation*. Washington: Brookings Institution. pp. 403–66.

Martin, Andrew (1991) *Wage Bargaining and Swedish Politics: the Implications of the End of Central Negotiations*. Stockholm: FIEF.

Mitchell, Deborah (1991) *Income Transfers in Ten Welfare States*. Brookfield: Avebury.

Mjøset, Lars (1986) *Norden Dagen Derpå*. Oslo: Universitetsforlaget.

Mjøset, Lars (1987) 'Nordic economic policies in the 1970s and 1980s', *International Organization*, 41(3): 403–56.

Mjøset, Lars et al. (1994) 'Norway: the changing model', in Perry Andersen and Patrick Camiller (eds), *The Contours of the West European Left*. London: Verso. pp. 55–76.

Moene, Karl Ove and Wallerstein, Michael (1993) 'The decline of social democracy', in Karl Gunnar Persson (ed.), *The Economic Development of Denmark and Norway since 1879*. Gloucester, UK: Edward Elgar.

Moene, Karl Ove and Wallerstein, Michael (1994) 'How social democracy worked: labor market institutions'. Paper delivered at the Conference on the Politics and Political Economy of Contemporary Capitalism, University of North Carolina, Chapel Hill, NC, 9–11 September 1994.

Moses, Jonathon (1994) 'Abdication from national policy autonomy: what's left to leave?', *Politics and Society*, 22(2): 125–48.

Nørby Johansen, Lars (1986) 'Denmark', in Peter Flora (ed.), *Growth to Limits: the Western European Welfare States since World War II*, vol. 1. Berlin: Walter de Gruyter. pp. 197–292.

OECD (1993) *OECD Economic Surveys: Finland*. Paris: OECD.

OECD (1994) *OECD Economic Surveys: Sweden*. Paris: OECD.

Olsson, Sven E. (1990) *Social Policy and Welfare State in Sweden*. Lund: Arkiv.

Palme, Joakim (1990) *Pension Rights in Welfare Capitalism: the Development of Old-Age Pensions in 18 OECD Countries 1930 to 1985*. Stockholm: Swedish Institute for Social Research.

Palme, Joakim (1993) 'Pensions and income inequality among the elderly: "The welfare state and equality" revisited'. Paper presented at Åbo Akademi, 3 January.

Pestoff, Victor (1991) 'The demise of the Swedish model and the resurgence of organized business as a major political actor'. School of Business Administration, University of Stockholm, Working Paper.

Pierson, Paul (1994) 'The new politics of the welfare state'. Paper delivered at the Conference of Europeanists, Chicago.

Pöntinen, Seppo and Uusitalo, Hanno (1988) 'Stability and change in the public support for the welfare state; Finland 1975–1985', *International Journal of Sociology and Social Policy*, 8(6): 1–25.

Pontusson, Jonas (1992) 'The political economy of class compromise: capital and labor in Sweden', *Politics and Society*, 20(3): 305–32.

Pontusson, Jonas and Swenson, Peter (1992) 'Markets, production, institutions, and politics: why Swedish employers have abandoned the Swedish model'. Paper delivered at the Eighth International Conference of Europeanists, Chicago, 27–9 March 1992.

Ragin, Charles (1994) 'A qualitative comparative analysis of pension systems', in Thomas Janoski and Alexander M. Hicks (eds), *The Comparative Political Economy of the Welfare State*. New York: Cambridge University Press. pp. 320–45.

Rothstein, Bo (1992) 'The crisis of the Swedish Social Democrats and the future of the universal welfare state'. Paper delivered at the Eighth International Conference of Europeanists, Chicago, 27–9 March 1992.

Rothstein, Bo (1994) *Vad Bör Staten Göra*. Stockholm: SNS Förlag.

Salminen, Kari (1993) *Pension Schemes in the Making: a Comparative Study of the Scandinavian Countries*. Helsinki: Central Pension Security Institute.

Saunders, Peter (1991) 'Noncash income and relative poverty in comparative perspective: evidence for the Luxembourg Income Study'. Paper delivered at the Conference on Comparative Studies of Welfare State Development, Helsinki, Finland, 29 August to 1 September 1991.

Schwarz, B. and Gustafsson, Björn (1991) 'Income redistribution effects of tax reforms in Sweden', *Journal of Policy Modelling*, 13: 551–70.

Stephens, John D. (1979) *The Transition from Capitalism to Socialism*. Urbana: University of Illinois Press.

Stephens, John D. (1994a) 'The Scandinavian welfare states: development and crisis'. Paper delivered at the World Congress of Sociology, Bielefeld, Germany, 18–23 July 1994.

Stephens, John D. (1994b) 'Welfare state and employment regimes', *Acta Sociologica*, 37: 207–11.

Stephens, John D. (1995) 'The future of the social democratic welfare state', *Nordic Journal of Political Economy* (in press).

Stephens, John D., Huber, Evelyne and Ray, Leonard (1994) 'The welfare state in hard times'. Paper delivered at the Conference on the Politics and Political Economy of Contemporary Capitalism, University of North Carolina, Chapel Hill, NC, 9–11 September 1994.

Svalforss, Stefan (1991) 'The politics of welfare policy in Sweden: structural determinants and attitudinal cleavages', *British Journal of Sociology*, 42(4): 609–34.

Svalforss, Stefan (1992) 'Den Stabila Välfärdsopinionen: Atityder till Svensk Välfärdspolitik 1986–92'. Unpublished paper, Sociologiska Institutionen, Umeå Universitet.

Titmuss, Richard A. (1974) *Social Policy*. London: Allen and Unwin.

van Kersbergen, Kees (1991) 'Social capitalism: a study of Christian democracy and the post-war settlement of the welfare state'. PhD dissertation. European University Institute, Florence.

Vartiainen, Juhana (1994) 'The state and late industrialization', in Douglas Hibbs (ed.), *Politics, Growth, and Distribution*. Oxford: Oxford University Press.

3

Welfare States without Work: the Impasse of Labour Shedding and Familialism in Continental European Social Policy

Gøsta Esping-Andersen

Imperial Germany's social insurance reforms became the model for policy emulation in most European countries. As with Bismarck, social policy was motivated by concerns far removed from any egalitarianism. Chiefly, it was the creation of conservative elites who abhorred *laissez-faire* almost as much as the socialist menace, and who sought to rescue the old order with moral discipline, social pacification, and nation-building (Rimlinger, 1971; Flora and Alber, 1981). Bismarck's aim was not a welfare state but a welfare monarchy. In comparison with the universalistic egalitarian ideals that later came to define the British Beveridge plan or Scandinavian social democracy's 'people's home' ideal, the early architects of social policy on the Continent were authoritarian, étatist, and corporativistic.

Much of this conservative legacy has been carried over in contemporary welfare state institutions. In most other countries the modern welfare state was built by social democrats or left liberals; welfare state consolidation in postwar Europe was dominated by rightist or centre-right coalitions – Christian democracy in particular. Even where Christian democratic parties were marginal, such as in France or Spain, Catholic social doctrines still exert a visible influence on social policy.

The partisan roots of the European welfare states are, for two important reasons, worth stressing. For one, the Christian democratic 'subsidiarity principle' has institutionalized familialism in the sense of supporting the male-breadwinner/female-carer model with transfers. In particular the Southern European states are characterized by their very generous cash transfers and their almost non-existent provision of social services.[1]

The conservative-Catholic imprint affects also the politics of crisis and retrenchment today. The kind of ideologically fuelled partisan battles that are fought in the Anglo-Saxon nations, and even in Scandinavia, are conspicuously absent. The neo-liberal right is, on the Continent, a truly marginal player. These are probably the most consensual of all modern welfare states and this, as we shall see at the end of the chapter, helps explain why the welfare state edifice remains so immune to change, not-withstanding the urgency of major and quite radical reforms.

The implications of a social insurance dominated approach are twofold. The first is that social entitlements derive principally from employment rather than citizenship (as in the Nordic model) or from proven need (as in the more targeted systems in North America and the Antipodes). It is assumed that family dependants rely on the entitlements of the (usually male) breadwinner. A second implication is that social protection tends to be differentiated by occupational classes; that benefits will mirror accustomed status and earnings rather than redistributive ambitions. In brief, the realm of solidarity and risk-sharing is narrower and more particularistic.

The degree of status differentiation varies between nations and pro-grammes. In Germany, unemployment insurance is unified, pensions are divided into broad occupational classes (workers, salaried, miners, and civil servants), and health care is a labyrinth of 1200 separate regional, occupational, or company-based funds. In contrast, the French and Italian pension systems combine large occupationally mixed plans with a myriad of status-particularistic schemes. Italy's health care system is unified, while the French (and Belgian) is organized in broad occupational funds. Civil servants tend to be especially privileged in the continental European welfare states. As we shall see, the long-term financial solidity of social insurance is inversely related to the degree of status fragmentation.

The influence of Catholic social teachings remains a fetter on state provision of services, particularly those related to social care and family social reproduction. As a result, the continental European model is, in sharp contrast to the Nordic countries, service-lean yet very 'transfer-heavy'.[2]

The consequences for employment, as we shall see, are substantial. The lack of social services contradicts women's growing desire for employment and helps account for Europe's overall employment stagnation. As women nonetheless increasingly desire to work, and since high wage costs make private care alternatives unaffordable, the system imposes a severe trade-off between female careers and fertility. It is in this context that we must understand why Italy and Spain, today, exhibit world-record low fertility rates.

In broad terms, the accent on social insurance remained a source of strength and adaptability during the postwar decades' welfare state matur-ation. In comparison with the British or Nordic flat-rate schemes, social insurance was more easily upgraded in terms of benefit adequacy with rising incomes and an increasingly affluent middle class society. The substantially heavier financial burden which *full* income maintenance imposed was, until the 1970s, easily absorbed because of sustained growth with low inflation and unemployment (Gordon, 1988).

The perceived adequacy of social insurance across most social strata implies also very little demand for private sector coverage, especially in pensions. And since contributory social insurance instils a sense of individually earned contractual rights, these social security systems have enjoyed unusually broad public legitimacy. Despite mounting fiscal burdens, and the inescapable complaints about bureaucracy and the quality of services, the kind of anti-welfare-state revolts that erupted in Scandinavia, Britain and the United States are conspicuously absent, be it in Germany, France or Italy.

The primary focus of this chapter is on the problems and tensions that these particular welfare state models face as a consequence of sweeping social and economic change in the past decades. Rather than boost public employment, as in Scandinavia, their main policy response to 'deindustrialization' and unemployment has been to induce labour force exit. This approach may have had favourable consequences in terms of restoring competitiveness in traditional industries, such as autos. The longer-term effects, however, are quite problematic. It has resulted in very unfavourable population dependency ratios due to swelling numbers of retirees coupled to a stagnant and even shrinking workforce. The upshot is prohibitively heavy fixed labour costs which, in turn, discourage employment growth or, alternatively, spur the growth of informal sector jobs or self-employment. In brief, these systems find themselves locked into a self-reinforcing negative spiral, and are today particularly ill-suited to address pressures for greater labour market flexibility and women's demand for economic independence. In brief, the continental Western European welfare states are coming into conflict with the emerging needs of a postindustrial economy.

Before analysing these problems in greater depth, I shall provide a brief sketch of the principal characteristics of the postwar European welfare state models. In the third, and final, section I shall examine possible future scenarios on the basis of identifiable current trends.

The postwar model of social security

The postwar welfare state consolidation on the Continent meant essentially an elaboration and extension of existing social insurance in both income maintenance (accident, sickness, disability and old age pensions, unemployment) and health care. In some cases, like Germany and Italy, postwar reformers entertained ideas of a Beveridge-type universalistic system. However, the vested interests in maintaining the proven social insurance model were too strong. Pressures for more universalism translated instead into a patchwork policy of extending insurance to previously non-covered populations (such as the self-employed); of consolidating the myriad insurance funds under one general umbrella; and of building basic minimum income support programmes for those groups unable to participate in social insurance – principally persons with a weak labour force attachment. Hence, old social assistance programmes were upgraded, or similar plans were introduced from scratch (such as the Italian social pension, or the French and Belgian social minimum). Together with the emergence of universal family or child allowance schemes, then, an element of universalism and citizenship-based rights was coupled to the dominant insurance model.

If this is the general pattern, it also has its exceptions. Thus, Italy never introduced a genuine unemployment insurance, and national health care (since 1978) came to be a mix of universal citizen entitlement and insurance (financed via premiums from earned income as well as general revenues). In fact, Italy's lack of unemployment insurance has, in the high-unemployment era of the 1980s, additionally perverted the pension schemes, disability pensions in particular.[3] The Dutch pension system, like Italy's health care, combines insurance principles (it is contributory) with universal coverage and (generous) flat-rate benefits. For employees, there is a mandated second-tier occupational pension insurance. Also the Dutch disability pensions have played a major (and highly controversial) role in reducing labour supply. While most countries have introduced national standards in their means-tested assistance programmes, this is not so in the Mediterranean countries where social aid remains closer to the classical poor-relief model.

Besides cautious universalization, the single most important postwar change involved the adoption of the adequacy principle in cash benefits. This entailed a shift from contribution- to earnings-based benefit calculations and, hence, the adoption of a non-actuarial pay-as-you-go practice. The move was motivated by familialist and status maintenance concerns. In essence, the principle of a 'family wage' was extended to social transfers, as was the principle that social benefits should mirror accustomed status differentials. As a consequence, continental European, and especially Southern European, pension replacement rates are among the highest in the world.

Pioneered in Germany (1957) and then subsequently introduced by the other nations, benefit levels are now pegged to previous earnings (see Table 3.1). The average old age pension in the EC is 81 per cent of net earnings; the figure is around 66 per cent for sickness and unemployment. National variations are substantial, particularly with regard to unemployment and sickness. The social minimum programmes are much more residualistic. Hence, as seen in Table 3.1, the social minimum for the aged in no case approaches 50 per cent of per capita GDP. The consequence, as comparative research shows, is high poverty risks in groups, such as widows or single mothers, which depend on non-insurance transfers. In contrast, poverty rates are very low among standard career households. Poverty rates (for the mid 1980s) among retired couples and non-aged families with a full-time earner are as low as in Scandinavia. For households without a main (male) breadwinner, however, the safety net tends to be fragile. The child poverty rate for single-parent households is 18.7 per cent in Italy, 19.2 in France, and 26.7 in Germany (compared with 4.5 per cent in Sweden).[4]

Table 3.1   *Transfer benefit levels as a percentage of net earnings,*[1] *1990*

	Pensions	Sickness	Disability	Unemployment	Social minimum
Belgium	80	100	113	79	32
Germany	77	100	60	63	29
France	83	53	46	80	30
Italy	89	31[2]	56	26[2]	16
Netherlands[3]	67	70	69	74	41
Spain	98	60	32	80	28
EC 12	81	69	60	61	30

[1]   The social minima are expressed as a percentage of per capita GDP.

[2]   In Italy most employees have the right to full wage continuation during sickness. The unemployment benefit does not refer to the *Cassa Integrazione* system for industrial redundancies, which will typically replace 70–80 per cent of pay.

[3]   The Dutch data reflect the 1987 reform's reduction of replacement rates.

Source: European Community, 1993

Two issues are of particular importance for income replacement. The first has to do with employment and contribution requirements. Although the precise norms vary, the basic pension usually requires around 30 or 35 years' contribution. To arrive at maximum benefits, perhaps 40 or even 50 years (as in Germany) are required. These norms have been seriously weakened as governments sought to induce early retirement. In Italy, until recently, 25 years' employment sufficed for public sector workers, giving rise to the concept of 'baby pensioners'.

Still, as far as pensions are concerned, a long and stable employment career is still assumed. Hence, it is quite inevitable that social insurance tends to be male-biased. German data bring this out well. Female manual workers average only 22 years' contribution (36 years among males), and female white collar employees 27 years (38 among males). Only 8 per cent of females (compared with 53 per cent of males) arrive at 40 years' contributions (Scheiwe, 1994: Tables 9.3 and 9.4). The consequence is very low average pension benefits for women.[5]

The second issue concerns upper ceilings for contributions and benefits. If benefit ceilings are drawn relatively low, higher-income employees will naturally seek complementary private protection. A certain degree of redistribution would result if contribution ceilings were comparatively higher. A hallmark of the corporativistic principle in continental European social insurance is that the two tend to go together. In most countries, both ceilings are quite high; in some cases, such as Italy, they have been abolished altogether (Palme, 1990: European Community, 1993). In Germany, though, replacement rates begin to fall for persons earning twice the average wage; in Spain, at around three times the average wage (European Community, 1993: 88–90). The somewhat brusque decline in Germany (except for civil servants) explains why, there, complementary

Table 3.2   *Social security expenditures and the role of services, 1990*

	Social security expenditure (% GDP)		Services/transfers ratio[1]
	1980	1991	
Belgium	28.0	26.7	NA
France[2]	25.4	28.7	0.12
Germany (West)	28.7	26.6	0.16
Italy	19.4	24.4	0.06
Netherlands	30.8	32.4	NA
Denmark	28.7	29.8	0.33
Sweden			0.29

[1]   Social services excluding health care.
[2]   France is for 1989.

Sources: OECD, 1991; European Community, 1993

private pension plans are quite widespread among high-income groups (Esping-Andersen, 1990: Table 3.1).[6]

When even the elites perceive social insurance as adequate, the welfare state is likely to enjoy solid loyalties. But this also means heavy public expenditures which, if the schemes were fully funded, might not provoke crisis. The problem is that not only are they not fully funded, but they crave more and more government subsidization. Fears of imminent fiscal collapse may nurture more private insurance, but so far its role has been marginal. Private pension spending (1980 data) accounts for 1–4 per cent of *all* pension payments in continental Europe, compared with 10–12 per cent in Britain, Canada, and Japan, 17 per cent in the USA, and a full 20 per cent in Australia (Esping-Andersen, 1990: Table 4.3).

Catering to the upper strata has, however, its price in terms of egalitarianism. The top-quintile pensioner group in Germany receives almost 30 per cent of total *public* pension transfers, compared with 20 per cent in the UK. In contrast, the bottom German quintile receives only 11 per cent, compared with 17 per cent in the UK (West-Pedersen, 1994). In terms of *private* pensions, the distribution is much more skewed everywhere. The top-quintile pensioners receive 65–70 per cent of the total in Germany, as well as in the UK and the Netherlands.

The continental European welfare state is, in other words, distinct for its generous social transfer benefits and underdeveloped social care services – both mirroring its familialistic bias. The difference between Europe and Scandinavia in welfare state service commitment can be seen in Table 3.2.[7] Systematic cross-national comparisons of service delivery are rare but, to exemplify, Gustavsson and Stafford (1994) show that Swedish day care covers about 50 per cent of small children compared with 2 per cent in the Netherlands. Zimmermann (1993: 214) estimates the equivalent German rate at 1.4 per cent, while OECD (1990: 32) cites a figure around 5 per cent for Italy; France provides public day care centres for only 3.7 per cent of small children, but encourages a much larger network of private day care (OECD, 1990: 191).[8]

Differences in service provision have profound effects on the employment structure. In Denmark and Sweden, public sector employment in health, education and welfare services reached 25 per cent of the labour force in the late 1980s, compared with a range of 6–11 per cent in continental Europe (7 per cent in Germany, 11 per cent in both France and Italy) (Esping-Andersen, 1990: 158). The comparison with the Nordic countries is pertinent because also there high labour costs prohibit most families from consuming equivalent market services.

The lack of either market or state provided care is a source of low female activity *and* fertility rates. The resulting overall low employment levels imply very unfavourable ratios of dependants to actives, meaning a very high marginal tax on the few that actually do work. In addition, as I shall discuss below, it is arguable that suppressed female employment is becoming a chief obstacle to flexibilization.

Expenditures and finances

The great strength of social insurance is that it nurtures a sense of equity: you get what you have earned and you earn what you get. In terms of securing broad legitimacy, this is a strong point in the 'continental model'. Originally, social insurance was meant to be strictly actuarial: benefits were supposed to be directly related to contributions. Originally, financing was shared equally between employers and employees.

Today, all are pay-as-you-go systems and their financial structure has changed. In part, as a means of dampening wage growth via the 'deferred wage' strategy, employers and government now absorb a larger share of the financial pie. Of total social security finances, employers now account for 50–60 per cent and employees for 30 per cent, the remainder being covered by general government revenues. Owing to expensive early retirement and rising deficits, government subsidization of pension schemes has risen sharply in the past decade.

The rise in benefit levels, combined with a massive increase in beneficiaries (due to ageing, early retirement, and the inclusion of non-insured groups) over the past decades, has produced internationally extremely high financial requirements. The result is fiscal imbalances and rising labour costs. Fixed labour costs as a percentage of the total wage bill (for a married worker with two children) hover around 50 per cent in Belgium, France, Germany, Italy, and the Netherlands (European Community, 1993:83). This, as we shall see, arguably contributes to Europe's chronic employment problem.

As seen in Table 3.3, the financial status of the European social security systems has, with few exceptions, deteriorated. To cover contribution shortfalls, government subsidies have grown which, in turn, adds to current

Table 3.3 *Social security finances in selected*
European countries, 1980–91: differences
between contributions and benefit expenditures
(per cent)

	1980	1991
Belgium	−5.9	−3.2
France	+1.7	+0.9
Germany	+3.1	+5.2
Italy	−3.9	−4.3
Netherlands	NA	−2.4
Spain	NA	−1.1

Source: OECD, 1991

budget deficits. It is estimated that about half of Italy's current annual public debt (at about 13 per cent of GDP) goes to cover revenue shortfalls in the social security system.

There was a noticeable slowdown in social expenditure trends during the 1980s but, except for Germany and Belgium, total spending as a share of GDP was higher in 1991 than in 1980 (see Table 3.2). Annual growth rates (in constant prices) averaged around 1–1.5 per cent in Belgium, Germany and the Netherlands; 3 per cent in France; and 4.5–5.0 per cent in Spain and Italy. Besides a catch-up effect in the latter cases, the common thrust behind rising expenditures, and thus financial burdens, can be traced to the burden of social insurance in managing the social and economic problems of the past two decades.

The rising financial burdens are mainly concentrated in three programmes. One is rising expenditures due to high and persistent unemployment. 'Passive' unemployment compensation expenditures absorb (1992) between 1.5 and 2.0 per cent of GDP in our countries (except Italy where they are masked as pension payments or *Cassa Integrazione* expenditures). The rising burden of transfers to the unemployed has, moreover, the unfortunate effect of crowding out 'active' labour market measures such as training, job creation, and mobility measures (OECD, 1993). The second area is health care where rising costs are closely related to population ageing. Thus OECD (1988: Table 31) estimates that, by year 2000, up to 50 per cent of all health spending will go to the aged. Thirdly, as we have seen, population ageing and early retirement have produced a cost explosion in pensions. The financial difficulties of pension funds are aggravated by their occupational fragmentation: the decline of some labour force groups, like miners and manual workers, means fewer contributions and generally more early retirement.

The ratio of pensioners to contributors has been worsening in all the European countries. In Italy, the number of pensioners as a percentage of contributors rose from 60 per cent in 1971 to 84 per cent in 1987, and will soon reach parity. Record low fertility rates will seriously worsen the dependency burden in future decades.

To put it differently, Europe's welfare states have become 'pensioner' states, not because ageing is more advanced than elsewhere, but rather because of their policy bias in favour of passive income maintenance and labour supply reductions. Thus, the ratio of social spending on the aged to that on the non-aged is generally much higher (the average is around 1.5) than in, say, Scandinavia. Italy is an extreme case where, in 1990, almost five times as much was spent on pensioners as on the non-aged. And, in contrast to the Nordic countries, the pro-aged bias is strengthening over time.[9]

Where pension schemes are occupationally exclusive, the fiscal imbalances will vary sharply according to structural change. Thus, today, member contributions in the German miners' pension scheme barely cover 30 per cent of expenditures; for the workers' scheme, roughly 70 per cent. In contrast, the salaried employee scheme is able to balance its expenditures with contributions (Statistisches Bundesamt, 1992: Tables 19.1 and 19.4.9).

We have already noted the possible negative employment effect of high social contributions and labour costs. An additional factor has to do with the punitive tax treatment (and social transfer effect) of wives' earnings that is built into some European tax systems. This additionally discourages female (full-time) employment in general, and mothers' labour supply in particular (Gustavsson and Stafford, 1994; Zimmermann, 1993). Thus, for a one-child family in which the male earns average wages, the wife's decision to work full-time (at earnings equal to the male) would have negative consequences for net disposable income. In France, the effect is modest (an elasticity of 0.93), but it can be quite severe in other countries (an elasticity of 0.71 in Belgium, 0.58 in Germany, and 0.52 in the Netherlands). This contrasts with perfect neutrality in Sweden. For families with three children, the punitive effect is substantially stronger (calculations based on European Community, 1993: Table 24).

Thus, if we combine the tax-benefit effect of wives' employment and the widespread absence of child and other family services, we have also identified a primary cause of the generally low female activity rates. In turn, female inactivity has the double effect of holding down the size of the actively employed population which finances the welfare state, and per-petuating the family's dependence on the male breadwinner's earnings and entitlements. This translates into high transfer levels.

A diagnosis of contemporary welfare state problems

The European welfare states, as they exist today, were moulded in the social, economic, and demographic conditions that obtained in the 'Fordist' era of full employment. Many of the assumptions that underpinned continental European social policy in this era were also policy objectives.

Primary among the underlying assumptions was stable and vigorous non-inflationary growth with full employment. Hence, whether or not governments actively committed themselves to a Keynesian counter-cyclical regime (which, indeed, was hardly the case in France, Germany or Italy), they could assume growth via the sustained expansion of domestic and international demand for their manufacturing goods.

Most European countries experienced after the war a heavy outflow of unskilled rural populations. This latent welfare problem was primarily resolved by the expansion of industrial mass production. Relying chiefly on the market to secure high wages and job growth (and, thereby, rising aggregate consumer demand), the chief task of welfare policy was to secure families during the passive stages of the male breadwinner's life cycle – old age in particular. At the micro-level, working class families could count on lifelong income security. Thus was born the standard worker and the standardized life course.

On the basis of these premises, the welfare state was a success. All evidence suggests that old age poverty diminished drastically with the upgrading and universalization of pensions (Mitchell, 1991). The welfare state's relative passivity with regard to the active years of the life cycle, limiting itself to assuring against unanticipated sickness or disability, and against the (assumed) marginal risk of unemployment, remained until recent years a minor problem.

Contemporary demographic and labour market changes imply that this residual attention to the active phase of the life cycle is becoming problematic. Marital instability is rising everywhere, creating in its wake a bundle of new poverty risks. In countries like Belgium, Germany and France, single-parent households now account for roughly 10–12 per cent of all child families. They have a high incidence of poverty – 27 per cent are poor in Germany, 19 per cent in France and Italy (own calculations based on LIS data) – and they are increasingly reliant on public assistance. In France, for example, the number of one-parent families on social assistance grew by 185 per cent in 1978–86 (Room, 1990: 52). A very similar story emerges among the unemployed. Between 1970 and 1986, the unemployed's share of all assistance recipients jumped from less than 1 per cent to 33 per cent in Germany, from 3 to 67 per cent in the Netherlands (Room, 1990: 62).

The postwar full-employment concept was usually limited to the male breadwinner. As agriculture and urban self-employment declined, the working class, even the unskilled, could count on well-paid industrial employment. It was this context that permitted policy makers to assume (and actually encourage) women to be full-time, full-career housewives. In this respect, social policy and industrial relations acted in tandem. The family's virtually complete dependence on the male earner's income and entitlements meant that unions came to battle for job security (seniority principles, the regulation of hiring and firing practice) and the 'family wage'. The principle of a family wage has nowhere become as institutionalized as in continental Europe, in wage bargaining as in the social benefit structure. This helps account for the comparatively very high income replacement rates in social security.

In other words, social policy both assumed and created the 'standard worker family'. Indeed, in response to severe manpower shortages in the 1960s, the strategic choice of countries like Germany, Belgium and France to draw on foreign workers, rather than domestic women, only helped reinforce this logic. While women's labour force participation began to accelerate in Scandinavia and North America from the 1960s onward, it remained basically stagnant in the continental European economies until the 1980s, after which female activity rates began to rise.

Linked closely to the model family, the postwar welfare state premised itself on a set of socio-demographic assumptions. Primary among these was the organization of the (male) life cycle between inactivity and employment. Thus, entry into the labour force was assumed to occur at age 15–16 and retirement at 65, thus permitting 40–45 years of active employment (with social contributions) before retirement. As regards the female life cycle, it was assumed that a short period of employment in youth would be followed by more or less permanent withdrawal at time of marriage and having a family. This would, in turn, safeguard the availability of women for full-time social care of children and, later, of the aged family members.

Put as briefly as possible, the postwar welfare state assumed full-time, lengthy, and unbroken male careers followed by relatively few years of retirement prior to death, and full-time female careers dedicated to social reproduction activities. This principle not only was stronger on the Continent than elsewhere, but also has been perpetuated until today. Hence, its labour force is comparatively very masculine, and very protected.

As elsewhere, these underlying conditions no longer obtain. And, again as elsewhere, the impending crisis of the system is chiefly attributed to population ageing. Certainly, the continental European nations do exhibit an unfavourable age profile. Yet, there are several reasons why ageing may not be the chief problem. The dependency burden is primarily a function of fertility and retirement behaviour, and both are intrinsically welfare state issues. The crisis of ageing in Europe is, to a great extent, the by-product of the welfare states' labour reduction strategy.

A second set of conditions that no longer obtain has to do with employment structure. On the one hand, industrial employment is declining rapidly, and services constitute today the chief source of job growth. On the other hand, it is widely acknowledged that the labour market requires greater flexibilization. The latter, as is well known, involves both negative and positive trends: on the negative side, a departure from the standardized, secure employment relationship in favour of more precarious, temporary contracts and greater wage differentiation; on the positive side, greater adaptability to new skill and technology requirements in the workforce (Rodgers and Rodgers, 1989). In both instances, workers are decreasingly able to count on the 'Fordist' promise of lifelong job stability with steadily rising pay.

The post-OPEC policy response in continental Europe differed sharply from that of both Scandinavia and the neo-liberal deregulation approach favoured in Britain, the United States, and the Antipodes. Rather than following the 'labour cheapening' strategy of flexibilization and labour market deregulation that characterizes the Anglo-Saxon political economies, or the public-employment-led strategy of the Nordic countries, the dominant approach in Europe has been to manage labour market problems via supply reductions. To a (relatively modest) degree this led to a re-export of foreign guest workers, but the dominant policy came to concentrate on early retirement of male workers and discouragement of female participation, often combined with hours reduction, the hope being that this would ease youth unemployment.

This strategy, it is clear, is intricately linked to the social insurance system. Hence, besides marginal benefit adjustments and the like, a common trait in our group of countries is the visible lack of any major attempts to scale back or reform social security (except very recently, as we shall see below). Indeed, the political economy of these nations came to hinge on preserving the welfare state edifice.

There is a convincing case to be made that welfare state suppression of labour supply will have positive net welfare consequences if, that is, it is mainly unqualified workers, or workers with redundant skills, who are eased out of the labour market. A hallmark of the modern economy is that demand for unskilled workers is in rapid decline. One response would be to allow their wages to decline accordingly – the American approach in a nutshell. This has clearly negative distributional consequences. The other, as in Scandinavia, is to provide sheltered publicly subsidized employment. The continental strategy of easing them out via welfare programmes is based on three increasingly questionable assumptions. One is that the resulting productivity dividend will more than offset the financial cost of passive income maintenance. The second is that those whose supply is effectively suppressed are, indeed, unqualified low-productivity workers.[10] And the third is that the current surplus of unskilled manpower is transitory; that the problem will go away once the process of industrial restructuring has been completed.[11]

As we have seen, social expenditures continue to rise as the ratio of inactives to actives worsens. In addition to this source of revenue shortfall, the drastic curtailment of the average worker's active contributing years adds to the financial disequilibrium. Thus, compared with the orthodox assumption of 40–45 active years, the average worker in our countries will enter into employment around age 18–20 and retire at age 55–59. This, with heightened probabilities of unemployment and job loss along the life cycle, amounts to maybe an average of 35 or at most 40 years' active employment, i.e. a decline of 10–20 per cent in terms of financial contribution.[12] Our average worker will also collect pension benefits for many more years than the orthodox model assumed, owing partly to earlier withdrawal, partly to longevity. Since 1950, male life expectancy (at birth) has risen 5.9 years, female 8.5 years. Hence, a male who today retires at age 60 can count on 17–18 years' pension, a female on 20–22 years.

Combining and averaging the two, the standard individual worker pays 15 per cent less towards retirement and collects 30 per cent more than was the case in the golden 1950s.

The *real* demographic problem in continental Europe is not ageing but low fertility and low activity rates. Hence, in contrast to the Nordic countries, German, Italian or Dutch women face a rather powerful trade-off between careers and family formation. Italy's fertility rate is today the world's lowest (1.3), followed by Spain, and Germany; Ireland and Sweden, albeit for different reasons, enjoy the highest. In fact, Gustavsson and Stafford (1994) argue that Sweden's increased fertility is positively related to access to day care facilities *and* flexible employment conditions (part-time and flex-time, and liberal conditions for paid absence). These are exactly the elements lacking in the continental European welfare states' policy menu.[13]

The consequence of basic demographic trends is a rising age-dependency ratio. Age dependencies, however, are manageable depending on produc-tivity performance (GDP growth) and labour supply behaviour. Thus, the demographic scenario is subject to changes in retirement decisions, to the average age of employment entry, to male and female activity rates, to immigration, and to economic performance. The point is that the European welfare states have managed these variables in such a way as to seriously aggravate the underlying problem.

The employment problem

Why are the continental European welfare states so uniquely incapable of generating employment growth? For the EC as a whole, the employment share among the working-age population actually fell from about 64 per cent in 1968 to 57 per cent in 1988 (European Community, 1989). In contrast, the United States, starting at the same level, arrived in 1988 at 72 per cent; and Sweden at more than 75 per cent.

In part, the European decline has to do with male early retirement. Male participation rates have declined, 1960–85, by 15–20 per cent in Germany, the Netherlands, Belgium, and Italy, compared with 6 per cent in the US and Canada. And, in part, it has to do with relatively stagnant rates of female participation. Compared with around 80 per cent in Sweden, overall female participation is only 50 per cent in Belgium and Germany, 55 per cent in France, and 40–45 per cent in the Netherlands, Italy and Spain (OECD, 1993).

Since the mid 1980s, female participation has risen, especially in the young cohorts in Germany and the Netherlands where part-time employment has become common. Nonetheless, the total level of net job generation has fallen far short of supply, thus creating very high and chronic unemployment levels, especially among youth. Except for Germany, average unemployment levels have hovered around 10 per cent through the last decade. The incidence of long-term unemployment is now between 50 and 70 per cent of all unemployment in Belgium, Italy, Spain and Germany; about 40 per cent in the Netherlands and France. And, as perhaps the most sensitive indicator of labour market exclusion, youth unemployment rates tend to be extremely high in countries like Italy (33 per cent), Spain (35 per cent), France (22 per cent) and Belgium (20 per cent).

In other words, the employment conditions in continental Europe display all the characteristics of 'insider–outsider' labour markets. Thus, low levels of unemployment among adult male workers combines with huge populations of excluded or marginalized workers. In general terms, this can be ascribed to industrial job decline combined with very sluggish service employment growth. What is unique within our countries is the slow rate of service growth and, in some sectors, actual stagnation and decline (particularly in personal services). Thus, from the mid 1970s to the mid 1980s, the EC average rate of service growth was less than half the American.

As neo-liberal critics repeatedly assert, 'Eurosclerosis' is the stepchild of the welfare state and industrial relations institutions working in tandem. The lack of service job growth (except in the high-end services, such as business, finance and the like) can be attributed to the classical cost disease problem (Baumol, 1967). Since most personal and social services enjoy only modest, if any, productivity improvement they will fail to create jobs if wages and labour costs follow trends in high-productivity sectors. Egalitarian and high-wage (family wage) structures, as exist throughout Europe, will therefore render private sector services, like laundry, carwash, bellhops, or day care, inordinately expensive. One solution is to furnish services via public sector employment. Another is to encourage wage flexibility.[14] For obvious welfare state related reasons, neither alternative has been possible in continental Europe. To safeguard the family wage, unions cannot allow low-wage markets; social contributions raise fixed labour costs, thus making the hiring of one additional worker marginally very costly. And, fixed social contributions have been rising steeply. Catholic familialism aside, the very heavy transfer burdens (and public debt payments) with which European welfare states are already burdened would prohibit any significant public employment strategy.[15]

The result, then, is weak public *and* private sector service employment growth. With the continuation of traditional industrial relations practice and job rights legislation, the consequence, in turn, is an increasingly closed and rigid 'insider' labour market with ever narrower ports of entry. Hence, low female participation and massive youth unemployment exist in concert with a secure, predominantly male, insider labour force which relies precisely on the guarantee of lifelong employment with high wages and heavy social contributions in order to ensure family welfare across the life cycle.

The point is that the particular kind of welfare-state/family/work nexus that characterizes the continental European model has an inbuilt tendency to eat the very hand that feeds it. Unable to promote employment expansion, it reverts to labour supply reduction policies which, for males, mean unemployment and pension costs; for women, the necessary continuation of male breadwinner dependencies. In both cases, this translates into extremely high labour costs and labour market rigidities because the 'insiders' are compelled to defend their employment security. As such, the labour market remains rigidly closed and incapable of major job provision.

The strengthening of insider–outsider cleavages poses obstacles to greater flexibility. From the employer point of view, what counts is wage flexibility (setting wages according to productivity and profits), functional flexibility (such as greater adaptability to new technologies), and employment flexibility (capacity to hire and fire according to need). From the individual and family point of view, flexibility means the capacity to manage dual-career marriages with family obligations, the rising probability of family breakups, the increased possibility of mid-career changes, such as unemployment, reschooling, and occupational change, and generally more differentiated and less standardized life cycles.

The continental European welfare state model conspires to inhibit either of these flexibility needs. The 'insider' labour force is trapped in its dependence on lifelong job security and will thus, via its collective organizations, resist attempts to weaken the 'standard employment relationship'. This entrapment is obviously tightened by the shortened span of active contribution years: if a decent pension requires at least 35–40 years' employment, workers will logically struggle to minimize whatever employment securities might emerge.

Of course, the welfare state may relax the conditions pertaining to eligibility, or otherwise subsidize career risks. This is, indeed, a major element in social security reform over the past decades. On the one hand, welfare states (especially the German) grant implicit contributions during education, unemployment, and military service, thus allowing individuals the possibility of arriving at standard contribution records despite early retirement and employment interruptions. On the other hand, they seek to nurture familialism by granting pension points (or even mothers' salaries) to women who choose to leave the labour force. Here, flexibility is bought at the expense of additionally unbalanced social security budgets and/or of consolidating the traditional gender division of labour.

The alternative road to flexibility, which at present appears much more pervasive, implies an exit from the conventional welfare-state/employment nexus. Data here are, by nature, much scarcer, but there is little doubt that employers as well as employees are given particularly strong incentives to re-create the market, so to speak, behind the back of the welfare state. Thus, to escape high fixed labour costs, employers and employees jointly underdeclare wages (and thus contributions) up to the ultimate years of employment which are taken into consideration for benefit purposes. This is notoriously common in the Italian system. Similarly, early retirees and employers have a common interest in an informal employment relationship because the former no longer need to accumulate entitlements. Hence, an estimated 50 per cent of early retired males in Italy continue to work; a similar figure has been cited for laid-off workers in the *Cassa Integrazione*. An alternative is to farm out production in the form of homeworking. According to the most conservative estimates, 700,000 women in Italy, and 500,000 in Spain, produce informally out of their home, being paid piece rates without any form of social contributions; other estimates for Italy put the number at 2 million (European Community, 1989; Dallago, 1990).

Two other trends point towards a similar scenario. One is the rising proportion of self-employed – often disguised franchise workers – especially in Belgium, France, Italy and Spain. In fact, compared with other types of 'atypical' employment like temporary workers, this is a main source of employment generation, especially in labour intensive services like restaurants, hotels and entertainment (OECD, 1993: European Commuunity, 1989). The other is black economy activity which, however, has probably not grown as much as many assume and which, regardless, tends to involve mainly persons already employed (moonlighting) or recently retired. Nonetheless, there seems to be much higher levels of black economy activity in precisely those nations with high welfare state induced labour costs and employment rigidities, while this does not seem to be the case with high-taxation nations, such as Sweden. Thus, in Northern Europe, black economy work may account for 5 per cent or less of GDP, while in Italy and Spain the level is around 10–20 per cent (European Community, 1989).[16]

All these forms of irregular employment are examples of labour market actors dodging the rigidities and high costs of the regular economy. They have in common one factor which is detrimental to the welfare state: they draw on its benefits without contributing fully to its finances. Thus the vicious circle worsens additionally. As to flexibilization, there is mounting evidence that *partial* flexibilization policies – such as liberalization of temporary contracts – may actually deepen the insider–outsider divide. Spain is an illustrative case since, here, temporary workers account for virtually all net job growth in the 1980s; their share is now almost a third of total employment. Yet, their chances of attaining a more permanent employment relationship is exceedingly small (10–15 per cent). Indeed, it has been shown that the wage and job-security privileges of the permanently employed 'insiders' have strengthened precisely because firms can regulate their labour force at the margin through easily dismissable temporaries (Bentolila and Dolado, 1994).

Future welfare state scenarios

All the advanced Western welfare states have experienced a degree of socio-economic transformation for which they were ill-prepared, mainly because their construction reflects an economic, family, and demographic structure that no longer obtains. There are substantial differences in nations' policy responses to these changes. The continental European countries have, so far, followed a distinctly own trajectory in which welfare state induced labour supply reductions figured prominently. One result has been to nurture the emergence of rigid 'insider–outsider' labour markets with consequent marginalization and peripheralization, particularly among youth and women workers.[17] The strategy's reliance on existing social security programmes has led to a major cost explosion to the point where several nations' social insurance funds are threatened with bankruptcy unless continuously subsidized by public monies.

In response to the self-reinforcing negative spiral of these systems, families and labour market actors often seek flexibility solutions outside the formal system: people take irregular employment which escapes tax contributions and employment legislation; women, facing a naked trade-off between employment and children, delay and reduce fertility. It should be evident that the more that individuals opt for informal flexibility solutions, the more they help tighten the noose around the system's neck. The system is such that individual rationality adds up to collective irrationality.

Public confidence in the welfare systems' continued capacity to deliver on expected benefits appears in many countries to be falling (European Community, 1993; Grasso, 1989). There has thus in recent years been a shift towards private pension savings plans, in the form of either company occupational pensions or individual annuity plans, especially in Belgium, France, Germany, and the Netherlands, but also in Italy. Fears of impending benefit reductions or tightened eligibility rules also have the perverse effect of accelerating the run on early retirement schemes.

Welfare state reform has, so far, been limited to marginal adjustments: dampening cost growth via delayed or diminished benefit indexation or via spending caps in health care. Some countries, especially the Netherlands, have taken more direct measures to reduce replacement rates and to encourage private sector insurance. Retirement age is now being raised, most recently in Italy, but this can for obvious reasons occur only very gradually and will, at best, see positive results only in the longer run. In order to combat fiscal fraud, but also to restore greater actuarialism to the system, there is a noticeable trend to return to contribution-based (rather than earnings-based) entitlements in pensions. The reform currently being implemented in Italy may, in fact, spearhead similar reforms elsewhere.

On the labour market front the policy profile is similar. Relaxation of part-time employment legislation has, in the Netherlands, helped promote a surge in women's employment; in Italy, however, hardly at all. The explanation is quite simply that employers have very little incentive to offer part-time contracts given the high fixed overhead costs. Similarly, there have been some marginal efforts to lower wage costs and flexibilize job access for youth by government wage subsidization.

However, it is quite clear that marginal adjustments either on the social insurance front or in the labour market will not suffice to bring the systems out of disequilibrium. And, as in the case of temporary contract workers in Spain, more sweeping reforms may actually have perverse effects if they are implemented only selectively. Of course, temporary contracts *do* help provide first-entry labour market opportunities for women and youth in particular. But all evidence, for Spain as well as for France, indicates that they nourish dualisms while hardly generating additional *net* employment growth. Partial flexibilization may actually deepen the abyss between the core and periphery workforce.

In general, it is evident that a system premised so heavily on the family-wage logic and career-long contributions imposes severe rigidities on people's life cycle behaviour at the micro-level, and suboptimal labour force participation levels at the macro-level. Hence, the most pressing issue for these welfare states is how to encourage, at once, a major expansion in the supply and demand for employment. Lower labour costs is one solution, but it does not address women's trade-off between work and family. Without an adequate supply of family care services, women's entry into the labour market may still rise (as it does), but at the long-term cost of extremely low fertility.

The lack of adequate social care provision also risks creating a peculiarly perverse kind of inequity. A dual-career couple within the privileged occupational strata will both earn the 'family wage' and accumulate rights to two 'family social wages'. For them, the lack of public day care is a minor problem since they will be able to afford nannies and maids. This is not likely to be the case for most families; hence, households' earnings power may easily polarize. What is also likely to polarize is families' capacity to manoeuvre and adjust flexibly in today's labour market. The individual earner's risk of change, mobility, or job loss is much reduced in the context of a two-career household. In contrast, the traditional male breadwinner household will logically see such events as a threat. It is therefore logical that trade unions will continue to uphold traditional job rights and favour strong labour market protection policies.

It is virtually certain that tomorrow's family and labour markets will demand a drastic reduction in the household's social care responsibilities. It is also becoming increasingly evident that the distribution of social risks along people's life cycle is shifting towards the active adult stages: in part because of changing family behaviour, including divorce and the rise of single-parent households; in part because the labour market will decreasingly offer the kind of classical life-time employment guarantees it once did. On both counts, the continental European 'pensioner' welfare state model is singularly ill-equipped.

Since the financial situation of these welfare states is already so over-loaded, it is difficult to envisage any major new reform departures along the lines sketched above. It is, however, equally difficult to imagine radical deregulation strategies of the neo-liberal kind. Continental Europe's welfare systems were built by the conservatives and these very same forces remain essentially dedicated to their survival. Since, as I have suggested, the population is also locked into dependency on these systems, it is difficult to imagine broad-based support for any drastic welfare state roll-backs. It is symptomatic, indeed, that most conservative-led governments today seek solutions that imply a reinforcement of the existing edifice. Thus, in 1994 the German government passed a social insurance plan for care of the elderly, and the new conservative French government intends to raise additional taxes so as to create subsidized jobs for the unemployed, extend mothers' parental leave, and improve old age pensions.

At the same time, of course, cuts are a must – especially in the most financially unbalanced systems such as Italy's. A common characteristic of cutbacks, however, is that they are explicitly meant to safeguard – not destroy – the existing edifice. This is plainly the principle behind the ongoing pension reforms in Italy: sustaining the programme by slowly raising retirement age and by strengthening the importance of contributions for benefit calculations. And those that propose more privatization do so half-heartedly. For one, it is obvious to all that if privatization means company welfare plans, the idea is simply unrealistic given employers' already burdensome fixed labour costs. A gradual, albeit probably slow, rise in individual private welfare plans is under way. But it is uncertain whether this, in the long run, will result in a major 'system change'. In part, it is fuelled by uncertainty regarding the viability of public schemes, and if the latter are brought on a surer financial footing, the thrust may be limited to a relative small, high-income clientele. And, in part, a massive surge in individual or group insurance is unlikely unless governments grant favourable tax concessions. It is difficult to see how governments can afford such today.

If the combination of familialism and suboptimal activity rates defines a crucial element of the continental European welfare state crisis, it is not easy to see a positive-sum solution in the short to medium run. Since a surge of costly social services is an unrealistic prospect, while women's integration in the economy is likely to rise, Europe's very low fertility rates are likely to continue. Financial crisis will clearly compel governments to scale back early retirement practices, and in this respect the labour shedding strategy will abate. But where is job growth going to come from? How is the deepening gulf between insiders and outsiders going to be closed?

Notes

1 This group of welfare states includes (West) Germany, France, Italy, Austria, Belgium, Spain and Portugal. The Netherlands is a partial exception in that important elements of her income maintenance system are closer to the Nordic universalistic model. Since a detailed examination of so many nations is impossible in this chapter, my approach is to concentrate on Germany (as the leading and most comprehensive exponent of the social insurance approach), and Italy (as an example of a less complete and unusually 'familialistic' welfare state). Other nations will be discussed less systematically.

2 Thus, the 1990 ratio of social services (excluding health care) to social transfer payments is 0.16 in Germany, 0.12 in France, and 0.06 in Italy, whereas in Denmark it is 0.33 and in Sweden 0.29. (Note that the US ratio is also a low 0.07, here mainly due to the encouragement of market alternatives) (OECD, 1991). Put differently, a third of the Scandinavian welfare states is dedicated to servicing family needs; in the continental European nations, typically only one-tenth. Non-health social services include day care and youth services, care of the aged and disabled, home help services, and the like, but also employment-related services such as rehabilitation schemes and employment exchanges.

3 Thus, disability pensions (which are not subject to normal contribution requirements) have been granted at the rate of three times as much in the high unemployment areas of the south as in the north. Besides the objective of diminishing unemployment, they have also been a chief means of political clientelism. On the specific clientelistic aspects of the Italian system, see Paci (1989). Italy's only genuine unemployment protection scheme is the *Cassa Integrazione*, meant to guarantee incomes among the partially or fully laid-off workers in the 'primary sector' economy. Since it is financed by the general pension funds (INPS), the currently very high redundancy rates add substantially to pension insurance deficits.

4 These figures are based on own calculations on the Luxembourg Income Study (LIS) data sets using the standard 50 per cent of (equivalent) median income as the poverty benchmark. Similar results for 1980 (without Italy) are provided in Mitchell (1991). The Nordic (and to an extent the Dutch) universal flat-rate pensions (with automatic supplements) ensure that no one will fall below 50 per cent of median income (see also Palme, 1990). A recent EC study (European Community, 1993) has tried to simulate key cases. Thus, a single aged person with an interrupted career would receive about 60 per cent of the standard pension in France, Germany and the Netherlands, only 23 per cent in Italy, but 93 per cent in Denmark.

5 For females who worked during their life, the average pension benefit is less than half the male's. For females entitled to a widow's pension, the benefit is about 60 per cent of the male's average pension (Scheiwe, 1994: Table 9.5).

6 On the financing side, contribution ceilings are very high in France and Germany, and non-existent in Belgium and Italy. As was the case in the recent US social security reforms, the abolition or upward adjustment of contribution ceilings has been a means to raise additional revenues. There are some indications that growing concern with the financial viability of existing pension schemes is giving rise to private plans, be it of the occupational type or individual annuity schemes. In France, life insurance type plans are growing at the rate of 20–25 per cent per year; in Belgium there is a rapid growth of company plans (Grasso, 1989: Appendix). Also the Netherlands has recently liberalized conditions for private schemes.

7 Note, however, the widespread kindergarten tradition for pre-school children, a system that is virtually universal in Italy. Indeed, its origins are closely tied to the Church. Note also the sometimes important role played by religious voluntary organizations in the field of care for socially disadvantaged and needy persons.

8 A study conducted by the European Community (1990: 10) had fairly similar results. If private day care solutions are included, however, France's and Belgium's coverage rates approximate 20 per cent of small children.

9 Thus, between 1980 and 1990 the ratio rose from 1.36 to 1.49 in France; from 3.18 to 4.75 in Italy; and from 0.95 to 1.14 in Belgium. In Denmark it fell from 0.76 to 0.55; in Sweden from 0.86 to 0.83. A slight decline is also registered for Germany (from 1.39 to 1.35). Calculations based on OECD, 1994: Tables 1b and 1c.

10 The validity of the second assumption is quite shaky. We know that there is very little difference in early retirement behaviour between unskilled workers and qualified (even professional) workers. We also know that women's educational attainment today equals – and in many countries even surpasses – that of men.

11 Also this assumption is questionable since it will hold only if new labour force cohorts enter with the kinds of skills that are, and will be, in demand. However, it is widely recognized that existing education and training systems fall far short in this regard.

12 The average academically trained employee will enter first job at age 25–26 (in Italy) or 28–30 (in Germany). All data suggest that their retirement choices are not very different from

manual workers, i.e. they are likely to contribute little more than 30–35 years. When we also consider their higher pension benefits and longer life duration, the contribution–pension cost ratio for this group will be substantially worse. For more detailed data on retirement behaviour, see Kohli et al. (1993).

13 The lack of day care and similar facilities does not unequivocally arrest women's employment. Participation rates among the younger cohorts are steadily increasing everywhere. This may be the main factor behind declining fertility. Part-time employment may help combine both if, that is, employers go along. In Italy they evidently do not, citing the punitively high fixed labour costs. However, as Kloosterman (1993) suggests, Holland's introduction of more flexible wage schemes and lowered social costs in the 1980s has given a formidable boost to female (part-time) employment, while female full-time jobs have hardly changed at all.

14 Recent data on earnings differentials bring this out. While the lower-quintile income earners in America, Britain (and also Australia) have lost substantial ground over the last decade, this has not been the case in either Germany or Italy (see OECD, 1993; Gottschalk, 1993).

15 Public debt as a percentage of GDP was, in 1989, 128 per cent in Belgium, 99 per cent in Italy, and 79 per cent in the Netherlands. Germany (with 43 per cent) and France (with 36 per cent) would clearly be better positioned were it not for the upward trend (OECD, 1991).

16 Zimmermann (1993: 233–4) suggests, however, that there has been a noticeable rise in black economy work in Germany between 1960 and 1980.

17 As popular discourse across many European nations suggests, strong insider–outsider divisions risk producing social dualisms. Thus, the French speak of the *société de deux vitesses*; the Germans of the *Zweidrittelgesellschaft*. In the case of France, the factual base of marginalization is brought out in a recent United Nations report (United Nations European Region, 1993: 49). In the age group 18–24, 26 per cent were unemployed and another 25 per cent muddled through by doing *petits boulots*.

References

Baumol, W. (1967) 'The macroeconomies of unbalanced growth', *American Economic Review*, 57: 415–26.

Bentolila, S. and Dolado, J. (1994) 'Spanish labour markets', *Economic Policy*, April: 55–99.

Dallago, B. (1990) *The Irregular Economy*. Aldershot: Dartmouth.

Esping-Andersen, G. (1990) *The Three Worlds of Welfare Capitalism*. Oxford: Polity Press.

European Community (1989) *Employment in Europe*. Luxembourg: EC.

European Community (1990) *Childcare in the European Communities 1985–1990*. Bruxelles: European Commission.

European Community (1993) *Social Protection in Europe*. Luxembourg: EC.

Flora, P. and Alber, J. (1981) 'Modernization, democratization, and the development of welfare states in Western Europe', in P. Flora and A. Heidenheimer (eds), *The Development of Welfare States in Europe and America*. New Brunswick, NJ: Transaction Press. pp. 37–80.

Gordon, M. (1988) *Social Security Policies in Industrialized Countries*. Cambridge: Cambridge University Press.

Gottschalk, P. (1993) 'Changes in inequality of family income in seven industrialized countries', *American Economic Review*, 2: 136–42.

Grasso, F. (1989) 'L'evoluzione degli squilibri del sistema pensionistico', in R. Brunetta and L. Tronti (eds), *Welfare State e Redistribuzione*. Milano: Franco Angeli. pp. 409–66.

Gustavsson, S. and Stafford, F. (1994) 'Three regimes of childcare: the United States, the Netherlands, and Sweden', in R. Blank (ed.), *Social Protection versus Economic Flexibility*. Chicago: University of Chicago Press. pp. 333–62.

Kloosterman, R.C. (1993) 'Three worlds of welfare capitalism?' Unpublished paper, University of Utrecht.

Kohli, M., Rein, M. and Guillemard, A. (1993) *Time for Retirement*. Cambridge: Cambridge University Press.

Mitchell, D. (1991) *Income Transfer Systems*. Avebury: Aldershot.

OECD (1988) *Employment Outlook*. Paris: OECD.

OECD (1990) *Lone Parent Families*. Paris: OECD.

OECD (1991) *National Accounts. Detailed Tables*. Paris: OECD.

OECD (1993) *Employment Outlook*. Paris: OECD.

OECD (1994) *New Orientations for Social Policy*. Paris: OECD.

Paci, M. (1989) *Pubblico e Privato nei Moderni Sistemi di Welfare*. Napoli: Liguori.

Palme, J. (1990) *Pension Rights in Welfare Capitalism*. Stockholm: SOFI.

Rimlinger, G. (1971) *Welfare and Industrialization in Europe, America and Russia*. New York: Wiley.

Rodgers, G. and Rodgers, J. (1989) *Precarious Work in Western Europe*. Geneva: ILO.

Room, G. (1990) *New Poverty in the European Community*. London: Macmillan and the Commission of the European Communities.

Scheiwe, K. (1994) 'German pension insurance', in D. Sainsbury (ed.), *Gendering Welfare States*. London: Sage. pp. 132–49.

Statistisches Bundesamt (1992) *Statistisches Jahrbuch fur Deutschland*.

United Nations European Region (1993) *Welfare in a Civil Society: Report for the Conference of European Ministers for Social Affairs*. Vienna: European Centre.

West-Pedersen, A. (1994) 'What makes the difference? Cross-national variations in pension systems and their distributional outcomes'. Paper presented at Workshop on Convergence and Divergence, Sorö, Denmark, 9–11 June.

Zimmermann, K. (1993) 'Labor responses to taxes and benefits in Germany', in A.B. Atkinson and G.V. Mogensen (eds), *Welfare and Work Incentives*. Oxford: Clarendon Press. pp. 192–240.

4

Needs-Based Strategies of Social Protection in Australia and New Zealand

Francis G. Castles

For much of the past century – although to different degrees in different periods and to different degrees in the two countries – Australia and New Zealand have been the clearest examples of a particular approach to social protection. That approach rests on guaranteeing minimum levels of social protection to those who meet certain conditions. One such condition is need, with the emergence, in these countries, of the world's most comprehensive systems of means tested income support benefits. Means testing is not, of course, unique to the Antipodes, but what has been unique is a further set of guarantees providing minimum income levels for those in employment also supposedly related to a social policy definition of need. Together these guarantees have underpinned a model of the welfare state quite unlike those of Western Europe and North America.

Earlier this century, the emergent Antipodean nations were frequently regarded as laboratories for path-breaking social experiments. In 1913, an American scholar felt it appropriate to point to 'the ideals which have animated the Australian people and the Australian lawmakers in placing on the statute book the body of social legislation which has drawn the eyes of all the World to Australia, and which marks the most notable experiment yet made in social democracy' (Hammond, 1913: 285). In 1949, the ILO would note that the New Zealand Social Security Act of 1938 has 'more than any other law, determined the practical meaning of social security, and so has deeply influenced the course of legislation in other countries' (ILO, 1949: iii). More recently, however, the combination of low aggregate social expenditure and widespread means testing manifested by these nations gave them the reputation of being amongst the worst laggards of social development during the Golden Age of the welfare state. Now, with the Golden Age but a memory, an account of the features making the Antipodean welfare state model distinctive may be instructive in widening the repertoire of policy options for those seeking to achieve the basics of social protection in an era in which 'choices of restraints and innovation' (Heidenheimer et al., 1990: 17) are unquestionably the order of the day.

The wage earners' welfare state

Social protection by other means

During the third of a century or so following the Second World War, the Antipodean nations were amongst those for which a very strong case can be mounted that the exigencies threatening disruption to the 'working class life course' (Myles, 1990: 274) had been largely tamed. In 1950, Australia's and New Zealand's GDP per capita levels were respectively fifth and sixth highest in the world (Summers and Heston, 1991) and in both countries there was an extensive and state regulated system of minimum wages leading to greater wage compression than in most other comparable nations (Lydall, 1968: 153; Easton, 1983). Nor were the wage packets of most workers much reduced by taxation, with a very strong preference for progressive income taxation on the well-off rather than on indirect taxes or social security contributions that impacted on ordinary wage earners.

Most important of all, in both countries, a combination of Keynesian demand management and measures protective of local industries had led to extremely low levels of unemployment. In New Zealand 'in March 1956 only 5 unemployment benefits were being paid, and thus there was some substance to the claims of politicians that they knew the unemployed by name' (Shirley, 1990). According to the economists, Australia 'enjoyed brimful employment' in the 1950s (Karmel and Brunt, 1962) and an increase to over 2 per cent in 1961 very nearly toppled the long-running Liberal government and forced it into instant reflationary measures. Australia maintained full employment until the mid 1970s and New Zealand until the early 1980s. Given these conditions, plus the strong ties of family dependency implicit in high fertility rates, low divorce rates (UN, 1970) and rates of female labour market participation well below OECD norms until the late 1960s (OECD, 1992: Table 2.8), it is arguable that wage earners and those dependent on them experienced a relatively high level of social protection throughout this period.

On the surface, at least, it would not appear that the same could be said of those outside the labour force and dependent on social security. In Australia, all social security benefits other than child allowances were incomes tested and, in New Zealand, the only exceptions to incomes testing were, again, child allowances plus a universal, but income taxed, super-annuation benefit payable at age 65. In both countries, all benefits were flat-rate and all were financed directly from the General Exchequer. After 1960, Australia and New Zealand were the only OECD countries without any form of contributory social insurance, a fact which does much to explain the lack of pressure for greater universalism: contributions not only fund benefits, they also create a view that all should benefit!

Replacement rates in Australia varied from genuine subsistence level (unemployment and sickness benefits) to no more than the basis for a frugal existence (the age pension) (see Henderson et al., 1970). In New Zealand, overall expenditure levels were high at the beginning of the period

(ILO, 1972), allowing very generous provision in certain areas. However, over a long period of right-wing political dominance, benefit levels were eaten away by inflation. In 1972, Labour governments were elected in both countries with a mandate to increase welfare spending, but that followed a decade in which the Antipodean nations had been the only ones in the OECD experiencing a decline in income maintenance expenditure as a percentage of GDP (OECD, 1976). It is these features which have made contemporary European observers and domestic critics alike point to the weaknesses of the Antipodean welfare states.

Nonetheless, for the period discussed here, the evidence does not suggest that inadequacies in the benefit systems translated into working class life courses that were more subject to fluctuation than in other advanced nations. The most obvious reason why this should have been so was, of course, the fact that unemployment was minuscule and almost entirely frictional. But there were other factors intrinsic to the design of Antipodean social policy which also served as important offsets to the supposed weaknesses of the welfare state system. Incomes tests on unemployment, sickness and invalidity benefits are of rather less practical significance than is sometimes supposed by the social policy community (cf. Esping-Andersen, 1990: 78), given that the conditions which define entitlement automatically prevent disqualification on income grounds. Over time, moreover, there was a gradual shift in emphasis, with means tests designed less to target the very poor and more to exclude the middle class. Universal superannuation in New Zealand and progressive age pension incomes test liberalization in Australia made for an increasingly residual definition of the excluded rather than the included group, with the prevailing notion being one of a welfare state in retirement for 'the battlers' (the preferred Australian term) or 'the ordinary bloke' (a New Zealand formulation).

Apart from these factors, mitigating the supposedly deleterious effects of widespread means testing, were others modifying the impact of relatively low, flat-rate benefits. Most important was the institution of supplementation for dependants on the basis of need, so that a relatively small flat-rate unemployment or sickness benefit might be doubled or trebled where a beneficiary supported a spouse and dependent children. It should be remembered, too, that flat-rate benefits are singularly more favourable to maintaining the living standards of those at or below average wage levels than to preserving the life styles of those in higher income echelons. All other things being equal, the means tested, flat-rate, welfare state is far more redistributive than the universal, income-related one (see Åberg, 1989).

As important as these intrinsic factors were institutional arrangements, rarely considered aspects of the welfare state as such, which mitigated the impact of low and/or declining transfers in these countries. It is these distinctive institutional features of the Antipodean welfare states that explain why sickness and, in particular, old age were not, for the great majority, significant threats to income maintenance across the life cycle.

Although spending on social insurance sickness benefits in this period was extremely low by OECD standards (Varley, 1986) and remains so (Kangas, 1991), the reason was that the same system of wage regulation which enjoined minimum wage levels also guaranteed workers stipulated numbers of sickness leave days paid for by the employer at full wage rates. In Australia, this obligation dated back to the interwar period, and meant that, in practical terms, Australia was a pioneer in respect of this form of social provision (Castles, 1992).

Looked at from a comparative perspective, two factors mitigated the impact of old age on poverty in the Antipodes. The first arose from a far more youthful age profile than in most parts of Europe. The second, which served to offset the low replacement rate of pensions, was a highly institutionalized and culturally ingrained system of private home ownership, with figures for owner-occupation being around 70 per cent in both countries during much of the post-war era (on New Zealand, see Thorns, 1984; on Australia, see Kemeny, 1980). For older couple households, ownership free of mortgage obligations is nearly universal, with recent figures for both countries of around 85–90 per cent (on New Zealand, see Thorns, 1993, 98; on Australia, see Gruen and Grattan, 1993: 184). Since home ownership leads to an appreciable diminution of the need for cash income (see St John, 1993: 124), this must be regarded as a very important offset to the low replacement rates of income support payments in these countries.

This system resting on wage compression and low-level, needs-based, income support did not, of course, mean that poverty and destitution in these countries was wholly absent. There is, however, no reason to suppose that gaps in Australasian safety-net provision at this time were any greater than in other advanced nations. They were, however, differently located. The author of Australia's major poverty study of the late 1960s, Ronald Henderson, argued that the crucial difference between Australia and most other OECD countries lay in the lower percentage of the poor to be found in the workforce. In the OECD, overall, half the poor were working, a figure which contrasted with around a quarter in Australia, and suggested that 'the high level and comprehensive coverage of minimum wage legislation in Australia . . . meant that Australia had a much smaller group of "working poor"' (Henderson, 1978: 169). Given that, in New Zealand, the prevailing architecture of the welfare state was also based on 'enforcing minimum wage regulations and subsidising those outside the wage system with selective benefits' (Davidson, 1989: 250), it seems reasonable to suppose that the New Zealand system was similarly biased.

The use of wage regulation as the primary instrument of social protection and the distinctive pattern of social policy outcomes resulting from it have been the basis for labelling the Antipodean nations as 'wage earners' welfare states' (Castles, 1985: 102–9), a description and, in many cases, a designation which has achieved some currency in both countries (on Australia, see e.g. Brown, 1989: 51 and Bryson, 1992: 89–99; on New

Zealand, see the analysis of Davidson, 1989 and the comments of Walsh, 1993b: 190 and Rudd, 1993: 240). The typical life cycle profile produced by the wage earners' welfare state in this period is clearly distinguishable from those emanating from other welfare state types – most notably in its unusually equalizing thrust within both the working population (reduced wage dispersion) and the group dependent on benefits (flat-rate provision) combined with a somewhat greater discrepancy between the two life cycle stages as a result of the system's lesser generosity to all beneficiaries other than those on below average wages or with above average needs.

Origins and logic

In very simple terms, what made for a distinctive set of strategies of social protection in the Antipodes was a different historical context. Perhaps to a greater degree even than in Europe and Scandinavia, social advances were a function of growing affluence and working class politics. However, what was different about the Antipodes was that these countries were rich from the latter part of the nineteenth century onwards (for Australia, see Maddison, 1991; for New Zealand, see Rankin, 1992: 46–9) and that, in these newly democratized settler societies, the labour movement was politically strong far earlier than in Europe (the world's first Labour government was a minority government in the State of Queensland in 1899). This meant that the push for social amelioration occurred in a quite different intellectual climate to that of Europe of the 1930s and 1940s – a climate in which the issue of addressing the problem of want was seen in terms of what was commonly called 'the problem of wages' rather than of state expenditure for welfare.

Turn-of-the-century Antipodean social reformers with strong labour movement support set out to tackle 'the problem of wages' directly, with their most important innovation being courts of arbitration with the power to set wage rates. The outcome was to make wage awards subject to forces other than those of the market, and, in particular, to allow some room for wage-fixing on the basis of social policy criteria. Contemporary New Zealand commentators talked of a 'theory of fair wages . . . sufficient to give the worker a decent living according to the colonial standard' (Le Rossignol and Stewart, 1910: 239) and the Australian Court of Arbitration suggested that a 'fair and reasonable wage' was one which met 'the normal needs of the average employee regarded as a human being living in a civilised community' (Higgins, 1922). Since the 'average employee' of the time was a male, and since his 'normal needs' included his domestic responsibilities, a 'fair wage' was very rapidly defined as a wage sufficient to support a wife and two or three children. In this sense, the notion of the 'family wage' has been at the heart of Antipodean social and wages policy since the first quarter of the century.

But by itself, the institution of compulsory arbitration could not be regarded as a sufficient basis for resolving the issue of social protection in a capitalist economy. Getting an adequate wage was one part of the problem; the other, as amply demonstrated by recent economic conditions, was getting a job. What made compulsory arbitration the basis for a distinctive strategy of social amelioration was that it was fashioned into a more or less explicit political deal, which has been dignified by some authors as a 'historic compromise' paralleling those of Scandinavia in the 1930s (on Australia, see Castles, 1988: 110–32; on New Zealand, see Davidson, 1989: 177–87). The substance of this deal was that fair wages were to be complemented by policy measures, in principle, regarded as ensuring the capacity of employers to provide sufficient high-wage jobs. These policy measures, which in combination have been described as constituting a strategy of 'domestic defence' (Castles, 1988), involved high levels of tariff protection to restrict foreign competition and to foster the basis of a domestic manufacturing industry, and controls on migration designed simultaneously to exclude low-wage ('Asiatic') labour and to allow population growth within parameters set by the need to maintain a reasonably tight labour market.

The logic by which a strategy of domestic defence was transformed into the wage earners' welfare state is transparent enough. To the degree that wage regulation delivered all male employees an adequate family wage, and in so far as the assumption was that all women and children were dependent on male wage earners, it followed that only when men were unemployed or had been insufficiently provident to provide for their old age could there be a need for additional intervention by the state. But with wages as the frontline weapon against poverty and, supposedly, sufficient high-wage jobs generated by the protection of tariff walls and controls on migration, social policy could be doubly residual: to be given only to the poor and only where it was apparent that the wages mechanism was inadequate. In other words, the unusually needs-based character of income support measures in the Antipodean nations was a function of the fact that the needs of most families were supposed to be guaranteed by a wage-setting process which gave heed to social policy objectives.

These considerations explain why schemes of social expenditure in these countries have tended to be selective and laggard and why the tax state has been both small and redistributive in emphasis. Targeting benefits only to those in need followed from seeing them as a secondary safety-net only for those who somehow fell through the mesh of the primary wage control mechanism. With the exception of the means tested age pension, other benefits tended to be introduced rather later than in many European countries, because the initial assumption was that private savings from supposedly adequate wages would be sufficient to meet short-term emergencies such as frictional unemployment or to insure privately for foreseeable medical costs. Certainly from the latter part of the nineteenth century until the Second World War, these were countries in which small scale savings societies, often organized as friendly societies, with a clientele largely of ordinary working men, flourished mightily.

Only when the assumption of wage adequacy proved demonstrably inaccurate over a long period of time were new benefits introduced and, even then, the initial tendency was to seek remedies through the wage awards system, as was the case in respect of sickness leave. The logic by which an emphasis on fair wages led to means testing and the small tax state was replicated on the revenue side. An aversion to heavy tax burdens on average working families, and, hence, a strong preference for reliance on progressive income taxes, followed naturally from the conception that wages from employment were the legally established minimum required for a civilized existence. Overall, the closely intertwined set of preferences for redistributive instruments on both the expenditure and the revenue sides of the tax-transfer system gave the wage earners' welfare state in its heyday a distinctively egalitarian or 'radical' cast (see Castles and Mitchell, 1993).

Judicially determined wage levels set on the basis of social policy considerations also account for other important features of the Antipodean wage earners' welfare state. The extremely low levels of female (particularly married) labour force participation in both countries were a direct consequence of the family wage concept, which led the arbitration courts to set female base wage rates at around half those of men on the ground that women generally were not responsible for the support of dependants (on Australia, see Bryson, 1992: 167–70; on New Zealand, see Brosnan and Wilson, 1989: 21–34). Given this legally institutionalized construction of female dependency, feminist commentators have properly seen the Antipodean model of the early post-war decades as a 'male wage earners' welfare state' (Bryson, 1992; Du Plessis, 1993). Finally, the high wage rates stemming from the relative affluence of these nations, together with the relatively low dispersion of wages produced by the arbitration system, created circumstances highly propitious to high levels of private home ownership, with mortgage repayments serving, in effect, as a functional alternative to European earnings-related welfare as a means of horizontal life cycle income distribution. Certainly, by the 1950s and 1960s, governments in Australia and New Zealand were treating home ownership as a welfare good to be provided for all classes of the population through subsidized or interest-regulated loans, with the most dramatic instance of the equation between ownership and welfare being the New Zealand Labour initiative in 1958 of permitting the 'anticipation' of some part of future child benefits as a lump sum payment towards private house purchase (Thomson, 1991: 39–40).

The story told here of an evolving economic policy strategy of domestic defence contributing to the maturation of a wage earners' welfare state is, of course, an ideal typical representation of developments occurring over many decades and with many important differences in the two Antipodean nations. In this context, the difference that most demands attention is that which led to New Zealand developing a system of social security in the 1940s and 1950s which, in all respects bar its selectivity, was as extensive as any in the world. This difference is attributable most particularly to the fact that, as in Scandinavia, the party which assumed the reigns of government after the Depression of the 1930s was Labour. Over a period of 14 years of continuous majority rule, Labour sought to marry the institutional design of a comprehensive and generous social security state, including the world's first national health service, with the wage guarantees for the broad mass of wage earners provided by the arbitration system. Arguably, the resulting welfare state was highly ambiguous – 'neither fish nor fowl' – but it was sufficient to convince contemporary observers that New Zealand was amongst the world's leaders in social security development.

In the first half of the post-war period, the wage earners' welfare state in New Zealand re-emerged by stealth as more or less continuous government by the right-wing National Party undermined the generosity of social security provision. Nevertheless, the First Labour Government left an important legacy of legitimation for a welfare state along European lines, which resurfaced with legislation by the Third Labour Government, 1972– 5, to introduce a funded, earnings-related, superannuation scheme. But the ambiguities built into New Zealand's welfare state were to continue. Basing its appeal on what has been described as 'a blatant electoral bribe', the National Party returned to office with a 'national superannuation' scheme which was reasonably generous in replacement rate terms, but extra-ordinarily so in reducing the age of entitlement to 60 and in offering the benefit as a demogrant. The ambiguities – and obvious future fiscal difficulties – lay in tying the old to the new by making superannuation flat-rate and funding it from the Exchequer on exactly the same basis as the other benefits of the wage earners' welfare state.

By contrast, whilst never as generous, the Australian development was far more consistent. Although the Australian Labor government of the 1940s had brought into existence the standard range of social security schemes – child, unemployment, sickness and widows' benefits – all, bar the child benefit, were in the traditional selective, ungenerous and flat-rate mould of the 1908 pension and represented an extension of the residual safety-net of the wage earners' welfare state, not its supersession. The wartime Labor government had unsuccessfully attempted to create a national health system along New Zealand lines, but otherwise believed that the crucial tasks of post-war economic reconstruction were full employment and economic growth which would make welfare 'palliatives . . . less and less necessary' (Chifley, 1944: 1). Its long-term Liberal successor never challenged the existing social policy model and believed that it had proved successful in wiping out absolute poverty in Australia (Wentworth, 1969: 3). When Labor next came to office in 1972–5, it finally succeeded in introducing a national health system, increased the generosity of benefits and even took a cautious step towards universalism in respect of pensions for those over 70. However although, as in New Zealand, ideas of earnings-related pensions were in the air, they were ultimately rejected because of 'the clash of principle between this earnings-related scheme and the traditional Australian practice of flat-rate benefits according to need'

(Henderson, 1978: 175). Finally, the Fraser Liberal government which took office in 1975 saw monetarism as the correct response to the developing economic crisis and had absolutely no intention of moving beyond the traditional confines of Australia's low-taxation welfare state.

Changing the shape of social protection

A new social laboratory

If it is appropriate to regard the Antipodes at the turn of the last century as a social laboratory in which state experiments were carried out for the greater edification of other nations, the same may be no less true of the last two decades of this century. In the 1980s and early 1990s, Australia and New Zealand were amongst a group of largely Anglo-American nations which did more than simply seek incremental and piecemeal ways of coping with the economic and social policy consequences of major new disruptions in their external economic environment (Castles, 1993: 3–34). Instead, departing from a premise that the end result of many decades of state intervention had left a substantial legacy of economic inefficiency, these countries committed themselves to making a substantial overhaul of their entire panoply of economic and social policy institutions and, in particular, sought to reshape institutions in such a way that they would become more responsive to market disciplines. This more comprehensive policy response to the economic disruptions of the 1970s is generally seen as emanating from the ideas of the 'new right', although in Australia – and perhaps a significant indicator of differences in that nation's approach – a rather less overtly political label of 'economic rationalism' (see Pusey, 1991; King and Lloyd, 1993) has found some favour, at least in regard to the home-grown product.

Nor can it be said that the policy response of the Antipodean nations was merely a minor echo of the new right mainstream of Thatcherism in the United Kingdom and Reaganomics in the United States. What makes the dramatic economic and social reforms of the past decade in Australia and New Zealand so fascinating is that they were initiated by governments traditionally associated with the interventionist state and with measures of social protection. In Australia, the architect of reform was a Labor government that was first elected in 1983, and which has subsequently proceeded to win the next four elections. In New Zealand, economic reform directions were established by the Fourth Labour Government which ruled from 1984 to 1990, and were markedly accelerated, particularly in the labour market and social policy areas, by its National Party successor.

The kinds of economic policy and welfare outcomes associated with the new right triumphant – a greater emphasis on price stability than un-employment, labour market deregulation, reduced taxation, cuts in public expenditure and stringent targeting of benefits, and greater inequality in the distribution of income – are simultaneously the outcomes often associated with a post-industrial future in which the supposed fate of the welfare state is 'poor, nasty, brutish and short'. In a sense, then, it would appear that the Antipodean nations over the course of the past decade provide a perfect laboratory for testing the limits of those theories which suggest that the economic reforms set in motion by contemporary societal developments are inimical to the maintenance of social protection at the levels established in the early post-war decades. Two countries on the periphery of the world economic system embarked on extensive policy reforms explicitly designed to make their economies respond more efficiently to market signals under the auspices of governments without any previous predilection for pro-market interventions or for rightist outcomes. Had the experience of the two countries been a common move towards outcomes uniformly destructive of social progress, it might have been argued that this was proof sufficient that, even in countries with a tradition of social protection and under governments supposedly committed to socially protective goals, the very fact of seeking to conform to the demands of international competitiveness was an inevitable recipe for the destruction of the welfare state.

In fact, as the remainder of this chapter demonstrates, whilst welfare state outcomes in Australia and New Zealand manifested certain common trends over the period, they were, in substantial ways, very different. A vital component of that difference was the fact that, despite quite similar economic objectives, the governments in the two countries sought to achieve their ends by quite distinctive policy means. At a minimum, this seems to imply that the future trajectory of welfare state development is far more open than some commentators appear to believe. Just as important, the tenor of the account offered here, as of the previous section, which noted the pivotal role of labour movement politics in articulating the agenda of social protection in the Antipodes, suggests that, however much the general trajectory of welfare state development is shaped by broad societal and economic developments, an account which leaves out political choice and agency will always be, to some degree, flawed.

Processes of economic and social change

The areas in which common trends have been most apparent are those in which economic and social factors have impinged most directly on the life cycle prospects of workers and potential workers. They are the areas in which the forces unleashed by the breakdown of the post-war economic settlement and post-industrial transformation have been least mediated by policy, whether because policy has been ineffective, because policy-makers have consciously retreated from former interventionist strategies or because the transformation has been at a level too fundamental to admit of policy solutions. Table 4.1 summarizes a variety of these outcomes in Australia and New Zealand and contrasts them with those of other groupings of advanced nations featuring in this volume.

What Table 4.1 shows is the extent to which the world had changed since

Table 4.1   *Economic and social indicators of economic slowdown and post-industrial change*

	Australia	New Zealand	North America	Continental Europe[1]	Scandinavia
Economic slowdown					
Per capita growth 1979–90[2] (%)	1.6	0.8	1.7	1.8	2.2
Unemployment 1992[3] (%)	10.7	10.3	9.4	10.2	8.8
Labour force composition					
Service sector 1980–90[2] (%)	65.9	59.3	68.9	60.4	63.0
Male labour force 1992[3] (%)	85.8	82.2	84.2	77.2	83.4
Female labour force 1992[3] (%)	62.5	63.2	68.5	54.7	74.9
Part-time employment 1992[3] (%)	24.5	21.6	17.2	16.1	20.4
Social structure					
Divorce rate 1990 (or nearest)[4] (per 1000)	2.5	2.6	3.9	1.5	2.5
Tertiary education 1991[5] (%)	38.6	44.8	79.7	36.2	41.4
Female tertiary education 1991[5] (%)	42.0	48.0	87.8	34.8	44.9

[1] Average for Belgium, France, Germany, Italy and the Netherlands.

Sources:
[2] From OECD, 1992.
[3] From OECD, 1993.
[4] From UN, 1992.
[5] From UNESCO, 1993.

the end of the Golden Age. A decade or more of low economic growth and cyclical recessions had by the early 1990s everywhere produced levels of unemployment uncontemplated in the 1950s and 1960s. The character of the labour force had also changed. Everywhere services had become dominant, everywhere male participation rates had declined significantly and everywhere women were entering the labour force in unprecedented numbers. In respect of social structure the transformation was no less pronounced, with increased rates of family break-up, a more educated population and, within that population, far greater opportunities for women.

However, despite these common trends, there were, as emphasized by Gøsta Esping-Andersen in his contributions to this volume, quite major differences between different national groupings, especially with respect to labour force development. Of the groupings, continental Europe experienced a lesser move towards service employment, a higher attrition of the male workforce and a lower rate of entry by female workers. By contrast, Australia and New Zealand's male workforce is comparable with that of the North American and Scandinavian nations. However, in respect of female participation rates, the Antipodes lags behind these latter groupings, although clearly on a trajectory towards their higher levels, with part-time employment as the vehicle of that transformation. In respect of social structure, it is again clear that continental Europe is different, with the Antipodean nations rather similar to Scandinavia in respect of marriage break-up, and falling somewhere between Scandinavia and continental Europe in respect of educational expansion.

Turning to the specifics of the Antipodean development, it is apparent that, from the mid 1970s onwards, the economic and labour market outcomes, which through the 1950s and 1960s had been the main testimony to the success of the wage earners' welfare state in delivering a decent and even-tenored standard of life, had begun to deteriorate or to be transformed. Relative GDP per capita levels in both countries remained in the top half of the OECD distribution until the mid 1970s, but declined appreciably thereafter as a consequence of slow productivity growth and a serious downturn in the terms of trade. In 1985, Australia had a GDP per capita level 98 per cent of the OECD average and New Zealand 90 per cent; in 1992, the Australian figure was 91 per cent and the New Zealand level was 76 per cent (Easton, 1993: 11). By the latter date, New Zealand, with an economic growth rate shown in Table 4.1 to be substantially lower than even the modest norm for the period, had a GDP per capita which, amongst the OECD nations, only exceeded those of Ireland, Greece, Portugal, Spain and Turkey (OECD, 1994).

The decline in the Antipodean nations' relative economic standing was, of course, one of the most significant factors promoting a sense of the need for policy change that might lead to enhanced international competitiveness. In particular, it promoted moves to financial deregulation and the phasing out of the barriers of external protection which had been such a central component of the traditional 'domestic defence' strategy. Deregulation across all spheres of policy was a particularly compelling platform for policy reform in nations which had historically seen economic regulation as the sovereign remedy for all problems, and, most particularly, for problems perceived as emanating from the international economy. Hardly surprisingly, this new deregulatory ethos, signalled by the defeat of conservative governments which had confronted the economic crisis of the late 1970s by a further battening down of the regulatory hatches, made for substantial pressures on the no less traditional wage earners' welfare state strategy of wage compression in a full employment economy.

Research suggests that, as late as the mid 1980s, the dispersion of male earnings in Australia was still relatively low compared with a range of other OECD nations, being roughly comparable with that of Sweden, but that it increased markedly thereafter (Bradbury, 1993). An emerging trend towards greater wage inequality in Australia over the past decade or so is compatible with evidence concerning the progressive disappearance of the middle of the income distribution as part-time employment at low wages has been substituted for full-time jobs at standard wage rates (Gregory, 1993). Similar wage distribution trends were also clearly apparent in New Zealand during the period of the Fourth Labour Government and have continued under the National government (Brosnan and Rea, 1992). Whilst some critics have argued that these trends constitute a particular cause for condemnation of domestic economic policy in these nations, in actual fact the wage distribution tendencies described are common to many OECD countries, and criticism, if that is appropriate, should be directed more to the removal of the barriers that had hitherto insulated these countries from world market trends. However the consensus of economists in both countries, and not merely those with new right and economic rationalist views, is that such barriers could not have lasted much longer in any case and that, whatever their past rationale, they had, by the early 1980s, become wholly counter-productive.

Transformation rather than deterioration is the appropriate description for other aspects of the change occurring in these decades. Greater service employment was partly a function of enhanced productivity levels in other economic sectors, and was accompanied by a great expansion in educational opportunity and economic independence for women. However these nations rated in comparative terms, the structural shifts which occurred were of mammoth proportions. In Australia, services grew from 50.1 per cent of civilian employment in 1960 to 69.0 per cent in 1990 and, in New Zealand, from 46.8 to 64.8 per cent (see OECD, 1992). Female labour force participation as a percentage of the female population from 15 to 64 grew from a level well below the OECD average to one somewhat above it – in Australia, from 34.1 per cent in 1960 to 62.5 per cent in 1992 and, in New Zealand, from 31.3 to 63.2 per cent over the same period (OECD, 1993). In Australia, part-time employment as a percentage of total employment increased from 11.9 to 24.4 per cent between 1973 and 1992, and in New Zealand the comparable figures were 11.2 and 21.6 per cent (OECD, 1993). Finally, turning to the educational correlates of employment change, between 1980 and 1991 tertiary enrolment ratios in Australia increased from 25.4 to 38.6 per cent (for females, from 23.4 to 42 per cent), and in New Zealand from 28.6 to 44.8 per cent (for females, from 23.7 to 48 per cent) (see UNESCO, 1993).

One area in which transformation was somewhat less pronounced than in many OECD nations was in respect of the reduction in the male labour force stemming from the decline in industrial manufacturing and the more general labour market deterioration since the early 1970s. In Australia between 1960 and 1992, the reduction was only 11.4 percentage points; in New Zealand, it was 11.6 points. Together with the figures for the expansion in the female labour force, this demonstrates that Australia and New Zealand did not utilize labour supply reduction strategies of the kind common in Western Europe during this period (see Esping-Andersen, 1990; von Rhein-Kress, 1993). However, unlike the Scandinavian countries, the expansion of aggregate labour supply in these countries was not a function of an expansion of public employment. Rather the employment story of these countries into the mid 1980s, at least, is quite analogous to that of the other Anglo-American countries during the same period, with the main factor facilitating female labour force entry being a taxation system providing substantial incentives to part-time work and the precise level of overall employment depending on a particular government's willingness to utilize measures of fiscal stimulus.

It is not the case that the changes in workforce composition which have taken place in Australia and New Zealand in this period have been inherently inimical to the life cycle security of most wage earner families, although they have certainly altered the typical profile of the interface between family and work. Indeed, the fact that it is now the norm for most families during early and later stages of the life cycle to have more than one member in some form of paid employment may have been an important factor in maintaining the very high level of Antipodean home ownership despite two decades of economic slowdown and periodic unemployment (Castles, 1994). On the other hand, part-time working for men and employment for married women have made the wage earners' welfare state notions of the 'family wage' and female dependence increasingly antediluvian.

That is all the more so as a result of changes in social mores and legal norms. Divorce law reform in both countries since the 1970s has markedly facilitated family break-up, and crude divorce rates per 1000 of the population are amongst the highest in the world (see UN, 1992; and see Table 4.1). As a consequence, the percentage of sole-parent families has also increased greatly: in New Zealand, from 5 per cent of households in 1971 to 9 per cent in 1991 (Statistics New Zealand, 1993), and in Australia, from 6 per cent of family households in 1976 to 9 per cent in 1991 (Australian Bureau of Statistics, 1994). While changing workforce composition *per se* may not undermine the security of the standard wage earner life course, family break-up clearly does, and, in common with the experience of most other advanced nations, single-parent households in these countries are likely to be those with the greatest risk of poverty.

Employment and social changes relating to women, unquestionably, have been the single most important manifestation of post-industrial transformation in Australia and New Zealand in the past two decades. One interesting response, and hardly one that would have been expected on the basis of the more apocalyptic prognoses of the consequences of postindustrial change, has been the development of a strong women's policy machinery within the bureaucracies of both nations, and a series of policy changes under the two Labour governments (but not National) which have created greater gender equality within the welfare system (on Australia, see Sawer, 1990 and Shaver, 1993; on New Zealand, see Curtin, 1992) and have modified and extended (i.e. by childcare subsidies) the welfare state to facilitate still greater female labour force participation. On this score, it would appear that the most recent periods of Labour rule in these countries have seen initiatives pushing Australia and New Zealand in policy directions more Scandinavian than continental European (low female labour force participation) or North American (no state involvement).

However, the Antipodean nations still have a very long way to go. A wage earners' welfare state premised on female dependency is hardly the best nurturing environment for an income support system which caters adequately for women seeking to combine labour force participation and caring duties within the family. There remain many impediments. For single mothers, these include the lack of generosity of benefits (although cf. Table 4.2 below and associated comment) and means tests imposing high effective marginal tax rates which deter women from re-entering the work-force to an appreciably greater degree than in Scandinavia or, indeed, other Anglo-American nations. For all working women, there is the difficulty of the very limited range of benefits facilitating workforce re-entry and job retention. These are clearly important targets for welfare reform in these countries.

Interestingly, although the wage earners' concept has been an impediment to some of the substance of women's welfare needs, what shift there has been towards greater gender equality has owed not a little to the traditional mechanisms of the wage earners' welfare state. The arbitration system, which had once stood as institutional guarantor of the family wage, became in the late 1960s and early 1970s a mechanism actively promoting equal pay for women through award decisions. As a consequence, in recent decades, Australia and New Zealand have maintained relatively low gender wage inequalities by international standards, only now under threat as a result of the recent decentralization, and, in New Zealand, destruction of traditional wage-fixing institutions (on New Zealand, see Hammond and Harbridge, 1993). Most recently, the Australian trade union movement has been pressing for both maternity and parental support payments to become a new type of occupational benefit established under the wage award system, bearing first fruit in a lump sum, means tested (but along standard Australian lines, only excluding the top 15 per cent of income earners) maternity benefit announced in the May 1995 budget. In general, the use of the state as a 'user-friendly' mechanism to achieve women's welfare goals is one which has strong resonances with the regulatory and interventionist modes of Antipodean government that gave birth to the wage earners' model.

Obviously, the change which has broken most dramatically with the even-tenored working class life cycles of the immediate post-war decades has been the growth of unemployment. As of 1993, the jobless figure was around 11 per cent in both countries, although declining to below 9 per cent by mid 1995 (all unemployment figures bar the most recent are from OECD, 1993). In Australia, Labor in 1983 inherited around 10 per cent unemployment from its monetarist predecessor and in the early 1990s again experienced levels of this magnitude, not least as a consequence of a high real interest rate policy at the end of the 1980s. In the interim, however, there was a substantial decline in unemployment to a low of around 6 per cent in 1989. In New Zealand, unemployment was to some extent contained by Keynesian and state-led investment policies until the mid 1980s, standing at less than 6 per cent in 1983 and under 4 per cent in 1986. Thereafter, unemployment in New Zealand was to increase annually to 1993, not so much in tune with cyclical trends in the world economy, but rather as a consequence of the policy initiatives of the Fourth Labour Government and its successor, and, in particular, its successive use of monetarist and real interest rate remedies against inflation from the mid 1980s onwards.

The wage earners' welfare state in jeopardy

To say the very least, the broadly common outcomes of economic policy development in these countries over the past decade mean that there are major areas in which the wage earners' welfare state either no longer delivers or in which it delivers outcomes markedly less favourable than was previously the case. The Antipodean economies and labour markets no longer guarantee living standards comparable with the best in the world, no longer guarantee full employment and no longer guarantee a high level of wage equality, although they do still appear to provide an extraordinarily high level and, indeed, standard of home ownership. Moreover, the guarantees that are no longer there were precisely those on which rested the claim for the efficacy of the Antipodean welfare strategy *vis-à-vis* European welfare state models. Nevertheless, from the mid 1980s onwards, there also were major differences in labour market policies and labour market outcomes between the two countries, and differences also in the tax policies which transformed the economic rewards of labour market participation into family incomes. These differences very clearly demonstrate the greater commitment of the Australian Labor government than its New Zealand Labour and National counterparts to insulating its natural constituency of support amongst average and below average income earners from the full impact of its programme of economic deregulation.

One very important area of difference has been in employment policy. In New Zealand, thorough going economic restructuring initiatives were taken to remove external barriers to trade, to corporatize state enterprises as a precursor to privatizing them, to reduce assistance to industry and agriculture, to remove price controls and, above all, to reduce inflation. However, there were no serious efforts to address the likely employment effects of these policies, and, indeed, they took place at the same time as the active labour market schemes already in existence were being phased out (Shirley et al., 1990: 84–6). On the contrary, what Roger Douglas, the Labour Finance Minister, and the Treasury, seen by many commentators (Jesson, 1989; Easton, 1994b) as the intellectual powerhouse of the monetarist and Hayekian doctrines shaping policy from 1984 onwards, wanted was for their measures to bite with immediate effect so as to realize structural adjustment gains as rapidly as possible. The result was to decimate employment in whole areas of the economy and regions of the country.

In Australia, by contrast, a deregulatory thrust which was of major dimensions by OECD standards, but nevertheless far less gung-ho than in New Zealand, was managed by tripartite industry plans and negotiated micro-economic reform in the context of government and trade union negotiated policy settings encouraging stable business expectations and high levels of investment (Chapman et al., 1991). Labor's primary policy instrument in this was a consciously established set of corporatist or quasi-corporatist arrangements and understandings known as the Accord, which, for more than a decade, have made the government and trade unions partners in the process of economic transformation (see Matthews, 1991: 191–218; Gruen and Grattan, 1993: 111–34). A telling contrast, pertinent to both the style and content of labour market policy on both sides of the Tasman in the latter half of the 1980s, was that whereas in New Zealand, policy was driven by a Chicago School enthused Treasury, in Australia policy was presided over by a Prime Minister (Bob Hawke) who had been President of the Australian Confederation of Trade Unions (ACTU) for many years. In employment terms, at least, the difference made by this contrast of policy approaches was extremely dramatic. Between 1982 and 1990, Australia recorded employment growth of 2.6 per cent per annum, much the best performance in the OECD, whilst New Zealand, with an average of 0 per cent per annum, was the second worst performer after Ireland (OECD, 1993: 5).

The other crucial area of difference related to issues concerning wages, conditions of employment, and taxation of income from employment. In Australia, the Accord mechanism was initially used, in conjunction with the traditional arbitration machinery, to manage the decline in real wages adjudged necessary to enhance competitiveness, whilst simultaneously providing continuing minimum wage guarantees for workers in low-wage industries. Whilst wage inequality has clearly increased in Australia, there has been, at least, some attempt to preserve wage fairness. Changes on the industrial relations front have also seen a progressive shift towards more decentralized, enterprise-based, wage-setting (Plowman, 1990: 155–6), but the Accord mechanism has prevented any serious undermining of those features of the centralized industrial relations system protecting minimum wage levels and working conditions and preventing wage break-outs. The demands of competitiveness also impinged in the area of taxation, where economic rationalist reformers argued that progressivity reduced the incentives stemming from what they saw as necessary wage inequalities. However, again as a consequence of the Accord relationship between Labor and the trade unions, the government backed away from plans to impose a general consumption tax in return for a reduction in marginal rates of taxation. Although reducing the top marginal rate from 60 to 49 per cent, the traditional wage earners' welfare state aversion to consumption taxes triumphed. Instead, Labor instituted both a capital gains tax and a progressive fringe-benefits tax on business expenses, measures very much against the regressive trend of 1980s OECD tax reform (cf. Heidenheimer et al., 1990: 209–14).

The crucial difference between the two countries in respect of managed wage restraint was the absence in New Zealand of a working relationship between unions and the Labour government in any way comparable to the Australian Accord (Sandlant, 1989). The absence of such a relationship also showed up clearly in the tax arena, with a complete lack of popular, much less trade union, consultation prior to the imposition of a general consumption tax and a far less progressive income tax regime than any contemplated in Australia, with a top marginal rate of 33 per cent (Heidenheimer et al., 1990: 211). On the other hand, and with the exception of radical reforms in respect of state sector employment, industrial relations was an area in which the Fourth Labour Government, perhaps for once mindful of traditional allegiances, manifested rather less deregulatory zeal than was its wont (Walsh, 1991). However, the National Government after 1990 was far less circumspect, seeing labour market deregulation as the major missing building-brick in the edifice of economic restructuring. The Employment Contracts Act, passed in 1991, did away with almost 100 years of labour market protection, abolishing the last remnants of the arbitration system and severely curtailing the right to strike, as well as removing much of the basis of trade union freedom to organize. According to one commentator, the consequences are already apparent in 'a substantial, perhaps irreversible, fall in trade union membership and collective bargaining coverage, the continued erosion of employment conditions and employment security, a growing sense of employer strength and (in some quarters) militancy' (Walsh, 1993a: 74).

Rolling back or refurbishing the welfare state

If the keystone of the institutional arch of the wage earners' welfare state used to be the institutions of wage control which regulated and pacified the conflict of labour and capital, then the Employment Contracts Act marks the end of the wage earners' welfare state in New Zealand. The contrast here with Australia is one not just of outcomes, but of the integrity of institutions and of their potential for social protection. As we have already noted, the Australian labour market has offered a markedly lower degree of protection over the past decade, but it does still contain institutions designed to resolve the conflicts of labour and capital by adjudicating the outcomes of the wage bargaining process; it does maintain important protections against the exploitation of weaker groups of workers in the labour market; and there are still tax mechanisms which seek to moderate the growing inequality of wages. Moreover, in the adverse external circumstances of the past decade, and with the general realization that it is impossible any longer to pursue the traditional strategy of domestic defence, the established wage-fixing apparatus has been made more flexible without undermining its inherited legitimacy and has been simultaneously augmented by the development of quasi-corporatist links between Labor and the trade unions. In Australia, arguably, the verdict on what has happened in the labour market in the Labor decade is that, whilst the traditional institutional props of the wage earners' welfare state have ceased to operate as effectively as in the past, there has been a genuine attempt to refurbish their role as, at least, a secondary line of defence of life cycle security for the broad mass of wage and salary earners.

In the traditional wage earners' model, wage control was the primary instrument of welfare and social security was residual. Now, the roles have been reversed, partly as a consequence of the failure of the traditional labour market strategy, but also because, as in many other countries, changes in mores, family structures and patterns of female labour force participation have transformed traditional ties of family dependence. Under these circumstances, it might have been reasonable to assume that New Zealand, with a stronger policy tradition of universalism and expenditure generosity, would have responded more positively than Australia. In fact, the reverse has been the case and, as of the mid 1990s, it seems clear that social protection through social security rests on firmer foundations in Australia than in New Zealand and, indeed, arguably, on firmer foundations than in any other English-speaking nation.

This has not happened as a consequence of any sudden shift towards universalism or massive growth of generosity on Australia's part. On the contrary, in respect of social security income maintenance expenditure, the Labor decade has been one in which selectivism has been intensified, with an assets test imposed on age pensions, and the one non-income-tested benefit, the child allowance, becoming tested against both income and assets. There have been a whole host of more minor adjustments designed to target need more precisely and to encourage the transition from benefits to labour market participation, the latter emphasis being the theme of Labor's major Social Security Review of the latter part of the 1980s. Crucially, however, the budgetary impetus for such change has come from a wish not so much to cut back public expenditure as to control its growth. In consequence, means tests have been drawn not at the line separating the poor from the rest, but rather at the line which obviates 'middle class welfare'. In the new stringently targeted Australian world of means tests, the one-child family earning less than $60,000 (approximately US$42,000) still receives child benefit, and 72 per cent of the aged qualify for the age benefits (Gruen and Grattan, 1993: 192).

Moreover, real benefits, whilst they have not increased substantially, did move up gradually over the course of the 1980s (Saunders, 1991: 302) and, taking account of both social wage and indirect tax changes, the living standards of the bottom three income deciles improved by 5 per cent or more over the period from 1984 to 1988–9 (Saunders, 1994: 183). There is also some evidence that this trend of the high employment growth years has been maintained in respect of unemployment and family benefits throughout the recessionary period of the early 1990s (Harding, 1994: 16). Indeed, family poverty, and particularly that of one-parent families, has been a specific target of Labor policy, with the introduction of an additional child payment for low-income families and the very substantial enhancement of the rent allowance as a means of targeting family poverty arising from the lack of private home ownership. If recent simulation estimates are to be believed, these measures appear to have been rather successful, leading to a marked decline in both poverty rates and poverty gaps for families with children between 1989–90 and early 1994 (Harding, 1994: 15–17).

In New Zealand, initial social policy measures by the Fourth Labour Government had some similarities to the tighter targeting measures in Australia, with a whole series of cost containing modifications of the existing system. Given the flagrant generosity of certain aspects of national superannuation – its status as a flat-rate demogrant from age 60 – it became an early candidate of the new government's zeal for budget stringency. The imposition of a tax surcharge on the benefit effectively amounted to an incomes test on the benefit. As an additional means of containing superannuation costs, the government further announced the gradual phased-out eligibility of the 60–65 age group. In the area of family support, the real value of universal child benefits was allowed to decline, despite evidence of increasing family poverty, but, as in Australia, a new targeted benefit was introduced for families with low incomes. By 1987, major divisions emerged within Labour, with those who had earlier spearheaded economic reform arguing for a major rationalization and cut-back of social expenditure. This view was contested, not least by a major Royal Commission on Social Policy, which reaffirmed a commitment to a New Zealand society in which there is 'a sense of community responsibility and collective values that provide an environment of security' (Royal Commission, 1988: 11). Labour, nevertheless, went into the 1990 election with proposals for a single base-rate for all benefits other than superannuation that would have meant substantial reductions for many classes of beneficiaries (O'Brien and Wilkes, 1993: 79).

These proposals lapsed when the Nationals won in 1990, but, as in the labour market arena, the new National Government took up the running where Labour left off. The National Government's new policy programme, 'Welfare that works', included a scheme for a global system of abatement of all forms of social assistance, including health and hospital care. So far, this has proved too complex to implement, and the piecemeal introduction of parts of the package has compounded existing poverty traps resulting from means testing. In its initial form, the programme also included a proposal to make superannuation a direct, means tested, benefit targeted exclusively at the poor, but this generated enormous opposition and National had to be satisfied with an increase in the surcharge, a three-year freeze on benefit levels and an acceleration of the timetable for making benefits payable from age 65. Despite these reverses, moves towards 'an ever more tightly targeted welfare state' continued apace (St John and Heynes, 1993: 3), with the total abolition of the universal child benefit and a means tested regime of health care that much diminished the concept of a universal, national health system (Kelsey, 1993: 85–8), being only amongst the more conspicuous examples. Moreover, in its early months in office, National reduced real benefit levels for virtually all classes of beneficiaries, leading to an estimated increase in poverty of no less than 40 per cent over the two-year period 1989–90 to 1991–2 (Easton, 1993: 1–23).

Although it is not possible to measure benefit replacement rates in the Antipodean nations as percentages of prior earnings as in the European and Scandinavian earnings-related systems, a rough and ready comparative yardstick may be provided by relating benefits to GDP per capita in much the same manner as Esping-Andersen does in his analysis of the social minima in Western Europe (Chapter 3). This is done in Table 4.2, which examines the replacement rates of various benefits for claimants with and without spouses and specified dependants. The contrast between the countries at the end of the period we have been examining shows the extent to which Australia has now caught up with New Zealand in the area of income support. In respect of both unemployment and sickness benefits, Australia is now somewhat the more generous of the two nations and, for unemployment beneficiaries between 21 and 24 years of age, it is appreciably so. In respect of single parents, New Zealand remains marginally more generous than Australia, and only in respect of age superannuation does New Zealand maintain a large margin of advantage.

There is, in fact, an almost point for point reversal in the welfare policy transformation that has taken place in New Zealand and Australia since the advent of Labour governments in both countries in the first half of the 1980s. In respect of income maintenance expenditure, New Zealand started

Table 4.2 *Benefit rates as a percentage of per capita GDP, 1993*

Benefit	Australia	New Zealand
Unemployment		
Under 18	14.4	20.4
Youth	26.4 (18–20 years)	25.6 (18–24 years)
Full	34.7 (21 years +)	30.8 (25 years +)
Couple	57.9	51.3
Couple + 2 children	76.3	69.3
Sickness		
Full	34.7	32.1
Couple	57.9	58.3
Couple + 2 children	76.3	73.1
Single parent		
+ 1 child	47.1	53.8
+ 2 children	56.4	62.9
Aged		
Single	34.7	43.9
Couple	57.9	67.6

Sources: calculated from official data from the Australian Department of Social Security and the New Zealand Department of Social Welfare. Since New Zealand benefits are taxed, the figures in the table are calculated net of tax. Figures for families with children include all applicable child benefits

out both more generous in respect of all forms of income maintenance expenditure and less selective. However, by the mid 1990s the changes we have described had led to a situation in which some benefit levels were higher in Australia and only age benefits remained markedly more generous in New Zealand. Moreover, Australian incomes tests, again with the exception of age pensions, cut in at rather higher levels than in New Zealand. In the early 1980s, New Zealand also possessed a national health system which, dating back to the late 1930s, had some claim to be the oldest in the world, whilst the Australian Liberals had just abolished Labor's Medibank scheme introduced for the first time in 1974. But in 1984, Australia's new Labor government restored the universal, national health scheme under the name of Medicare and less than a decade later New Zealand made user charges a major component of its once universal health care system. Finally, even New Zealand's long-standing record as the more generous provider of age pensions may well disappear over the course of the coming decades. Initially introduced in the traditional wage earners' welfare state context of a general wage award, the Australian arbitration system delivered an earnings-related, employer-funded, scheme in 1986. This has now been codified in legislation and expanded, so that nearly all Australian wage earners will eventually benefit from a scheme which, by early next century, will be funded by 9 per cent employer, 3 per cent employee and 3 per cent general revenue contributions. Although contributions are compulsory, they go into privately administered funds and are not generally counted as part of public expenditure. According to official estimates, a retiree on average wages in the year 2031 might expect superannuation benefits amounting to 60 per cent of pre-retirement income (Clare and Tulpulé, 1994).

The enormous difference between the termination points of these processes of welfare state transformation is poignantly underlined by a juxtaposition of the titles of recent books published in the two countries. In 1992, a group of well-known New Zealand social scientists contributed to an edited volume called *The Decent Society?* (Boston and Dalziel, 1992), the question mark prefiguring a critical onslaught on the entire policy record of the National Party Government which had used 'the decent society' as its 1990 election slogan. In complete contrast, an Australian book, co-authored by a social policy specialist and an economist, and based on extensive survey research using analytical techniques similar to those of the Scandinavian level-of-living studies of the 1970s, could use the title *Living Decently* (Travers and Richardson, 1993) to epitomize its conclusions as to the character of the life courses of average Australians in the late 1980s.

This history of a decade of welfare reversal in the Antipodes is of more than parochial interest. The willingness and capacity of the Australian Labor government to introduce reforms to the system of social amelioration as significant as universal health care and earnings-related superannuation offer an extraordinary contrast to the 'there is no alternative' brand of public expenditure cut-backs in New Zealand and the United Kingdom in the same period. Interestingly, too, the superannuation reform was initiated as an adjunct to the wages system and may, properly, be considered an extension of the wage earners' welfare state. Indeed, the usual myopia of domestic and foreign commentators concerning features of the Antipodean welfare model applies to this scheme, which, presumably because it counts as neither public expenditure nor taxation, is frequently unmentioned in debate on social security development in the Labor decade – an omission roughly equivalent, in real terms, to describing the Swedish system of social protection without mentioning the ATP system of age superannuation. The contrast between the social policy initiatives of the Australian and New Zealand governments in these years is a still more clear-cut instance of the difference in policy stances already noted in the area of labour market reform. What both differences demonstrate is that there are, in fact, alternatives: that policy may be harnessed to refurbishing the welfare state, as in Australia (see Castles, 1994), or to destroying any kind of welfare state, as in New Zealand. In this account, policy clearly matters.

Some lessons

That policy matters is one important lesson that may be drawn from this analysis of the development of social policy in the Antipodean nations before, during and after the Golden Age. There are others. Another emerges as a kind of a postscript to the emergence of differences between the two nations' responses to economic disruption and postindustrial change in the past two decades. This is a lesson that human institutions – and, perhaps, particularly institutions of social protection (see Polanyi, 1944) – are often more resilient than we give them credit for. That lesson is clearly underlined by recent developments in New Zealand which offer some prospect of preserving what is left of the welfare state and, perhaps, even reversing some of the losses. After almost a decade in which the New Zealand Treasury's views have been pushed through Parliament by majority governments with both Labour and National partisan labels, in 1993 the electorate used the referendum mechanism to ditch the first-past-the-post electoral system blamed for producing majority governments unresponsive to popular opinion (Mulgan, 1994). Arguably, governments elected under the new system will be more wary of policies designed to 'crash through or crash'. It should give aid and comfort to those who favour the cause of social development when, however belatedly, attacks on established standards and institutions of social protection inspire popular reaction and counter-attack.

A further lesson is that while policy matters, it is not the only thing that matters. The world of the Golden Age cannot be recovered by policies which wish it so. Policy options are broadly shaped by the economic forces and social and cultural structures which shape a generation's dilemmas and opportunities. Sadly, this generation's dilemmas involve many of the same kinds of economic constraints and trade-offs that characterized the choices of the pre-Golden-Age generation. More hopefully, in areas such as greater female emancipation and greater educational opportunity, at least some of the options offered by a postindustrial society seem to allow for an extension of the limits of social protection beyond those allowed by the institutional structures of the Golden Age. That the sexist assumptions of the wage earners' welfare state have been subject to a slow process of dissolution over the past two decades is a gain not a loss for social development in Australia and New Zealand.

A final lesson provides a challenge to those who are too ready to assert that there is one best way of pursuing the cause of social development. The countries examined in this chapter have frequently been criticized for low levels of social protection implicit in low income support replacement rates. In the Golden Age, the best retort was to point to the wage earners' welfare state's capacity to deliver 'social protection by other means' (Castles, 1989) – through guaranteed wage levels and high levels of home ownership. Even today, however, with wage guarantees under threat or destroyed, there remain some defences of a system resting on needs-based guarantees, as, of course, there are also for systems resting on social insurance (the entrenchment of entitlements) or universalism (equality of treatment).

Table 4.2 above shows that the Antipodean systems of income support do genuinely adjust for need stemming from dependency. The figures in that table cannot be compared with the social minima reported by Esping-Andersen (see Table 3.1), because the latter are not adjusted for additional payments for dependants. However, very recent research (Bolderson and Mabbett, 1995), which compares replacement levels (as a percentage of the average production worker's wage) for single beneficiaries and for couples with two children in respect of age, invalidity and unemployment benefits in Sweden, the Netherlands, France, Germany, Britain, the USA and Australia, does allow some tentative conclusions to be drawn. As one might expect, for single beneficiaries, flat-rate benefits lead to replacement levels in Australia generally lower than in most other countries. However, for couples with two children the results are quite different and Australia is in the top half of the distribution for every type of benefit. For second-string unemployment benefits (i.e. when social insurance is exhausted and social minima apply), Australia is second only to the Netherlands. New Zealand does not figure in this analysis, but extrapolation from Table 4.2 suggests that quite similar conclusions must apply in this case also. What this means is that in the area where a needs-based system should deliver – i.e. where need is greatest – it does, at least, deliver outcomes at least as satisfactory as those of most other types of welfare state. That is a feature of such systems which may be of very considerable appeal to nations seeking to establish viable systems of social protection for the first time or to streamline existing systems under the pressure of fiscal exigency.

References

Åberg, R. (1989) 'Distributive mechanisms of the welfare state – a formal analysis and an empirical application', *European Sociological Review*, 5(2): 167–82.

Australian Bureau of Statistics (1994) *Australian Social Trends 1994*. Canberra: AGPS.

Bolderson, H. and Mabbett, D. (1995) 'Mongrels or thoroughbreds: a cross-national look at social security systems', *European Journal of Political Research*, 28: 119–39.

Boston, J. and Dalziel, R. (eds) (1992) *The Decent Society? Essays in Response to National's Economic and Social Policies*. Auckland: Oxford University Press.

Bradbury, B. (1993) 'Male wage inequality before and after tax: a six country comparison'. University of NSW, Social Policy Research Centre Discussion Paper, no. 42.

Brosnan, P. and Rea, D. (1992) 'Rogernomics and the labour market', *New Zealand Sociology*, 7(2): 188–221.

Brosnan, P. and Wilson, M. (1989) 'The historical structuring of the New Zealand labour market', Victoria University of Wellington, Industrial Relations Centre, Working Paper no. 4.

Brown, R.G. (1989) ' Social security and welfare', in K. Hancock (ed.), *Australian Society*. Cambridge: Cambridge University Press.

Bryson, L. (1992) *Welfare and the State*. London: Macmillan.

Castles, F.G. (1985) *The Working Class and Welfare: Reflections on the Political Development of the Welfare State in Australia and New Zealand, 1890–1980*. Sydney: Allen and Unwin.

Castles, F.G. (1988) *Australian Public Policy and Economic Vulnerability*. Sydney: Allen and Unwin.

Castles, F.G. (1989) 'Social protection by other means: Australia's strategy of coping with external vulnerability', in F.G. Castles (ed.), *The Comparative History of Public Policy*. Cambridge: Polity Press.

Castles, F.G. (1992) 'On sickness days and social policy', *Australian & New Zealand Journal of Sociology*, 28(1): 29–44.

Castles, F.G. (1993) 'Changing course in economic policy: the English-speaking nations in the 1980s', in F.G. Castles (ed.), *Families of Nations*. Aldershot: Dartmouth.

Castles, F.G. (1994) 'The wage earners' welfare state revisited: refurbishing the established model of Australian social protection, 1983–1993', *Australian Journal of Social Issues*, 29(2).

Castles, F.G. and Mitchell, D. (1993) 'Worlds of welfare and families of nations', in F.G. Castles (ed.), *Families of Nations*. Aldershot: Dartmouth.

Chapman, B.J., Dowrick, S.J. and Junankar, P.N. (1991) 'Perspectives on Australian unemployment: the impact of wage-setting institutions', in F.H. Gruen (ed.), *Australian Economic Policy: Conference Proceedings*. ANU: Centre for Economic Policy Research. pp. 21–57.

Chifley, J.B. (1944) *Social Security and Reconstruction*. Canberra: Government Printer.

Clare, R. and Tulpulé, A. (1994) 'Australia's ageing society', EPAC, Background Paper no. 37.

Curtin, J.C. (1992) 'The ministry of women's affairs: where feminism and public policy meet'. MA dissertation, University of Waikato.

Davidson, A. (1989) *Two Models of Welfare: the Origins and Development of the Welfare State in Sweden and New Zealand, 1888–1988*. Uppsala: Acta Universitatis Upsaliensis.

Du Plessis, R. (1993) 'Women, politics and the state', in B. Roper and C. Rudd (eds.), *State and Economy in New Zealand*. Auckland: Oxford University Press.

Easton, B. (1983) *Income Distribution in New Zealand*. Wellington: NZ Institute of Economic Research.

Easton, B. (1993) 'Poverty and families: priority or piety?' Unpublished paper, Economic and Social Trust on New Zealand, Wellington.

Easton, B. (1994a) 'Economic rationalism in New Zealand', 'Australia, New Zealand and economic rationalism: parallel or dividing tracks'. Institute of Ethics and Public Policy, Monash University, Occasional Paper no. 7, pp. 15–30.

Easton, B. (1994b) 'The ideas behind the New Zealand reforms', *Oxford Review of Economic Policy*.

Esping-Andersen, G. (1990) *The Three Worlds of Welfare Capitalism*. Cambridge: Polity Press.

Gregory, R.G. (1993) 'Aspects of Australian and US living standards: the disappointing decades 1970–1990', *The Economic Record*, 69(204): 61–76.

Gruen, F. and Grattan, M. (1993) *Managing Government*. Melbourne: Longman Cheshire.

Hammond, M.B. (1913) 'Judicial interpretation of the minimum wage in Australia', *Annals of the American Academy of Political and Social Science*.

Hammond, S. and Harbridge, R. (1993) 'The impact of the Employment Contracts Act on women at work', *New Zealand Journal of International Relations*, 18: 15–30.

Harding, A. (1994) 'Family income and social security policy'. Unpublished paper, University of Canberra, National Centre for Social and Economic Modelling.

Heidenheimer, A.J., Heclo, H. and Adams, C.T. (1990) *Comparative Public Policy*, 3rd edn. New York: St Martin's Press.

Henderson, R. (1978) 'Social welfare expenditure', in R.B. Scotton and H. Ferber (eds), *Public Expenditures and Social Policy in Australia*, vol. I. Melbourne: Longman Cheshire.

Henderson, R.F., Harcourt, A. and Harper, R.J.A. (1970) *People in Poverty: a Melbourne Survey*. Melbourne: Cheshire.

Higgins, H.B. (1922) *A New Province for Law and Order*. London: Constable.

ILO (1949) *Systems of Social Security: New Zealand*. Geneva: International Labour Office.

ILO (1972) *The Cost of Social Security*. Geneva: International Labour Office.

Jesson, B. (1989) *Fragments of Labour*. Auckland: Penguin.

Kangas, O. (1991) *The Politics of Social Rights*. Stockholm: Swedish Institute for Social Research.

Karmel, P.H. and Brunt, M. (1962) *The Structure of the Australian Economy*. Melbourne: Cheshire.

Kelsey, J. (1993) *Rolling Back the State*. Wellington: Bridget Williams Books.

Kemeny, J. (1980) 'The political economy of housing', in E.L. Wheelright and K. Buckley (eds), *Essays in the Political Economy of Australian Capitalism*, vol. 4. Sydney: Australian and New Zealand Book Company.

King, S. and Lloyd, P. (1993) *Economic Rationalism: Dead End or Way Forward?* Sydney: Allen and Unwin.

Le Rossignol, J.E. and Stewart, W.D. (1910) *State Socialism in New Zealand*. London: Harrap.

Lydall, H. (1968) *The Structure of Earnings*. London: Oxford University Press.

Maddison, A. (1991) *Dynamic Forces in Capitalist Development*. Oxford: Oxford University Press.

Matthews, T. (1991) 'Interest group politics: corporatism without business?', in F.G. Castles (ed.), *Australia Compared*. Sydney: Allen and Unwin.

Mulgan, R. (1994) *Politics in New Zealand*. Auckland: Auckland University Press.

Myles, J. (1990) 'States, labor markets and life cycles', in R. Friedland and A.F. Robertson (eds), *Beyond the Marketplace*. New York: Aldine de Gruyter.

O'Brien, M. and Wilkes, C. (1993) *The Tragedy of the Market: a Social Experiment in New Zealand*. Palmerston North: Dunmore Press.

OECD (1976) *Public Expenditure on Income Maintenance Programmes*. Paris: OECD.

OECD (1992) *Historical Statistics 1960–1992*. Paris: OECD.

OECD (1993) *Employment Outlook*, July. Paris: OECD.

OECD (1994) *OECD Observer*, June/July. Paris: OECD.

Plowman, D. (1990) 'The stone the builders rejected', in M. Easson and J. Shaw (eds), *Transforming Industrial Relations*. Sydney: Pluto Press. pp. 145–59.

Polanyi, K. (1944) *The Great Transformation*. New York: Rinehart.

Pusey, M. (1991) *Economic Rationalism in Canberra*. Melbourne: Cambridge University Press.

Rankin, K. (1992) 'New Zealand's gross national product: 1859–1939', *Review of Income and Wealth*, 38(1).

Royal Commission on Social Security (1988) *Towards a Fair and Just Society*. Wellington: Government Printer.

Rudd, C. (1993) 'The welfare state: origins, development and crisis', in B. Roper and C. Rudd (eds), *State and Economy in New Zealand*. Auckland: Oxford University Press.

St John, S. (1993) 'Income support for an ageing society', in P.G. Koopman-Boyden (ed.), *New Zealand's Ageing Society*. Wellington: Daphne Brasell Associates Press.

St John, S. and Heynes, A. (1993) 'The welfare mess'. Unpublished paper, University of Auckland, Department of Economics.

Sandlant, R.A. (1989) 'The political economy of wage restraint: the Australian accord and trade union strategy in New Zealand'. M Arts thesis, Auckland, Department of Political Studies.

Saunders, P. (1991) 'Selectivity and targeting in income support: the Australian experience', *Journal of Social Policy*, 20(3): 299–326.

Saunders, P. (1994) *Welfare and Equality: National and International Perspectives on the Australian Welfare State*. Melbourne: Cambridge University Press.

Sawer, M. (1990) *Sisters in Suits: Women and Public Policy in Australia*. Sydney: Allen and Unwin.

Shaver, S. (1993) 'Women and the Australian social security system: from difference towards equality'. University of NSW, SPRC Discussion Paper, no. 41.

Shirley, I. (1990) 'New Zealand: the advance of the right', in I. Taylor (ed.), *The Social Effects of Free Market Policies*. London: Harvester/Wheatsheaf.

Shirley, I., Easton, B., Briar, C. and Chatterjee, S. (1990) *Unemployment in New Zealand*. Palmerston North: Dunmore Press.

Statistics New Zealand (1993) *All About Women in New Zealand*. Wellington.

Summers, R. and Heston, A. (1991) 'The Penn World Table (Mark 5): an expanded set of international comparisons, 1950–88', *Quarterly Journal of Economics*, 106(2): 327–68.

Thomson, D. (1991) *Selfish Generations*. Wellington: Bridget Williams Books.

Thorns, D. (1984) 'Owner occupation, the state and class relations', in C. Wilkes and I. Shirley (eds), *In the Public Interest: Health, Work and Housing in New Zealand*. Auckland: Benton Ross.

Thorns, D. (1993) 'Tenure and wealth accumulation: implications for housing policy', in P.G. Koopman-Boyden (ed.), *New Zealand's Ageing Society*. Wellington: Daphne Brasell Associates Press.

Travers, P. and Richardson, S. (1993) *Living Decently*. Melbourne: Oxford University Press.

UN (various dates) *UN Demographic Yearbook*. New York: United Nations.

UNESCO (1993) *UNESCO Yearbook*.

Varley, R. (1986) *The Government Household Transfer Data Base 1960–1984*. Paris: OECD.

von Rhein-Kress, G. (1993) 'Coping with economic crisis: labour supply as a policy instrument', in F.G. Castles (ed.), *Families of Nations*. Aldershot: Dartmouth.

Walsh, P. (1991) 'The State Sector Act 1988', in J. Boston, J. Martin, J. Pallot and P. Walsh (eds), *Reshaping the State: New Zealand's Bureaucratic Revolution*. Auckland: Oxford University Press.

Walsh, P. (1993a) 'The Employment Contracts Act', in J. Boston and P. Dalziel (eds), *The Decent Society? Essays in Response to National's Economic and Social Policies*. Auckland: Oxford University Press.

Walsh, P. (1993b) 'The state and industrial relations in New Zealand', in B. Roper and C. Rudd (eds), *State and Economy in New Zealand*. Auckland: Oxford University Press.

Wentworth, W.C. (1969) 'Social services and poverty', in G.C. Masterman (ed.), *Poverty in Australia*. Sydney: Australian Institute of Political Science.

5

When Markets Fail: Social Welfare in Canada and the United States

John Myles

Like Scandinavia, North America occupies a special place among modern welfare states. Compared with their European counterparts, Canada and, especially, the United States are typically portrayed as welfare state 'laggards' (Kudrle and Marmor, 1981). Modern social legislation came later than elsewhere and, when it did, often retained an adherence to traditional 'liberal' principles of means-testing and modest social benefits (Esping-Andersen, 1990). North American levels of income inequality are high by international standards (Smeeding, 1991) and, until the 1980s, unemployment ranged well above European levels (McBride, 1992; Therborn, 1986).

To a much greater degree than elsewhere, twentieth century North Americans have looked to the market as their primary source of 'welfare'. And for most of this century, they have had good reasons for this view. The resistance by early American labour leaders to European-style social insurance programmes had a real material base. As the American labour leader Samuel Gompers (1910) observed at the turn of the century, the average American city-dweller could hardly imagine the poverty then prevailing among European workers.

For most of this century, Americans have believed in the market because, for many, the market worked. Despite modest social programmes, North American workers enjoyed enviable levels of economic well-being during the 'Golden Age' of postwar expansion. With wages well above European levels and an expanding economy, North America was still the 'land of opportunity'. The 'great wage compression' of the 1940s and 1950s reduced inequality in the labour market (Goldin and Margo, 1992) and rapid productivity growth brought 'middle class' living standards to North American workers and their families (Levy, 1988). An active Veterans Administration provided housing programmes, educational allowances, and a plethora of other social benefits for a generation returning from war (Amenta and Skocpol, 1988: 108). Despite a weak welfare state, unionized and public sector workers won increasingly generous pension, health care and other income security provisions at the bargaining table (Stevens, 1988).

Table 5.1   *Earnings inequality, selected countries, c. 1990: ratio of lower*
and upper earnings deciles to the median and average five-year change in the
1980s

	Canada	US	Germany	France	Sweden	Norway
Decile ratios:						
D1/D5	0.42	0.40	0.71	0.65	0.74	0.76
D9/D5	1.85	2.22	1.64	1.96	1.54	1.50
Change in 1980s:						
D1/D5	−0.01	−0.03	0.03	0.01	−0.02	0.02
D9/D5	0.03	0.03	0.01	0.02	0.00	0.02

Source: adapted from OECD, 1993: Table 5.2

Since the 1970s, all this has changed. By the end of the 1980s North America, and especially the United States, had consolidated its reputation as the 'land of inequality'. Wage and earnings levels have been stagnant since the 1970s. Workers in the lowest earnings decile in Canada and the United States earn about 40 per cent of median earnings compared with 70 per cent or more in Germany and Scandinavia (Table 5.1). Labour market incomes have polarized, expanding the ranks of the 'working poor'.[1]

In the United States, 'market failure' has resulted in real declines in aggregate social welfare. Family incomes have become more unequal and child poverty has returned to 1965 levels, the year Lyndon Johnson declared America's War on Poverty. Between 1973 and 1987, the income of the poorest 20 per cent of families fell by 22 per cent while that of the richest 20 per cent increased by 25 per cent.

To date, rising labour market inequality in Canada has been offset by social transfers (Economic Council of Canada, 1991). The final distribution of family incomes and child poverty has scarcely changed since the 1970s (Love and Poulin, 1991; Myles and Picot, 1995). However, 'market failure' has meant a sharp rise in demand for transfers and has added to the growth of a public sector debt that is now well above the OECD average (OECD, 1994a: 43).

Paradoxically, however, the very weakness of North American labour market institutions and welfare states is now regarded as the reason for the comparative success of both national economies in generating jobs and restraining the growth of long-term unemployment (OECD, 1994b). The low levels of North American labour market regulation, payroll taxes and social benefits are now held out as models of labour market 'flexibility' to be emulated by the high unemployment European economies. As the OECD (1994b: 35) remarks, allowing wage differentials to widen could be expected to increase employment growth and North America appears to provide evidence that it does.[2]

But widening wage differentials creates a new set of dilemmas for welfare states, not unlike those created by high unemployment. As Keynes and Beveridge recognized, the foundations of social welfare in capitalist economies lie in the labour market. For them, full employment, not generous welfare states, provided the key to economic well-being. Full employment meant low demand for social transfers and a large tax base to finance generous social programmes for the aged, the sick, and the minority of persons without jobs. Generous welfare states were possible only so long as most people found their 'welfare' in the market most of the time.

Widening wage differentials create a similar problem. The ranks of the 'working poor' expand, demand for social transfers rises, and government revenues decline since low wage earners pay few taxes.

In the post-Cold-War era, Western nations appear to be caught in the dilemma of choosing between 'two ways' again, with no 'third way' in sight. The high-wage/low-employment model of continental Europe limits the growth of an American-style underclass but at the price of creating an insider–outsider problem between those with and without those jobs. The low-wage/high-employment strategy of the United States has sustained employment growth but at the price of levels of inequality and poverty widely considered unacceptable by postwar standards.

Canada provides a counterpoint to the American model in much the same way that Scandinavian countries provide a counterpoint to continental Europe. During the 1980s, Scandinavia, and especially Sweden, avoided the European disease of low employment by means of a massive programme of public employment that now appears to have reached its limits. Thus far Canada has avoided the American disease of rising poverty and inequality largely via social transfers. By the 1990s, however, a large public debt was forcing cutbacks and a massive restructuring of social programmes along American lines (Battle and Torjman, 1995).[3]

Postwar social programmes were designed around three basic models: (1) a residual *social assistance* model of means-tested benefits for the poor inherited from the prewar era; (2) the industrial achievement model of *social insurance* based on labour market performance; and (3) a citizenship model of *universal* social benefits. The United States relied almost exclusively on the first two models, providing social insurance for those not expected to work (the elderly and the disabled) and residual means-tested programmes for the working age population. Canada adopted a mixture of all three, including universal health care, family allowances and old age security as citizenship entitlements.

In the social policy debates of the 1990s, all three designs have been challenged. Traditional social assistance programmes are seen as 'welfare traps' that discourage labour market entry and higher incomes for the poor. Social insurance programmes, intended to provide security to middle income workers, are attacked for wasting scarce transfer dollars or as 'out of control' because of the demographic pressures of population ageing. Canada has abandoned the citizenship design entirely as a model for income transfers. Only in health care is the citizenship strategy unquestioned for reasons of both political popularity and the cost advantages of national health insurance over the American private insurance model.

The challenge to contemporary welfare states is to address the new life cycle distribution of economic risk that has resulted from economic restructuring and new family forms. Concretely, this means addressing the new economic insecurities and risks faced by *working age* families because of a rapidly changing labour market, high divorce rates and single parenthood while simultaneously sustaining traditional postwar programmes that now support a rapidly expanding *elderly* population.

Two broad social policy responses have been proposed to adapt to the negative effects of the low-wage/high-employment strategy. *Social investments* in education, job training and other active labour market initiatives are proposed to hasten labour market re-entry and mobility up wage ladders. *Selective wage and income subsidies* modelled on the lines of a negative income tax (NIT) are seen as ways of modernizing traditional social assistance that will maintain work incentives and avoid welfare traps.

The aim of this chapter is to describe the origins and possible outcomes of the dilemma in North America. The first section describes the existing structure of North American welfare institutions. In the second section, the political dynamics that shape social politics in Canada and the United States are described. In the third section, I consider alternative strategies now under discussion to accommodate to the 'market failures' of the past two decades. The chapter concludes on a pessimistic note for two reasons. The first is the 'fiscal deficit' facing Canada and the United States and the limits this imposes on state capacities to invest in significant social experimentation. More important, however, both societies confront a 'democratic deficit' that limits the representation of those most affected by economic restructuring in the political process. In the present context, the 'third way' implies the capacity to identify and implement positive-sum solutions to new forms of economic security. The democratic deficit makes this unlikely.

North American welfare states

The United States emerged from the Second World War with the basic building blocks of its current welfare state already in place, a product of Roosevelt's New Deal. It included social insurance for the elderly, unemployment insurance (UI), and a social assistance programme (aid to families with dependent children, AFDC) aimed at widowed and divorced mothers with children. The disabled were added to the social security system in 1955. Canada passed unemployment insurance legislation in 1940, introduced universal family allowances in 1944, and in 1951 passed the Old Age Security Act that provided $40 a month to all citizens age 70 and over.

During the long postwar boom from the 1940s to the 1970s, however, the market was the main source of welfare and security for North American workers. And the market succeeded in at least three ways. First, the quarter-century that followed the Second World War brought constantly *rising real living standards* stemming from rapidly increasing productivity. Structurally generated 'upward mobility' – between generations and over the life course – took place at unprecedented levels. As Levy (1988: 78–82) shows for the United States,[4] a young man who left home at age 18 in the 1950s would, by age 30, be earning about 15 per cent more than his father had earned when the young man was living at home. In the 1950s a man who made the transition from age 40 to 50 would, on average, have realized a 34 per cent increase in real income.

Second, unlike the 1980s, the labour market brought more, not less, *equality*. The 'great compression', as it has been called (Goldin and Margo, 1992), brought a marked decline in wage inequality during the 1940s and 1950s, the result of wartime wage controls, an increased demand for unskilled labour and a comparatively strong labour movement.

Third, the market became a source of *income security*. Following the Second World War, American unions, frustrated by Congress's refusal to establish national health insurance and to extend social security, began pressing – successfully – for private sector social benefits (Stevens, 1988).[5] The federal government encouraged these efforts. In 1948 the National Labor Relations Board (NLRB) ruled that employers were required to bargain over pensions. The effects spilled across the border to Canada where large numbers of industrial workers were employed by American firms, organized by affiliates of American unions, and therefore eligible for the same benefits.[6]

By the 1960s, some of the flaws in this market-driven model were already apparent. Some groups (the elderly) and regions (Appalachia, the maritime provinces) had missed the rising tide of postwar prosperity. Private social benefits won at the bargaining table had divided the labour market into a 'core' of high wage workers with generous social benefits and a 'secondary' labour market with low wages and limited security. The result was a flurry of social policy reform in both nations. In 1965 President Johnson proclaimed his 'Great Society' and a 'War on Poverty'. Not to be out-visioned, Canada's Pierre Trudeau announced his agenda for the 'Just Society'.

The War on Poverty, however, did not depart from the basic market-driven model of social welfare of postwar America. As Rebecca Blank (1994) points out, *The Economic Report of the President* (GPO, 1964) which laid out the intellectual foundations for the War on Poverty placed its emphasis on economic self-sufficiency. James Tobin (1994: 147), a co-author of the report, observes that the War on Poverty relied mainly on the 'market magic of general prosperity and growth' to solve the poverty problem. Employment, not transfers, would provide the solution. Government initiatives took the form of programmes to improve the earnings opportunities for individuals – Head Start, education grants, job training, public health, community action programmes – not more income transfers or public services. Improved schooling and job opportunities augmented by civil rights legislation to remove barriers to employment and housing were aimed at creating what Jill Quadagno (1994) has called the 'equal opportunity welfare state'.

The exception to the rule was social provision for the elderly. The Medicare Act of 1965 made public health insurance available to those 65 and over. Between 1969 and 1972 social security benefits for the elderly were raised three times, resulting in a net increase of 23 per cent, and benefits were indexed against inflation.

Canada, in contrast, pursued a 'transfer-intensive' social reform. The brief period between 1965 and 1971 (Guest, 1985) brought universal health insurance, and major reforms to social assistance and unemployment insurance. Sickness insurance was added to the UI programme. Two new programmes for the elderly were created: the earnings-related Canada and Quebec pension plans (C/QPP) and the guaranteed income supplement (GIS).

As the following two decades were to show, the transfer model proved the more successful of the two strategies. Poverty among the elderly declined significantly in both countries. And in the 1980s, Canadian transfer programmes offset rising inequality among working age families. Universal health coverage in Canada not only provided more equal access to health care but also proved more effective at containing exploding health care costs (Evans et al., 1991). In contrast, the absence of a well developed transfer system in the United States meant that rising labour market inequalities translated into more inequality in family incomes. And without national health insurance, there was an explosion in health care costs while leaving over 30 million Americans without coverage.

The design of liberal welfare states

It is by now almost academic convention to classify the welfare state regimes of Australia, Canada, the US and the UK among the so-called 'liberal' welfare states (Esping-Andersen, 1990). Richard Titmuss's classical distinction between 'residual' and 'institutional' welfare comes close to what is conventionally understood by liberal social policy: public intervention occurs only after the two traditional sources of support – family and market – break down. Assistance tends to be minimal, is intended to be short term, and is often punitive and stigmatizing in nature.

The empirical basis for the North American countries' reputation as liberal welfare states is highlighted in Table 5.2. Compared with European countries, both nations have continued to rely on more intensive use of means-tested (residual) forms of welfare on the one hand, and private, market-based, insurance on the other. Greater reliance on means-testing and private insurance means a smaller share of national income flows through the public purse and aggregate social spending is smaller as a result.

In the United States, means-tested assistance for the non-elderly is provided in the form of cash payments (AFDC), food stamps, and medical

Table 5.2 *Means-testing, private welfare and social spending*

	Canada	United States	18 OECD countries
Means-tested benefits as % of social expenditure	16	18	6
Private insurance:			
Private pensions as % of total pensions	38	21	13
Private health spending as % of total	26	57	22
Social expenditure as % of GDP:			
OECD estimate 1986	22	18	25
ILO estimate, 1985	16	12	19

Source: benefits and private insurance data adpated from Esping-Andersen, 1990: Table 3.1

Table 5.3 *Social assistance for the non-elderly*

	Canada	US
Maximum monthly social assistance benefit, 1987:		
Single individual	$266	NA
Single parent + two children	$627	$384
Weighted annual average total public assistance		
for a family of four, 1990	$14,932	$8,684
Poverty rate, and poverty gap, single-parent		
family with 2 children, 1986–7:		
Poverty rate (US definition, per cent)	26	41
Poverty gap	$2519	$4172

Figures expressed in national currencies.

Sources: monthly benefit and poverty data, Blank and Hanratty, 1993; public assistance, Banting, 1992a

insurance (Medicaid). Traditionally, AFDC was restricted to single-parent families. In the 1960s, states were allowed to add a programme for unemployed fathers to AFDC and about half did so. Since 1990 states have been required to provide coverage to two-parent households when the principal wage-earner is unemployed but only for six months in any year (Banting, 1992a).

The primary means-tested assistance programme in Canada is social assistance. Unlike the American system, single persons and childless couples are included and benefit levels are considerably higher than in the United States (Table 5.3). As a result, poverty rates among welfare-dependent households are lower than in the United States and the 'poverty gap' – the difference between current income and the poverty line – is smaller.

The United States has experimented modestly and Canada extensively with a modern variant of means-testing (Banting, 1992a). Traditional means-testing is based on a test of assets as well as income, requiring families to 'spend down' their resources to qualify. Beneficiaries are often subject to intrusive surveillance by public officials and moral codes of behaviour. And there is often considerable administrative discretion in

Table 5.4 *Old age minimum benefits and poverty levels among the elderly*

	Canada (1987)	United States (1986)	Average 12 OECD countries (1984–7)
Minimum benefit as % of median income:			
Single person	54	34	52
Couple	59	37	59
% 65+ with less than 50% of median income	6.8	22.4	6.4

Source: adapted from Smeeding et al., 1993

deciding eligibility and benefit levels. In the modern variant, criteria other than income are not considered. Eligibility is determined solely by an income test based on income reported in an annual tax return. There is no surveillance of beneficiaries and administrative discretion is limited to that normally associated with the auditing of tax returns.

The implicit model underlying liberalism's modern face is the negative income tax (NIT) or guaranteed income (GI) initially proposed by then US Treasury Department economist Milton Friedman in 1943 (Moynihan, 1973: 50). Under an NIT model, low income people are entitled to their pre-tax income as well as a government income supplement. The basic idea of the NIT design was simple: in good years workers would pay taxes to governments, in bad years governments would pay taxes to workers.

The most significant exemplar of this design is Canada's guaranteed income supplement (GIS) for the elderly, introduced in 1966. GIS provides single persons with a guaranteed income equal to 54 per cent of the median for single households and 59 per cent for couples (Table 5.4). In contrast, the United States relies on a traditional means-tested programme (supplemental security income, SSI) for the elderly with limited resources. Together with food stamps, SSI provides a couple with 37 per cent and single persons with 34 per cent of median household income. The result is a Luxembourg Income Study (LIS)-based elderly poverty rate of less than 7 per cent in Canada compared with 22 per cent in the United States.

In 1979, Canada began reforming its family programmes along NIT lines with the introduction of a refundable child tax credit. By 1993 the family allowance and child tax exemptions had been rolled into a single child tax benefit (CTB) that provides a refundable tax credit to all low income families with children. Benefits go to both the working and non-working poor and rise proportionately with the number of children. In 1993, the CTB provided $1020 per child with additional supplements for children under seven and for large families. A small 'earned income' supplement (up to $500 per family) is provided to 'working poor' families.

The US has taken much more modest steps in modernizing its means-tested programmes. After the failure of Richard Nixon's Family Assistance Plan (FAP) that aimed to provide a guaranteed annual income for all American families, the US implemented the more modest earned income tax credit (EITC) for the 'working poor' in the early 1970s. EITC excludes the 'non-working poor' (such as welfare mothers) and makes only small adjustments beyond the first child. In 1991, the maximum credit was $1192 for the first child and only $1235 for families with more children. Nevertheless, US social policy gives some indication of following the Canadian trajectory. The annual cost of the once modest EITC grew from $2 billion to $12 billion between 1980 and 1992. And President Clinton's 1993 budget added $20 billion over five years while cutting billions from 'middle class' programmes such as Medicare.

NIT-like programmes draw broad support from the business community as an alternative to both social benefits for middle income workers and minimum wage laws (Haddow, 1993; Quadagno, 1994). Because the marginal tax-back rate on such programmes is low, policy analysts view them as an alternative to the 'welfare traps' created by traditional social assistance programmes. Since they are administered through the tax system, they are less visible and easier to legislate than traditional social programmes. For beneficiaries, they carry none of the stigma or social control associated with traditional means-testing.

Organized labour is more ambivalent since NIT programmes also subsidize and encourage low wage employers and threaten to become substitutes for minimum wage laws and traditional social insurance programmes (Haddow, 1993; Myles 1988). Under an NIT design, the role of the welfare state changes: instead of providing income security (social insurance) for average workers its task is to provide wage subsidies to a growing pool of low wage and underemployed workers.

Nevertheless, because of the unusual political coalitions they create and the potential solutions they offer to high social insurance costs, the growth of low wage employment, and the 'welfare traps' of traditional social assistance, NIT-like designs have a strong possibility of becoming the model of choice for future welfare reforms. In Canada, income-tested supplements have replaced universal citizenship entitlements in the field of income security (Banting, 1992a). And advocates of income-testing are proposing that social insurance programmes be revised along NIT lines in both Canada (Courchene, 1994) and the United States (Peterson, 1993).

Social insurance

Canada and the United States have followed the *social insurance* model – earnings-related income security – in two main areas: old age security and unemployment.

The elderly in both Canada and the United States rely on public pensions – the Canada and Quebec pension plans and old age security in Canada, and old age security income (OASI) in the United States – for most of their income. Until the 1970s, income replacement rates for 'average' workers (Table 5.5a) were quite low in both countries. The exception was the traditional single-earner couple in the United States who

Table 5.5   *Old age security*

(a) Pension replacement rates for workers with average wages in manufacturing, 1969–80 (per cent)

	Canada	United States	Average 12 OECD countries
Single worker:			
1969	24	30	40
1980	34	44	49
Aged couple:			
1969	41	49	50
1980	49	66	61

(b) Pension replacement rate for low, average and high earners, 1989 (per cent)

	Low earnings	Average earnings	High earnings
United States	58	42	24
Canada:			
Without GIS	61	45	22
With GIS	87	51	NA

Sources: (a) Aldrich, 1982; (b) Banting, 1992a

benefit from a 50 per cent supplement for a dependent spouse. Both systems were 'modernized' as a result of legislative changes in the mid 1960s in Canada and the early 1970s in the United States. Replacement rates rose through the 1970s and for average workers were quite similar in the two countries by the end of the 1980s (Table 5.5b). As noted above, however, the two countries diverge sharply in their treatment of low income seniors.

Despite the importance of social insurance in the income packages of the elderly, the 'liberal' character of North American welfare states remains evident in their more extensive reliance on private pensions and property income. In Canada and the United States, public transfers account for about 60 per cent of the income of the population over 65 compared with 70 to 85 per cent in the European and Nordic countries (Smeeding et al., 1993: 8). As Smeeding et al. show, the result is greater income inequality among the elderly (see also Korpi and Palme, 1994).

Unemployment insurance (UI) in the United States is entirely state run and benefits and eligibility criteria differ widely among states. Summary statistics for the US in Table 5.6 are state weighted averages. Before the Canadian UI reforms of 1971, Canadian benefits were below US levels (Table 5.6). Because of the reforms, Canadian benefit levels, benefit duration and average replacement ratios are now well above those of the United States. Unlike the United States, Canada's UI system also provides sickness, parental and maternity benefits. Because of high unemployment, a

Table 5.6   *Unemployment insurance*

	Canada	US
Ratio of average weekly UI benefit to average weekly earnings:		
1968	0.24	0.34
1989	0.44	0.35
Maximum weekly benefit, 1991	$396	$186
Maximum benefit duration (weeks)	50	26
Average duration of UI claims 1989 (weeks)	18.1	13.2
Ratio of average weekly UI recipients to average weekly unemployment rate, 1989	0.99	0.27

Source: adapted from Card and Riddell, 1993

Table 5.7   *Public expenditures on labour market programmes as a percentage of GDP, 1990–1991*

	Canada	United States	Average 18 OECD countries
Total	2.46	0.76	2.37
Active measures	0.54	0.27	0.81
Income maintenance	1.92	0.50	1.52

Source: adapted from OECD, 1993: Table 2.B.1

high rate of labour force participation and more generous benefit and eligibility conditions, Canada spends a larger share of GDP on unemployment compensation than the OECD average (Table 5.7). The United States, in contrast, spends decidedly less.

Citizenship entitlements

The model of citizenship entitlements – benefits that accrue to individuals independently of need or labour force participation – is quite foreign to the American social policy tradition. The closest approximation is Medicare which, despite being insurance based, provides health coverage for 99 per cent of the population over 65.

In contrast, Canada established a universal programme of family allowances in 1944 and universal old age security benefits in 1951. Both provided a monthly flat benefit payment to all citizens (a demogrant) irrespective of need or contributions. Universal insurance to cover hospital fees was established in 1957 and was extended to include physician fees and related services in 1966.

Canada abandoned the tradition of demogrants in 1988 with the creation of an income-tested 'clawback' of family allowances and old age security from high income earners. In 1993, family allowances were folded into the income-tested child tax benefit. Because the income level at which the 'clawback' of old age security takes effect is only indexed to inflation above

3 per cent, it will gradually work its way down the income scale eliminating all but low income seniors. National health insurance, however, has thus far remained politically inviolable for reasons of both its political popularity and the obvious advantage it provides in containing health care costs compared with the United States.

Welfare state effectiveness

The consequences of Canada's more comprehensive and transfer-intensive welfare state became apparent in the 1980s. During the 1980s, the United States became the paradigmatic case of the 'new inequality'. Wages and earnings distributions polarized and the American 'middle class' declined as a share of the population. High divorce rates and out-of-wedlock births exposed more children and adults to the threat of poverty as dual-earner households became the standard for maintaining a middle class life style. In theory, an 'effective' welfare state would offset these developments. In practice, AFDC and UI programmes have eroded in value since the 1970s, exacerbating the trend toward greater inequality with the most notable result being a sharp rise in child poverty from approximately 15 to over 21 per cent between 1979 and 1990 (Hanratty and Blank, 1992).

Despite similar labour market trends, Canadian households experienced little change in the distribution of economic well-being during the 1980s (Love and Poulin, 1991; Blackburn and Bloom, 1993) for two reasons. First, hourly wage inequality grew much less than in the United States largely because of labour market institutions – stronger unions and minimum wage levels (DiNardo and Lemieux, 1994). Second, changes in the earnings distribution were largely offset by the tax-transfer system. Hanratty and Blank (1992) estimate that in 1979 Canadian social assistance and child benefits provided an average combined benefit that was 14 per cent more generous than the comparable combination in the United States. By 1986, the gap had grown to 42 per cent. Between 1970 and 1986 the Canadian poverty rate (measured by US standards) moved from 6.9 points *above* the US level to 4.5 points *below* it.

OECD (1994c) data on public expenditures for social protection also show that Canadian transfers were more responsive to the new circumstances of the 1980s. Between 1980 and 1990, Canada moved sharply upward in social protection expenditures, converging on the OECD average (Table 5.8). In the United States the share of transfers to the non-aged actually declined as a percentage of GDP, a result of the declining relative value of two of the major programmes available to non-elderly Americans – AFDC and unemployment insurance. Between 1972 and 1990, median adjusted AFDC benefits for a family of four declined from $761 per month to $435 per month (Blank, 1994: 179). UI recipients as a percentage of the unemployed peaked at 52 per cent in 1975 and then declined to 29 per cent in 1990 (Card and Riddell, 1993: 180).

Table 5.8   *Public expenditures on social protection as a percentage of GDP*

	Canada	United States	EC	Other OECD
Total:				
1980	14.37	14.10	21.60	18.20
1990	18.79	14.58	21.69	21.15
Non-aged:				
1980	5.73	4.47	7.23	6.04
1990	7.58	3.54	7.46	7.60

Source: adapted from OECD, 1994c: Tables 1b and 1c

Explaining the difference: social cleavages in federal states

Canada and the United States represent two alternative responses to the economic restructuring and new macro-economic environment of the 1980s. In the United States, modest programmes of social protection for the non-elderly followed the downward drift in wages and earnings at the low end of the labour market. Transfers to working age households declined as a share of GDP and family income inequality and child poverty rose. The result was a general decline in aggregate social welfare despite strong employment growth. This outcome was more a byproduct of the welfare state design of the 1960s than of a neoconservative revolution in American social policy in the 1980s. The 1960s and early 1970s consolidated a design rooted in the New Deal: national social insurance for the elderly and a decentralized, largely means-tested, system of social protection for the working age population. The US Social Security Act of 1935 and subsequent legislation left powers over eligibility and benefit levels in crucial areas such as unemployment insurance and AFDC in the hands of the states. The result of this decentralized system of social expenditures has been *fiscal competition* among jurisdictions that puts downward pressure on social spending (Marmor et al., 1990; Pierson, 1994: 35), a pattern evident in the decline in AFDC and unemployment benefits since the 1970s.

Fiscal federalism, rather than fiscal competition, became the foundation for welfare state construction in postwar Canada. During the 1930s, the inability of poorer provinces and municipalities to meet the relief burden of the Great Depression set in motion a process of 'massive centralization' of responsibility for income security in Canada (Banting, 1987: 63). The result was a common set of national standards in key areas of social policy such as unemployment insurance, child benefits and old age security that produced large inter-regional transfers from richer to poorer regions. In the 1960s, the redistributive impact of national standards in social spending was complemented by a complex mix of direct federal–provincial equalization payments.

The decentralized character and anti-transfer bias of American social programmes are tied to the fundamental cleavage that continues to shape the politics of social policy in the United States, namely race (Piven and Cloward, 1994; Skocpol, 1988; Quadagno, 1988; 1994). The New Deal politics of the 1930s was driven and constrained by an unusual coalition inside the Democratic Party that included both northern labour and a southern planter-merchant oligarchy struggling to preserve a preindustrial plantation economy based on indentured black labour. As Jill Quadagno (1988) has shown, control over key Congressional committees allowed the southern wing of the Democratic Party to exclude southern blacks from the New Deal in the name of 'state rights'. Eligibility criteria and benefit levels for old age assistance, unemployment insurance, and aid to dependent children were left to the discretion of the states since programmes that created national standards would have undermined the southern economy. Agricultural workers were excluded from OAI since even the meagre sum of $15 a month would provide more cash than a cropper family might see in a year.

During the 1960s, both labour market policy (Weir, 1992) and the development of new social programmes (Quadagno, 1994) collided with and were deflected by the struggle for civil rights by African Americans. The mass migration of southern blacks to urban America because of the mechanization of southern agriculture brought them into direct competition with white urban workers for jobs and housing. The urban riots of the 1960s and subsequent racialization of President Johnson's War on Poverty created a white backlash and the defection of the white working class from the New Deal coalition. Labour market programmes focused on the fringes of the labour market (the urban and especially the black 'poor'), had little impact on the private economy, and did little to win enduring political support as a strategy to achieve broad economic goals (Weir, 1992: 62). As Quadagno (1994: 197) concludes: 'Rather than responding to the need for jobs, housing and social services that the black migration brought to the urban centers, the nation turned its back on the cities.'

Efforts to expand the transfer side of the welfare state stumbled on similar grounds. As Quadagno shows, major opposition to FAP came from southern Democrats where FAP would have revolutionized the local economy. According to Department of Health Education and Welfare (HEW) estimates, beneficiaries under FAP would increase the 'welfare rolls' in New York by 30–50 per cent, but in the low wage south by 250 to 400 per cent. More importantly, as Quadagno points out (1994: 184), FAP would triple the median wage of southern farm workers, totally under-mining local labour markets. In the final vote in the House, 79 of the 155 negative votes came from the 11 Deep South states.

The Reagan administration built on this fault line in American politics to achieve electoral victory and to pursue its politics of retrenchment. During the Reagan era the very word 'welfare' became synonymous with single black American mothers and their children.

The politics of region and ethnic division created a different dynamic in Canadian federalism. Regional cleavages in Canada have been formed along three main divisions: (1) an industrialized core in central Canada overlapped by the cleavage between the French (Quebec) and the English (Ontario); (2) a Western economy based in agriculture and resource extraction where primary producers were compelled by a protectionist economic policy to purchase expensive inputs and consumer goods from the core; and (3) an economically underdeveloped region in the east.

Creating a nation out of a country of 'regions' and 'two founding peoples' has always been the major challenge for Canadian political elites. And since the 1920s,[7] the welfare state has been the 'pot of glue' to which these elites have turned to hold the country together even when party ideology has dictated otherwise.[8] As Banting observes (1992b):

> The welfare state is a central component of the politics of national integration on a territorial – as distinct from a class – basis. . . . Federal welfare programmes, whether delivered directly to individuals or through provincial governments are powerful tools of inter-regional redistribution. They represent one of the few ways in which the federal government can fashion appeals that cut across linguistic and regional divisions. As a result social policy reinforces the political legitimacy of a federal state that is under constant pressure from powerful centrifugal forces.

Universal programmes produced inter-regional transfers that created demand for goods produced in central Canada reflecting the protectionist strategy that was Canada's main response to the Great Depression (Turegun, 1994). As a result, Jenson (1990) observes, Canada emerged from the war with a centralized system for income security but one constructed around a 'politics of place' rather than a 'politics of class'. Whereas, the Beveridge reforms in the United Kingdom were presented as a strategy to break down traditional divisions of class, Canadian reforms were 'justified as a means of eliminating inter-regional disparities in benefits' (Jenson, 1990: 664). Postwar social reconstruction meant reconstructing the *nation*, of providing all *Canadians* with common social rights irrespective of their geographical, not social, place in the Canadian mosaic.

Until the 1960s, Quebec played a role similar to that of the American south in the United States, blocking social legislation that threatened to impinge on provincial sovereignty and the dominant place of the Catholic Church in the provision of social services. Quebec's Quiet Revolution in the 1960s, however, brought to power a secularizing elite with a strong étatist orientation (Banting, 1992a). During the critical period of the 1960s, French-Canadian elites played a major role in expanding both the quantity and quality of public programmes.

During the 1960s, fiscal federalism acquired an institutional form in which economic and social strategies were worked out through federal–provincial negotiations. As a political regime, this represented a departure from a pure liberal model of politics in which only individuals are represented. Like the corporatist models in which collectivities are represented on a functional basis (labour, capital), the federal–provincial model gave representation to collectivities (e.g. French Canada, poorer provinces) on a territorial basis. Throughout the 1980s, 'fiscal federalism' put a hard upper limit on the extent to which conservative-minded 'reformers' in Ottawa could cut back on social commitments. As Banting (1992b) points out, the most important and effective opponents of retrenchment in unemployment insurance are provincial premiers from poorer regions, not organized labour.

The disadvantaged in the United States have no comparable institutional mechanism by which their interests are represented in the political process. The poor tend not to vote in American elections (Piven and Cloward, 1988) and gain attention only through periodic outbursts of violence and social unrest (Piven and Cloward, 1994).

Welfare state politics in the 1990s

We can summarize our survey of recent trends in North American welfare states in terms of the three alternative models of distribution noted earlier:

Citizenship entitlements have always been weak in the United States and, except for health care, have been abandoned in Canada.

Social insurance programmes, notably old age security and unemployment insurance, have been modified both as a cost-saving measure (old age security) and to maintain work incentives in a low wage economy (unemployment insurance). Canadian UI transfers remain high by international standards but are now targeted for reduction.

Traditional social assistance models based on means-testing for the poor are also under attack. In the United States, the rejection of traditional social assistance such as AFDC has moralistic and racial origins (see below). But both liberals and conservatives agree that traditional social assistance with strict means-testing creates 'welfare traps' that discourage work effort and do little to help the poor.

The main challenge to contemporary welfare states is to address the new life cycle distribution of economic risk that has resulted from economic restructuring and new family forms. Concretely, this means addressing the new economic insecurities and risks faced by working age families because of a rapidly changing labour market, high divorce rates and single parenthood while simultaneously sustaining postwar social insurance programmes that now support a rapidly expanding elderly population.

The North American variant of this challenge is shaped by an economic regime in which employment is maximized by allowing wages to be set at market-clearing levels. In practice, this was achieved by allowing wages and earnings at the bottom of the market to decline in both real and relative terms. The upshot is that the American strategy of relying on economic expansion and employment growth to ensure economic well-being no longer suffices. Job growth constrains the expansion of the 'welfare poor' but only by expanding the ranks of the 'working poor'. Low wage jobs also reinforce 'welfare traps' and work disincentives unless benefit levels follow the downward drift in wage levels, as they have in the US.

Proposals to adjust social programmes to accommodate a low wage economy are of several types:

Workfare One approach to increasing work effort among the poor is to increase the share of total income from earnings even if this results in a dollar for dollar replacement of transfer income with work income (Blank, 1994: 169). Hence, except for those obviously unable to work (the disabled), all those unable to support themselves should be required to provide labour in return for public support. Welfare traps are eliminated through coercion. The purpose is not to enhance welfare but to enforce moral and cultural standards of behaviour on the poor.[9]

Wage subsidies If high employment now depends on accepting a large number of low wage jobs, one response is to redesign social transfers along the lines of a negative income tax for the 'working poor'. The exemplar is EITC, an income-tested programme that subsidizes low earnings of 'working poor' families with children. The implicit model is a negative income tax for families that satisfy two conditions: employment and the care of children.[10]

Income subsidies Canada's child tax benefit removes the employment condition and provides income subsidies for all low income households with children present. Child-based income subsidies designed along NIT lines address new needs created by low wage employment and by the growth of single-parent families.

Social investment Proposals to shift social expenditures from 'passive', social insurance models to 'active' labour market programmes that provide job training and job search assistance to those affected by structural unemployment are now commonplace. Unlike social transfers that can leak out of the economy to purchase imports, social investment in human capital remains at home, and can raise labour productivity and the earnings potential of workers. Social investments in active labour market policies are proposed to ensure early exit from non-employment (social assistance), unemployment and low wage employment.

The Canadian experience indicates that wage and income subsidies can stabilize the distribution of income at least for a while. As a general strategy, however, they quickly reach their upper limits for both cost and work incentive reasons. All NIT models (including the US EITC and Canada's CTB) are defined by three parameters: the guarantee level (the maximum benefit); the tax-back rate (the rate at which benefits are reduced as earnings rise); and the break-even point (the income level at which benefits disappear). A high guarantee level is desirable to ensure adequate incomes and a low tax-back rate is desirable to encourage people to work.

But a high guarantee level combined with a low tax-back rate means the break-even point is very high and so are the costs. Consequently, most NIT-type proposals for the working age population provide a low tax-back rate (to maintain work incentives) but also a low guarantee level (to contain costs). Blanchard (1995: 51) estimates that wage subsidies sufficient to restore US wage differentials of a decade ago would cost in the order of 4 to 5 per cent of GDP.

Although employers favour NIT models as an alternative to minimum wages, wage subsidies can also become a perverse industrial strategy to the extent that they subsidize the labour costs of low wage employers, hence encouraging the expansion of low wage and part time employment.

Social investment in education, job training and other active labour market policies is now widely hailed as a major cure for non-employment, unemployment, and low wages. Rather than insist that the welfare state redistribute income to achieve 'point-in-time' equality, the aim of the social investment strategy is to maximize opportunities to achieve life-time equality. Enthusiasm for this strategy is reinforced by the growing wage gap between well educated and poorly educated workers in the United States and the growing unemployment gap between the well educated and poorly educated in both countries.

While there is little doubt that education and training can improve the labour market opportunities of the disadvantaged, there are at least two reasons to doubt that more social investment is a cure-all for labour market polarization. The first is cost. James Heckman (cited in Blanchard, 1995: 51) estimates that it would cost approximately 3 per cent of US GDP per year in education and training expenditures to restore American wage differentials to 1979 levels. This is a difficult target to reach in a country that has invested little in active labour market programmes in the past (see Table 5.7). Enthusiasm for active labour market policies is also muted by the ambiguous results of previous experiments (Blank, 1994).

Second, the assumption behind the social investment strategy is that supply will create its own demand: putting more highly skilled workers on the market will produce more highly skilled jobs. Those who consider the problems of wages and employment to be largely determined by the demand side (Nakamura and Lawrence, 1993) are sceptical about the possibility that supply side strategies by themselves will provide a solution. Juhn and Murphy (1995), for example, find that there has been no change in the overall rate of growth in demand for skill in the United States since the 1940s. What has changed is the concentration of demand at the very highest skill levels, a demand that is unlikely to be met through upgrading the skills of workers in the large mass occupations.

The enthusiasms of policy analysts, however, do not by themselves create policies. The main obstacles to moving toward a more active version of liberal interventionism – to shift toward a system of social investments and wage subsidies – are political. Decentralized and fragmented power in the American state make significant policy changes difficult. Low wage workers and minorities are not effectively represented in the political process. As a result, anti-poverty policies 'are less a matter of demands poor people make in the political process and more a function of what other people decide to do to and for them' (Heclo, 1994: 397). The politics of race continues to divide the natural constituencies for a more activist role by government.

In Canada, increasing economic integration with the United States is shifting the east–west axis of economic activity that sustained the politics of 'fiscal federalism' in the past. As north–south trade flows expand, the enthusiasm for interregional equity among the richer provinces declines (Courchene, 1994). High government debt has led to offloading of social expenditures by the central government to the provinces. And the revival of the Quebec sovereignty movement in the 1990s encourages fiscal decentralization and impedes the search for *national* as opposed to regional solutions. As a result, Canadian social policy stands on the verge of following the American path of fiscal competition between regions and provinces.

In the intermediate future, the single most important constraint on policy innovation in both countries is limited state capacity to raise revenues to finance new initiatives. Corporate tax concessions, the deindexing of tax brackets, reductions in marginal tax rates, and reliance on debt financing have created enormous pressure to check expenditures rather than raise revenues to embark on new and untested social strategies. Whereas electoral competition in the postwar years typically took the form of bidding for votes with expanded social programmes, in the 1990s parties vie with one another by promising 'middle class' tax cuts and 'less government'.

Because of these politically systemic obstacles to pursuing an activist version of the liberal model, it is unlikely that North America will provide the testing ground for new social experiments in the provision of social welfare in postindustrial capitalism. Canadian experiments in the use of NIT-type programmes to provide income-tested income subsidies (such as the child tax benefit) are likely to expand at the expense of traditional social insurance programmes (such as unemployment insurance). In the United States, locally based (i.e. state level) 'social investment' strategies will also bear watching (Osborne, 1988).

North American states, however, suffer not only from a fiscal deficit but also from a democratic deficit. The comparative weakness of political institutions able to represent competing social and economic interests makes the search for non-zero-sum solutions difficult. In the United States, the decline of organized labour has left both the industrial and the postindustrial working classes without a political voice. Inner-city mayors have no institutional power in either regional or national politics. In Canada, fiscal federalism is in decline. As a result, 'market magic' rather than democratic politics will shape the future welfare of the liberal economies.

Postscript: North American welfare politics in 1995

It is always dangerous to project future developments on the basis of the immediate political and economic climate of the day. Hence, my emphasis in this chapter has been on long-term patterns of change in both the labour market and welfare state policy in North America. To simply pass by recent developments in welfare state politics in the two countries, however, would leave a large gap in the story.

For a brief moment following President Clinton's election in 1992, liberal Democrats in the United States were hopeful of turning around more than a decade of anti-welfare state rhetoric and policy-making. Hopes were high that the United States would soon implement some form of national health care. The failure of the Clinton health care agenda, a Republican victory in both House and Senate in 1994, and the possibility of a Republican Presidential victory in 1996 has changed all this.

The main target of the Republican agenda to date has been 'welfare' – social assistance programmes for the 'welfare poor'. Apart from Medicaid, however, there are few savings to be had by reducing or even eliminating these programmes. AFDC, for example, accounts for less than 1 per cent of the federal budget. To realize the larger goals of the Republican 'Contract with America' – debt reduction and a smaller role for the federal government – attention must turn to the large and virtually universal programmes for the elderly, social security and Medicare.

During most of the 1980s, programmes for the elderly were considered sacrosanct by both liberals and conservatives in the United States for electoral reasons. The elderly were seen as a large and cohesive voting block able to punish any politician who threatened their 'entitlements'. To date, Republicans have trodden softly on these issues.

More instructive, perhaps, was the direction taken by the Entitlements Commission, chaired by Senators Kerrey and Danforth in the summer and autumn of 1994. Heavily influenced by the Concord Coalition headed by former investment banker Peter Peterson, the aim of the Commission co-Chairs was to sharply reduce spending by income-testing all social benefits including Medicare and social security. The basic design as outlined by Peterson (1993) is very close to the negative income tax model – reducing social transfers to middle and upper income groups combined with some enrichment of programmes for low income groups.

Although the Commissioners failed to reach a consensus, there is a strong sense in Washington circles that the agenda remains very much alive. While Republicans are generally hesitant to cut welfare for the rich, elements of the Concord strategy could well become the grounds for a successful coalition between Republicans and conservative Democrats. Here, the Canadian experience of the past decade is also instructive.

When the Conservative government of Brian Mulroney came to power in 1984, one of its first forays into social policy was an effort to eliminate the universal old age security programme, the first tier of Canada's public pension system. Such a proposal was actually introduced in early 1985 but was subsequently withdrawn after several months of public uproar and great embarrassment for the Conservative Finance Minister, Michael Wilson.

In 1988, the Conservatives took another tack and this time succeeded. Under the rubric of cutting 'welfare for the rich', an income test was introduced for all seniors with incomes of more than $54,000 per year. Few tears were shed for these high income seniors and the measure passed without resistance. The key to the legislation, however, was long term in nature. The cut-off point at which the income test becomes effective was only indexed to inflation that exceeds 3 per cent per year. Consequently, the income test will slowly work its way down the income hierarchy until only low income seniors are beneficiaries. In his February 1995 budget, Finance Minister Paul Martin gave notice of his intent to accelerate the process. This strategy of 'social policy by stealth', as it has become known, has been widely used in other programme areas as well.

Canadian and American social policy began to diverge sharply during the 1960s. Whether they will now reconverge remains to be determined. The 1995 Canadian budget included a reduction in federal transfers to the provinces and moved to a system of 'block funding' for expenditures on social assistance, health care, and post-secondary education. There is now considerable speculation that as federal transfers decline, the provinces will engage in the sort of 'fiscal competition' characteristic of the United States with an ensuing downward spiral in social spending.

In both countries, 'market failure' has created a new trajectory for social policy. The social insurance model of the postwar decades is being sharply questioned and a new model based on providing wage and income subsidies for workers in a low wage economy has come to the fore. How vigorously this emergent strategy will be pursued remains to be seen.

Notes

Special thanks to Keith Banting, Gøsta Esping-Andersen and Jill Quadagno for comments on previous versions of this chapter.

1 For the United States, see Levy and Murnane (1992); for Canada, see Morissette et al. (1994).

2 Although Canadian unemployment levels approach European levels, this is due to high levels of labour force participation, not stagnant job growth (Card and Riddell, 1993).

3 The 1994 Canadian federal budget made substantial cuts in unemployment insurance benefits. The 1995 budget brought sharp reductions in federal transfers to the provinces for health, education and social assistance. Further reforms in old age security and unemployment insurance are anticipated in 1996.

4 For Canadian evidence see Myles et al. (1993).

5 As Stevens (1988: 141) notes, 55 per cent of the strikes in 1949 in US industry and 70 per cent of the strikes in 1950 were over health and welfare issues in labour contracts.

6 Ironically, during this period at least, economic integration spurred the development of the public sector as well. American industrialists pressed Ottawa to pass the Old Age Security

Act of 1951 (Murphy, 1982). In the absence of this 'first tier' in the Canadian pension system, firms would have been required to pay the full cost of the pensions then being negotiated at the bargaining table.

7 Until the 1920s, as Smith (1989) observes, patronage rather than the welfare state was the main instrument used by prime ministers 'to create and hold constituency loyalties'. For the role of patronage in shaping the American welfare state see Orloff (1988).

8 This paradox was most evident during the Conservative regime of John Diefenbaker during the late 1950s and early 1960s. Diefenbaker's pan-Canadianism led to the national development policy, the extension of hospital insurance, and the Royal Commission on Health Services which resulted in the adoption of national health insurance when the Liberals returned to power (Smith, 1989: 138–41). The paradox became more apparent during the free trade election of 1988 when the Mulroney Conservatives were compelled to articulate a most un-Conservative commitment to Canada's welfare state institutions to show they were not selling out Canadian identity.

9 There has been a clear shift in the normative order since the 1960s when 'good' mothers were expected to be in the home and 'working mothers' were thought to be a source of youth delinquency. The dramatic rise in women's labour force participation has altered expectations so that now even single mothers are expected to be employed.

10 Single persons with low earnings are also eligible for EITC: however, the benefit is extremely modest.

References

Aldrich, Jonathan (1982) 'Earnings replacement rates of old-age benefits in 12 countries, 1969–80', *Social Security Bulletin*, 45(11): 3–11.

Amenta, Edwin A. and Skocpol, Theda (1988) 'Redefining the New Deal: World War II and public social provision in the United States', in Margaret Weir, Ann Shola Orloff and Theda Skocpol (eds), *The Politics of Social Policy in the United States.* Princeton, NJ: Princeton University Press. pp. 81–122.

Banting, Keith G. (1987) *The Welfare State and Canadian Federalism.* Kingston and Montreal: McGill–Queen's University Press.

Banting, Keith G. (1992a) 'Economic integration and social policy: Canada and the United States', in Terrance Hunsley (ed.), *Social Policy in the Global Economy.* Kingston: Queen's University Press. pp. 21–44.

Banting, Keith G. (1992b) 'Neoconservatism in an open economy: the social role of the Canadian state', *International Political Science Review*, 13: 149–70.

Battle, Ken and Torjman, Sherri (1995) *How Finance Reformed Social Policy.* Ottawa: Caledon Institute of Social Policy.

Blackburn, McKinley and Bloom, David (1993) 'The distribution of family income: measuring and explaining changes in the 1980s for Canada and the United States', in David Card and Richard Freeman (eds), *Small Differences that Matter: Labor Markets and Income Maintenance in Canada and the United States.* Chicago: University of Chicago Press. pp. 233–65.

Blanchard, Olivier (1995) 'Macroeconomic implications of shifts in the relative demand for skills', *Economic Policy Review*, 1(1): 48–53.

Blank, Rebecca (1994) 'The employment strategy: public policies to increase work and earnings', in Sheldon Danziger, Gary Sandefur and Daniel Weinberg (eds), *Confronting Poverty: Prescriptions for Change.* Cambridge: Harvard University Press. pp. 168–204.

Blank, Rebecca and Hanratty, Maria (1993) 'Responding to need: a comparison of social safety nets in Canada and the United States', in David Card and Richard Freeman (eds), *Small Differences that Matter: Labor Markets and Income Maintenance in Canada and the United States.* Chicago: University of Chicago Press. pp. 191–231.

Card, David and Riddell, Craig (1993) 'A comparative analysis of unemployment in Canada and the United States', in David Card and Richard Freeman (eds), *Small Differences that Matter: Labor Markets and Income Maintenance in Canada and the United States*. Chicago: University of Chicago Press. pp. 149–90.

Courchene, Thomas (1994) *Social Canada in the Millennium: Reform Imperatives and Restructuring Principles*. Montreal: C.D. Howe Institute.

DiNardo, John and Lemieux, Thomas (1994) 'Diverging male wage inequality in the United States and Canada, 1981–1988: do unions explain the difference?', Irvine Economic Paper no. 93-94-16.

Economic Council of Canada (1991) *Employment in the Service Economy*. Ottawa: Economic Council of Canada.

Esping-Andersen, Gøsta (1990) *The Three Worlds of Welfare Capitalism*. Princeton, NJ: Princeton University Press.

Evans, R.G., Barer, M.L. and Hertzman, C. (1991) 'The 20-year experiment: accounting for, explaining and evaluating health care cost containment in Canada and the United States', *Annual Review of Public Health*, 12: 481–518.

Goldin, Claudia and Margo, Robert (1992) 'The great compression: the wage structure of the United States at mid-century', *The Quarterly Journal of Economics*, CVII(1): 1–34.

Gompers, Samuel (1910) *Labor in Europe and America*. New York and London: Harper.

GPO (1964) *Economic Report of the President*. Washington, DC: US Government Printing Office.

Guest, D. (1985) *The Emergence of Social Security in Canada*. Vancouver: University of British Columbia Press.

Haddow, Rodney S. (1993) *Poverty Reform in Canada, 1958–1978: State and Class Influences on Policy Making*. Montreal: McGill–Queen's University Press.

Hanratty, Maria and Blank, Rebecca (1992) 'Down and out in North America: recent trends in poverty rates in the United States and Canada', *Quarterly Journal of Economics*, CVII(February): 233–54.

Heclo, Hugh (1994) 'Poverty politics', in Sheldon Danziger, Gary Sandefur and Daniel Weinberg (eds), *Confronting Poverty: Prescriptions for Change*. Cambridge: Harvard University Press. pp. 396–437.

Jenson, Jane (1990) 'Representations in crisis: the roots of Canada's permeable Fordism', *Canadian Journal of Political Science*, XXIII(4): 653–83.

Juhn, Chinui and Murphy, Kevin (1995) 'Inequality in labor market outcomes: contrasting the 1980s and earlier decades', *Economic Policy Review*, 1(1): 26–32.

Korpi, Walter and Palme, Joakim (1994) 'The strategy of equality and the paradox of redistribution'. Swedish Institute for Social Research, course pack.

Kudrle, Robert T. and Marmor, Theodore R. (1981) 'The development of welfare states in North America', in Peter Flora and Arnold J. Heidenheimer (eds), *The Development of Welfare States in North America*. London: Transaction Books.

Levy, Frank (1988) *Dollars and Dreams: the Changing American Income Distribution*. New York: W.W. Norton.

Levy, Frank and Murnane, Richard (1992) 'U.S. earnings levels and earnings inequality: a review of recent trends and proposed explanations', *Journal of Economic Literature* 30: 1333–81.

Love, Roger and Poulin, Susan (1991) 'Family income inequality in the 1980s', *Canadian Economic Observer*, September: 4.1–4.13.

Marmor, T., Bradshaw, J. and Harvey, P. (1990) *America's Misunderstood Welfare State*. New York: Basic Books.

McBride, Stephen (1992) *Not Working: State, Unemployment and Neo-Conservatism in Canada*. Toronto: University of Toronto Press.

Morissette, Rene, Myles, John and Picot, Garnett (1994) 'Earnings inequality and the distribution of working time in Canada', *Canadian Business Economics*, Spring: 3–16.

Moynihan, Daniel P. (1973) *The Politics of a Guaranteed Income: the Nixon Administration and the Family Assistance Plan*. New York: Vintage.

Murphy, Barbara (1982) 'Corporate capital and the welfare state: Canadian business and public pension policy in Canada since World War II'. Master's thesis, Carleton University, Ottawa.

Myles, John (1988) 'Decline or impasse? The current state of the welfare state', *Studies in Political Economy*, 26 (Summer): 73–107.

Myles, John and Picot, Garnett (1995) 'The changing economic position of young families and children: the impact of declining earnings, the transfer system and changing demographics'. Business and Labour Market Analysis Division, Statistics Canada, Ottawa.

Myles, John, Picot, Garnett and Wannell, Ted (1993) 'Does post-industrialism matter? The Canadian experience', in Gøsta Esping-Andersen (ed.), *Changing Classes: Stratification and Mobility in Post-industrial Societies*. London: Sage. pp. 171–94.

Nakamura, Alice and Lawrence, Peter (1993) 'Education, training and prosperity'. Bell Canada Papers on Economic Growth and Public Policy, October.

OECD (1993) *Employment Outlook*, July. Paris: OECD.

OECD (1994a) *Canada*. OECD Economic Surveys. Paris: OECD.

OECD (1994b) *The OECD Jobs Study: Facts, Analysis, Strategies*. Paris: OECD.

OECD (1994c) *New Orientations for Social Policy*. Social Policy Studies no. 12. Paris: OECD.

Orloff, Ann Shola (1988) 'The political origins of America's belated welfare state', in Margaret Weir, Ann Orloff and Theda Skocpol (eds), *The Politics of Social Policy in the United States*. Princeton, NJ: Princeton University Press. pp. 77–80.

Osborne, David (1988) *Laboratories of Democracy*. Boston: Harvard Business School Press.

Peterson, Peter (1993) *Facing Up: How to Rescue the Economy from Crushing Debt and Restore the American Dream*. New York: Simon and Schuster.

Pierson, Paul (1994) *Dismantling the Welfare State? Reagan, Thatcher and the Politics of Retrenchment*. Cambridge: Cambridge University Press.

Piven, Frances Fox and Cloward, Richard A. (1988) *Why Americans Don't Vote*. New York: Pantheon.

Piven, Frances Fox and Cloward, Richard A. (1994) *Regulating the Poor*, rev. edn. New York: Vintage.

Quadagno, Jill (1988) *The Transformation of Old Age Security*. Chicago: University of Chicago Press.

Quadagno, Jill (1994) *The Color of Welfare: How Racism Undermined the War on Poverty*. New York: Oxford University Press.

Skocpol, Theda (1988) 'The limits of the New Deal system and the roots of contemporary welfare dilemmas', in Margaret Weir, Ann Shola Orloff and Theda Skocpol (eds), *The Politics of Social Policy in the United States*. Princeton, NJ: Princeton University Press. pp. 293–312.

Smeeding, Timothy (1991) 'Cross-national comparisons of inequality and poverty', in L. Osberg (ed.), *Economic Inequality and Poverty: International Perspectives*. Armonk, NY: M.E. Sharpe. pp. 39–59.

Smeeding, Timothy, Torrey, Barbara and Rainwater, Lee (1993) 'Going to extremes: an international perspective on the economic status of the U.S. aged'. Luxembourg Income Study, Working Paper no. 87.

Smith, David (1989) 'Canadian political parties and national integration', in Alain Gagnon and Brian Tanguay (eds), *Canadian Parties in Transition: Discourse, Organization and Representation*. Scarborough, Ont.: Nelson, pp. 130–51.

Stevens, Beth (1988) 'Blurring the boundaries: how the federal government has influenced welfare benefits in the private sector', in Margaret Weir, Ann Shola Orloff and Theda Skocpol (eds), *The Politics of Social Policy in the United States*. Princeton, NJ: Princeton University Press. pp. 133–48.

Therborn, Goran (1986) *Why Some People are More Unemployed than Others: the Strange Paradox of Growth and Unemployment*. London: New Left Books.

Tobin, James (1994) 'Poverty in relation to macroeconomic trends, cycles and policies', in

Sheldon Danziger, Gary Sandefur and Daniel Weinberg (eds), *Confronting Poverty: Prescriptions for Change*. Cambridge: Harvard University Press. pp. 147–67.

Turegun, Adnan (1994) 'Small state responses to the Great Depression, 1929–39: the white dominions, Scandinavia and the Balkans'. PhD dissertation, Carleton University, Ottawa.

Weir, Margaret (1992) *Politics and Jobs: the Boundaries of Employment Policy in the United States*. Princeton, NJ: Princeton University Press.

PART TWO
EMERGING NEW
WELFARE STATES?

6

Options for Social Policy in Latin America: Neoliberal versus Social Democratic Models

Evelyne Huber

Social policy in Latin America today stands at the crossroads between market-determined, private, individualistic and inegalitarian models on the one hand, and market-correcting, public, solidaristic, and egalitarian models on the other hand. The hegemony of neoliberalism in business and banking circles, in international financial institutions, and among governments in core countries and ruling technocrats in many Latin American countries during the 1980s seemed to tilt the balance towards the former models. Yet, as the social costs of economic neoliberalism and of state abdication of social responsibilities have become all too visible and questions of governability of new democracies have come to the forefront, the latter models are getting a serious second look both in international institutions and among the governments in the region. The main obstacle to the pursuit of these latter models in the 1990s is the balance of social and political power that has shifted squarely towards capital and away from organizations representing mass interests, most importantly unions, in the course of the structural adjustment policies. This chapter explores the costs and benefits of attempts to pursue these alternative models, focusing on the cases of Chile and Brazil, with secondary comparisons with Argentina and Costa Rica. Additional comments on general trajectories are used to situate these cases in the larger Latin American context.

The economic crisis of the 1980s had a profound impact on social policy, leading to an increase in poverty and at the same time to a reduction in social expenditure, a deterioration of public services, and severe fiscal imbalances in social insurance schemes. The reactions to these problems have ranged from the neoliberal solutions of individualization and privatization to the social democratic solutions of universalization and consolidation of public schemes. Chile followed the neoliberal route and Costa Rica the social democratic route; Argentina has adopted some elements of privatization and Brazil has *de jure* (though not *de facto!*) virtually universalized coverage and improved the benefits of the poorest sectors.

Background

The three most important areas of social policy in Latin America have been pensions, health care, and price subsidies and controls.[1] Social assistance has traditionally been underdeveloped (Tamburi, 1985: 76). Expenditures for pensions and health care have accounted for between two-thirds and virtually all of total social benefits expenditures (Table 6.7). Price subsidies and controls, of course, are captured neither by data on social expenditures nor by any other comparable data. Their importance only becomes clear if one takes account of the proportion of income spent by poor people on basic foods and transport and of the extent to which basic foods and transport used to be subsidized and/or sold at controlled prices before the austerity and structural adjustment policies of the 1980s. Only 7 out of 34 Latin American and Caribbean countries have family allowances and unemployment compensation (Mesa-Lago, 1994: 16). Compared with welfare states in advanced industrial societies, unemployment insurance, like social assistance, is sorely underdeveloped. Given the persistently high levels of unemployment in most Latin American countries, such an insurance has been considered prohibitively expensive; where it exists, the benefits are extremely limited.

The two central problems in the development of social insurance in virtually all countries have been the *de facto* limitation of coverage by the existence of a large informal sector and the high degree of fragmentation and of inequality of entitlements (Tables 6.1–6.4). In most Latin American countries, the right to transfer payments and services is based mainly on the insurance principle and linked to paid employment, which means that large sectors of rural and urban poor remain excluded. Only in six Latin American countries (excluding the non-Spanish-speaking Caribbean) are more than 60 per cent of the population covered by social security (in Argentina, Brazil, Chile, Costa Rica, Uruguay, and Cuba); in another six countries between 30 and 60 per cent are covered (in Colombia, Guatemala, Mexico, Panama, Peru, and Venezuela); and in the remaining countries an even smaller percentage enjoys coverage (in Bolivia, the Dominican Republic, Ecuador, El Salvador, Honduras, Nicaragua, and Paraguay).[2] The figures on total social security benefits expenditures as a percentage of GDP confirm this picture. Only Argentina, Brazil, Costa Rica, Cuba, Chile, Panama, and Uruguay spend 4.6 per cent or more on

Table 6.1 *Percentage of economically active population covered by social security programmes (including health)*

	Argentina	Brazil	Chile	Costa Rica
1970	68	27	69	38
1979–80	52	49	64	49

Source: Isuani, 1985: 95

Table 6.2 *Distribution of total economically active population by sector (per cent)*

	Year	Urban informal	Rural traditional	Total non-formal
Argentina	1950	15	8	23
	1980	19	6	26
Brazil	1950	11	38	48
	1980	17	28	44
Chile	1950	22	9	31
	1980	20	9	29
Costa Rica	1950	12	20	33
	1980	12	15	27

Source: Isuani, 1985: 93

Table 6.3 *Distribution of nonagricultural economically active population (per cent)*

	Year	Self-empl./domestic serv./unpaid fam.	Small enterprise	Total
Argentina	1980	25.6	13.0	38.6
	1985	30.4	13.3	43.7
	1990	30.8	14.9	45.7
Brazil	1980	24.0	9.9	33.7
	1985	30.2	14.5	44.7
	1990	28.6	23.9	52.5
Chile	1980	36.1	14.3	50.4
	1985	34.2	19.1	53.3
	1990	31.7	18.3	50.0

Source: Schoepfle and Pérez-Lopez, 1993: 251, 256

social security benefits; the next highest spender is Bolivia with 2.3 per cent, half the Brazilian level (Table 6.4). The problem of fragmentation and inequality was most pronounced in the countries that had established their programmes early and then expanded them to ever larger groups. The gradual expansion of insurance schemes resulted in a multitude of schemes for different employment categories with different contribution requirements and different benefits. On the whole, these schemes did more than reproduce the inequality in the labour market; they aggravated inequality

Table 6.4   *Total social security benefits as a percentage of GDP*

For Latin America				For several OECD nations	
Argentina	8.9	Guyana	0.9	Austria	21
Barbados	2.1	Honduras	0.7	Spain	15
Belize	1.0	Jamaica	1.2	France	25
Bolivia	2.3	Mexico	2.0	Germany	23
Brazil	4.6	Nicaragua	2.0	Greece	12
Colombia	2.2	Panama	5.3	Italy	20
Costa Rica	6.3	Peru	2.0	Norway	20
Cuba	11.3	St Lucia	0.2	Switzerland	13
Chile	9.9	Surinam	2.1	Sweden	31
Dominica	0.4	Trinidad and		UK	16
Ecuador	2.1	Tobago	0.6		
El Salvador	1.4	Uruguay	7.0		
Grenada	1.7	Venezuela	1.1		
Guatemala	1.0	USA	12.1		

Source: The Cost of Social Security 1981–1983, OECD

by imposing some of the burden of financing on groups not covered, mainly through indirect taxes and through the passing on of employer contributions to prices in protected markets (Mesa-Lago, 1983: 89–91). Though these problems had long been recognized by international and domestic experts and politicians alike, attempts to bring about unification and standardization of social insurance failed repeatedly because of the determined resistance of privileged groups. Only the military regimes of the 1960s and 1970s were able to effect some degree of unification and standardization in Argentina, Chile, Brazil, Uruguay, and Peru.

The development of social policy in Latin America has to be understood in the context of the political economy of import substitution industrialization (ISI). ISI created urban constituencies for social insurance, that is, employed middle and working classes with an interest in protection from loss of earnings due to accidents, illness, and old age. Typically, these groups were better organized than the self-employed, the unemployed, and the workforce in the rural sector and thus had their needs met to a much greater extent. Politically, passage of social insurance schemes with relatively generous benefits for those covered was facilitated by the fact that employers did not really have to absorb the costs of their contributions but rather could pass them on to consumers because they were operating in protected markets. Therefore, the crisis of ISI and the subsequent opening of markets was bound to lead to conflicts over the financing of social insurance. However, the financial problems in the social security systems predated the opening of markets.

In the countries with the older and more developed social insurance programmes, the maturing of the pension programmes, increasing life expectancies, rising costs for curative health care, widespread evasion of contributions, and very poor investment returns on the reserves contributed to severe financial strains and crises even before the economic crisis of the 1980s. The debt crisis and the general fiscal crisis of the state in the 1980s then also brought less developed systems into severe financial difficulties. Social insurance revenues declined as a result of rising unemployment in the formal sector, falling real wages, growing evasion, and the inability of the state to live up to its financial obligations towards social security. Runaway inflation eroded the value of pension benefits and forced adjustments that, despite their delay and inadequacy from the point of view of the recipients, imposed a heavy financial burden on the systems.

The stabilization policies imposed by the International Monetary Fund (IMF) to deal with the balance-of-payments crises entailed not only reductions in expenditures for social services and transfer payments but also reductions of subsidies of basic foodstuffs and public transport. These reductions, combined with rising unemployment and falling real wages, caused increased poverty. The combination of the financial crisis of the existing systems and their glaring inability to deal with the intensifying problem of poverty opened the door for reforms of existing systems, ranging from the radical overhaul and privatization of the Chilean system to efforts to move further towards universalistic public provision of pensions and health care in Brazil. Other countries pursued a mix of reshaping of some programmes, an increase in contributions, and the addition of some new programmes, particularly programmes targeted at the very poor.

Chile and Brazil span the spectrum from a radical neoliberal response to the problems of a highly developed but very fragmented, inegalitarian, and expensive system in Chile, to the gradual move toward a universalistic system of coverage in the context of the legacy of a fragmented and inegalitarian system in Brazil. The Chilean system of social policy is headed in the direction of a two-class system and a residual welfare state, where those who can insure themselves through the market enjoy good protection, whereas the state helps the poorest sectors only. Brazil has created the legal foundations for a universalistic welfare state, aiming to provide basic income security to all citizens, but the implementation of these policies has been hampered by the inadequate extractive capacity of the state and the inability of the political system to pass reforms that would reduce social spending for privileged groups. Argentina and Costa Rica fall near these opposites. Argentina adopted a pension reform with part of the new system modelled after the Chilean one but maintaining a universalistic public system, and Costa Rica has advanced further than any other Latin American country in the extension and reform of a welfare state inspired by the social democratic principles of universality and equity.

These four countries also followed different paths of adjustment to the debt crisis and the crisis of ISI, and they developed different export strategies. Chile has come to compete successfully in the international market on the basis of raw materials and cheap labour, a strategy facilitated by the Pinochet government's anti-labour policies. Brazil has maintained higher levels of protection and is competing in the international market also on the basis of more sophisticated manufactured products. Other Latin American countries are looking to the Chilean and Brazilian models. In the present conjuncture of immediate-past but still lingering neoliberal hegemony, the former model appears more attractive and has been followed, for instance, in Argentina and Peru. However, in the longer run the Brazilian/Costa Rican model of gradual economic reform combined with a socially interventionist state may well come to look more attractive, particularly under democratic rules of the game and the need for political leaders to consolidate democratic regimes.

The development of social policy after the Second World War

The key to understanding the differences in social policy patterns between advanced industrial societies and Latin America is the nature of late and dependent development and its effect on the occupational and class structure. The growth of the export economies based on agrarian products or minerals generated urbanization and growth of the state before any significant industrialization. The exceptions are Argentina and Uruguay whose meat and wool exports created subsidiary industry. This meant that the urban middle classes became larger compared with the industrial working class than at comparable stages of development in advanced industrial societies. The number of state employees, private sector white-collar employees, intellectuals and professionals, artisans, shopkeepers, and small entrepreneurs grew, and as they organized they acquired some political influence. The same was true for those workers in sectors crucial to the export economy, such as railroad, port, and maritime workers, as well as miners and oil workers. From the 1930s on, ISI did enlarge the working class, but again not to the same degree as at comparable stages of development in advanced industrial societies. Moreover, in the industrial as well as in the tertiary sector there was a predominance of small enterprises. These small enterprises tended to be characterized by paternalistic labour relations, and many of them operated in the informal sector, that is, outside the coverage of labour laws, social security legislation, and contractual labour relations with regular money wages.[3] This situation made labour organization outside the strategic sectors very difficult, and the weakness of labour organization meant that there were no strong working-class pressures for the establishment of universalistic and egalitarian systems of social insurance. Land tenure patterns, with the exception of Costa Rica and a few regions in some other countries, were dominated by large holdings. Large landholders exercised local domination and significant political influence at the national level, such that rural workers remained largely unmobilized and disenfranchised until the 1960s or 1970s. Thus, there was no potential to form worker–peasant alliances in support of universalistic social policy.

The process of state building and consolidating state power was a difficult one in most Latin American countries. The independence wars and later border wars and armed confrontations among different elite groups thrust the military into a prominent position in national politics. Consolidation of state power in the sense of the successful establishment of a monopoly of organized force by the central state was generally achieved by the beginning of the twentieth century, but the military in most cases retained a politically influential position. Brazil constitutes an important exception to these generalizations, as the easy achievement of independence perpetuated the presence of a well consolidated state apparatus. Nevertheless, the military remained an important part of this apparatus as well and played a crucial role in politics, supporting or opposing presidents and candidates until 1964, when it seized power to rule in its own right until 1985.

The development of social insurance in Latin America reflected this constellation of forces. Virtually uniformly, it began with the military, civil servants and the judiciary. Then followed coverage for the best organized and strategically located sectors of the middle and working classes, such as journalists, bank workers, teachers, railroad and port workers and the merchant marine, and only then for larger sectors of the working class such as in mining, public services, and manufacturing.[4] Voluntary or compulsory extension of the system to self-employed workers was a next step. However, many of the self-employed and most of those employed in the informal sector either remained formally excluded from the social insurance system or were self-excluding by evading contributions. Extension of coverage to the rural sector also came very late, if at all, in accordance with the lack of political power of the rural lower classes. In the rural sector, though, only a small percentage of the labour force is in relatively stable dependent employment, and even where coverage was extended to the urban and rural self-employed, contributions from the self-employed generally require the equivalent of employer plus employee portions and thus are too high for the vast majority of the rural poor.

Whereas the constellation of forces outlined above shaped the general sequence of social security expansion, the timing and the particular types of policy patterns were shaped by the political histories of the different countries, which in turn reflect the interaction of state building with the class structures and class alliances shaped by the particular pattern of economic development. The group with the highest coverage includes the countries that had comparatively long histories of democratic rule (Chile, Uruguay, and Costa Rica, along with the English-speaking countries of the Caribbean)[5] and two countries that had regimes making strong incorporation attempts towards the urban working classes (Vargas in Brazil and Perón in Argentina).[6] In the second group, only Colombia and Venezuela had substantial periods of democracy, but in both cases these democracies were initiated by pacts among elites. These pacts deliberately reduced the saliency of electoral competition and excluded autonomous popular movements and potential challengers to the status quo, such that political pressures for social policy reforms remained weak. Finally, the group with the lowest coverage is made up of countries at much lower levels of industrialization that had only brief experiences with democracy or none at all before the 1980s.

To point out that the countries with the most democratic histories or the most extensive labour incorporation attempts also had the earliest and most developed welfare state programmes is not to argue that these programmes were elaborated and pushed through by political alliances of middle and working classes. Rather, their introduction was a response of political elites to middle-class pressures for particularistic benefits and to labour militancy, a response that was frequently inspired by the European example (see e.g. Malloy, 1979). Where pressures from middle and working classes had been able to effect a democratic opening of the political system, such as in Uruguay and Argentina, the electoral constraint induced elites to grant benefits like pension programmes to the best organized groups. But even in countries that retained oligarchic systems with elections or outright authoritarian rule, such as Brazil, concerns about the disruptive potential of labour prompted elites to use social security legislation selectively to coopt and control militant groups. Accordingly, the social policy patterns developed akin to the European Catholic/conservative/corporatist patterns identified by Esping-Andersen (1990).

Chile

The Chilean system of social protection developed along the lines of the general sequence outlined above, but with more parliamentary input after 1932 than in most other countries. As a result, it came to offer wide coverage for all social risks, but it also became probably the most fragmented system in Latin America. This fragmentation was a result of clientelistic links between different groups of employees and political parties or individual politicians. It reflected the combination of a decentralized and politically diverse labour movement with parliamentary representation of left-wing parties that were in competition with centre and right-wing parties for popular electoral support.

By the early 1970s, Chilean social protection was very comprehensive as to social risks and offered coverage to between 60 and 70 per cent of the population (Mesa-Lago, 1978: 41; Tamburi, 1985: 77; Raczynski, 1994: 72). It was very costly in comparison with other Latin American countries as well, a result of a gradual and clientelistic expansion of benefits to ever larger groups. In 1971 social security expenditure reached 17 per cent of GDP (Mesa-Lago, 1989: 105), a figure that was brought down to 11 per cent by 1980 and compared with a range of 9–11 per cent among the highest spenders in Latin America in 1980 (1989: 40). However, it was rather inegalitarian in financing and benefits.[7] For instance, the average pension for the military was eight times higher than the average pension for blue-collar workers, and the pension fund for bank employees was five to seven times higher (Mesa-Lago, 1989: 130). Finally, the system was truly chaotic administratively, with 35 withholding funds, 150 different pro-grammes, and some 2000 legal texts that had remained uncompiled and uncoordinated (Raczynski, 1994: 17). Several reform attempts directed towards gradual standardization and unification failed because of deter-mined resistance from privileged groups. The Allende government had a comprehensive reform project to create a universalistic welfare state, but all it could accomplish was the extension of coverage to the self-employed and greater accessibility of welfare assistance (Borzutzky, 1983: 212–13).

It was only the military government under Pinochet (1973–89) that made reform possible through ruthless repression of any popular political organization and dissent. The systems covering the military and the police, though, were exempt from the reforms. In the period 1974–9 the reforms eliminated the most glaring and costly privileges, standardized eligibility rules and cost-of-living adjustments for pensions, introduced uniform benefits for unemployment, uniform payments and a common fund for family allowances, a uniform minimum pension and expanded welfare pensions, and uniform entitlement conditions for health care. They also eliminated employer contributions to the pension funds (Mesa-Lago, 1989: 109–10). The most dramatic reform came in 1981, with the privatization of the pension and health systems. Though this reform predated the general Latin American debt crisis of 1983, it has to be seen as part and parcel of the Chilean neoliberal structural adjustment programme and thus will be discussed in the context of the changes of the 1980s.

Brazil

In Brazil President Vargas (1930–45) used social security as a tool in his pursuit of an explicitly corporatist system in which the state promoted labour organization and control through a system of official recognition of unions by the Ministry of Labour. He extended protection to all organized sectors of the urban working class and changed the system from a company-based one to one based on occupational categories, enshrined in the 1934 constitution (Malloy, 1979: 68). The administration of the various social security institutes, many of which also began to offer health care and housing loans, was headed by a chairman appointed by the President of the Republic and an administrative council with equal representation of employers and employees, the latter elected through officially recognized unions. In the period of restricted democracy from 1945 to 1964 the electoral imperative turned this provision into a source of power for organized labour and thus of resistance against unification of the system. Also, the social security institutes became prime sources for patronage employment.

As in Chile, significant reform was only implemented under the bureaucratic-authoritarian regime that seized power in 1964 and linked the reform effort to its primary goal of weakening organized labour. Labour representation in the administration of social insurance was abolished and six major social security institutes were merged into one. Again, the military and civil servants kept their own privileged funds. Whereas the bureaucratic-authoritarian regime's main approach to urban labour was repressive, it embarked upon an inclusionary corporatist project *vis-à-vis* the newly mobilizing rural workforce. In 1971 it established a system for the entire rural sector that did not require contributions and granted flat rate benefits of one-half of the highest national minimum salary and free access to health care. This scheme was financed by a combination of a payroll tax on urban employers and a tax on the value of agricultural products paid by wholesalers. Both the cash and health care benefits were administered by officially recognized rural syndicates of workers or employers (Malloy, 1979: 133). In 1972 domestic workers were granted social security protection as well, and in 1974 those urban elderly or invalids who had at one point made contributions to the system (Weyland, 1991: 245).

By the late 1970s, then, the Brazilian system of social security legally covered some 70–80 per cent of the urban economically active population (EAP) and in theory the entire rural one. Official government figures gave a coverage rate of 93 per cent of the population (Malloy, 1979: 134). Notably excluded was the urban informal sector, some 17–34 per cent of the EAP (Tables 6.2 and 6.3), depending on the measurement (Isuani, 1985: 93; Schoepfle and Pérez-Lopez, 1993), except for those who had made contributions at some point. However, rural benefits were extremely low, and disbursement was tied to patronage. Moreover, medical facilities were highly unequally distributed and entirely insufficient in rural areas. The heavy reliance on curative rather than preventive medicine and on contracting private providers aggravated this situation. Before the elections coming up in 1978 a major effort was made to bring sanitary and basic medical facilities to the underdeveloped north-east, and despite many problems they managed to reach several million people by 1979 (Weyland, 1991: 275). In the urban sector, efforts were made to reach the poor through social assistance programmes, but resource constraints kept the effects minimal (Weyland, 1991: 248). In terms of total benefits expenditures as a percentage of GDP, Brazil with 4.6 per cent was the lowest of those countries with the most developed welfare states in Latin America (Table 6.4).

Argentina

In Argentina, Juan Perón, Minister of Labour in the military government that seized power in 1943, and then President from 1946 to 1955, established the foundations of a comprehensive system of social security. His quest for power was based on mobilizing, incorporating and controlling labour, and social security formed part of this strategy. He first established pension funds for different categories of police, then for commercial and industrial workers (1944–6), and in 1954 for permanent workers in agriculture and for self-employed, professionals, and entrepreneurs (Mesa-Lago, 1978: 164–5). He also extended health care to some of the categories that already had pension coverage: he built military and public hospitals, the latter to supplement the mutual health care insurance funds established by unions and the charity hospitals established by the Eva Perón Foundation to provide free medical care to the whole population. Thus, Perón's legacy was a social security system with very wide coverage for pensions and health care, but great heterogeneity and inequality, and with significant influence by the unions in the administration of welfare funds, the *obras sociales*, whose main responsibility was the management of health care schemes. In this period, the Argentine economy had essentially full employment, and thus the employment-based insurance schemes formed the basis of a welfare state, albeit of a highly corporatist, segmented, and inegalitarian variety. The bureaucratic-authoritarian government of Onganía (1966–70), then, effected some unification. Existing pension funds, except those for the military and the police, were merged into three funds, one for blue- and white-collar workers in the private sector, one for public employees, and one for the self-employed. The first two are governed by the same legislation. Health insurance continued in its fragmented form.

As of the early 1980s, then, whereas the pension system was relatively unified and had wide legal coverage, the health system was still very complex, with many different public funds coexisting with public health programmes at the national and provincial levels, resulting in unequal access to care even for those who were covered. Reliable coverage figures for health care are virtually impossible to obtain because of the possibility of multiple affiliations. Pension coverage by this point was restricted by the decline of industrial and public employment in the period 1976–80. Isuani (1985), basing his figures on the percentage of the EAP paying contributions, estimates that in 1970 68 per cent of the EAP were covered but in 1979–80 only 52 per cent.[8] Coverage for unemployment was extremely restricted, as only construction workers were covered. Family allowances covered all employed persons (except for domestic employees), as well as pensioners and recipients of means-tested benefits who had dependents. Within the Latin American context, Argentina had one of the most generous welfare states, with total social security benefits expenditures of 8.9 per cent in 1980 (Table 6.4).

Costa Rica

Compared with Argentina, Brazil and Chile, Costa Rica had a very low level of industrialization and thus a much weaker labour movement, such that the initiation of a social security system for workers came some 20 years later, despite the existence of a more democratic political system. Costa Rica's economy was based on coffee and banana exports, the latter entirely under the control of United Fruit. In 1941 a reformist government instituted a pension and health/maternity insurance programme (Rosenberg, 1979: 122). This programme was compulsory for all employees below a certain income limit, in the public and private sectors. Thus, unlike in the other cases discussed here, the Costa Rican system of social insurance started out as a unified one, under the Costa Rican Social Insurance Institute (CCSS), and it remained essentially so, except for some small separate funds being added (Mesa-Lago, 1989: 45). Implementation of the programmes, though, was very slow, reaching only a quarter of the economically active population by 1960 (Rosenberg, 1979: 124).

The next significant reform was initiated and passed in 1961 by a legislature dominated by the National Liberation Party (PLN), a party with social democratic leanings. The reform took the form of a constitutional amendment stipulating that the Social Insurance Institute was to universalize coverage within a decade. Though this goal was not nearly achieved, with only 43 per cent of the population having coverage by 1971 (Rosenberg, 1979: 124), the amendment was a strong impetus pushing the system towards universalistic and standardized coverage. An integrated national health service was established in 1973, with the transfer of all hospitals to the Social Insurance Institute. By 1980, 95 per cent of physicians had salaried positions in the social security system, and though about one-third of physicians had some form of private practice, only 14 per cent of consultations were made by private physicians (Casas and Vargas, 1980: 268). The Ministry of Health retained responsibility for preventive and primary care, particularly through a community and rural health programme, which was very important because of insufficient accessibility of social insurance health facilities in rural areas.

By 1980, some 75 per cent of the population had social security coverage for health care and roughly 50 per cent for pensions (Tamburi, 1985: 77; Isuani, 1985: 95); those who did not were either self-employed or employed workers whose employers evaded registration and contributions. Uninsured people with a low income could receive health care as indigents or for a small fee (Casas and Vargas, 1980: 273; Mesa-Lago, 1989: 53). Whereas the great majority of the insured belonged to one single fund, there remained in existence 18 special pension funds for different categories of public employees with more flexible conditions and higher pensions (Mesa-Lago, 1985: 337). In terms of total social security benefits expenditure, Costa Rica ranked third among our four cases with 6.3 per cent of GDP (Table 6.4).

Comparative perspectives

As of 1980, then, the four cases discussed exemplified the most developed Latin American welfare states (Table 6.4).[9] They also illustrate the different paths to welfare state expansion (Tables 6.5–6.7). In Argentina and Brazil the first legislation was passed by conservative elites in response to labour militancy and later corporatist regimes used social security programmes in

Table 6.5 *Total social security expenditure and benefits as a percentage of GDP*

	Argentina		Brazil		Chile		Costa Rica	
	Expenditure	Benefits	Expenditure	Benefits	Expenditure	Benefits	Expenditure	Benefits
1965	—	—	4.3	3.4	12.1	9.8	2.3	1.9
1975	6.8	6.6	5.7	4.9	11.0	10.1	5.1	4.6
1980	9.3	8.9	4.8	4.6	10.7	9.9	7.1	6.3
1981	8.8	8.0	5.8	5.2	10.0	9.5	7.2	6.5
1982	6.8	6.3	6.1	5.6	15.6	14.3	5.9	5.2
1983	7.3	6.8	5.6	5.2	14.3	13.0	6.3	5.6
1984	7.3	6.8	5.1	4.6	14.7	13.4	7.0	5.6
1985	5.9	5.8	4.8	4.5	13.5	12.3	7.4	6.1
1986	6.1	5.9	5.0	4.6	13.1	12.0	7.3	6.0

Source: The Cost of Social Security 1981–1983, 1984–1986, OECD

Table 6.6 *Social security receipts by origin (per cent)*

	Argentina			Brazil			Chile			Costa Rica		
	Insured	Employer	State	Insured	Employer	State	Insured	Employer	State	Insured	Employer	State
1965							19.6	42.0	33.8	25.1	37.7	26.0
1975	22.8	70.3	5.0				16.3	46.5	32.2	23.8	47.8	20.1
1980	38.3	49.3	10.2				20.5	38.3	34.2	27.6	45.9	20.4
1981	33.6	25.3	37.4	4.9	83.0	9.3	40.0	11.8	39.5	23.5	38.7	31.7
1982	34.1	25.9	37.2	17.3	75.5	4.5	32.2	2.6	52.7	23.3	38.8	31.9
1983	34.5	27.2	36.0	15.2	74.7	8.0	31.1	2.1	48.9	28.4	47.0	18.6
1984	33.0	31.9	28.9	21.2	65.0	10.9	31.8	2.1	52.6	25.0	52.5	4.3
1985	30.6	41.4	19.6	17.2	72.6	4.3	29.1	2.0	48.6	24.2	52.1	2.9
1986	31.3	45.6	19.5	38.5	53.5	3.8	30.1	2.0	48.9	25.5	49.2	2.6

Source: The Cost of Social Security 1981–1983, 1984–1986, OECD

Table 6.7   *Distribution of benefit expenditures (per cent)*

	Argentina			Brazil			Chile			Costa Rica		
	Sickness/ maternity	Pensions	Unem- ployment	Sickness/ maternity	Pensions	Unem- ployment	Sickness/ maternity	Pensions	Unem- ployment	Sickness/ maternity	Pensions	Unem- ployment
1975	14	58	–	47	51	–	25	34	1.8	77	15	–
1980	24	58	–	38	54	–	24	44	4.3	80	15	–
1981	23	60	–	37	58	–	4	57	6.1	67	29	–
1982	25	61	–	36	60	–	18	64	3.9	68	28	–
1983	27	59	–	34	62	–	15	68	3.6	70	27	–
1984	26	59	–	32	63	–	15	70	2.6	67	25	–
1985		81	0.7	35	60	–	16	71	1.8	66	26	–
1986		77	0.8	32	63	–	17	71	1.1	66	27	–

Source: The Cost of Social Security 1981–1983, 1984–1986, OECD

their efforts to build up and control the labour movement. In Chile and Costa Rica the welfare state was shaped under democratic auspices but with a different political centre of gravity, with conservatism being stronger in Chile and social democracy stronger in Costa Rica. Accordingly, the Costa Rican welfare state was the only one to develop in a relatively unified and solidaristic way; the other three developed into highly fragmented and inegalitarian structures.[10] Military regimes in the 1960s and 1970s then effected some degree of unification, but great inequalities continued to exist. Coverage remained far from universal; about a third and more of the population remained *de facto* without coverage. Among those covered, income maintenance and health care benefits still varied by category of previous employment. Even for those people for whom medical benefits were supposed to be available through public institutions or publically financed providers, access varied greatly by geographical location because of differential availability of health care institutions.

In general, those insured for pensions were also insured for sickness/maternity, both for cash payments and for medical care. There were some provisions for those without or with insufficient social insurance coverage, but benefits were very low. All four countries had legally guaranteed minimum pensions and provisions for means-tested pensions (called family allowances in Costa Rica but available only for people over 65).[11] In addition, Chile had a special programme of family allowances for the needy, and Costa Rica and Brazil had social assistance programmes; but in Brazil, for instance, this accounted for less than 1 per cent of total social security expenditure. Unemployment insurance did not exist at all in Costa Rica and only for construction workers in Argentina, though Argentina had legislation that required employers to pay severance pay. In Brazil unemployment insurance covered only workers with 120 days of employment in the same large enterprise; over 50 workers had to be laid off in a period of 2 months for coverage to become effective; and in Chile only those with 52 weeks of coverage during the previous 2 years and registered for employment and able and willing to work were covered.

The financing structure of social security varied among the four countries (Table 6.8).[12] In Argentina, after a 1980 reform that abolished employer contributions to the pension system, employers and workers contributed roughly equal percentages of earnings to social security; in Brazil and Costa Rica, employers paid the lion's share; whereas Chile had eliminated employers' contributions altogether by 1981.[13] The difference in the changes in employer contributions at that point reflected the differences in the strength of the neoliberal impulses in the four countries. Chile had gone furthest in opening its markets and reducing the role of the state in the economy, followed by Argentina, whereas Brazil and Costa Rica still maintained more protected markets.

Since the informal sector is defined as those income-earning activities that are carried on outside the reach of labour and social security legislation and other forms of state regulation, in a social environment

Table 6.8　*Sources of contributions to social security as a percentage of earnings*

	1981			1991		
	Insured	Employer	Government	Insured	Employer	Government
Argentina						
Pensions	11	–	139% contribution of insured and means-tested federal pensions	10	11	90% of contribution + means-tested subsidies for non-contributors
Sickness/maternity	4	4.5	–	3	5.4	–
Work injury	–	All	–	–	All	–
Unemployment	–	4 Construction only	–	–	4 Construction only	–
Family allowances	–	12	All for pensioners and means tested	–	9	All for pensioners and means tested
Total	15	20.5		13	29.4	
Brazil						
Pensions	8	11	Various taxes	8–10	21.5	Special taxes
Sickness/maternity		(included in above)			(included in above)	
Work injury	–	0.5–2.5	0.5% of value of agricultural products	–	2	–
Unemployment	Union dues	–	–	–	–	
Family allowances	–	4	–	–	4	All
Total	8	15.5–17.5		8–10	27.5	–

Table 6.8 *(continued)*

	1981			1991		
	Insured	Employer	Government	Insured	Employer	Government
Chile						
Pensions	Old/new 19/13	–	Special subsidies	Old/new 19/13.5	–	Special subsidies
Sickness/maternity	4/4	–	Partial subsidy	6/7	–	Partial subsidy for public system
Work injury	–	1–4	Subsidies	–	4–8	Subsidies
Unemployment	–	–	Subsidies	–	–	All
Family allowances	–	–	Subsidies	–	–	All
Total	23/17	1–4		25/20.5	4–8	
Costa Rica						
Pensions	2.5	4.75	0.25% of covered earnings	2.5	4.75	0.25% of covered earnings
Sickness/maternity	4	6.75	0.25% of covered earnings	5.5	9.25	0.25% of covered earnings
Work injury	–	All	–	–	All	–
Unemployment	–	–		–	–	
Family allowances	–	5	Sales tax	–	–	3% of sales tax
Total	6.5	16.5+		8	14+	

Source: USDHHS, 1982, 1992

where similar activities are regulated (Castells and Portes, 1989: 12),[14] by definition employers in the informal sector evade the payment of social security contributions. Tables 6.1–6.3 show different measures of the percentage of the economically active population in the urban informal sector and in the rural traditional (and thus informal) sector, and the percentage covered by social security. Argentina, Chile, and Costa Rica (along with Uruguay) were the Latin American countries with the traditionally smallest total informal sectors and the highest degrees of social security coverage. Nevertheless, even in these countries between a quarter and a half of the labour force (depending on the measures used) remained outside the formal sector and thus outside the social security system by 1980. From 1980 to 1990, then, informality in the nonagricultural sector increased even further.[15]

If we look at the distribution of the labour force by sector, we find a low percentage in industry compared with Europe. In 1980, Argentina with 34 per cent had the highest percentage of the labour force in industry of any Latin American country; in Brazil 27 per cent were in industry, in Chile 25 per cent and in Costa Rica 23 per cent. This put the Latin American countries clearly at the lower end of the range of 25–35 per cent in continental Europe. If the continental European experience suggests that a welfare state model built around stable industrial employment simply does not work well under such conditions (Esping-Andersen, Chapter 3 in this volume), this is even more true for Latin America. It is further important to note that even in the formal industrial sector employment conditions became increasingly precarious in the late 1970s and 1980s, particularly in Chile and Argentina as a result of changes in labour legislation. Workers employed in the formal sector under a short-term contract or without any contract at all did not come under social security coverage.

The majority of self-employed remained without coverage, even where there were schemes that formally included them.[16] Partly this is due to the fact that contributions for self-employed were much higher than for employees and therefore the self-employed evaded payment, and partly it is due to the high proportion of self-employed who operate in the informal sector, avoiding any contact with public authorities. Given that the size of the informal sector is a lasting structural problem, the only way significantly to expand social security coverage would be to break with the employment nexus and establish a non-contributory scheme where entitlement is based on citizenship. Brazil is the only one of the countries discussed here that established a non-contributory social insurance system for the rural sector, but given that the system was administered by official syndicates of rural workers and employers, it also had a strong bias towards the formal sector. Financing such schemes on a large scale and with benefit levels to eliminate destitution would require a significant strengthening of the extractive capacity of Latin American states. This also applies for a potential expansion of social assistance, i.e. income-support programmes for those in need and without any social insurance coverage.

Chile and Argentina, and to a lesser extent Brazil, then, strongly resembled the conservative, corporatist welfare state regime identified by Esping-Andersen (1990; and Chapter 3 in this volume) as typical of the continental European welfare states. The basis of the welfare state was the social insurance principle, not citizenship rights; there were virtually no services outside health care; and social assistance programmes were of minimal impact. The family remained crucial in providing a safety net for the sick and the old. Female labour force participation rates were comparatively low: under 30 per cent of the female population over 15 years of age in Argentina, Chile, and Costa Rica, and somewhat above it in Brazil. The big difference between the European and Latin American variants of these welfare states was the much more restricted coverage of the latter, owing to the structural differences in the labour markets, with the much larger informal sectors in Latin America. Thus, despite very extensive formal legal inclusion, the Chilean and Argentine systems reached at best some 70 per cent of their population.

For the covered parts of the population, pension benefits were relatively generous if unequal, probably most unequal in Brazil, followed by Chile and then Argentina. The exception to this generosity was the non-contributory scheme for the rural sector in Brazil, with benefits equal to one-half the minimum wage only. These welfare states reinforced class and status distinctions and made the nexus to the labour market pivotal. There was no adequate safety net for those outside the formal labour market. Accordingly, poverty rates in 1980 ranged from 10 per cent in Argentina to 45 per cent in Brazil (CEPAL, 1990).[17]

In contrast, Costa Rica was more like an embryonic social democratic welfare state, conforming to the principles of universal coverage (in health only), standardization of benefits, unification of administration, and some aspects of solidaristic financing. Except for different categories of civil servants, all those insured belonged to the same pension scheme, with the same conditions and benefits, and there was a safety net for the uninsured in the form of means-tested pensions. However, pensions were earnings-related and the social assistance pensions were only about one-fifth of the average pension. The health care system was the same for everybody: those insured in the general and the special funds, as well as the uninsured who were entitled to virtually free medical care. In addition, Costa Rica had a strong community and rural health programme, for preventive and primary care for urban and rural poor communities, run mainly by the Ministry of Health but in coordination with the Social Security Institute. The principle of solidarity operated in the form of state financing of the programmes for the indigent. After the abolition of income ceilings, the pension benefits structure had a progressive character, but given the relatively large percentage of the population that had no pension coverage, the overall incidence of the pension system was probably at best distributively neutral. As of 1980, one of the glaring lacunae in the Costa Rican system from a social democratic point of view was unemployment insurance. Nevertheless, in consideration of Costa Rica's level of income per capita, which was significantly lower than those of Brazil and Chile, its poverty rate of 24 per cent in 1980 compared favourably with that of these two countries. This is even more so for life expectancy, which in 1984 was 73 years for Costa Rica, compared with 70 years for Chile and 64 years for Brazil (IBRD, 1986).

The impact of social security on the labour market is complex. Certainly, the fact that coverage is tied to participation in the formal sector enhances the attractiveness of this sector. But it is far from clear that this influences the behaviour of labour maket participants, as for them formal sector work is much more attractive anyway because of higher wages, other protective labour legislation, and greater stability of employment. Wilson (1985: 263) argues that the financing of social security through payroll taxes reduces formal sector employment because it creates a cycle whereby these taxes are passed on to consumers in the form of higher prices, informal sector workers have limited capacity to absorb these prices, demand for products from the formal sector is reduced, which in turn means restricted employment in the formal sector. This argument is plausible in principle, though its importance is limited because of the range of goods for which a decrease in price would substantially increase demand from the informal sector. One certainly could accept the argument, though, that high social security contributions imposed on payrolls increase the incentives for employers to carry on at least part of their operations in the informal sector. Wilson further argues that payroll taxes increase the incentive to substitute capital for labour, though he recognizes that this effect is confounded by the favourable credit policies and subsidies for capital goods typical of ISI promotion policies. The main point to be made with regard to payroll taxes is their effect on labour markets via the competitiveness of domestic products in protected versus open markets. The levels of payroll taxes that were compatible with production for protected markets did not remain so with production for open and internationally competitive markets.

The economic crisis of the 1980s and its impact on social policy

In the 1980s Latin America underwent the most severe economic crisis since the Depression. Chronic balance-of-payments deficits linked to the exhaustion of the ISI model of growth had been aggravated for the non-oil producers by the two oil shocks and dealt with in the 1970s by heavy borrowing from international commercial banks. When international interest rates rose in the early 1980s, and at the same time recession in the developed world and changing terms of trade reduced the export earnings of Latin American countries, many of them became unable to service their debt burdens. The reaction of the banks in the form of an abrupt halt to lending to Latin American countries forced severe adjustment measures. Latin America became a net exporter of capital in the 1980s.[18]

The crisis forced a critical examination of all aspects of the post-war development model. The conclusions reached in this critical examination centred around the exhaustion of ISI and the role of the state in promoting ISI. The chronic balance-of-payments problems suggested that a shift in emphasis from ISI to export-led industrialization was necessary. Since the state had played the major role in promoting ISI, the state's role in the economy would have to be modified. Moreover, the external deficits were accompanied by internal deficits and strong inflationary pressures, and an improvement in economic performance would also require a reduction of public sector deficits and thus of inefficiency and waste in the state apparatus.[19] There was virtually general acceptance of this diagnosis. However, this diagnosis could potentially lead to a range of corrective measures. What happened in practice was that the crisis gave enormous leverage to international financial institutions, particularly the International Monetary Fund (IMF), private banks, and creditor governments, where a neoliberal view of the economic world was dominant. These agents, with the support of domestic groups who for economic or political reasons favoured the reorientation, imposed, under the label of 'structural adjustment', harsh austerity policies, measures to reorient production towards exports, and a general programme of state shrinking on the Latin American countries. Initially, with a few exceptions such as Pinochet in Chile and the junta in post-1976 Argentina, most governments resisted these impositions. However, in the course of the 1980s, two developments favoured the pursuit of both austerity and liberalization policies. First, episodes of runaway inflation made the imposition of harsh austerity policies more urgent and also made the population more willing to accept them. Second, the liberalization measures that were taken created their own internal support constituencies among their beneficiaries in the financial and export-oriented sectors which, combined with the intensity of the pressures, slowly made the 'Washington consensus'[20] hegemonic in many Latin American countries.

In the neoliberal view the state came to be qualified almost by definition as bloated and inefficient. Moreover, since the state had played such a prominent role in ISI, it was falsely concluded that a turn towards export-oriented industrialization would require a radical withdrawal of the state from its economic roles. Despite evidence to the contrary from the successful East Asian industrializers and small states in Europe, indiscriminate state shrinking became a cornerstone of the radical neoliberal agenda.[21] In addition to austerity, the dominant theme in prescriptions for reinvigorating the Latin American economies came to be liberalization. Liberalization was to include deregulation of trade (lowering of tariffs and elimination of import controls), financial flows (removing foreign exchange controls and relaxing restrictions on private financial institutions and on foreign investment), and prices (elimination of price controls and subsidies), as well as privatization of state enterprises. Such deregulation and privatization would shrink the bloated state and make the market the supreme guiding force in economic decisions, and the market would dictate a reorientation from ISI to export-led growth.

The combination of austerity and liberalization policies induced or reinforced a severe contraction of economic activity, a shrinking of employment in the formal sector, particularly in the public sector, falling real incomes, and a decline in social services. Budget cuts necessitated layoffs in the public sector, cutbacks in social expenditures, and cutbacks of subsidies for basic foods, public transport, and utilities. The reduction or elimination of such subsidies, along with massive devaluation (prescribed by the IMF), led to astronomical price increases for these goods and services, in many cases virtually overnight. Given the high percentage of their income spent on these goods and on public transport by the poor, these price increases hit them particularly hard.[22]

Declines in social expenditures are only partly reflected in the ILO figures for social security expenditure as a percentage of GDP: in Argentina these expenditures declined from 9.3 per cent in 1980 to 6.1 per cent in 1986; in Brazil they remained virtually stagnant in the period, at 4.8 and 5.0 per cent; in Chile they even increased from 10.7 to 13.1 per cent, though this has to be seen in the light of the drastic contraction between 1974 and 1980, when Chile pursued a radical neoliberal economic course, and of the costs of the privatization of the pension system (see below); and in Costa Rica they also remained relatively constant at 7.1 and 7.3 per cent (Table 6.5). If we look at total social expenditures, by central and provincial governments, and including education, health, housing, pensions, and others, we find significant declines during the 1980s and slow recoveries by 1990 to levels still below those of 1980 (Carciofi and Beccaria, 1993).[23] There was a pronounced difference in magnitude of the decline between Chile, where the most radical neoliberal model was implemented, and the other countries. Typically, what suffered most in these declines were investments in facilities and supplies, such as for schools and hospitals, and salaries for teachers, nurses, and in many cases administrative employees. Over the course of the decade, then, this affected delivery of services.

Declining real wages of public and private sector employees and the loss of formal sector employment meant that more people were pushed into poverty. Privatization of state enterprises in Chile and Argentina was preceded or accompanied by layoffs, and import liberalization in Chile, Argentina, and Costa Rica caused contraction or bankruptcy of private industrial firms. A CEPAL study (1990: 42) showed increases in the percentage of the population below the poverty line from 1980 to 1986 of the following magnitude: Argentina from 10 to 16 per cent; Brazil stagnant at 45 per cent;[24] Costa Rica from 24 to 27 per cent; Peru from 53 to 60 per cent; Venezuela from 25 to 32 per cent. A study prepared for UNICEF/ CEPAL by Carciofi and Beccaria (1993: 56) showed similar increases, though somewhat lower levels overall owing to a different calculation of the poverty line; this study showed a poverty rate for Chile of 38 per cent in 1986, compared with 17 per cent in 1970 (no data available for 1980).

Problems of social security programmes

The existing social security programmes in Latin America, even in the most advanced cases, were poorly equipped to deal with the social costs of the structural adjustment policies. They had some pre-existing problems resulting from structural weaknesses, and these problems were compounded by the impact of the economic crisis. As of 1980, the pension programmes in Argentina, Brazil, and Chile had some common problems that endangered their financial stability already. Given that they had been in existence for roughly half a century, they had matured and the ratio of active to passive insured had deteriorated significantly. Particularly in Chile and Brazil, benefits in the privileged systems and time-for-service pensions[25] were expensive. Investment yields from pension reserves were extremely low, as these reserves were partly used for investment in the health systems or for government securities, and during highly inflationary periods there was actual decapitalization. Other problems affected both the pension and health systems, such as evasion of payments by employers and the self-employed, or long delays of such payments, particularly under high inflation. The state on its part accumulated large debts to the systems because it postponed its payment obligations as third-party contributor. Moreover, administrative expenditures were excessively high owing to multiplicity of institutions and the use of social security agencies for patronage employment. Finally, the rising international costs of medical technology were driving up the costs of health care.

The economic crisis of the 1980s caused greater deficits because of declining revenue due to falling real wages, declining formal sector employment, and a greater burden put on public health facilities due to the greater levels of poverty. Also, the state debt to the systems increased.[26] Inflation played havoc with the pension systems and put the issue of adjustments into the centre of the political struggle. The authoritarian governments used various methods to understate the extent of inflation and thus reduce pressures for adjustments of wages and pensions. The result was a deterioration in the real value of pensions. The structural adjustment programmes also brought the issue of employer contributions to the top of the political agenda. The slashing of tariffs and other import restrictions and the emphasis on export diversification meant that employers could no longer simply pass on payroll taxes to the consumers. Thus, the material self-interests of employers combined with the ideological bent of proponents of neoliberal policy to reduce employer contributions. The magnitude of these reductions, of course, depended on the nature of the adjustment process and the relative political strength of these actors.

Approaches to reform

Attempts to deal with the financial problems of the social security systems on the one hand and with the social costs of structural adjustment policies on the other hand were part and parcel of the different countries' general approaches to the reshaping of their political economies. There were a few obvious measures that most countries took, such as the elimination of particularly costly privileges, some administrative coordination, and reduction of investments in facilities. However, beyond these basic measures, the various governments chose different combinations of available options, such as (1) increases/decreases in contributions from the insured, employers, and the government, and imposition of user fees; (2) reduction of benefits across the board or for specific groups; (3) reduction of administrative expenditures, e.g. for personnel; (4) a shift in emphasis from expensive curative health care to more cost-efficient public health measures and primary care with ambulatories and paramedics; (5) the establishment of new programmes outside the traditional social security programmes, targeted at particularly vulnerable groups; and (6) structural changes responding to a radical redefinition of the responsibilities of the state and the market with regard to social security. The combinations chosen reflected the different governments' visions of an appropriate model of the relationship between state and market, and state and civil society, as well as the realities of the new position of these countries in the international economy.

Chile

The military government under Pinochet in Chile (1973–89) pursued the most radical neoliberal restructuring of economy and society in Latin America.[27] Its shock programme of austerity and adjustment measures in 1975–6 went even further than the IMF demanded. The reason for this radicalness was that the economic policies formed an integral part of Pinochet's political project which included not just physical repression of pre-existing political organizations but also a critical weakening of labour and the left through a destruction of their social bases. The government sought to construct an atomized, depoliticized society where there would be no basis for collective action and the state would no longer be at the centre of the issue of distribution. Instead, the market was to determine the allocation of resources, though with a little help for capital in the form of legal restrictions on the formation of unions and collective bargaining.

In the period up to 1981 the government slashed total state expenditures from some 40 to 30 per cent of GDP (Vergara, 1986: 89), reduced the state bureaucracy by some 5 per cent per year (Foxley, 1986: 31), sold off all but 24 of the 479 state enterprises (Vergara, 1986: 90), slashed tariffs from an average of 94 per cent to an average of 10 per cent (Borzutzky, 1983: 247), deregulated the financial sector, and guaranteed foreign investment the same treatment as domestic investment. The results of these policies were partial deindustrialization, as weaker enterprises in traditional sectors such as textiles, shoes and leather, and garments, faced by import competition and high interest rates, were forced out of business (Foxley, 1986: 40–1). At the same time, the late 1970s saw a consumption boom spurred by foreign borrowing and imports, and a concentration of assets in the economy in the hands of a few major groups based on financial institutions. By late 1981 the boom turned to bust, as the financial system got into crisis and the government began to take over banks and other financial institutions to save them from bankruptcy. The halt of foreign loans in the wake of the regional debt crisis further aggravated the decline of the Chilean economy. By 1983, close to a third of the labour force was unemployed. The response of the government was twofold: on the one hand, it concluded an orthodox stabilization agreement with the IMF, and on the other hand it continued to take over failing banks and the enterprises controlled by these banks, and it assumed the external debt of the banks. However, these takeovers were emergency measures and did not signify a change in the economic policy course; rather, after the economic crisis was over, the banks and enterprises were reprivatized.

The same emphasis on reduction of the state's role and expenditures and reliance on the market also characterized the regime's social policy. Though social expenditures as a percentage of total public expenditures recovered to previous levels after a steep decline in 1974, this meant lower real expenditures as total public expenditures were reduced drastically. Moreover, two new programmes absorbed a large part of expenditure: an emergency employment programme and a subsidy paid to employers for the hiring of new workers. Overall per capita social spending in 1979 was at 83 per cent of the level of 1970, with major declines in housing, social security, and health, and large increases in public assistance and employment. The decline in social security spending reflected largely the decline in the average amount paid for pensions and family allowances (Vergara, 1986: 97–102). By 1989, the index of per capita public social expenditure (in 1985 pesos) was still below the base year 1970, standing at 92 (Raczynski, 1994: 71).

Comprehensive social security reform was delayed for quite some time owing to internal bureaucratic disagreements between more corporatist-oriented technocrats and the radical neoliberals, before the latter won decisively. Between 1974 and 1979, though, employer contributions were greatly reduced, unemployment compensation and family allowances were made uniform, and the real value of pensions and family allowances was greatly reduced through lags in adjustment to inflation. In 1979, reforms eliminated the most costly pension privileges, such as time-for-service pensions, unified the retirement age at 65 for males and 60 for females, and unified the system of pension adjustment and tied it to the consumer price index (Borzutzky, 1983: 298).

A 1980 law established a new pension system based on compulsory private insurance for wage and salary earners, with full capitalization; participation by the self-employed is voluntary. Every individual has to pay his/her own contribution into an individual account administered by a private for-profit pension fund (*administradora de fondos de pensiones*, AFP), and the contributor's pension will be determined by these contributions plus the returns on the investments of the pension funds, minus the charges for administration. Thus, the adequacy of pensions will depend entirely on the general performance of the Chilean economy, particularly the level of real wages and the relationship between inflation and interest rates. Employers make no contributions to the new system; nor does the government, except for the guarantee of a minimum pension to those with 20 years of contributions, and obligations resulting from the transition.[28] Every new entrant into the labour force is required to join the new system. Those previously insured had 5 years to choose between the old and the new system, but once they left the old system, they could not return to it. The attractiveness of the new system was enhanced by a massive advertising campaign and by lower contributions of the insured than under the old system, 19.5 to 20.7 per cent in the new system versus 25.6 to 27.7 per cent in the old system. In order to motivate people to switch to the private system, the government issued recognition bonds to the new system for the contributions that each insured had made to the old system; these bonds will become effective in full at the time of retirement.

The AFPs are regulated by the government with regard to their investments, but not the amount they can charge in the form of commissions and fees. Presumably, competition would take care of this aspect. However, the new system became rapidly highly concentrated, with three AFPs controlling 68 per cent of all deposits by 1991. The commissions typically consist of a flat fee and a percentage of the contributions, which means that they have a regressive impact (Diamond and Valdés-Prieto, 1994).[29] Ironically, the administrative expenses associated with the new system probably exceed those of the old system, even though the old system was criticized as inefficient and too expensive (Diamond and Valdés-Prieto, 1994: 309). By 1991, 90 per cent of the insured were registered in the new private scheme; those remaining in the old system were mainly people close to retirement. In 1988, about one-fifth of the labour force was not covered by social security, most of them self-employed. However, only 56 per cent of the labour force was both registered for social security and contributing, whereas 24 per cent was registered but not contributing. There are multiple reasons for this state of affairs. Some of those registered but not contributing were temporary workers, or workers without contracts, or unemployed; for others their employers deducted the contributions but delayed forwarding them to the AFPs. In addition, there was considerable underreporting of earnings, as many with low incomes only made contributions to get a minimum pension. The minimum pension guaranteed to those insured, though at the equivalent of US $75 per month in 1991 not sufficient to meet basic needs, was more than twice the public assistance pension which amounted to the equivalent of US $36 in 1992 (Mesa-Lago, 1994: 117–21).

The transition, then, imposed considerable costs on the government, given that it had to cover deficits in the old system where contributions declined radically compared with pension obligations, and that it had to transfer funds into the new system. These costs amounted to 4–5 per cent of GDP per year in the 1980s and early 1990s (Diamond and Valdés-Prieto, 1994: 279–80). The entire reform amounted to a massive transfer of assets from the public to the private sector. By 1991 AFPs controlled funds equivalent to 34.5 per cent of GDP, and estimates are that they will control assets equal to 50 per cent of GDP by the year 2000 (cited in Mesa-Lago, 1994: 124). This costly process of privatization could be carried out without macro-economic disruptions only because the government had built up a fiscal surplus before undertaking the reforms and because it continued to keep other expenditures extremely low.

In health care, the public system was reorganized and in addition a private system of health insurance was created for middle- and upper-income earners. In 1979, the government unified the blue- and white-collar health systems and decentralized the new public health system into regional systems, to be reimbursed by the central government on a services rendered basis (Borzutzky, 1983: 337–8). Those insured in the private pension system are eligible to join private health plans (*institutos de salud previsional*, ISAPRES), which offer a variety of benefits and may construct their own facilities or contract with private providers. Even for most middle-income earners the premiums charged by ISAPRES in addition to the mandatory health insurance contribution are too high. Accordingly, by 1990 only 16 per cent of the population were affiliated with ISAPRES, but their contributions amounted to more than 50 per cent of mandatory contributions for health insurance (Carciofi and Beccaria, 1993). ISAPRES spend four times the amount that the public sector spends per capita, and in addition they make substantial profits (Vergara, 1994: 257, n.10). Thus, the lower-income/lower-contribution people remained with the public system, which also serves indigents. Investments and salaries greatly decreased in the public system during the 1970s and 1980s, which means that developments were headed in the direction of a two-class system of health care.

In the 1970s, at the same time as it reduced overall social expenditure, the government created or reactivated a number of programmes targeted at the very poor. Of particular importance were the emergency employment programme, which in 1983 provided temporary employment to 13.5 per cent of the labour force, as well as health and nutritional programmes for poor mothers and infants before and after birth, a means-tested school lunch programme, and pre-school day care centres for poor children with nutritional and other health problems. As a result, there was not only no deterioration but actually an improvement in some basic social indicators like infant mortality despite the impact of the economic crisis and austerity programmes.[30] One should note, though, that the effectiveness of these health and nutrition programmes was in large part due to the structure and coverage that the public health service had achieved under the old system (Raczynski, 1994: 80). In the early 1980s, total social expenditures increased from 17 per cent of GDP in 1980 to an average of 22.3 per cent in 1982–4, reflecting the costs of the pension reform and of the unemployment and emergency employment programmes, before declining again to 14 per cent in 1990 (Carciofi and Beccaria, 1993). While most of these reduced expenditures continued to be targeted at the poorest groups, they were simply inadequate to ameliorate poverty in a meaningful way.

The new Chilean model of integration into the world economy is heavily based on exports of raw materials – agricultural goods, minerals, and forestry products – increasingly complemented by light manufacturing. For most of these manufacturing and particularly agricultural activities to be profitable, cheap labour is essential. Accordingly, social security contributions based on the payroll, except for work injury, were eliminated by the military government and not reimposed by the democratic government. In contrast, contributions from the insured as a percentage of their income are the highest among our four cases (Table 6.8). The economic transformation has brought about a significant change in the Chilean labour market in the past decade, a change that keeps large sectors of the employed labour force in precarious and poorly paid employment. Whereas unemployment had fallen to 5.7 per cent in 1990, average and minimum wages had not returned to their 1981 levels (Díaz, 1993: 21). In 1987, 54 per cent of workers and employees in the formal sector earned below 2.5 times the value of the per capita poverty line, the minimum for satisfying the needs of a basic nuclear family (León, 1994: 41). Labour's position was so weak that growth of productivity was consistently higher than growth of wages. A very large proportion of waged workers are employed on the basis of informal labour relations, even in firms that are operating in the formal sector. They are hired on an individual basis, with or without temporary contract, as unions and collective bargaining are kept out of these enterprises – a situation that is possible because of the labour code's emphasis on flexibility in labour markets. Large firms take advantage of this situation by subcontracting with medium and small firms, with the result that the proportion of core workers with stable employment under formal labour relations is small compared with the large proportion of part-time and temporary workers (Díaz, 1993: 13). This has clear implications for social security coverage in that the latter groups of workers either are not covered at all or only make sporadic contributions that might at best be sufficient to entitle them to a minimum pension.

The weakness of labour and other mass organizations has also meant that there were no effective pressures pushing the democratic governments to change course in social policy. Whereas the Aylwin government did make some important progress by raising taxes in order to increase social spending and by increasing the legal minimum wage, it continued the safety net approach to social policy and did not even put a change in the institutional parameters of the two-class system of social protection on the political agenda. As a result of the increases in social spending and in the minimum wage, combined with rising average wages due to decreasing inflation and a certain tightening of the labour market, poverty was reduced from 40 per cent in 1990 to 34 per cent in 1992 (Díaz, 1993: 22).

Still, social policy for the poor retains the character of charity and remains focused on immediate consumption (Vergara, 1994: 251–5). One innovation has been the Fund for Solidarity and Social Investment aimed at improving community-based social welfare infrastructure and increasing productivity of micro-enterprises and the informal sector. The fund, though, receives 1 per cent of public social expenditure only (Graham, 1994: 42–5). Moreover, even at higher levels of funding it would have a limited impact, given that a large proportion of the poor are in precarious waged employment connected to the formal sector (Díaz, 1993: 25).

Brazil

In contrast to Chile, the neoliberal impulse was much weaker in Brazil and the entire approach to economic policy under the military and then the new democratic governments remained much more statist. The post-1964 military government's entire development project had been based on extensive state involvement coupled with disregard for popular and labour interests. Unlike the Chilean military government, though, which ruled unencumbered by electoral considerations until 1988, the Brazilian military government had begun a process of liberalization and democratization in the 1970s and thus came to face demands from within the ranks of its own supporters as well as from the opposition for distributive policies. Throughout the 1980s, then, pressures from the IMF and from domestic technocrats favouring orthodox adjustment measures faced opposition from a combination of traditional politicians concerned with the maintenance of their power bases through patronage and left-wing politicians who favoured a social democratic approach to economic and social policy. However, whereas the general approach remained statist under the New Republic inaugurated in 1985, the very patronage basis of Brazilian politics obstructed the efforts by reformist forces to implement significant redistributive policies.

In late 1982 Brazil was forced to turn to the IMF and implement several rounds of severe austerity policies, which plunged the country into a deep recession. As growth recovered in 1984 and 1985, so did inflation, reaching a 300 per cent annual rate by early 1986 (Baer et al., 1989: 34–5). The new democratic government of President Sarney launched a heterodox stabilization plan to bring inflation under control without sacrificing growth.[31] The Plan Cruzado among other measures contained a price freeze and a partial wage freeze, limits to indexation, and the creation of a new currency. The plan was successful temporarily, but price freezes were maintained for too long and the budget deficit was not brought under control, such that inflation returned with great force by early 1987 (Baer et al., 1989: 37–9; Pang, 1989: 132–6). A moratorium on the commercial bank debt provoked highly negative reactions from the international financial community and the US government and consequently was of short duration, as was another attempt at heterodox stabilization (Pang,

1989: 137–9). The repeated failures to bring inflation and the budget deficit under control opened the way for President Collor after his election in 1990 to embark on a neoliberal offensive with rapid liberalization and privatization in conjunction with orthodox austerity measures. However, this project was cut short by Collor's impeachment in 1992, as his successor took a more statist position again. The main economic problems remained inflation and the budget deficit, both of which called for reforms to increase state revenue.

Total social expenditures of the federal government as a percentage of GDP stood at 9.25 per cent in 1980, increased in 1981 and 1982, fell in 1983 and 1984, and then increased steadily again, reaching 10.78 per cent in 1989.[32] Broken down by area, expenditures declined after 1982 for pensions and social assistance and remained slightly below the 1981 level by 1989, whereas they increased for health and education (Azeredo, 1992). In the early 1980s the social security system underwent a severe fiscal crisis, in part for the same reasons it did in other countries, such as increasing unemployment and declining real wages during the recession, but another important part was the escalation of health costs due to the system of private delivery of services where increasingly decisions were driven by the medico-pharmaceutical complex. The government responded to this crisis by decree, circumventing opposition in Congress even from within its own party, imposing increases in the payroll tax of 2 per cent for employers and a sliding scale for the insured, an increase in the wage base from 15 to 20 minimum wages, taxes on pensions, and a 2 per cent tax on luxury goods earmarked for the social security system.

Under the new democratic government of Sarney, the Ministry of Social Security and Social Assistance (MPAS) was given to the progressive wing of the opposition PMDB.[33] From these positions, progressive technocrats pushed for truly universalizing reforms and improvements of benefits for the poorer sectors. In the mid 1980s, at least some 30 per cent of the urban population was *de facto* without coverage, despite their legal inclusion in the system, and the bulk of the rural population received minimal benefits. The reformers attempted to reduce the contribution for the lowest paid to induce more of the marginal population to join the system. To compensate for these low contributions and increases in benefits for the poorest, they advocated an elimination of costly privileges like time-for-service and special pensions, controls on charges by private health care providers, and a correction of the privatizing and curative tendencies in the health system. Urban labour and pensioners organized by urban labour supported only parts of these reforms, not universalization for fear of losing benefits they enjoyed, and added demands for a recalculation of pensions that would benefit pensions of higher value. The MPAS accepted some of these demands, with the result that the reform package required additional resources and met with the stern opposition of the Ministry of Finance. The entire project then went to the Constituent Assembly, where politicians accepted demands for the preservation of higher benefits, including time-for-service pensions, along with an extension of welfare pensions equal to one minimum wage to anybody over 65, and the stipulation that any income-replacing benefit had to be at least equal to one minimum wage. They also imposed new taxes on sales and profits of firms to increase social security revenues (Melo, 1992). These measures did help the urban and rural poor in principle, but they made only minimal progress toward solving the problem of financing and thwarted the redistributive thrust of the reforms.[34] Accordingly, the conflict between the MPAS and the Ministry of Finance continued, the latter's position being strengthened by imposition of severe IMF austerity conditions.[35] Finally, a measure was passed to strengthen the financial base of the pension system by raising the minimum years of contributions to qualify for a regular pension from 5 years by 6 months every year, beginning in 1992, until the minimum reaches 15 years (US Department of Health and Human Services, 1992).

In health care some progress towards universalization was made in 1987 with provisions that entitled anybody to free health care, not just in emergencies, and eliminated the need to produce social security records. Still, the realization of this universal right remained highly deficient owing to the insufficient availability of facilities, particularly in poorer regions. In 1987 the reformers launched a project for unified and decentralized health systems (SUDS) which entailed a significant transfer of resources and responsibilities to the state level to bring about a better coordination of the health care activities of the social security system and the Ministry of Health and thus improve health care for the poor. However, these initiatives did not have the desired results as the transfers were taken advantage of by many state governments to pursue their own goals, such as increasing the pay for medical personnel or reducing their own health expenditures. Moreover, the reformers failed in their efforts to strengthen state controls over private providers of health care and thus reduce expenditures driven by the latters' interests.

In sum, whereas by the late 1980s the Brazilian pattern of social policy approximated a universalistic welfare state on paper, in reality it fell far short of this ideal, both at the level of absolute provision of income replacements and services and in the dimension of equity. Legally, every Brazilian had the right to free health care based on his/her citizenship, over 90 per cent of the population was covered by social security, and the needy were entitled to social assistance pensions no lower than one minimum wage. However, access to health care was sorely lacking in many poor areas, non-payment of contributions left many low-income earners without coverage, and the requirements for documenting a social security pension or social assistance claim were beyond the record-keeping abilities of most low-income people. This situation perpetuated the tradition of patronage in Brazilian politics, as low-income claimants needed an intermediary to deal with the social security and social assistance bureaucracies. Accordingly, control over social security agencies remained a coveted political prize for parties and individual politicians at all levels of government, and the tendency to overstaff such agencies with political supporters remained strong. The strength of the patronage tradition in Brazilian politics, in turn, has made it extremely difficult to form cohesive parties and legislative majorities for truly redistributive and solidaristic social policies.

Newly elected President Fernando Henrique Cardoso has clearly recognized these institutional deficiences and has made the strengthening of parties and the construction of party coalitions in Congress, along with reforms to improve the capacities of the state, his strategic priorities. He emphasized assumption of the social debt as a key goal of his administration. Two early suggestions were the establishment of a community solidarity programme to combat hunger and poverty in cooperation with NGOs, and a longer-term plan to provide a basic income to some 7 million poor families without visible means of support (*Latin America Weekly Report*, 20 October 1994). Thus, the thrust of Brazilian social policy reforms will remain directed towards a universalistic basic security system.

Argentina

Compared with Chile, Argentina had weaker and shorter-lived neoliberal impulses, though they were much stronger than in Brazil and Costa Rica. The first push of neoliberalism ended in an economic disaster and the transition to democracy, the second one is still ongoing and tempered in the area of social policy by opposition articulated through democratic channels. The Argentine welfare state up to the late 1970s had been constructed around the assumption of virtually full employment of an essentially urban labour force. Therefore, it was poorly equipped to handle the changes in the labour market resulting from the economic policies of the late 1970s and the economic crisis of the 1980s. It could not stem the 'Latinamericanization' of Argentina, that is, the increase in poverty rates resulting from the growth of the informal sector and of open unemployment.

The military government that seized power in 1976 embarked upon a neoliberal project similar to that of its Chilean counterpart. It imposed extremely harsh orthodox austerity policies, import liberalization and deregulation of the financial system. The result was an extremely rapid accumulation of foreign debt and a flood of imports, leading to deindustrialization, a financial crash, and subsequently a severe economic crisis and fiscal crisis of the state. The military government's statization of the private foreign debt saddled its democratic successor governments with huge debt service obligations. The new democratic government of Alfonsín was inaugurated in December 1983, in the midst of this economic crisis. Alfonsín resisted IMF austerity pressures and opted for a heterodox approach instead, hoping to bring inflation under control without plunging the country deeper into recession. He imposed the Plan Austral in 1985, but neither this plan nor subsequent more orthodox policies were successful in bringing inflation under control.

The repeated failures of stabilization attempts opened the way for a turn to neoliberalism. Menem, the candidate of the Perónist party, won the 1989 elections in the context of a severe recession and hyperinflation of over 3600 per cent per year. He began to turn away from his campaign promises immediately and imposed an orthodox stabilization package; later he embarked on a rapid liberalization of trade, reduction of public sector employment, and privatization of state enterprises, and in 1991 he introduced free convertibility of the currency. In the area of social policy, he attempted to emulate the Chilean pension reform, but widespread opposition and in particular congressional reluctance forced many modifications and maintained strong state involvement.

The post-1976 adjustment measures and the economic crisis of the 1980s had drastic consequences for the Argentine labour market, particularly for domestic industry and wage earners.[36] Industrial output declined, and the proportion of blue-collar workers engaged in manufacturing declined 40 per cent in the first period and an additional 12 per cent in the second one. Average real wages in the industrial sector in 1991 were only one-third of what they had been in 1974 (Smith, 1991: 66). Open unemployment and visible underemployment increased to a combined total of 19 per cent in 1993 in the Greater Buenos Aires area (Lo Vuolo and Barbeito, 1993: 134); roughly another quarter of the labour force worked in the informal sector (1993: 134). Accordingly, poverty rates increased to 39 per cent of households in the metropolitan region by 1987 (Golbert and Fanfani, 1994: 19).[37] The provision of social services was increasingly delegated to provincial and municipal authorities, so that by the early 1990s the federal government had only a significant role in the pension system and universities. Real social expenditures per capita only surpassed the level of the beginning of the decade in 1987 and declined by 27 per cent from 1980 to 1990 (Carciofi and Beccaria, 1993).

The pension system entered the 1980s in financial crisis already because of its maturation, high life expectancy, low retirement ages, and repeated bouts of very high inflation, and the declining levels of employment and real wages further aggravated the financial problems.[38] The value of real pensions declined by 25 per cent from 1981 to 1988 and another 30 per cent from 1988 to 1991 (Mesa-Lago, 1994: 149), and the system accumulated a large debt to pensioners. This gave rise to numerous lawsuits against the pension system for non-compliance with its obligations, and in 1986 the system was declared in a state of emergency. Subsequently, a number of measures were taken to pay the debt according to a schedule of priorities, and in 1993 revenues from the privatization of the state oil company were allocated to the pension system, but the basic problem remained unresolved and the debt kept on accumulating (Isuani and San Martino, 1993: 34–9).

In June 1992 the government submitted a reform project for the entire pension system to Congress which was finally passed, after many modifications, in October 1993. Despite the government's neoliberal economic offensive, the pension system emerging from Congress was a mixed one, combining universalistic, basic security, and statist aspects with individual-istic and private features. Coverage under the new system remains compulsory, including for the self-employed; the three main existing funds were unified; and retirement age will gradually be raised for all to 65 years. The public system will continue on a pay-as-you-go basis and provide a basic pension for all insured that varies only with the time of contribution; it will be financed by the 16 per cent employers' contribution and the equivalent from the self-employed, as well as special earmarked taxes and the proceeds from the sale of the state oil company (Mesa-Lago, 1994: 152–5). For a supplementary pension, based on their 11 per cent contri-butions, employees and the self-employed can choose between remaining in the public system and joining the new private system. If they choose the private system, their contributions will go into individual accounts admin-istered by private pension funds, and as in the Chilean system, the eventual portion of the pension coming from this account will be determined by the amount of contributions plus the investment returns and minus commissions. In addition, individuals who contributed to the old public system will be compensated for those past contributions at the time of their retirement. The private accounts can be administered not only by private corporations but also by non-profit organizations, including unions or cooperatives. The new private funds began operating in mid 1994, and in just a few months the shortfall in contributions to the public system contributed to a deficit of crisis proportions in that system.

On the face of it, this reform maintains the aspirations of a universalistic welfare state. However, the characteristics of the Argentine labour market will keep these aspirations from being realized. Coverage remains based on participation in the formal labour market, which excludes a substantial part of the population. Moreover, the total contribution of the self-employed will amount to 27 per cent of their earnings, which will certainly perpetuate the high evasion rate even among formal sector self-employed and thus result in far from universal coverage. Finally, the non-pension components of the welfare state do not conform to a universalistic pattern. In the area of unemployment, coverage is highly limited; by mid 1993, when there were some one million unemployed, only 84,000 received unemployment benefits (Lo Vuolo and Barbeito, 1993: 44–5). Family allowances are also tied to status of dependent employment. Social assistance is of minimal impact in relation to need, with less than 1 per cent of GDP allocated to a variety of programmes (Lo Vuolo and Barbeito, 1993: 50–1). The health care system is not a universalistic one either, though everyone is entitled to receive free medical care from public institutions, the majority of which are financed by provincial governments. Employees and their dependants are covered by health insurance through the *obras sociales*, financed by employer and employee contributions and administered by unions. Supervision and coordination of the health care system are highly deficient, resulting not only in quality differences between different *obras sociales*, between them and the public system, and within the public system by region, but also in excessive expenditures driven by the interests of private providers (Lo Vuolo and Barbeito, 1993: 39–42) and blatant corruption.

Costa Rica

Costa Rica deserves attention because it is the only Latin American country that had built a pattern of social policy with social democratic aspirations, and because it is a rare case of a small country that could resist pressures for a move to a neoliberal model and instead could protect this pattern. The country benefited from its strategic location with regard to the Reagan administration's policy towards Nicaragua; it received significant US aid and was not exposed to the same pressures from international financial institutions for neoliberal structural adjustment policies as other countries with similarly massive foreign debts. Thus, it was able to resist orthodoxy and protect the poorer sectors from bearing disproportionate costs of austerity and adjustment. By the 1990s, when the Nicaraguan conflict had lost its saliency and thus its utility for Costa Rica, there was a much more widespread recognition of the social costs of orthodox adjustment policies and thus less pressure from international financial institutions and from the US government for radical neoliberal approaches.

Costa Rica was hit early by the debt crisis and was the first country to put a moratorium on its debt payments. The newly elected Monge government had to impose a stabilization programme from mid 1982 to the end of 1983 (Nelson, 1989: 144–5). Monge as the PLN candidate had a long-standing social democratic commitment and close relations to labour, and he insisted on a gradual approach to stabilization and a mix of orthodox measures such as steep cuts in the government deficit and wage restraint with decidedly non-orthodox ones such as strict foreign exchange controls and an incomes policy favouring the lower paid. The same basic orientation also shaped the post-1983 structural adjustment programme. General austerity policies continued, but they were accompanied by a social compensation plan and resistance to drastic state shrinking. Business had to share in the costs of adjustment through tax increases and increases in utility rates, and the costs of declining real wages and formal sector employment were countered with temporary public employment programmes, unemployment assistance, food aid, and an increase in the minimum wage. The state was also relatively successful in promoting non-traditional exports (Nelson, 1989: 148–9).

Overall, there were no dramatic changes in social policy in the 1980s.[39] Rather, the government took a step-by-step approach to improve the financial situation of the Social Insurance Institute (CCSS), and it instituted special assistance programmes to cushion the effects of austerity policies on the poor. The CCSS increased contributions from employers, employees, and the government for health care, and contributions from the government to the pension system. Moreover, the retirement ages were increased to 60.5 years for females and 62.5 years for males, and new entries into the costly civil servants' system[40] were closed, such that all new civil servants will be incorporated in the CCSS under standardized conditions.

The efforts to preserve universalistic social policies in health care and to use social assistance programmes to mitigate the impact of the economic crisis and of the austerity policies on the weaker social sectors were successful in the sense of continuing progress in basic social indicators *and* reducing poverty rates.[41] Zuvekas (1992) presents figures from eight different studies of poverty that show different levels of poverty due to different methodologies, but a consistent pattern of increases in the early 1980s and then a decrease to slightly below the 1980 level by the end of the decade. Whereas programmes targeted at the poorest sectors also prevented a deterioration of social indicators in Chile, the great increases in the poverty rates in Chile and Argentina stand in stark contrast to the slight decline achieved in Costa Rica.

Interpretation of present trends and future options

In the 1970s and 1980s the fiscal crisis of the state forced adaptations in the social policy patterns of all four countries, but these adaptations took very different forms in accordance with the changes in the countries' political economies and the governments' larger political agendas. Chile has pursued the most radical programme of economic liberalization. Much of domestic industry was destroyed and primary emphasis was put on diversification of exports. However, the new insertion in international markets is based heavily on exports of primary and light manufactured goods relying on cheap labour and a highly flexible labour market. In accordance with its pro-capital and anti-labour policies, the Pinochet government transformed the Chilean welfare state in the direction of a two-class system. It created a publicly supported private scheme, whereby the state guarantees basic minima for those whose private pension accounts do not yield a sufficient income but leaves the profits from the administration of the funds in the hands of the private companies. Given that the high levels of economic growth needed to generate returns sufficient to accumulate large individual pension accounts are unlikely to prevail, a large proportion of pensioners is likely to require public subsidies to arrive at a minimum pension. Insufficient accumulation will be a particular problem for low-income earners because their contributions get penalized by a regressive structure of fees and commissions. Moreover, the precarious employment conditions of a majority of waged workers will make it difficult for them even to accumulate the 20 years of contributions required to receive a minimum pension and will make them dependent on the low social assistance pension. It is mainly for this reason and because even the minimum pension is insufficient to meet basic needs that one cannot look at the Chilean model as a basic income security model, despite the state guarantee of a minimum pension. The responsibility of employers for the welfare of their employees has reverted to the state of the early twentieth century, limited to work injury. This entire pattern fits with Chile's new integration into the world economy outlined above.[42] The only positive development in Chilean social policy has been the strengthening of the unemployment scheme, though in order to make a real difference it would require a stronger financial base founded upon an enlarged tax base, a problem to which I shall return.

Proponents of the Chilean model point to the beneficial effect of the privatization of the pension scheme on the capital market. It is certainly true that the Chilean capital market has grown greatly since the 1980s. However, the primary goal of social policy should be to improve human welfare and combat poverty, not to strengthen capital markets. Furthermore, whereas the stronger capital market has helped spur economic growth, it has not generated a development model that provides secure and adequately paying jobs significantly to reduce mass poverty. Without large-scale governmental efforts to upgrade the skills of the labour force and promote higher-skill/higher-wage manufacturing for export, accompanied by greater protection for union organization to ensure better distribution of the benefits from increases in productivity, continued economic growth is unlikely to solve the problem of poverty.[43] Such efforts would require rebuilding state capacity to pursue an industrial policy, as well as a deliberate decision to strengthen labour *vis-à-vis* capital. Such a reordering of relations between the state and the private sector and between labour and capital is made extremely difficult by the hegemonic position of large capital in the Chilean political economy. The position of large capital has been strengthened by the economic concentration generated by the Pinochet government's policies of liberalization and privatization on the one hand, and by its drastic weakening of labour and the grass-roots organizations of left-wing parties on the other hand.[44]

Brazil exhibits an entirely different pattern of participation in the world economy. Aside from subregional integration with Argentina, Uruguay, and Paraguay through Mercosur, it has maintained a more protectionist stance, and it also has a much larger internal market and a much more industrially based export structure than Chile. Collor's programme of privatization and liberalization was both gradual and selective, lifting tariffs primarily on consumer goods (Sola, 1994: 155–9). As a result, Brazil did not suffer from deindustrialization; rather, the index of industrial production, set at 100 in 1981, stood at 124 by mid 1994. By far the largest proportion of exports are manufactures, with a strong participation of transport and mechanical equipment and chemicals, i.e. comparatively high skill branches (ECLAC, 1994). Accordingly, along with Argentina, Uruguay and Costa Rica, Brazil has one of the highest levels of employer contributions to the social security system in the region.[45] Brazil's major unresolved economic problem, which has serious effects on social policy, is the fiscal crisis of the state and the attendant strong inflationary pressures.[46]

The stabilization attempt undertaken under Cardoso's direction in 1994 showed promising early results and undoubtedly contributed heavily to his victory in the presidential elections. Should he be able to forge the political coalitions necessary to solve the fiscal crisis, Brazil could become an example of a country undertaking successful adjustment measures that did not correspond to the neoliberal blueprint, while continuing to move towards increased state responsibilities for the welfare of the majority of the population.

Given its large rural sector, Brazil has achieved impressively large legal coverage. Brazil is the only country that adopted a non-contributory scheme of social insurance for part of its poor population, the rural sector, as early as the 1970s. This scheme entitles its members now to pension benefits of one minimum wage and to health care. The question is, of course, why this solution was chosen rather than the simple extension of free medical care (as in Costa Rica) and a minimal universalistic citizenship pension to the rural sector. In fact, one could argue that non-contributory social insurance is a contradiction in terms. The answer lies, of course, in the politics of social policy. The rural scheme was designed to give power to officially recognized syndicates as they were entrusted with the administration of benefits. A universalistic scheme would neither encourage membership in such syndicates nor give much discretionary power and thus the means to build clienteles to local political leaders. It also might lead to larger numbers of claims in the absence of the filter function performed by the rural syndicates. Lastly, it would require provision of health services through a national health system instead of private providers contracted by the syndicates. The Brazilian system, then, demonstrates the problem of transforming a *de jure* universalistic welfare state into a *de facto* one in the context of legacies of a segmented and inegalitarian pattern of social policy based on private provision of services and a political system characterized by clientelism and weak political parties.

Costa Rica implemented severe austerity policies but not according to the neoliberal blueprint and sustained its direction towards a universalistic welfare state in the 1980s. It came closer to reaching this goal in health care than any of the other countries, and it initiated an important reform which will facilitate progress towards this goal in the pension system in the future. In contrast to Brazil, the health care system is based on the predominance of public provision of services and the rural sector is included in the general contributory system, on a mandatory basis for employees and a voluntary basis for the self-employed. Contribution requirements are minimal, amounting to contributions in the month preceding the onset of illness only. Moreover, contributions to sickness insurance for the low-income self-employed are kept low, at 5 per cent of their earnings, and their costs are supplemented by the state.

Costa Rica heavily supported the development of non-traditional exports in agriculture and assembly-type manufacturing with a variety of tax incentives and subsidies, but did not reduce employer contributions to social security. The end of the special treatment for Costa Rica because of the Nicaraguan conflict has put new urgency on the need to increase exports to bring the trade deficit down and will keep the issue of labour costs and thus employer contributions to social security highly salient throughout the 1990s. The outcome, of course, will be shaped not just by the pressures of international economic competition, but also by the political power distribution. The Chilean option is not the only one available. If employer contributions need to be reduced for reasons of international competition, financing of the public health and pension system can be put to a greater extent on a tax basis.

In addition to the requirements of the new political economies, changes in social policy have also responded to the attempts of governments and opposition to use social policy for political ends, both to promote their ideological visions of a desirable social order and to build, or destroy, support bases. The Pinochet government in Chile privatized social security with the intent of supporting the atomization, individualization, and thus depoliticization of civil society. It did so with a complete disregard for any opposition from popular and even middle class groups, as well as for the distributional consequences of its policies for the poorer sectors. The only exception were a few special programmes targeting the poorest and most vulnerable groups. Under the two democratic governments in Chile, the new power distribution has heavily favoured capital. The process of economic concentration and the dependence on foreign capital, combined with the emasculation of union strength through physical repression and the drastic shrinking of traditional bases of union organization, have produced a situation where pressures from capital against significant labour and social policy reforms easily outweigh pressures in support of such reforms from labour and other popular groups.[47] In contrast, in Argentina civil society and particularly the labour movement had remained stronger than in Chile, despite repression of unions under the 1976–83 military government and a serious weakening of their base through deindustrialization. Accordingly, they were capable of defending the existing health care system and the principle of public responsibility for a major part of the pension system. Thus, despite Menem's rapid moves in a neoliberal direction, his government's pension reform programme only emulated the Chilean model in its supplementary part.

In Brazil, the military government also pursued a development project that was anti-labour and pro-capital. Nevertheless, in contrast to Chile, it attempted to build organized support bases in the rural sector and thus created the non-contributory scheme to be administered by the officially recognized syndicates. Electoral considerations during the long period of transition from authoritarian rule further promoted the allocation of resources to social policy on a patronage basis. After the return to democracy, the former opposition gained a foothold in important bureaucratic positions and used those as well as their influence in Congress to promote universalistic and egalitarian reforms. However, the very patronage bases of Brazilian politics that had facilitated the introduction of social policy programmes now obstructed the reform of these programmes in a more universalistic and redistributive direction. The political organization of popular movements and unions was simply not strong enough to overcome these obstacles, in particular due to the lack of links to disciplined parties. In contrast, in Costa Rica the strength of the social democratic PLN and of civil society, in the form of labour unions, cooperatives, and peasant associations, facilitated the government's continued pursuit of a comparatively egalitarian pattern of social policy. Even during the most severe period of austerity the government managed to protect the social achievements, and the PLN as well as the opposition parties remained responsive to popular interests.

The prospects for future developments in all four countries, but particularly in Brazil and Costa Rica, have a similar bottom line: to transform legal mandates into reality, specifically those with universalistic aspirations, significant additional resources will have to be allocated to social policy. Since the constraints of international competition will militate against increasing employer contributions and thus labour costs, more of these resources will need to come out of general revenue. Accordingly, governments will have to increase state revenue. At 1990–1 levels of revenue of 15 per cent of GDP in Argentina and Costa Rica, 24 per cent in Brazil, and 27 per cent in Chile (IDB, 1993) there is certainly room for increase. The need to increase state revenue has been recognized and tax reform has been high on the political agenda of the governments in these countries. Whether governments will be able to increase revenue depends first on the political coalitions that can be formed in support of tax reform, second on the capacity of the state apparatus to enforce tax legislation, and third on a rate of economic growth that enlarges the tax base.[48] Improvement of state capacity is crucial not only for enforcement of tax legislation but also for managing social policy. Duplication, inefficiency, and corruption have led to disproportionate administrative expenditures in the social security systems of Latin American countries. Accordingly, administrative reform should enjoy a high priority in efforts to make the welfare state more universalistic.

What are the lessons to be drawn from the preceding analysis for Latin American countries with social policy patterns at still lower levels of development? The central problems in Latin America are poverty and un- or underemployment. Poverty is not concentrated among the elderly and the sick but affects a large proportion of people of working age and their children as well. Therefore, traditional employment-based welfare state schemes are inappropriate solutions. They perpetuate poverty among those without access to more or less stable employment in the formal sector and their families. To address the problem of poverty in old age and sickness for the entire population, non-contributory schemes, or schemes with minimal contribution requirements, for those in the informal sector are needed. A system of basic flat rate pensions, financed out of general revenue and with entitlement based on citizenship, would meet these needs. This system should be complemented by a public system of contributory, non-subsidized, capitalized pensions.[49]

Health care is arguably the most important welfare state programme in the Latin American context. The entire population needs it and, as the Costa Rican example demonstrates, it is within the technical (if not political) capabilities of most Latin American countries to establish an effective and close to universalistic system. Again, a combination of contributory and non-contributory coverage is needed, but the facilities for both categories should be the same, lest the facilities of the non-contributory scheme be underfunded and inadequate. Of particular importance is an emphasis on preventive and primary health care for poor areas. It is difficult to imagine how such a system could be constructed on the basis of other than public provision of services; private providers are likely to impose their own preferences for expensive curative care in major urban areas and they are more likely to overtreat patients and overcharge the public purse.

Other important programmes for the welfare of Latin American populations are nutritional programmes for poor children and mothers, as well as subsidies for basic foodstuffs. The argument that such subsidies also benefit middle- and upper-income earners is true, but they do so to a much lesser extent because of the lower percentage of their income that these groups spend on basic foodstuffs. Moreover, such subsidies are much cheaper to implement than alternatives like the means-tested distribution of food or food stamps, and they are not subject to the abuses for patronage purposes typical of the latter type of programmes.

The 'social funds' approach, or the targeted emergency programmes currently advocated and partly financed by international financial institutions, can make important contributions to alleviating poverty, but caution has to be exercised lest they become mere palliatives. Such programmes can be very helpful, as long as they do not detract from the basic task of building permanent universalistic programmes and institutions. The danger is that such programmes lead to a diversion of resources and to duplication because of the creation of new institutions to administer them. They can be of greater long-term benefit if they are tied to a reform of and integrated into existing institutions and programmes to better serve the most vulnerable groups. A second danger is that such programmes, by virtue of being targeted, increase the discretion of political leaders and bureaucrats with regard to the allocation of resources and thus the incentives for patronage and corruption.

Five basic points emerge from these reflections that policy-makers in Latin American countries at lower levels of welfare state development should learn from the experience of countries with relatively advanced welfare state programmes. First, the initial design of the social policy model is of great importance. If a model is set up with segmented and unequal programmes, it will be very difficult to change it in a universalistic and egalitarian direction later, because the privileged groups will resist such changes and they tend to be politically more influential than the potential beneficiaries of reforms. This is a matter of concern not just for policy-makers with egalitarian values but also for those concerned with the financial solvency of welfare state schemes; entitlements of relatively small groups can put a heavy financial strain on the entire system. Second, if health care programmes are to contribute to national development by improving the health of the mass of the population and thus of the future labour force, the health care system has to be set up on the basis of public facilities. Private providers will claim large amounts of resources for curative medicine and resist an allocation of resources to preventive and primary care in poor areas. Like privileged groups of beneficiaries, private doctors, hospitals, and drug companies are generally in politically strong positions to defend their interests, once they have been allowed to assume an important role in the health care system of a country. In the case of many states, the establishment of an effective public health system would require previous administrative reform of the state apparatus. Third, given the new more open economic environment, traditional financing methods based heavily on employer contributions will have to be changed. Financing from general revenue does not increase labour costs and thus does not reduce the competitiveness of national production. Fourth, welfare state policies have to be conceived broadly and not confined to social insurance. To reach the quarter or more of the economically active population outside the formal sector, non-contributory schemes have to be developed for pensions and health care. In addition, nutritional pro-grammes need to be integrated with other welfare state policies as they directly affect levels of health and poverty. Fifth, in all welfare state programmes the discretionary power of bureaucrats and politicians should be kept to a minimum in order to minimize opportunities for corruption and for the building of patronage bases. Universalistic rules, then, are desirable not only from the point of view of equity but also from the point of view of efficiency, as corruption and patronage inevitably result in a waste of scarce resources in Latin American welfare state programmes.

Notes

I would like to thank Sergio Berensztein, Pamela Graham, and Leonard Ray for research assistance on this chapter, and Gøsta Esping-Andersen, Jonathan Hartlyn and John D. Stephens for comments on an earlier draft. I would also like to thank the Swedish Collegium for Advanced Study in the Social Sciences where revisions on this chapter were completed. This chapter is a shortened version of the paper written for the UN World Summit. The original version has been published as a Working Paper by the United Nations Research Institute for Social Development in Geneva and can be obtained from them.

1 Education and, depending on the country, housing have been additional important components of social policy. Given the orientation of this volume, though, this chapter will

concentrate on traditional social security aspects of social policy, primarily pensions and health care.

2 The figures on coverage in this section are all drawn from Mesa-Lago (1994: 21–2). Getting accurate figures on coverage is extremely difficult, and accordingly estimates of coverage rates vary rather widely among different sources. Mesa-Lago has been working on this subject for 30 years and is generally recognized as a leading authority. Thus, for the purposes of this section, which are simply classificatory, his figures can be accepted as good approximations. For the discussion of the cases, a variety of figures will be considered. Mesa-Lago's (1989; 1994) figures are generally higher than those from other sources (e.g. Isuani, 1985: 95; Tamburi, 1985: 77). The most difficult country is Brazil: Mesa-Lago gives a figure of 96 per cent of the economically active population for 1980, Isuani gives 49 per cent, and Tamburi gives 25 per cent in 1970 and indicates missing information for 1981. Isuani's figure is clearly too low, because it is very close to the figure for the percentage of the workforce paying social security taxes (Weyland, 1991: 581) and thus excludes all those covered under the non-contributory rural scheme. Mesa-Lago's figure is close to official government figures and represents legal entitlements, which of course are much higher than the proportion of those having a social security record, data for which are lacking. Coverage of the population at large through health insurance more or less parallels that of pension coverage (Mesa-Lago, 1994: 21–2).

3 Portes and Walton (1981: 67–106) develop this conceptualization of the informal sector, and Portes (1985) discusses the development of the informal sector in Latin America and shows that it remained larger than at comparable stages of development in the United States.

4 Historically, the first programmes established were typically for occupational risks, followed by maternity and sickness insurance and pensions for invalidity, old age, and survivors. By 1980, virtually all countries in Latin America and the Caribbean had these three types of coverage (Mesa-Lago, 1994: 16).

5 For an analysis of the relationship between economic development and democracy, see Rueschemeyer et al. (1992). Chile was a restricted democracy until 1970, as illiterates and thus a large proportion of the rural population were excluded. However, in the urban sector electoral competition led to an extension of benefits to all sectors of the working class. In the late 1960s, when the Christian Democrats competed with the left in the mobilization of the rural sector, benefits were extended to that sector as well.

6 To some extent, the countries with the highest coverage are also the most developed ones, and at the other end those with lowest coverage the least developed ones. However, there are important exceptions that demonstrate the importance of political dynamics in shaping social policy. Costa Rica's GNP per capita in 1980 was lower than that of the other members of the first group, but its particular political history had produced a social policy pattern that came closer to a social democratic welfare state than any other in Latin America. Jamaica's GNP per capita was slightly lower even than Costa Rica's, but the political constellation with two highly competitive parties based on coalitions between middle and working classes had led to an expansion of social policy. On the other hand, Mexico's GNP per capita in that year was higher than that of Brazil and Chile, but the growth orientation of successive Mexican governments had led to a relative neglect of social policy and the hegemonic position of the PRI had shielded policy-making elites from popular pressures in that area.

7 The report on the system ordered by President Alessandri (1958–64) estimated that the uninsured paid 41 per cent of the social security costs through taxes and the transfer of employer contributions to the costs of goods and services. Moreover, only 42 per cent of uninsured contributions went to the blue-collar fund that served 70 per cent of all insured (Borzutzky, 1983: 98–113). On the other hand, looking mainly at public social spending on different income brackets and citing figures from Foxley et al. (1979), Raczynski argues that in 1969 the social security system had a mildly progressive impact (1994: 24–5, 43). However, she does not take into account the fact that employers in protected markets passed on their social security contributions to prices, which affected uncovered groups along with covered ones. Looking just at those covered, another study for the early 1970s in Chile showed that social

security had a slightly progressive effect from the highest to the lowest of the insured (cited in Mesa-Lago, 1985; 329).

8 His figures for the percentage of the population of pension age receiving pension benefits are 58 per cent in 1980 and 61 per cent in 1990; for the population over 70 it is 72 per cent at the end of the 1980s (Isuani and San Martino, 1993: 18–25).

9 Chile and Argentina as the highest spenders were at roughly 70–80 per cent of the lowest spenders among the advanced industrial countries, such as the US with 12 per cent in 1980, but way below the medium and high spenders, such as Austria with 21 per cent and Sweden with 31 per cent. In Argentina, Brazil, and Chile, where pension systems had been introduced comparatively early and therefore had matured, the bulk of social security spending went to pensions; in 1986 Argentina spent 77 per cent on pensions, Brazil 63 per cent, and Chile 71 per cent. In Costa Rica, with a much younger pension system, only 27 per cent of social security spending went to pensions, and 66 per cent went to sickness/maternity insurance and health care (Table 6.7).

10 For instance, only the Costa Rican pension system had a redistributive component, with a replacement rate based on the average of the highest 48 monthly salaries during the last 10 years of coverage and structured as follows: 70 per cent of the first 300 colones, 50 per cent of the next 300, 40 per cent of the next 300, 35 per cent of the next 2400, and 40 per cent above 3300 colones, plus an increment of 0.125 per cent for each month of contributions (USDHHS, 1982). The qualification for retirement was 57 and 408 months of contributions or 65 and 120 months. There are no good comparative studies of the distributive impact of Latin America social insurance (see e.g. Musgrove, 1985: 187–208). Most case studies point to a regressive or neutral impact (Mesa-Lago, 1983: 95), particularly where coverage is very restricted. The potentially most progressive part is health care; Mesa-Lago (1991: 106) cites figures for Brazil and Chile (under the old system) that show that lower-income groups paid a lower percentage of the total contributions to the health care system but received a higher proportion of health benefits, and in Costa Rica the health benefits increased the percentage of total income of the poorer 60 per cent, and mostly of the poorest 20 per cent of the population. Raczynski (1994: 25) confirms the redistributive impact of public health spending under the old system in Chile.

11 All the information on characteristics of social security programmes presented in this section is drawn from US Department of Health and Human Services (1982).

12 All the percentage totals refer to contributions for pensions, sickness/maternity and medical care, and family allowances. They are calculated from USDHHS (1982).

13 In Argentina the contributions were 16.5 per cent for the employers and 15 per cent for the workers; the government theoretically paid 139 per cent of the contributions of the insured to the pension system. Before the reform, employers had paid over 30 per cent for all social security contributions. Employers paid 15.5–17.5 per cent in Brazil and 16.5 per cent in Costa Rica, compared with 8 per cent for employees in the former and 6.5 per cent in the latter country. In Costa Rica, the government was to contribute 0.5 per cent of total covered earnings as well as yields of a sales tax; in Brazil the government was to contribute various taxes. In Chile, blue-collar workers' contributions were 23 per cent of their earnings, with the government contributing special subsidies to various funds. Prior to the 1974–9 reforms, the employers' contribution had reached 38 per cent or more of the payroll (Mesa-Lago, 1985: 344), and it was brought down to 27 per cent before being eliminated altogether.

14 For a discussion of the origins and changes of the concept of informality, see Portes and Schauffler (1993: 3–8).

15 The estimates for self-employed and employees in small enterprises do not distinguish between high- and low-income earners, and the total does not include workers hired informally by larger enterprises.

16 For instance, in Brazil in 1977, 75 per cent of the self-employed working population was without coverage, particularly the very low-income self-employed, with over 90 per cent, and still 29 per cent of the high-income self-employed (Isuani, 1985: 96; see also Lopes, 1994: 15).

17 CEPAL defines the poverty line as two times the cost of a nutritionally balanced basic food basket for metropolitan/urban areas, and 1.75 times the cost of a basic food basket in rural areas. Chile was not included in this CEPAL report, but León (1994: 4) cites CEPAL

figures for 1987 of 38 per cent. The Chilean government's own figures were 24 per cent for 1978 and 26 per cent for 1988, which appears grossly understated given that in 1982 almost one-third of the labour force was unemployed and a survey under the new democratic government in 1990 showed a poverty rate of 40 per cent (Díaz, 1993: 21–2).

18 According to PREALC (1988: 10) estimates, the average annual transfer abroad (net capital transfers plus the variation in the terms of trade) for 10 Latin American countries amounted to 6.9 per cent of GDP in 1983, 7.5 per cent in 1985, and 5.3 per cent in the period 1985–90.

19 The literature on the debt crisis, the exhaustion of the ISI model, and structural adjustment is voluminous. See e.g. Nelson (1989); Feinberg and Kallab (1984); Handelman and Baer (1989); Canak (1989); Haggard and Kaufman (1992).

20 The 'Washington consensus' became a convenient label for the neoliberal adjustment policies pushed particularly hard by the Reagan administration and the IMF (Williamson, 1990). However, Feinberg (1990: 21) points out that even in the Washington of the 1980s, e.g. in parts of the US Congress, the Brookings Institution, and the World Bank, there was considerable opposition to the radical neoliberal model.

21 The defenders of neoliberalism object to the validity of these models on the grounds that the East Asian and small European states are efficient whereas most Latin American states are not because of patronage and corruption. To a large extent, this characterization of Latin American states is correct. However, virtually all states have had efficient parts, and the implication for action is that the remainder of the state apparatuses should be reformed rather than demolished. There are simply no historical precedents of late developers that were successful in generating sustained growth, not to speak of equity, without state intervention.

22 The dramatic impact of such price increases led to many cases of spontaneous riots, looting of food stores, strikes, and other forms of protest (see Walton, 1989: 299–328).

23 In Argentina, total social expenditures fluctuated in the 1980s, beginning at 22 per cent of GDP in 1980 and ending at 20.8 per cent in 1990; in Chile there were similar fluctuations during the decade, beginning at 17 per cent in 1980 and declining to 14 per cent in 1990, after an increase to 22 per cent in 1982, the same level as in 1970; in Costa Rica they began the decade at 23 per cent and, after a steep decline to a low of 14 per cent in 1982, recovered to 21.5 per cent in 1989. If we look at the index of real social expenditures, with the index set at 100 in 1980, we see a decline to 85.5 in 1990 in Argentina; in Costa Rica we see a decline to 71 in 1982 and then a gradual recovery to 107 in 1989; comparable data for Chile were not given in that study, and Brazil was not included (Carciofi and Beccaria, 1993). Figures for Brazil from a separate CEPAL study (Azeredo, 1992) show fluctuations for total social expenditures for the federal government for the 1980s, beginning at 9.25 per cent of GDP and ending at 10.78 per cent in 1989. The same study offers a breakdown of expenditures for the federal and state governments for 1986, where the two levels of government are responsible for roughly equal proportions of the total, such that the figure comparable with those for the other countries in the Carciofi and Beccaria (1993) study above would be roughly 18.5 per cent in 1980 and 21.5 per cent in 1989.

24 Brazil was one of the countries that resisted radical neoliberal austerity and liberalization measures to a significant extent and instead sought other, more heterodox paths to adjustment.

25 Time-for-service pensions are pensions to which an employee acquires the right after a certain number of years of contributions, regardless of his/her age. The existence of such pensions leads to retirements well below the general pension age and thus, in pay-as-you-go systems, to high expenditures for long periods of retirement for their beneficiaries.

26 Argentina ran deficits in its social security system every year from 1980 to 1986, reaching a high of –3 per cent of GDP in 1981; the same is true for Chile, with a high of –7.7 per cent in 1982; Brazil ran deficits in its social security system of under –1 per cent of GDP in 3 years and broke even in the other three years between 1981 and 1986; only Costa Rica ran consistent surpluses in this entire period, ranging from 0.8 per cent in 1981 and 1982 to 2.6 per cent in 1985 (Mesa-Lago, 1994: 83).

27 For a discussion of its economic policies and their political underpinnings, see e.g. Foxley (1986).

28 The minimum pension in 1991 amounted to the equivalent of US$75 per month.

29 For instance, Mesa-Lago (1994: 123–4) estimates that in 1987 the commission represented an 18 per cent reduction in the deposit of an insured individual in the 10,000 pesos per month bracket, but only a 0.9 per cent reduction for someone with ten times that income; the commission burden for an average insured was some 9 per cent in 1991.

30 See Graham (1994: 21–53) for a discussion of anti-poverty programmes of the Pinochet and Aylwin governments.

31 Orthodox stabilization plans, as prescribed by the IMF, emphasize devaluation and a reduction or elimination of foreign exchange controls, cuts in the government deficit through reduction of expenditures and increase in revenue, wage controls, and lifting of price controls. Heterodox stabilization plans, generally frowned upon by the IMF, include more controls, for instance on prices, the operation of financial institutions, and foreign exchange.

32 As mentioned above, the federal government accounted for just slightly over half of total social expenditures in 1986, the other half being carried by state and municipal governments. Thus, to compare these figures to other countries, they should be doubled. The federal government accounted for two-thirds of social security and social assistance spending, slightly over one-third of spending on education, 71 per cent of health expenditures, but only 11 per cent of spending for housing (Azeredo, 1992).

33 This entire discussion of the reform attempts since 1985 is based on Weyland's (1991) extremely well researched study, unless otherwise noted.

34 The constitution did enshrine the principle of a universalistic and redistributive welfare system, despite specific decisions to the contrary by the constituent assembly. Subsequently, no effective reform programme was implemented to give substance to the social rights established in the constitution (Faria, 1994: 8).

35 This conflict had an additional dimension because the Ministry of Finance increasingly resorted to the use of social security funds to cover budget deficits (Melo, 1992).

36 Industrial output declined by 11.9 per cent from 1974 to 1983 and another 11.2 per cent from 1983 to 1990 (Smith, 1991: 66). As to wages, just looking at the 1980s, average real wages in 1993 were at 81 per cent of their 1980 level, and the minimum urban salary was at 49 per cent (ECLAC preliminary figures, cited in Powers, 1994). Open unemployment increased from 2.6 per cent in 1975 to 10.6 per cent in 1993 in the Greater Buenos Aires area, and from 6.4 to 8.8 per cent during this period in agglomerations in the interior; visible underemployment increased from 4.8 to 8.2 per cent and from 6.6 to 9.9 per cent in the two areas in the same period (Lo Vuolo and Barbeito, 1993: 134). Roughly another quarter of the labour force worked in the informal sector, including household help, the informal urban sector, migrant rural workers, and very small farmers (Lo Vuolo and Barbeito, 1993: 134). According to a major study of poverty by the National Institute of Statistics and Censuses, 37 per cent of households in the Greater Buenos Aires area fell below the poverty line in 1988, and the percentage in other urban areas was even higher (Powers, 1994).

37 On the one hand, between 1974 and 1987 there was a significant reduction of structural poverty as indicated by unsatisfied basic needs, mainly in shelter and access to sanitation and basic education, from 26 to 16 per cent of households in the metropolitan region; but on the other hand there was a great increase in impoverishment in this period, that is, in the proportion of households whose basic needs are met but that have income levels below the poverty line as indicated by the cost of a basic basket of goods and services, from 3 to 23 per cent (Golbert and Fanfani, 1994: 18–19).

38 These problems persisted despite a reimposition of the employer contribution to the pension system in 1984 and its increase to 16 per cent by 1991. The employee contribution was lowered from 11 to 10 per cent in 1987. Evasion of contributions reached 42 per cent among the employed in 1990 and 70 per cent among the self-employed (Lo Vuolo and Barbeito, 1993: 34–5).

39 Total government expenditures as a percentage of GDP fell drastically from 25 per cent in 1980 to 18 per cent in 1982, but recovered to 26 per cent by 1989. Total social expenditures

also declined from 16 per cent of GDP in 1980 to 13 per cent in 1982, but reached 16 per cent again in 1986 and remained at that level up to 1989. The area with the clearest decline was education, down from 6.1 per cent of GDP in 1980 to 4.5 per cent in 1989. Health expenditures declined as well, from 7.2 per cent in 1980 to a low of 5 per cent in 1985, and they did not recover to the 1980 level until 1989. Some analysts argue that expenditure cuts were particularly detrimental in preventive health care and thus affected the poorer sectors disproportionately (Chalker, 1994). In contrast, expenditures for social security and social assistance increased markedly, from 1.8 per cent in 1980 to 3.5 per cent in 1989.

40 In 1987, 42 per cent of pension expenditures went to only 20 per cent of pensioners in these special independent programmes (Mesa-Lago, 1994: 98–9).

41 The illiteracy rate declined from 10 per cent in 1980 to 7 per cent in 1990, infant mortality declined from 19.1 children under one year old per 1000 live births to 15.3, and life expectancy increased from 73 to 75 years.

42 In fact, when the open unemployment rate came down to 6 per cent in 1992, Chilean employers began to complain to the government about the danger this posed to wage levels and exports. In response, the Chilean government relaxed the controls on the borders to Bolivia, which meant that a large number of Bolivians could come into Chile as seasonal agricultural workers. I am indebted to Sergio Berensztein for bringing this point to my attention.

43 For a similar view, which sees the problem of poverty rooted in the income concentration and the extreme power imbalance in capital–labour relations that the military regime's policies brought about, see León (1994).

44 See e.g. Garretón (1994) for an argument about the weakness of social actors and the marginalization of vast sectors from the sociopolitical arena.

45 Argentina has gone further in economic liberalization than Brazil and suffered significant deindustrialization. Argentina's export base combines its traditional agricultural exports of beef and grain with manufactured exports. Compared with Chile's agricultural exports, beef, grain, and manufactured exports are less dependent on cheap labour, and thus there is less of a downward pressure on employer contributions. Accordingly, Argentina reimposed the employer contributions that had been abolished by the military government and raised them in the 1980s to deal with the fiscal crisis. However, employers are pushing hard for labour market flexibilization, particularly the reduction or abolition of severance pay. Argentina, Brazil, and Chile all have achieved consistent trade surpluses for the past ten years; the only exception being Argentina since 1992, in the wake of the appreciation of the exchange rate.

46 See Bresser Pereira (1993) and Sola (1994) for explanations of the sources and effects of the fiscal crisis. Sola argues that the 1988 constitution presents major institutional obstacles to a solution of this crisis, because it greatly strengthened the position of states and municipalities *vis-à-vis* the federal government.

47 Whereas business had agreed to slight tax increases in 1990 to boost social spending, by 1994 they already pressured the government to lower taxes again, despite the comparatively very low level of Chilean taxes.

48 The same arguments about coalitions and the balance of power as made for social policy reform apply here. The overwhelming strength of capital in Chile and the weakness of political parties in Brazil are serious obstacles to an increase in the tax burden on those who are most able to pay.

49 Mesa-Lago's (1991: 118) recommendations go in part along the same lines; he suggests a basic pension, maybe means tested, and in addition a supplementary programme tied to contributions, administered by public or private organizations. My reason for arguing for public over private supplementary pensions is that in practice public supplementary pension schemes are less unequal than private ones. Public mandates for privately administered supplementary pensions could theoretically neutralize this difference, but they would still leave the profits from the administration of the pension funds in private hands. As noted above, a prerequisite for making such a public system work well in Latin America is administrative reform.

References

Azeredo, Beatriz (1992) 'O financiamento do gasto publico social na Argentina, no Brasil e no Chile: subsidios para uma analise comparativa'. CEPAL Proyecto Regional sobre Reformas de Política para Aumentar la Efectividad del Estado en América Latina y el Caribe, HOL/90/S45.

Baer, W., Biller, D. and McDonald, C. (1989) 'Austerity under different political regimes: the case of Brazil', in Howard Handelman and Werner Baer (eds), *Paying the Costs of Austerity in Latin America.* Boulder, CO: Westview Press.

Borzutzky, Silvia (1983) 'Chilean politics and social security policies'. PhD dissertation, Department of Political Science, University of Pittsburgh.

Bresser Pereira, Luiz Carlos (1993) 'Efficiency and politics of economic reform in Latin America', in Luiz Carlos Bresser Pereira, José Maria Maravall and Adam Przeworski (eds), *Economic Reforms in New Democracies.* Cambridge: Cambridge University Press.

Canak, William L. (ed.) (1989) *Lost Promises: Debt, Austerity, and Development in Latin America.* Boulder, CO: Westview Press.

Carciofi, Ricardo and Beccaria, Luis (1993) 'Provisión y regulación pública en los sectores sociales: lecciones de la experiencia Latinoamericana en la década del ochenta', UNICEF/CEPAL Taller sobre Reformas de las Políticas Públicas y Gasto Social, Santiago, Chile.

Casas, Antonio and Vargas, Herman (1980) 'The health system of Costa Rica: toward a national health service', *Journal of Public Health Policy,* September: 258–79.

Castells, Manuel and Portes, Alejandro (1989) 'World underneath: the origins, dynamics, and effects of the informal economy', in A. Portes, M. Castells and L.A. Benton (eds.), *The Informal Economy: Studies in Advanced and Less Developed Countries.* Baltimore: Johns Hopkins University Press.

CEPAL (1990) 'Magnitud de la pobreza en América Latina en los años ochenta'. LC/L 533 (Mayo).

Chalker, Cynthia H. (1994) 'Social policy, equity, and adjustment: the case of Costa Rica'. Paper delivered at the XVIIIth International Congress of the Latin American Studies Association, Atlanta.

Diamond, Peter and Valdés-Prieto, Salvador (1994) 'Social security reforms', in Barry P. Bosworth, Rudiger Dornbusch and Raúl Labán (eds.), *The Chilean Economy: Policy Lessons and Challenges.* Washington, DC: Brookings Institution.

Díaz, Alvaro (1993) 'Restructuring and the new working classes in Chile: trends in waged employment, informality and poverty 1973–1990'. United Nations Research Institute for Social Development, Geneva, Discussion Paper 47.

ECLAC (1994) *Economic Panorama of Latin America 1994.* United Nations, Economic Commission for Latin America and the Caribbean.

Esping-Andersen, Gøsta (1990) *The Three Worlds of Welfare Capitalism.* Princeton, NJ: Princeton University Press.

Faria, Vilmar E. (1994) 'The current social situation in Brazil: dilemmas and perspectives'. Kellogg Institute, University of Notre Dame, Democracy and Social Policy Series, Working Paper no. 1.

Feinberg, Richard E. (1990) 'Comments', in John Williamson (ed.), *Latin American Adjustment: How Much has Happened?* Washington DC: Institute for International Economics. pp. 21–4.

Feinberg, Richard E. and Kallab, Valeriana (eds) (1984) *Adjustment Crisis in the Third World.* New Brunswick, NJ: Transaction Books.

Foxley, Alejandro (1986) 'The neoconservative economic experiment in Chile', in J. Samuel Valenzuela and Arturo Valenzuela (eds), *Military Rule in Chile.* Baltimore, MD: Johns Hopkins University Press.

Foxley, Alejandro, Aninat, E. and Arellano, J.P. (1979) *Redistributive Effects of Government Programs.* Oxford: Pergamon Press.

Garretón, Manuel Antonio (1994) 'The political dimension of processes of transformation in

Chile', in William C. Smith, Carlos H. Acuña and Eduardo A. Gamarra (eds), *Democracy, Markets, and Structural Reform in Latin America: Argentina, Bolivia, Brazil, Chile, and Mexico*. New Brunswick, NJ: Transaction Books.

Golbert, Laura and Fanfani, Emilio Tenti (1994) 'Poverty and social structure in Argentina: outlook for the 1990s'. Kellogg Institute, University of Notre Dame, Democracy and Social Policy Series, Working Paper no. 6.

Graham, Carol (1994) *Safety Nets, Politics and the Poor: Transitions to Market Economics*. Washington, DC: Brookings Institution.

Haggard, Stephan and Kaufman, Robert R. (1992) *The Politics of Economic Adjustment*. Princeton, NJ: Princeton University Press.

Handelman, Howard and Baer, Werner (eds) (1989) *Paying the Costs of Austerity in Latin America*. Boulder, CO: Westview Press.

IBRD (1986) *World Development Report 1986*. New York and Washington, DC: Oxford University Press for the World Bank.

IDB (1993) *Economic and Social Progress in Latin America: 1993 Report*. Baltimore, MD and Washington, DC: Johns Hopkins University Press, for the Inter-American Development Bank.

Isuani, Ernesto Aldo (1985) 'Social security and public assistance', in Carmelo Mesa-Lago (ed.), *The Crisis of Social Security and Health Care: Latin American Experiences and Lessons*. University of Pittsburgh, Center for Latin American Studies, Latin American Monograph and Document Series, no. 9.

Isuani, Ernesto Aldo and San Martino, Jorge A. (1993) *La Reforma Previsional Argentina: Opciones y Riesgos*. Buenos Aires: Miño y Dávila Editores SRL.

León Batista, Arturo (1994) 'Urban poverty in Chile: its extent and diversity'. Kellogg Institute, University of Notre Dame, Democracy and Social Policy Series, Working Paper no. 8.

Lopes, Juarez Rubens Brandao (1994) 'Brazil 1989: a socioeconomic study of indigence and urban poverty'. Kellogg Institute, University of Notre Dame, Democracy and Social Policy Series, Working Paper no. 7.

Lo Vuolo, Ruben M. and Barbeito, Alberto C. (1993) *La Nueva Oscuridad de la Política Social: Del Estado Populista al Neoconservador*. Buenos Aires: Miño y Dávila Editores SRL.

Malloy, James M. (1979) *The Politics of Social Security in Brazil*. Pittsburgh: University of Pittsburgh Press.

Melo, Marcus C. (1992) 'Explaining the failure to reform: social policy-making in Brazil's new republic'. Paper delivered at the XVIIth International Congress of the Latin American Studies Association, Atlanta.

Mesa-Lago, Carmelo (1978) *Social Security in Latin America: Pressure Groups, Stratification, and Inequality*. Pittsburgh: University of Pittsburgh Press.

Mesa-Lago, Carmelo (1983) 'Social security and extreme poverty in Latin America', *Journal of Development Economics*, 12: 83–110.

Mesa-Lago, Carmelo (1985) 'Alternative strategies to the social security crisis: socialist, market and mixed approaches', in Carmelo Mesa-Lago (ed.), *The Crisis of Social Security and Health Care: Latin American Experiences and Lessons*. University of Pittsburgh, Center for Latin American Studies, Latin American Monograph and Document Series no. 9.

Meso-Lago, Carmelo (1989) *Ascent to Bankruptcy: Financing Social Security in Latin America*. Pittsburgh: University of Pittsburgh Press.

Mesa-Lago, Carmelo (1991) 'Social security and prospects for equity in Latin America'. Washington, DC, World Bank Discussion Papers no. 140.

Mesa-Lago, Carmelo (1994) *Changing Social Security in Latin America: Toward Alleviating the Social Costs of Economic Reform*. Boulder, CO: Lynne Rienner.

Musgrove, Philip (1985) 'The impact of social security on income distribution', in Carmelo Mesa-Lago (ed.), *The Crisis of Social Security and Health Care: Latin American Experiences and Lessons*. University of Pittsburgh, Center for Latin American Studies, Latin American Monograph and Document Series no. 9.

Nelson, Joan (1989) 'Crisis management, economic reform, and Costa Rican democracy', in Barbara Stallings and Robert Kaufman (eds), *Debt and Democracy in Latin America*. Boulder, CO: Westview Press.

Pang, Eul-Soo (1989) 'Debt, adjustment, and democratic cacophony in Brazil', in Barbara Stallings and Robert Kaufman (eds), *Debt and Democracy in Latin America*. Boulder, CO: Westview Press.

Portes, Alejandro (1985) 'Latin American class structures: their composition and change during the last decades', *Latin American Research Review*, 20: 7–39.

Portes, Alejandro and Schauffler, Richard (1993) 'The informal economy in Latin America: definition, measurement, and policies', in Gregory K. Schoepfle and Jorge F. Pérez-Lopez (eds), *Work without Protections: Case Studies of the Informal Sector in Developing Countries*. Washington, DC: US Department of Labor, Bureau of International Labor Affairs.

Portes, Alejandro and Walton, John (1981) *Labor, Class, and the International System*. New York: Academic Press.

Powers, Nancy R. (1994) 'The politics of poverty in Argentina in the 1990s'. Paper delivered at the XVIIIth International Congress of the Latin American Studies Association, Atlanta.

PREALC (1988) 'Asumiendo la deuda social: qué es, cuánto es y cómo se paga'. Oficina Internacional del Trabajo, PREALC/318.

Raczynski, Dagmar (1994) 'Social policies in Chile: origin, transformations, and perspectives'. Kellogg Institute, University of Notre Dame, Democracy and Social Policy Series, Working Paper no. 4.

Rosenberg, Mark B. (1979) 'Social security policy-making in Costa Rica: a research report', *Latin American Research Review*, 15(1): 116–33.

Rueschemeyer, Dietrich, Huber Stephens, Evelyne and Stephens, John D. (1992) *Capitalist Development and Democracy*. Chicago, IL: University of Chicago Press.

Schoepfle, Gregory K. and Pérez-Lopez, Jorge F. (1993) 'Work and protections in the informal sector', in Gregory K. Schoepfle and Jorge F. Pérez-Lopez (eds), *Work Without Protections: Case Studies of the Informal Sector in Developing Countries*. Washington, DC: US Department of Labor, Bureau of International Labor Affairs.

Smith, William C. (1991) 'State, market and neoliberalism in post-transition Argentina: the Menem experiment', *Journal of Interamerican Studies and World Affairs*, 33(4): 45–82.

Sola, Lourdes (1994) 'The state, structural reform, and democratization in Brazil', in William C. Smith, Carlos H. Acuña and Eduardo A. Gamarra (eds.), *Democracy, Markets, and Structural Reform in Latin America: Argentina, Bolivia, Brazil, Chile, and Mexico*. New Brunswick, NJ: Transaction Books.

Tamburi, Giovanni (1985) 'Social security in Latin America: trends and outlook', in Carmelo Mesa-Lago (ed.), *The Crisis of Social Security and Health Care: Latin American Experiences and Lessons*. University of Pittsburgh, Center for Latin American Studies, Latin American Monograph and Document Series no. 9.

US Department of Health and Human Services (1982) *Social Security Programs throughout the World – 1981*. Washington, DC.

US Department of Health and Human Services (1992) *Social Security Programs Throughout the World – 1991*. Washington, DC.

Vergara, Pilar (1986) 'Changes in the economic functions of the Chilean state under the military regime', in J. Samuel Valenzuela and Arturo Valenzuela (eds.), *Military Rule in Chile*. Baltimore, MD: Johns Hopkins University Press.

Vergara, Pilar (1994) 'Market economy, social welfare, and democratic consolidation in Chile', in William C. Smith, Carlos H. Acuña and Eduardo A. Gamarra (eds), *Democracy, Markets, and Structural Reform in Latin America: Argentina, Bolivia, Brazil, Chile, and Mexico*. New Brunswick, NJ: Transaction Books.

Walton, John (1989) 'Debt, protest, and the state in Latin America', in Susan Eckstein (ed.), *Power and Popular Protest: Latin American Social Movements*. Berkeley: University of California Press.

Weyland, Kurt G. (1991) 'Democracy and equity: redistributive policy-making in Brazil's new republic'. PhD dissertation, Department of Political Science, Stanford University.

Williamson, John (ed.) (1990) *Latin American Adjustment: How Much Has Happened?*. Washington DC: Institute for International Economics.

Wilson, Richard R. (1985) 'The impact of social security on employment', in Carmelo Mesa-Lago (ed.), *The Crisis of Social Security and Health Care: Latin American Experiences and Lessons*. University of Pittsburgh, Center for Latin American Studies, Latin American Monograph and Document Series no. 9.

Zuvekas, Clarence Jr (1992) 'Costa Rica: the effects of structural adjustment measures on the poor, 1982–1990'. *Staff Working Paper No. 5*. Washington, DC: Agency for International Development, Bureau for Latin America and the Caribbean, Washington, DC, Staff Working Paper no. 5.

7

The East Asian Welfare States: Peripatetic Learning, Adaptive Change, and Nation-Building

Roger Goodman and Ito Peng

While the last couple of decades has seen a burgeoning of literature on East Asian countries, little is known outside the region about their social welfare systems. There are several reasons for this. First, and perhaps most obviously, is that there are very few written materials on the subject in English. Since only a few social welfare experts and researchers in the West speak or read an East Asian language, access to information is limited. Secondly, systematized social welfare itself has been a relatively new development amongst the industrialized East Asian countries. Even in Japan, which probably has the most 'advanced' social welfare system of all the industrialized East Asian countries, public and academic debates on the subject only began to develop after the 1970s. Given the relative youth of the subject, East Asian scholars of social welfare have, until very recently, tended to rely on and accept Western analyses of their own social welfare regimes rather than generate indigenous analyses.[1]

Another, perhaps less obvious, reason for the relative lack of *accurate* knowledge on social welfare systems in East Asia has to do with the way information on the subject has been used for ideological purposes by individuals and governments in both Western and East Asian countries to create a certain image of an 'oriental' system that may have little connection with ground-level reality. In the West the 'models' of small government, company/corporate welfare systems, and strong 'familial' traditions, for example, have been used by governments and individuals to argue variously for anything from the virtue of increased privatization and low public sector spending to the merits of shifting the social welfare burden on to the corporate sector and returning to the basics of family mutual aid (see Gould, 1993, for an overview of these debates). In a sense, these debates in North America and Western Europe about Japanese social welfare tell us more about those countries – and their own concerns – than they do about Japan. Hence, while, until recently, East Asian countries have been criticized in the West for being welfare laggards, in some quarters they are now being looked to as leaders in market-conservative social welfare. Similarly, political rhetoric in Malaysia, Thailand and elsewhere in Asia about 'looking to Japan' for models of development needs to be examined in the light of local political and economic conditions and debates about welfare provision. Finally, simplistic accounts of welfare have also been employed *within* Japan, Korea and Taiwan, particularly in recent years, to argue against the further expansion of public social welfare entitlement.

Some recent comparative social welfare research, however, has attempted to include Japan in its analyses (Mishra, 1990; Esping-Andersen, 1990; Heidenheimer et al., 1990). In most cases, though, analyses have sought to fit Japan into one of a variety of pre-existing social welfare models conceptualized from a Western framework rather than examining it in its own terms. One result of such a Western-focused approach has been that the social welfare regime found in Japan has been often regarded as an 'exception' to the rule rather than as a new pattern. The recent developments in the newly industrialized countries (NICs) of East Asia such as South Korea (also known as the Republic of Korea), Taiwan (Republic of China), Hong Kong, and Singapore, suggest that there may be a case for discussing what might be called 'East Asian social welfare regimes', which diverge from the 'Western' pattern (Jones, 1990; 1993; Midgley, 1986).

In this chapter we argue that although historically Japan, South Korea, and Taiwan may have actively adopted various aspects of Western social welfare, and reassembled and reconstituted them into their own systems according to their respective cultural, political, and social backgrounds, it would be difficult to demonstrate that these social welfare regimes have copied or even followed any particular Western pattern; instead, social welfare regimes in these countries need to be examined in their own particular contexts.

A good example of this thesis is the case of the Japanese social welfare system, particularly since the mid 1970s, where there has been a decisive divergence away from any Western pattern. This has prompted authors such as Baba (1978) to put forth the proposition that Japan should develop what might be called a 'Japanese-style social welfare system' (*Nihongata shakai fukushi*), a social welfare system notably characterized, first, by a particularistic social insurance system, and second, by a strong reliance on the family as the site of social welfare and service delivery. This proposition has been strengthened in subsequent years. The Japanese government positively endorsed such a model in the 1980s, as illustrated by the social welfare administrative/fiscal reform programme of 1981 (see Zenkoku Shakai Fukushi Kyōgikai, 1989 for recent debates on social welfare reforms and their implications in Japan). A similar observation can be made for South Korea. The recent re-emphasis on Confucian family ethics by the Korean state as a social welfare strategy to deal with the rapid nucleariz- ation of families, due in part to the movement of younger individuals and families from the rural areas to the urban centres, also points to an attempt to seek solutions from within its own traditional cultural framework rather than adapting Western patterns. We argue that there is a general shift away from the pattern of social welfare development along 'Western' lines, at least among the newly industrialized East Asian countries of Taiwan and Korea and post-industrial Japan.

Indeed, we believe that there is a good case for talking about the development of what might be called 'Japan-focused East Asian social welfare regimes' as seen in Taiwan and Korea. These regimes, like Japan, have incorporated many aspects of Western social welfare ideas, but, in practice, deviate fundamentally from Western experience. This does not imply that the developmental patterns followed by the social welfare systems found in these countries are destined to converge into one model, nor does it deny that potential links exist between these regimes and those found in the industrialized Western countries. What it suggests are, first, that we need to begin examining social welfare in East Asian countries as a regional cluster and from a different perspective than hitherto, and second, that there is a need to analyse further the nature of social welfare found in these countries in order to gain a more precise picture of their similarities and differences.

The chapter will be divided into four sections. In the first section we define the field of our study by identifying underlying similarities in the political, social, economic and historical development of the societies under study. The second section will provide a brief overview of the post-war developments in social welfare in these countries. This will be followed by a discussion of more current developments of what might be best described as 'Japan-focused East Asian social welfare regimes'. Finally, the last section of this chapter will consider current issues confronting these countries and their implications for social welfare.

Defining the field

There is much confusion over how to define common areas in Asia. The range of countries, traditions and histories within Asia as a whole makes it impossible, perhaps more so than with any other continent, to talk of any 'Asian culture' or 'Asian model'. Within Asia, it is common to talk about a number of regional blocs (often political and economic as much as cultural) such as South Asia (essentially the Indian sub-continent), South East Asia (ASEAN countries) and North East Asia (China, Japan, Korea, Taiwan and Mongolia). Other definitions centre on economic development models (the NICs of Hong Kong, Singapore, Korea and Taiwan) and commonly perceived cultural backgrounds, such as Confucianism (Japan, Vietnam, the NICs etc.). In this chapter, we take as our frame of reference what we call 'East Asia'. As Rozman writes:

> In a world comprised of thousands of nationalities, hundreds of countries, and more than a dozen regions, East Asia reigns with Western Europe . . . as probably the greatest and most enduring regional force in world history. . . . Increasingly East Asia stands for a rare combination of rapid economic growth and high social stability, extraordinary individual effort and persistent group support. (1991: 4–5)

There are certain common points in the three sustaining 'national tradi-tions' in the area, Japanese, Chinese and Korean – which are here studied in the forms of Japan, Taiwan and South Korea (henceforth Korea)[2] – which allow for the comparative study of welfare in these three societies that may point to the development of a heuristically valuable East Asian social welfare model. It is important to stress, however, that East Asian peoples themselves have rarely adopted a regional focus, and in the case of Japan have, at times, attempted consciously to distance themselves from their neighbours. Some of these common points are as follows.

Historical links are strong. Japan, in part in the quest for an empire which would lead to it being accepted as 'modern', annexed Korea in 1895 and colonized it in 1910. Taiwan was ceded to the Japanese following the Sino-Japanese war in 1895. Japan remained in both countries until 1945. The Japanese wanted to integrate the Korean and Taiwanese economies into the Japanese Empire (Long, 1991: 28ff) and hence instituted a process of assimilation. Although the colonial period was experienced very differ-ently by the two native populations – with great resentment in Korea,[3] more benignly in Taiwan – both were left with a number of vital insti-tutions, financial, industrial, educational and political, which still today have much in common with Japanese contemporary systems.[4]

All three societies draw on the common *language* of Confucianism and, to a lesser extent, Mahayana Buddhism in the construction of their ethnic identity. (The two are often combined in a religious and philosophical syncretism which is characteristic of the region.) The utilization of these powerful rhetorics differs considerably between different areas and at different times (see Morishima, 1982). This 'language' has been powerfully utilized in debates about constructing a social welfare system culturally 'appropriate' to each society. In post-war Japan it is often referred to as *Nihonjinron* (theories of Japaneseness) rather than Confucianism, though the rhetoric is also largely recognized as having Chinese roots in common with other neighbouring societies. In Taiwan, the state has effectively employed a blend of Confucianism and Dr Sun Yat-sen's political ideology (much of which was strongly influenced by Bismarckian political theory) to advance the notion of a welfare mix which strongly emphasizes the roles of family and state sectors rather than community and corporate sectors.

The language of Confucianism includes important notions such as: respect for seniors, filial piety, paternal benevolence, the group before the individual, conflict avoidance, loyalty, dutifulness, lack of complacency, striving for learning, entrepreneurship and meritocracy. Diligence and hard work are given particularly high social status. Working hours are still among the highest in the world. Much emphasis is placed on 'familial' ideas of solidarity, inside/outside distinctions, patriarchal authority, strict gender role separation and female subordination, long-termism and family continuity, and fear of bringing shame. Studies have stressed similarities between Korean, Chinese and Japanese kinship patterns and how these have been drawn on to construct 'family-like' businesses. A basic underlying principle of Confucianism is that of original virtue: good leadership can produce good behaviour in others, a powerful form of 'moral suasion'. It also involves ideas of collective responsibility and acceptance of hierarchies.

Each society has traditionally had highly centralized bureaucracies and, in the post-war period, one-party domination until the present period which is seeing each go through a process of rapid political change. Central government, especially central bureaucracies, have been seen as key in co-ordinating industrial policy and economic growth. They are staffed by the most able who are assumed to be working for the good of the people and are given high respect.[5]

Each society in the post-war period has seen a period of great economic hardship and national devastation followed by the injection of large amounts of anti-communist American aid and spurts of spectacular economic growth (in Japan 1952–73, average annual growth rate around 11 per cent; Taiwan 1960–80, 10 per cent; Korea 1960–80, 9.5 per cent), followed by recent slow-downs. Major shifts occurred in employment from primary to secondary and tertiary sectors, together with rapid urbanization and, in places, rural depopulation. It is often argued that Korea and Taiwan are following a similar trajectory to that of the Japanese economy some ten to twenty years later.[6] In all these societies, in terms of material goods, the quality of life is at least equal with that in Western nations. For political reasons, especially in Japan, there has been some income redistribution from urban to rural areas in the form of financial support to small farmers.

Each society in the recent period of economic growth has been able to call upon a relatively young, and very highly educated, population to drive that growth. While each population is still relatively young, long-term predictions show that rapidly increasing longevity combined with equally fast-falling fertility rates will dramatically change the population structures by the second and third decades of the next century and also necessitate long-term planning about the financial implications of social welfare. This is particularly crucial to Japan as it has the highest proportion of elderly amongst the three, and moreover, its elderly population is strongly skewed towards the very old. The Japanese statistics suggest that the percentage of people over the age of 65 will reach 25.5 per cent by the year 2020, almost double that of today and surpassing that of most of the industrialized nations in the West, including the US, the UK, Sweden, Germany and France. Moreover, those over the age of 80 will increase to more than triple the current proportion.

Each society shows comparatively high savings rates which may be connected with the lack of state provision of social welfare, especially in old age.[7] Similarly, some have explained in the same way the labour force participation rate of the elderly[8] and the proportion of multi-generational households, both of which are high compared with Western nations. Indeed, recent statements by the Korean government concerning the impending problems of an ageing society seem to suggest a state-led strategy to anticipate and 'construct' welfare 'problems' well in advance.[9]

Economic growth has essentially been based on an export economy involving heavy investment in big business and little investment in internal infrastructure such as housing, parks, mainline sewerage, museums etc. Improving the quality of housing where there has been relatively little government investment is a major issue in all three societies.

In all the societies under study, investment in the labour force has been seen as crucial to economic growth: hence the high proportion of students receiving extended education, over 90 per cent continuing to the non-compulsory educational sector. This phenomenon is often presented in the light of resource scarcity in all areas (particularly in oil, minerals and usable land) except people. Investment in education has significance both at the national level – where the state has sought to create a system to produce an effective workforce – and at the personal level where, as individuals are largely ranked according to their educational background rather than their family standing, education is the key to social status and financial security. Education is particularly effective in science and mathematics and concentrates largely on attention to detail, task repetition, group work and rote learning, skills which are successfully transplanted to the workplace.

Ideologies of meritocracy and classlessness have meant that those who fail in society have little to fall back on and are seen to be responsible for their own failures.[10] Disability – physical and mental – is also highly stigmatized, which explains in part why, in Japan, official statistics for those with a disability are as low as 3 per cent. Similarly, in comparison with some other industrialized nations, there is little protection for the 'weaker' members of society; minimum wage levels, unemployment benefit, job security and high work safety levels exist only for those who gain the elite, core positions. Labour markets, therefore, demonstrate profound core–periphery distinctions that have had crucial significance for the types of social welfare systems which have developed.[11]

Relatively high, and rapidly rising, rates of female labour force participation mean that women are an essential part of the peripheral workforce in all these societies – the 1989 labour force participation of women was 59.3 per cent in Japan, 45.3 per cent in Taiwan, 46.5 per cent in Korea[12] – but, in times of recession, the rhetoric of the division of labour by gender (male, public sphere; women, domestic sphere) may be evoked. The idea of women as providers of domestic welfare may also be drawn upon. Feminist movements in the Western sense have had little impact and often women find themselves doing part-time work and also looking after elderly relatives.

Throughout much of the post-war period, with the important exceptions of Japan in 1945–7 and Korea and Taiwan currently, unionism has been weak and essentially covering only those 25–30 per cent of the workforce employed on full-time, permanent contracts in large companies. Unionism does not cover the majority of the labour force who work in small, often family-operated, enterprises with little security. In Japan, big company unionism has generally concerned itself with defending the interests of business and its own elite workers.

It has been argued (see Marmot and Smith, 1989) that post-war low unemployment rates, low reported crime rates and high crime clear-up rates, decreasing infant mortality rates, low inflation, ideologies of racial (and not just ethnic) homogeneity (there are very few post-war migrants in any of the countries) and classlessness lead to more stable – and predictable – life courses which may explain rapidly increasing longevity patterns.

Highly centralized systems of authority (even if delivery and finance in certain areas might be decentralized) have put much effort into the construction of a sense of national identity (built around images of racial homogeneity and classlessness) which have been essential for economic development. The populations in each country have begun to see themselves as largely middle class – for example, according to national surveys, about 90 per cent of Japanese consider themselves 'middle class' – though this 'middle class' contains significant economic disparities (see Ishida, 1993). As we shall see, the idea of constructing a specifically 'Japanese-style social welfare system' drawing on a powerful indigenous rhetoric should be seen, in part at least, in the context of the construction of 'Japaneseness'.[13] Similar processes can also be detected in Korea and increasingly in Taiwan. Emphasis is still placed in public on putting the group, community or country before individual desires, though it is recognized that individuals also have private agendas in which they can invest (such as private, extra education for their children).

In each society, a substantial, and increasing, proportion of the elite have overseas experience, especially in the United States, and are returning with new ideas to challenge the current system (see Goodman, 1990).

Very broadly speaking, welfare policy has been dominated by economic rather than social considerations supported by some underlying ideas of anti-welfarism and, especially, by resistance to the provision of government-guaranteed social welfare. The ruling elites have generally only accepted the institutional concept of social welfare when confronting political crisis; when this is overcome they return to the 'residual concept of social welfare' (Park, 1990) by drawing on 'Confucian' cultural ideologies. This pattern is particularly noticeable in Japan from the 1960s.

Development of social welfare in Japan, Korea, and Taiwan

Pre-war conditions

It is worthwhile pointing out here that although social welfare in the modern, Western sense of the term[14] did not become fully established in Japan, Korea, or Taiwan until fairly recently, this does not mean that social welfare as a concept or as a practice did not already exist in these countries. Rather, throughout most of their histories, the primary social welfare roles were assumed by the family, and sometimes the local community. While public relief and public assistance were available, they were mostly in the form of charity and local mutual aid reserved for truly destitute individuals without any family support and the state was able to assume what may be called a position of 'peripheral non-responsibility'[15] with regard to social welfare towards its citizens through the imposition of a combination of Confucian and Buddhist rhetoric. While the Confucian rhetoric extolled the virtues of filial piety, diligence, and conflict avoidance, the Buddhist teachings further reinforced these values with the notions of karma – the idea of benefit and obligation – and of private charity and acceptance of the status quo (Peng, 1995).[16]

In Tokugawa Japan (1600–1867), for example, the state imposed the *Gonin Gumi Seido* (group-of-five system) to ensure mutual aid and obligation among families. The system identified a group of five families as the basic administrative and legal unit for the purpose of mutual aid, taxation, and social control. This was further reinforced by the Meiji state (1868–1912) in the form of *Rinpo Sōfu*, a system of neighbourhood watch and mutual aid associations. The system necessitated mutual dependence among family members and residents of local neighbourhoods and villages, and thus relieved the state from social welfare provision (Anderson, 1987; Dore, 1967; Peng, 1995). In Japan, this system of neighbourhood watch and mutual aid continued until the end of the Second World War; in many rural areas especially, forms of it can still be found today. In Taiwan and Korea, the Japanese colonial government also imposed similar systems.

Although social welfare policies in these countries from the late nineteenth century to the end of the Second World War amounted to little more than official affirmation and institutionalization of family support and local mutual aid, evidence suggests that there was a general improvement in the material welfare of people, at least until the Second World War. This has been attributed to the strong and centralized state which was able to direct economic growth throughout most of the first half of this century.[17] For example, in Japan, within a decade of the Meiji restoration, the feudal class system was abolished and a national compulsory education system put in place. The Meiji government also carried out a land reform in 1872, redistributing land and enabling many peasant farmers to own land for the first time since 1643. Moreover, throughout the Meiji period, the government also put significant investment into the development of modern economic and industrial infrastructures, including the railway system, and the construction and management of new industries such as cotton, textiles, steel, armaments and ship building (Akamatsu, 1990; Nish, 1992).

In Korea, the Japanese invasion of 1895 and subsequent colonization in 1910 ended the Choson dynasty and crushed the traditional status system. The Japanese colonial government (i.e. the Meiji state) imposed a series of institutional reforms in Korea similar to those already introduced in Japan. These included a cadastral survey and land reform between 1910 and 1918, and the introduction of a capitalist economic system through the establishment of modern heavy industries such as steel, chemicals, and hydroelectric facilities. Kim (1991) contends that the Japanese occupation left two contradictory legacies in Korea. First, it left a lasting imprint of 'militaristic, bureaucratic, authoritarian political culture' which, while it hindered the process of democratization, was nevertheless effective in shaping authoritarian statist economic development and social welfare policy. Secondly, it also created a strong sense of *han*, 'a complex state of emotional resentment and regret, caused by acute frustration and injustice and often creating a desire for revenge or a feeling of hatred', towards the military government (Kim, 1991: 140). Kwon (1995) argues that effectively social welfare policy in Korea has been constructed by powerful but unpopular regimes seeking to legitimize themselves.

The impact of Japanese colonial policies on Taiwan was similarly ambivalent. Although there is no question that the Japanese occupation of Taiwan and Korea was by and large an exploitative one – the occupying government exploited the labour and resources of the occupied country to support the Japanese war effort (Prybyla, 1991) – it left some important institutional structures: land reform was carried out in Taiwan between 1896 and 1906; the colonial government also built a modern transportation system and introduced new agricultural technology, as well as establishing a Japanese-style education system, and other economic and industrial infrastructures.

Post-war development

The Japanese, Taiwanese, and Korean economies underwent dramatic changes after 1945, the most profound being the introduction of large amounts of Western, particularly American, investment. Under the American occupational government (GCHQ) the Japanese social welfare system underwent a complete overhaul. As in the case of the post-war Japanese constitution, the social welfare system in Japan was also reconstructed based on American ideology.

Although the constitutional statements concerning social welfare may be based on an idealized Western (American) social welfare model, in reality, evidence suggests different outcomes. Interpretations of the new constitution have always been prone to come into conflict with ideas enshrined in the earlier Meiji civil code (*Minpō*).[18] In the child welfare system, for example, while the new constitution stipulates the rights of all citizens and the state's obligation to ensure such rights, in reality, the parental rights prescribed under the civil code have almost always taken precedence over those of children (Goodman, 1993; Kinoshita, 1991; Peng, 1992; Takahashi and Peng, 1992).

Similarly, while article 25 stipulates the government's obligation to ensure a minimum standard of living for all citizens, the Japanese Supreme Court has historically interpreted this statement as an 'expression of the state's political and ethical obligation' – what Burks (1985: 41) calls a 'program clause' – and has entrusted actual policy-making on social security to the judgement of the government legislature and administration as in the pre-war period (JNC-ICSW, 1988; 1990). Such an interpretation has meant that, except for a series of social welfare programmes initiated during the years under the occupying government in response to immediate post-war needs – such as the Daily Life Security Law (1946, revised in 1950), Child Welfare Law (1947), Law for the Welfare of Physically Handicapped Persons (1949), and Social Welfare Service Law (1951) – no new provisions on social welfare were made until the 1960s.

Indeed, the trajectory followed by the development of the Japanese social welfare system in the post-war period suggests that, with the exception of a brief episode in the early 1970s, priority has always been on economic growth and industrial development. In this sense, the basic orientation of the Japanese government towards social welfare has not changed significantly since the Meiji period. For example, even during the period of high economic growth between 1955 and 1975, the government kept the expenditure on social welfare relative to national income stable at around 2 per cent of the GNP (Bronfenbrenner and Yasuba, 1987; Tabata, 1990), while the lack of social welfare outlay was compensated by a high household saving rate at between 13 and 20 per cent (Tabata, 1990). It has also been argued that the immediate post-war social welfare vacuum was filled by the expansion of pre-war-style company welfare programmes (pensions, housing and health care) which were provided by the biggest companies for their full-time workers under pressure from their unions (Hiwatari, 1993).[19]

A similar kind of economic growth and industrial development pattern of social welfare can be seen in Korea and Taiwan. Korea was divided in 1945 and internal struggles within the South over the next five years left the country in chaos and disorder. The Korean War lasted for three years (1950–3), by the end of which the American-backed, anti-communist military regime under the leadership of Syngman Rhee took power in the South. This bureaucratic authoritarian regime remained until the democratization process of the late 1980s. The Korean War decimated the country's economic and industrial structures. Between 1953 and 1960, no social welfare programmes were established owing to the lack of an economic infrastructure.[20] Although the first five-year economic plan in 1962 marked the beginning of the welfare system in Korea, it remained subsidiary to economic and industrial development policies. Until the 1980s, much of social welfare in Korea was focused on employee pension and health care schemes, while the rest of the population had little option but to rely on individual work effort and family support and, failing that, on the livelihood protection (introduced in 1961), a very basic form of poor relief (Chang, 1985).[21]

Taiwan, on the other hand, experienced a brief moment of independence under the nationalist government immediately after 1945. However, the independent Taiwanese government was soon quashed in 1949 when

Chiang Kai-shek and the Kuomintang (KMT) government fled from the mainland and re-established themselves as the *de facto* government of the new Republic of China (ROC). During the Cold War era, the involvement of the People's Republic of China (PROC) in the Korean War (1950–3) further reinforced the political and strategic alliance between the anti-communist governments of Taiwan and the United States. Until the American recognition of the PROC in the 1970s, Taiwan benefited greatly from the American recognition of ROC status in international politics. Even after the American recognition of PROC, Taiwan continued to enjoy preferential treatment over imports into the US domestic market, in addition to ongoing American military and economic aid. After the American recognition of the PROC, however, Taiwan's international status declined: it was stripped of its seat at the UN and became increasingly marginalized in international politics. The pressures for political liberalization and social development in Taiwan after the 1970s can be partly attributed to the imperative need to avoid further international isolation. The pressure for democratization and social development was further strengthened after the death of Chiang Kai-shek in 1975.

During the first three decades following the end of the Second World War, all three countries – Japan, Taiwan, and Korea – experienced a period of high economic growth, and most scholars agree that, by and large, economic growth substituted for social welfare during most of the post-war period. In the case of Japan, major employers, having in the 1950s expanded their pre-war programmes, were reluctant to pay more for public welfare and jeopardize those programmes which had proved very effective in coopting and keeping good workers. The unions of these big companies were similarly indifferent to public welfare reforms, leaving only Sōhyō, representing workers in smaller firms, pressing for new policies. In Taiwan and Korea, the success of their import-substituting industrialization policies was to a large extent accounted for by the respective authoritarian regimes which played a large role in ensuring the exclusion of labour from decision-making and the frequent exploitation of workers, particularly women. For example, in both Taiwan and Korea, union strikes were prohibited, and unions which did exist were often organized by the state (see Lin, 1991 for an insightful analysis of labour unions in Taiwan). Moreover, in free export zones such as Kaoshiung and Masan some 80 per cent of the workforce has been female, the majority of whom are teenage girls from rural areas, and who have been paid at a third of the Japanese level, and one-fifth to one-tenth of the US level (Cumings, 1987).

In Japan, the 1960s saw a small expansion in social welfare for the first time since the war. These included the introduction of the following: welfare for mentally disabled persons (1960); national health insurance and national pension system (1961); welfare for the aged (1963); and maternal and child welfare (1964). The 1970s saw a further increase in public concern and a grass-roots political campaign for improving the 'quality of life'. This was illustrated by increasing community and public protest over issues like pollution and traffic accidents. Also, the late 1960s saw an emergence of political activism among the new generation of well-educated, middle-class youth and women's groups who were influenced by liberal Western ideas. For example, the late 1960s saw violent clashes between the state and the anti-war (Vietnam) student movement, and the rise of women's groups advocating such causes as increased child-care facilities for working mothers. These latter calls, to a large extent, met with support from trade unions and also companies who were keen that the state and not they should finance such expansion. As a result, Japan has a high level of provision of subsidized day nursery places with a current surplus of perhaps 20 per cent over the take-up rate (Peng, 1995).

Year One of the Welfare Era (*Fukushi Gannen*) introduced by the Japanese government in 1973 owed much to increasing public pressure for improved welfare, and the government's growing concern to shore up its declining support.[22] This period saw a fall in public support for the Liberal Democratic Party (LDP): in the 1967 Lower Diet election the party gained less than 50 per cent of the vote for the first time since its existence in 1955; in 1976, the party lost its majority in the Lower Diet (Tabata, 1990). Although much of the welfare improvement was seen in the massive increase in the benefit level of pensions,[23] indexing of pensions, and the introduction of free medical care for the aged, the public articulation of the idea that Japan had at last reached a stage whereby it could begin to call itself a new 'welfare state' was crucial to the public consciousness. Unexpectedly, the government's move towards the Welfare Era came to a sudden halt in 1974 when the oil crisis hit Japan along with most of the industrial countries. The unemployment rate in Japan rose threefold between 1975 and 1985, resulting in an increase in welfare expenditure. It is in this particular economic climate that the new neo-conservative backlash against the welfare state, at first in the form of a critique of the Western (particularly the British and American) experience, and then through the formulation of the idea of 'Japanese-style welfare', was to emerge (Shinkawa, 1990; Tabata, 1990; Hiwatari, 1993; Japan, 1993).

Beginning in the mid 1970s, there has been a trend in Japan towards an increasing concern for the rising cost of social welfare provision. The new political language of *fukushi minaoshi* (reconsideration of welfare) stressed that continuing welfare expansion would be dangerous for investment in a competitive economy.[24] A consensus was reached between a number of important interest groups – the Ministries of Health and Welfare and Finance, big business and their unions – each of which had its own agenda, that expansion in the field of welfare had to be curtailed. At the core of this consensus were again the managers and unions of big business, reflecting the bifurcated large-firm-company-welfare/small-firm-government-welfare system that had emerged in the 1950s (Hiwatari, 1993). The fiscal concern prompted an administrative/fiscal reform in 1981, the main aim being to reduce the central government's share of social welfare costs. The pressure for reform came partly from a genuine concern over future prospects for the Japanese economy, particularly in light of widespread anxiety over the rapidly ageing population. Another, less openly stated, cause of the reform movement was a general anxiety over the dangers of too much 'Westernization'. During the 1980s, the growth of the Japanese economy, in the face of economic instability in most Western industrialized nations, led to a sudden interest among Japanese scholars and opinion leaders in redefining Japan's position in the world. In short, the idea of moving away from following what had been viewed earlier as 'model' nations of the West gained significant ground in Japan during this time.

Following the administrative/fiscal reform of 1981, small but incremental changes were put in place to curtail welfare expansion and to shift a greater burden of social welfare back on to the individual and the community. These included: (a) putting surcharges on medical treatment for the elderly; (b) reducing the level of the coverage of health insurance; (c) increasing the entitlement age for national pensions (from 60 to 70 for men; 55 to 60 for women); and (d) imposing a 3 per cent sales tax.[25] More recently, the government has put much effort into promoting the idea of 'residential participation organizations', quasi-public-funded voluntary, mutual-help service banks run by local governments and community groups (Ichikawa, 1994). Such progress suggests increasing expectations of individual and community roles in social welfare, though such volunteer activity is frequently portrayed as returning to a 'traditional' provision of welfare.

The Japanese public seems to accept these changes without much resistance. This may be partly because the government has been very effective in raising public awareness about an ageing society and the potential costs this will entail. Also, the idea of developing a Western-style welfare state was actually only around a fairly short period of time and perhaps never took root. Rudd (1994: 17) argues that it is also due to the way in which 'the state has fostered the social stigma that many Japanese still attach to statutory social assistance'.[26] In addition, the economic slow-down in Japan since the end of the 1980s has further reinforced government and public anxiety over the rising cost of social welfare in the future. It has to be emphasized, therefore, that the reforms in the 1980s in Japan should not be seen as a neo-liberal assault on the welfare state but were largely reached by consensus, with only the left-wing (i.e. non-large firm) unions and the Socialist Party being in opposition. Certainly, the current problems of the Liberal Democratic Party should not be seen as punishment for introducing these reforms; if anything, evidence from the early 1980s suggests that they were rewarded by the electorate.

In Taiwan, despite the KMT's ideological slogans of *Min-Tsu Chu I* (the principle of nationalism), *Min-Chuan Chu I* (the principle of democracy), and *Min-Shen Chu I* (the principle of people's livelihood),[27] the first thirty years of the KMT rule were anything but free and democratic. Indeed, at least until the death of Chiang Kai-shek in 1975, Taiwan could be described more appropriately as an authoritarian military regime. During this period, the basic components of democratic society, such as freedom of speech, freedom of organization, and political activities were all prohibited as the country was in effect held under martial law that had been imposed in 1950 (Lin, 1993). Although Chiang Ching-kuo, who succeeded his father, initiated a series of reforms in the 1980s, his own sudden death in 1988 left the reform process incomplete. Under the Chiang Ching-kuo presidency (1978–88), martial law and the 'Emergency Decree' were abolished and opposition parties were allowed to organize themselves. This has been encouraged by the gradual replacement of the older generation of KMT party members by younger Taiwan-born politicians, many partly educated in the West. Moreover, there are also some signs of greater liberalization under the presidency of Lee Teng Hui (1988 to present).

As in the case of Japan and Korea, post-war social welfare development in Taiwan has been relatively modest, and has only begun to take off in recent years. While the government introduced the labour insurance scheme in 1958, this move was primarily motivated by the KMT's previous experience on the mainland, and was widely regarded in Taiwan as an appeasement measure to avoid potential worker revolts. Between 1958 and 1980, small incremental changes were made to the existing social insurance schemes, but no significant changes were seen. Most of the broader welfare measures in Taiwan were put in place in the 1980s, after the country had reached some measure of economic and democratic development.

Contemporary social welfare in Taiwan is still less organized than in Japan and Korea. For example, while no less than ten new major health insurance schemes have been introduced in Taiwan since 1980, they are all organized according to work/professional affiliations. Moreover, with the exception of the labour insurance scheme which covers approximately 37 per cent of the total population, none of the existing schemes individually covers more than 8 per cent of the population, and none of the new insurance schemes introduced since 1980 has coverage of more than 1 per cent. The percentage share of the premiums paid by the insured, employers, and government also varies from 0–100 per cent, depending on the scheme. Types of benefit also vary, although most cover medical benefits for sickness and injury, with or without additional cash benefits for other risks such as disability, old age, death, maternity, and funeral costs. The divisive nature of social insurance schemes in Taiwan is unlikely to diminish in the future.[28] On the contrary, the combination of the upsurge in interest-group politics since the mid 1980s and the lack of sectoral labour coalitions in the country have contributed to a further intensification of diversity and confusion, rather than aiding the unification of the social welfare system. A universal health care scheme has been promised for 1995–6, though its exact form and level of coverage – indeed whether it can be implemented at all – remains to be seen.

As in the case of Japan, in Taiwan there also exists a large gap between the constitutional statement concerning the state's obligations to provide social welfare and the reality of the existing social welfare system. Despite the state's obligation to provide social welfare, as outlined in articles 155 and 157 of the 'Chapter on Fundamental Policy' in the Taiwanese consti-tution, little has been actually done to achieve these goals. Part of the government's reluctance to develop social welfare lies in its own identity problem. Since the KMT has always regarded itself as the only legitimate government of China, and continues to publicly maintain its goal of reconquering and unifying with mainland China, economic development and defence have been given the highest policy priority. For example, in 1988, the central government spent 0.1 per cent of its social welfare budget on labour welfare, while 63.1 per cent was spent on military welfare (Lin, 1994). Social welfare has, therefore, received little attention or interest from the government; in part, the Taiwanese government has successfully used the argument of its ultimate goal to unify with mainland China to postpone social welfare reforms (Chow, 1985–6; Lin, 1993).

As in Japan and Taiwan, the lack of social welfare in Korea was, until very recently, compensated by high economic growth and high employment rates. For example, livelihood protection, the basic safety net, was introduced in Korea a good ten years after Taiwan (where medical relief for low-income families and labour insurance were established in 1950, and the Government Employees' Insurance Law was put into place in 1958) and Japan (where daily livelihood protection was enacted in 1947). A few employee pension, health care and industrial injury compensation schemes were introduced in the 1960s. However, significant progress was made during the 1970s when the government concentrated on consolidating the medical insurance system. The Medical Aid Act giving basic medical care to the poor was introduced in 1977, the same year as medical insurance for employees of private industries and companies was established. In 1979, a similar insurance scheme was given to civil servants and private school teachers. It was not until 1988, however, that the basic medical insurance scheme was extended to all rural residents; the scheme for all urban residents was established in the following year. The late 1980s also saw a push in Korea towards extending the already-established national pension schemes to rural and urban residents, although special pensions for workers in industry had been in place since 1960.

Given Korea's growing economy, its recent democratization process, and the recent nature of its social welfare development, there are good indications that social welfare may continue to expand in the near future. This is likely to be further facilitated by the fact that, unlike in Japan, Korea's elderly population is still relatively small and its youth relatively large (Korea, 1994). Despite these positive potential prospects for social welfare development in Korea, however, there are some signs of govern-ment attempts to reshape the Korean social welfare regime in recent years. For example, despite the relatively low elderly population (the proportion of population over 65 years of age was 3.9 per cent in 1980, 5.0 per cent in 1992), since the early 1980s a series of social welfare reforms have been introduced to address the issue of an ageing society. In 1981, the government enacted the Old Age Welfare Act to improve social welfare services for the elderly, and in 1982, the Charter of Respect for the Aged was promulgated to enhance 'the spirit of respect for the aged'. Activities associated with the Charter of Respect for the Aged include a special day of celebration to commemorate the elderly, and the public presentation of government awards to some two hundred 'dutiful sons, filial daughters-in-law, and typical traditional families' (Korea, 1994). This public emphasis on the elderly is motivated by concerns over the nuclearization of families caused by rapid industrialization and urbanization over the past couple of decades. Despite the increasing expansion of social welfare, therefore, the state's agenda remains that the family will continue to provide the main social welfare role.

Summary

Since it is clear that there are significant divergences in the patterns of social welfare obtaining in Japan, Korea and Taiwan, is there anything that they have in common that particularly characterizes them? At the simplest level, we might argue that Japan is characterized by (a) a system of family welfare that appears to negate much of the need for state welfare; (b) a status-segregated and somewhat residual social insurance based system; and (c) corporate occupational plans for 'core' workers. A case can be made that much of this pattern also holds for Korea and Taiwan. In both, there is a strong emphasis on the idea that family welfare negates much of the need for state support, and patterns of status segregation and a residual social insurance system can be seen in Taiwan's current health insurance system and Korea's pension system. The idea of corporate occupational plans is less obvious in Taiwan because of the relatively small number of large corporations but, if we look at gender segregation in the labour market, then we could argue that the core–periphery distinction pertains in Taiwan as in Japan and Korea. Certainly, in Korea and Taiwan, as in Japan, almost all insurance programmes began with those who could pay contributions and have only recently begun to incorporate the less well-off.

If we look at welfare expenditure as a percentage of GDP, then East Asian countries appear to be spending much less than some of their European counterparts – by some accounts, maybe 50 per cent of the UK level, 35 per cent of the Swedish. Such figures, however, mask important points. In Japan and Korea, for example, since the early 1980s and late 1980s respectively, universal rights to health care have been established, but the financing of these is largely through public agencies which collect the insurance premiums, with only limited government subsidy. Spending in this area, therefore, is not generally counted as government expenditure and hence the state should be seen as playing the role of what Kwon (1995) calls a 'regulator' rather than a 'provider'. He argues that when the expenditure of these private agencies is included in the equation, the comparative level of expenditure may look quite different.

Finally, the development of social welfare programmes in these particular East Asian societies can be described as 'piecemeal', often in response to immediate political and economic conditions rather than as part of an overall, coherent plan. As we shall see later, it is difficult to explain their post-war development in terms of right–left political movements – the development of working-class demands following industrialization or ideological concentration on employment over welfare – though elements of these ideas, of course, must be part of the overall equation and it must always be stressed that developments in Korea and Taiwan should be seen as differing from those in Japan to the extent that there was a fundamental lack of democracy in these countries until recent times.

Despite the expansion of social welfare in post-war years, all three countries have shown some resistance to adopting a totally 'Western' type of social welfare. Recent trends demonstrate an increasing reluctance to further extend social welfare rights and entitlement as they upgrade the quality of existing social welfare programmes.[29] The role of the family – and private transfers – in social welfare has also been consciously re-emphasized through various state propaganda. In Japan, the idea of an imminent social welfare crisis resulting from the 'ageing society' has been effectively utilized to reassert and increase the role of the individual, the family, and the voluntary sector, and to emphasize the importance of self-sufficiency and self-help in the 1980s (Zenkoku Shakai Fukushi Kyōgikai, 1989). This period has also seen, in Korea, the (re)institution of the rhetoric of Confucian tradition (e.g. filial piety, individual self-help, and family interdependence) in social welfare policies. In Taiwan, a similar idea is also found in the push for 'planned change' through mutual aid and community-building (Chao, 1988). Interestingly, in all three societies, political decision-makers have been able to draw on the same Confucian vocabulary as well as indigenous traditions to combat the demands for the development of a 'Western-style' welfare system. It is perhaps this ability to draw on – either positively or negatively – and synthesize Western, indigenous and regional (Confucian) discourses and 'traditions' which most characterize the social welfare systems of Japan, Korea and Taiwan.

Analysis

All three countries examined here have seen an expansion in, and reformulation of, social welfare over the past couple of decades. These developments, however, have been marked by an ambivalence in each society between the initial motivations for change, and their potential implications. In the case of Japan, the social welfare reforms which took place in the Meiji period, and again after the Second World War, were significantly motivated by the national objective to 'catch up' with the Western industrialized nations. The process of 'catching up' involved modernization, which, in turn, implied industrialization and Westernization. Until recently, this process involved adopting Western knowledge and technologies, and Western economic and industrial structures, while keeping the indigenous social institutional structures intact.[30] After the 1970s, however, the imperatives for economic and industrial modernization had waned given the country's economic progress and there was a shift to a more cautious intake of 'Western' models. In social welfare, the Japanese began to actively debate the development of what they call the 'Japanese-style social welfare model'.[31] A similar pattern can be observed in Korea and Taiwan. On the one hand, both Korea and Taiwan found it necessary to develop social welfare in response to international pressures and expectations in keeping with their status as industrialized countries; on the other, the post-war social welfare developments have also caused anxieties within these countries about becoming too 'Westernized'. This tension between a shift towards increased liberalism and personal autonomy, and fears that such would lead to the disintegration of family systems and local community social cohesion, can be seen, for example, in the reintroduction of traditional Confucian language in the social welfare debates of Korea. In Taiwan, the idea of 'planned change' focused on community-building and the restoration of a spirit of family and mutual aid in the 1980s also illustrates an attempt to moderate the Westernizing potential of social welfare development (Chao, 1988).

These competing impulses provide the key to understanding the development of what may be called the 'East Asian social welfare regimes'. Indeed, they raise the question of quite how systematic or planned were the social welfare programmes in these countries in the first place. A historical perspective for each country appears to suggest that social welfare developed, on the one hand, with little change in the indigenous value systems (for example, the notions of family-based support and community-based mutual aid remain today much as they did a century ago), and on the other, in a rather reactive manner – that is, in response to problems as they arose, rather than as coherent and rationally planned measures.

Interpretations of social welfare development in Japan, Korea, and Taiwan

Different authors have endeavoured to explain the pattern of social welfare development in East Asia. While most of these focus on Japan, some recent work has attempted to extend the analysis to other newly industrialized East Asian countries, such as Korea, Taiwan, Hong Kong, and Singapore. Some have argued that the weakness of the left-wing political parties and the labour movements in these countries – and their apparent inability to fight for the rights of the 'working classes' – accounts for the meagre level of welfare (Panitch, 1979; Cameron, 1978; Lin, 1991). Alternatively, others have pointed to the strength of the right-wing and conservative politics to explain the same phenomenon (Castles, 1978; 1981).[32]

Jones (1993; 1990) contends that the common patterns of social welfare systems found among the newly industrialized East Asian countries – Japan, South Korea, Taiwan, Hong Kong, and Singapore – as with their economic success is related to shared 'Confucian' moral and ethical traditions.[33]

The 'America-Pacific social welfare regime explanation' (Rose, 1989; Rose and Shiratori, 1986) questions the validity of 'conventional' assumptions about the universal convergence of social welfare along the lines of 'European-type' welfare regimes. It argues that not only does there exist what may be called an 'America-Pacific social welfare regime' – characterized by little government intervention and relatively low social welfare expenditure (as illustrated by the cases of the USA, Japan, Canada, and Australia) – but also that this 'model' might be considered the norm rather than the exception to the rule (given that these countries make up some three-quarters of the total population of the OECD countries).

Finally, the statist theorists (Amsden, 1985; Heidenheimer et al., 1990; Skocpol, 1985) regard the impressive record of economic development in Japan and the other newly industrialized East Asian countries as the result of active nation-building processes exercised by the state.

Each of these interpretations offers useful insights into the development of aspects of social welfare in Japan, Korea and Taiwan at particular points in their history. They do, however, have ethnocentric and ahistorical elements, partly due to the fact that they are grounded on certain theoretical presuppositions common to Western analysis. For example, Western assumptions about 'class' have limited applicability when examining Japan, Korea, or Taiwan where concepts of class and class conflict are not well formulated in the minds of most people, particularly in the post-war years. Indeed, lack of 'class consciousness' and a rhetoric of classlessness is encouraged by state propaganda in all three countries.

In contrast to the above interpretations, we suggest that the developments in social welfare observed in these countries may be explained by what we describe as peripatetic adaptive learning and development strategies with the prime goal of nation-building. The welfare regimes, according to this theory, are seen primarily as the result of internal and external pressures for basic national survival and nation-building. The fact that the social welfare agenda has often been set in response to national imperatives explains patterns of development which seem inconsistent in comparison with the Western experience.[34] In this section, we shall explain each of the component parts of our proposition, using Japan as a case study to illustrate our argument.

Nation-building imperatives

The idea that social welfare and economic development in these countries can be attributed to nation-building imperatives is not new (Amsden, 1985; Heidenheimer et al., 1990; Skocpol, 1985; Allen, 1981; Francks, 1992). In particular, those who look to the statist explanation of social and economic development have frequently attributed the impressive record of economic growth both before and after the Second World War in these countries to the strong state characterized by clear purpose, motivation, and the means and power to effect change. Accordingly, the idea that nation-building was the foremost imperative for these countries in the post-war era has been used to explain the strong role played by these governments in exercising their economic policies, and also to explain how social welfare came to be subordinated to the state's economic priorities. Furthermore, it has also been argued that, motivated by these nation-building objectives, the state was able to manipulate national support for its economic goals and deflect public pressure for social welfare development. This has been achieved through a variety of means, including the education system and the mass media. In the cases of Taiwan and Korea, in addition to the ethical/ ideological content of the school curriculum, there has also been active state control of labour unions and bans on civil activities, such as organizing public protests.

We are in agreement with these statist theories, in so far as they propose the idea that the state's leadership in economic development and agenda-setting has been based on the priority of nation-building. However, we question the extent to which the state, as an institution, has been able to maintain a clear purpose and a coherent and consistent set of policies with regard to social welfare. Rather, the development of social welfare over the past century indicates that beneath the rhetoric, the states' approach to welfare has been haphazard, and extremely pragmatic. In many ways, they have taken what may be called a 'learn-as-we-go' approach to social welfare, continuously seeking and taking information and models from abroad, and adapting them to their domestic situations.

Peripatetic learning

In reality, the social welfare systems found in Japan, Korea, and Taiwan are aggregations of different welfare models.[35] For example, it is widely recognized that contemporary social welfare in Japan has been largely based on Western models; and, in more recent years, in Taiwan and Korea not only on direct Western models but also on reconstituted Western models as established in Japan. Indeed, since the end of the last century, all three countries have actively sought and incorporated Western knowledge in formulating their social welfare systems. The Japanese import of Western models began as early as the 1870s (see Goodman, 1992). As part of the modernization programme, the Meiji state sent scholars and govern-ment bureaucrats to Britain, Germany, and the US, the leading industrial and welfare nations at the time, to 'learn' about their social welfare systems. The results of these Western contacts included, for example, the incorporation of the Bismarckian social insurance system, which still marks the pension and health insurance schemes today, and the Alberfield system which became the model of the pre-war *hōmeniin* and the post-war *minseiiin* system.[36]

Theoretical ideas found in the English Poor Law of 1834 were integrated into the construction of the *Jukkyū Kisoku*;[37] the basis of modern Japanese notions of charity work was also heavily influenced by the Oxford idealist traditions at the turn of the century (Peng, 1995). In the post-war period, Japanese social welfare theory was strongly influenced by the American model; the post-war social work profession in Japan closely followed American social work practices. Similar legacies can be seen in Korea and Taiwan. Indeed, still today, social welfare and social work education in all three countries are in practice closely based on British and American social welfare theories.

Despite the contemporary rhetoric of the 'Japanese-style social welfare system', Japanese welfare bureaucrats have continued to look to Western countries for models and ideas, and continue to be influenced by them. For example, since 1990, the Ministry of Health and Welfare has set up several research commissions to examine the future of social welfare for Japan. The Special Research Commission on Issues Related to Family Functioning and Birth Rates (Katei Shussan Mondai Sōgō Chōsa Kenkyūkai), set up in 1991, has been monitoring the developments in the EU and North America in an effort to learn from their experiences. In response to the issues concerning the ageing of society, the increased labour market participation of women, and changing family structures, the Japanese government is also looking to the West for ideas and information on policy direction. The government has sent individuals and research teams to Britain to study its community care plans; to Brussels and Denmark to get information on the harmonization of family and work; and to Canada for direction on child welfare and legislation on children's rights and family services (Takahashi and Peng, 1992; Peng, 1992; Peng et al., 1994).

These projects suggest, first, that Japanese social welfare developed out of learning from multiple sources rather than through a consistent application of a small body of theoretical ideas. Secondly, it also implies that, to some extent, social welfare development in Japan has been relatively unhampered by ideological constraints. Finally, it suggests that social welfare development in Japan has been largely issue-driven; the basis of policy development has been essentially pragmatic.

Adaptive learning and development

Although the pattern of social welfare development in Japan has involved importing a wide range of Western ideas, these ideas have not been simply adopted wholesale. In all three countries, foreign social welfare models have been restructured to suit the needs of the state, national purpose, and 'cultural' orientations. This has resulted in a selective adoption, and goes some way towards explaining the uneven patterns of development, and a certain element of divergence between the societies. For example, while the current overall policy framework of the Japanese government is one of further enhancement of the Japanese-style social welfare system (that is, a system built on individual self-help efforts and cooperation within the family and the community), in reality, some rather progressive changes have also been pushed forward. For example, the current government has accepted an increase in the consumption tax, from 3 per cent to 5 per cent by fiscal year 1995–6, to fund increased social welfare expenditure.[38] Apart from health and pension benefits, a significant amount of future expenditure will be allocated to new programmes focused on enhancing family functioning, such as improved child allowances.

Projections

It is perhaps easier to discuss long-term projections in Japan, South Korea and Taiwan than in most other parts of the world since each is characterized by their long-term goals of nation-building, even if actual policy and decision-making may be highly pragmatic and susceptible to change depending on the national and international environment. It is common, especially in Japan, to find reports setting out possible scenarios in a whole range of issues well into the middle of the next century. While each society may draw on its past in defining itself, it certainly does not rely on this or express any sense of complacency with its current position.

Pressure for change

This comes from a number of different directions.

Internally

1   The rising expectations of a growing middle class
2   a younger generation which has no memory of recent poverty and hence different ideas about work (in Japan known as the *shinjinrui*, the 'new generation')
3   internationalization of the society through overseas travel, media etc., which demonstrates other possibilities for economic investment than simply putting money back into business
4   a change in the industrial base from manufacturing to the service industry, leading to demands for more individualized, and less company-negotiated, benefits.

Externally

From Western societies worried about spiralling trade deficits and demands for more infrastructure investment to ease this (known in Japanese as *gaiatsu*).[39]

Management of change

The high status enjoyed by bureaucrats in each of the societies under study means that they – rather than politicians – are normally given the task of carrying out reforms. Change, therefore, can be implemented gradually and can be coordinated by a small group of elite, well-educated, respected officials.[40] Bureaucrats in these countries, moreover, are permitted to implement policy which elsewhere might be considered more fitting to the private than the public domain, such as programmes aimed at trying to increase the birth rate in Japan.

In Japan in particular, long-term forecasting is used as an effective means for raising public consciousness about pending social issues. This might be termed the 'shock syndrome' where the discovery of each new social trend is dubbed a shock, such as the 1.53 shock of 1992 – the 'discovery' that each woman was having only 1.53 children during her child-bearing years (way below the nominal 2.1 replacement level). These trends are explained only in the context of change in Japan and not the wider world context (1.53 is not a particularly low rate compared with some European societies).[41] This process is extremely effective. For example, Japan still has a relatively young population, although the public perception is that it is already one of the oldest. Most Japanese are aware that ageing will have a major impact on income structures and welfare provisions and hence accept that changes 'will have to be made' in order to secure the future of the society. The new consumption tax of the late 1980s was introduced partly under this guise.[42]

Current issues

Since Japan is economically the most advanced of our three case studies, it makes sense to discuss in detail the current issues in that country.

Recent social 'shocks' in Japan include: growing rates of juvenile delinquency; increasing rates of school truancy and school refusal; higher divorce rates; increasing age at marriage; rural depopulation. By some international standards there is little in these 'shocks' to be worried about. The most interesting debates, however, centre around potentially enormous labour shortages over the next two decades. Figures which were part of the common consciousness at the start of the 1990s indicated a shortage of a million workers by the end of the decade, and possibly two million by the year 2010. While the current recession has revised these figures, there is little doubt that there will be a future need for more workers and essentially these will have to come from one of two sources: female or migrant labour. Since much of the labour shortage is in areas where young Japanese now feel over-qualified (the so-called 3-K jobs, *kitsui*, *kiken* and *kitanai* – difficult, dangerous and dirty), the response since 1988 has been an increase in the number of migrant workers (mainly from less developed Asian and Middle Eastern countries).[43] In order to control the influx of such workers – and to reduce their effect on the supposed homogeneity of the workforce – the government has encouraged the entry of Latin Americans (mainly

Brazilians and Peruvians of Japanese origin) to take jobs on short-term contracts. In the three years from 1990, 15 per cent (about 150,000) of the total population of Latin Americans of Japanese descent entered Japan.[44]

The current economic recession in Japan has also brought other basic social policies to the fore. Despite the *fukushi minaoshi-ron* (reconsideration of welfare debate) following the oil crisis of 1973, it has proved not always easy (though generally possible) to remove entitlements which had already been granted.[45] On the other hand, great efforts have been made to support private practices and, in particular, the ideology of Japan's 'company welfare model' which is seen to negate the need for Western-style state welfare. (See Whittaker, 1990, for a detailed description of how flexibilization has been utilized to prevent the break-down of this company welfare ideology.)[46]

On the other hand, many in Japan argue that there are still major areas in social welfare where Japan should be learning lessons from Western systems. These include:

1 greater integration of people with disabilities and mental illness into the community (particularly in rural areas)
2 introduction of new services to deal with the influx of foreign workers from poorer countries who have been attracted to Japan because of its labour shortage and high wages: this is generally debated under the new powerful rhetoric of the internationalization (*kokusaika*) of society
3 re-examination of the use of drugs in health care and reduction in the power of the pharmaceutical companies
4 a greater role for women in the public sphere
5 the introduction/tolerance of more originality and creativity in the education system and society in general
6 greater emphasis on housing, public infrastructure, parks, museums, leisure activities, shorter working hours and so on.

There is much debate on all of the above ideas – the current buzzwords in Japan are internationalization, decentralization, privatization, and a new emphasis on social justice – but, as yet, few signs of implementation.

To summarize, it could be said that, in the field of social welfare, the most interesting debates in Japan (and largely mirrored in Taiwan and Korea) are on the issue of 'rights' – for which a whole new vocabulary has had to be constructed – and 'obligations', which draws on the traditional Confucian ideas that applied essentially to the elites in the pre-modern period (*samurai, yangban, literati*) but has been invoked consistently over the past decades in a number of different social contexts.

These debates represent tensions and 'internal cultural debates' in Japanese society over competing Western and Japanese 'models' for social development. In Korea and Taiwan, we can see similar debates being carried on and, to a very large extent, although it is politically difficult for their governments to admit as much, these debates are a reflection of what is happening in Japan as increasingly large numbers of Taiwanese and

Korean policy-makers and practitioners look to Japan for guidance in formulating their own policies. This is why we are arguing here that the East Asian welfare model is 'Japan-focused'.

It is probable that all three societies will continue to draw on Western,[47] indigenous and, in the case of Korea and Taiwan, Japanese models as the economic and political situations dictate. The history of each system has been a haphazard adaptation and combination of elements of other systems – an adopt and adapt process – that has allowed pragmatic change. Similarly, we argue, future social welfare policy decisions will be based on economic and political pragmatism, but will be legitimated by reference to either 'traditional' culture or 'Western' models.

Notes

Any chapter with as broad a theme as this will inevitably incur innumerable debts and we are glad to have the opportunity to acknowledge these here while emphasizing, of course, that we alone are responsible for any faults and mistakes which remain in the text. Thanks are due to: Ronald Dore, Howard Glennerster, Janet Hunter, Jane Lewis, Chao-Yin Lin, Michio Morishima, Robert Pinker (all LSE); Marcus Rebick (Oxford); Ian Gough (Manchester); Kazuhiro Ichikawa (Japan Lutheran College); Tsuzaki Tetsuo (Bukkyo University); and Haeng-Jin Kim (Ministry of Welfare, Korea). Versions of this chapter were given at the International Sociological Association, Bielefeld; the Nissan Institute for Japanese Studies, Oxford University; and STICERD, LSE; and we would like to thank the participants of those seminars for their extremely useful comments. We would also like to thank STICERD for its generous financial support to Ito Peng which allowed her to complete this project.

1 The large research project on social welfare carried out by researchers from the Tokyo University Institute of Social Science between 1979 and 1985 which included comparative analysis of the Japanese system was probably the first major attempt to break away from the previously dominant Marxist approach in Japan and attempt to study the Japanese case in its own context (for an overview of this project, see Institute of Social Science, University of Tokyo, 1985: 125–48).

2 China is not included in our discussion of East Asia because of the very different economic course it has followed over the previous forty years.

3 For this reason, comparative research between Korea and Japan today remains very problematic. Korea, in particular, resents the label of lagging behind Japanese development which is implicit in many of these comparisons.

4 Put differently, there is little, for example, that a Taiwanese or South Korean would find strange about the Japanese education system. This is a point which is often ignored by Western and Japanese scholars of Japanese education who see the system as somehow 'unique'.

5 The most prestigious jobs in the bureaucracy have generally been taken – some would argue reserved – for graduates from the top national universities (Tōdai in Japan; SNU in Korea; Taidai in Taiwan) who, simply by virtue of having got into those establishments, are perceived to be the most able products of the education system.

6 Some economists argue that Taiwan and Korea are following a typical dependence model of development evolving as semi-peripheral nations of Japan. As Barret and Chin (1987) point out, however, the recent evidence suggests that their patterns of development have diverged significantly from the predicted course of dependency nations.

7 For a counter-argument to this, see Horioka (1993).

8 For an excellent account of why Japan has such a relatively high proportion of working elderly among OECD countries, see Rebick (1993).

9 See, for example, a speech by Suh Sang-Mok (1992: 36–7), a member of the Korean

National Assembly at an international conference in 1992: 'The composition of the population in Korea will change drastically in the future. The elderly as a proportion of the total population will increase, while the economically active population will decrease as a proportion of the total population. For the next five to six years until year 2000, however, the working age population, those who are in their 30s and 40s, will increase and the labour productivity will reach its peak. The ageing of Korea is projected to take place at a rate that is much faster than that of Japan. Korea will probably become burdened with the elderly population by year 2020, and now should be the preparatory period for the eventual ageing of Korea that is expected.' In support of his argument, Suh only shows that the aged population (those over 65) is projected to increase from 4.7 per cent to 6.6 per cent of the total population between 1980 and 2000.

10 Overall, the state contribution to the total income packaging of the family is very low. If we take, for example, Japan, on average the total contribution of the state to the income package of the 'average' household (i.e. two-parent families with dependent children) looks something like this: 94.5 per cent salaries/wages; 1.0 per cent income from self-employment; 2.1 per cent transfer payment; 2.4 per cent other income. The income packaging structure of low-income families like those headed by lone mothers looks like this: 81.5 per cent salaries/wages; 1.4 per cent income from self-employment; 11.3 per cent transfer income; 5.8 per cent other income. This shows that the income packaging structure of workers in the periphery (like lone mothers: 87.5 per cent of them work) is less concentrated on the salaries/wages, and depends more on transfer income and other incomes, such as family support (Peng, 1995). Compared with some Western countries, the income packaging structures of families in Japan is very low on transfer payment (i.e. low dependence on state support; high dependence on the labour market incomes). For example, in Britain, the income packaging structure of average two-parent family households looks something like this: 76.5 per cent salaries/wages; 2.3 per cent income from self-employment; 20.9 per cent transfer payment; 0.3 per cent other incomes. That of lone-mother families looks like this: 21.3 per cent salaries/wages; 2.3 per cent income from self-employment; 66.6 per cent transfer payment; 9.8 per cent other incomes. Compared with this, the contribution of the state to Japanese families' total income package is very small. Although there is a welfare safety net in Japan, the uptake rate is very low for those who would be expected to benefit most: 11 per cent of lone-mother families; 5 per cent of all elderly households; 0.8 per cent of households with a disabled person. The total take-up rate for public assistance is only 1.5 per cent or 8 per 1000 population (Peng, 1995). The public assistance programme in Korea covers those with no income earning ability as well as those who live in poverty. This latter category however was set in 1990 for those whose monthly income is no more than 45,000 won (based on doing 65 hours work a week at the minimum wage). This is very low compared with the minimum monthly income calculated by the General League of the Korean Trade Unions at 185,383 won (Kwon, 1995: 126–7).

11 The core–periphery distinction works on two axes. Within big companies there is a major difference between permanent (normally male) and seasonal/part-time workers (normally female). Within industries, there is a major difference between large companies and small to medium firms which are often in a sub-contracting role which is highly vulnerable to market forces. According to some estimates (Woronoff, 1982), only about 25 per cent of Japanese workers qualify for the life-time employment, seniority promotion, company union protection jobs often described as the three pillars of Japanese employment. Essentially, there is a direct correlation between firm size and salary and bonus payment. Similarly, part-time, seasonal and small/medium firm workers receive roughly one-third of the company welfare benefits (in terms of housing as little as one-ninth) of workers in large firms (Hall, 1988: 10–18).

12 These figures (from OECD, 1991: 66–7) do not include the participation of workers over 65.

13 For a review of the *Nihonjinron* (theories of Japaneseness) literature, see Gluck (1985), Dale (1986) and Mouer and Sugimoto (1986).

14 By this we imply the form of economic aid and personal social services provided by the state based on some notion of the citizen's entitlement to public support.

15 This term was first used by Komatsu (1992) to describe social welfare in Meiji Japan.

16 The notion of Confucianism used here as 'statecraft' is not the same as the intellectual system upheld by scholars.

17 Of course, this was largely motivated by imperialist goals on the part of the Japanese state. Much of the social welfare implemented up to the 1930s – indeed the establishment of the Ministry of Health and Welfare itself – was due to concern about the poor physical condition of prospective recruits (see Johansson and Mosk, 1986). Similarly, a number of government pension plans were instituted in the late 1930s and early 1940s when the government was in need of contributions for generating general revenue (Fujita, 1984: 10; Collick, 1988: 210; see also Nenkin Seido Kenkyūkai, 1986).

18 *Minpō* has been long discussed as in need of reform. Beginning in 1994, there has been a visible attempt by the government to change much of this body of law, particularly the sections concerning family law such as the family register system (*Koseki*), the family name, and the divorce act.

19 By the mid 1980s, voluntary enterprise welfare provided by the biggest firms (5000+ employees) was roughly three times that provided by smaller firms (less than 300) (Hall, 1988: 13–15).

20 Korea did, however, benefit from a handful of relief programmes which were initiated by international aid organizations such as UNICEF (Suh, 1992), as well as massive American military and economic aid. Between 1945 and the mid 1970s, South Korea received some $13 billion in such aid, compared with $5.6 billion received by Taiwan (Ho, 1978).

21 See note 10 for current levels of this relief.

22 When Tanaka Kakuei became Prime Minister in 1972, he was also keen to mark his arrival by large national projects, such as the expansion of social welfare.

23 According to Rebick (1994: 192–6), Japan, as did Sweden and the US, saw increases in the real level of pension benefits through the 1970s and, in the case of Japan and Sweden in the 1980s too, the increases in Japan being the most dramatic with the employee pension increasing threefold on average. Public employee pensions are currently about 40 per cent of income including bonuses. It is much more difficult to get accurate rates on public company pension rates.

24 Some official projections suggested that, if the original 1970s reforms had continued, they would have resulted in more generous benefits and higher contributions than even the most welfare-oriented European countries.

25 In 1994, the government introduced a new bill which would raise the sales tax to 5 per cent in fiscal year 1995–6. A key and controversial element of policy of recent governments is that this sales tax should act, in part at least, as a form of national welfare tax (see Maruo, 1994).

26 In the early 1980s, Hiraoka (1984: 139) argued that the stigma attached to receiving welfare has been greatly alleviated 'by the awakening consciousness of the right to social welfare and other changes in people's values'. This conclusion was perhaps premature. It is estimated that still only about 25 per cent of low-income families take up their entitlement to public assistance (Soeda, 1990).

27 These three slogans constitute what is called the Three Principles of the People (*Sam Min Chu I*) which form the political platform of the KMT and go back to Dr Sun Yat-sen, the founder of the predecessor of the KMT party, who was strongly influenced by Bismarckian social insurance systems when he was in Europe in his youth.

28 For example, in 1989 farmers won a special farmers' social health insurance programme after what can only be described as very aggressive lobbying.

29 There are many – indeed an increasing number of – groups advocating the development of ideas of human rights in all areas of society, including welfare provision. However, this movement has been consistently met with the counter-argument that such ideas – often enshrined in UN Conventions on Rights – are the last bastion of Western-derived Judaeo-Christian imperialism and hence not relevant to the context of East Asian societies, which have very different concepts of 'the person' and his or her relation to the wider society and the state (for an overview and a number of case studies on this issue, see Goodman and Neary, 1996).

30 There have, of course, been some important changes in social structures in Japan. For

example, the traditional family system, the *ie* system, was legally abolished after the Second World War. However, in reality, many practices originating from that family system, such as the rules of inheritance, still remain.

31 Perhaps the most extreme example of this movement is Nakagawa's (1979) claim that by the end of the 1970s Japan was already a 'welfare super-power'. A rather better-argued account, but along the same lines, can be found in Vogel (1980: 184–203). A very similar account for Korea, but fifteen years after Japan, can be found in Pae (1992: 393–4) who argues in a chapter unambiguously entitled 'Korea: Leader of the Nations in Social Welfare' that essentially countries divide into two types – economic priority and welfare priority states – and that in the former category, which he clearly identifies as superior, Korea is the leading nation: 'There is no doubt that the Korean model of welfare services can be a good reference for other countries, because of its high PQLI [public quality of life index], yet not drifting into . . . lavish expenditures of welfare services, and gearing towards continued economic development on the basis of the principles of the government's energetic role for export promotion/market economy, individualism, private enterprise, and privatization.'

32 For an excellent critique of explanations of social welfare development in post-war Japan in terms of simplistic left–right struggles, see Collick (1988).

33 As mentioned earlier, we feel that it is crucial to make a distinction between the influence of Confucian 'traditions' and the utilization of Confucian 'vocabulary' by political elites to develop a certain type of welfare system.

34 The closest approximation to our model can probably be found in the work of Pempel (1982; 1989) who attributes the Japanese case to 'creative conservatism', pointing to a close relationship between: (1) major corporations; (2) a 'small' but activist state; (3) a highly competitive oligopolistic domestic market; and (4) labour market oriented social welfare.

35 We call this 'peripatetic' rather than eclectic learning to stress the manner in which Japanese, Taiwanese and Korean policy-makers have historically travelled the world to look at alternative systems at first hand in the search for knowledge.

36 This is a system whereby a large number of voluntary individuals carry out the provision of social services in the local community under the guidance of a small number of professional, qualified social workers. The system changed its name in the post-war period because of the widespread belief that during the war the system acted as a means of controlling the local population; even in the post-war period, some have argued that *minseiiin* are more interested in maintaining local stability than acting as advocates for their client, though there is no doubt that they do provide a more locally based service than Western 'professional' systems. For a good ethnographic introduction in English to the *minseiiin* system, see Ben-Ari (1991: 125–89).

37 Poor Relief Regulation: a legal provision of the Meiji era enacted in 1874 and which remained in force until the enactment of the Poor Relief Law of 1929. It provided relief to the poor, aged and sick who absolutely could not be cared for by their own families and community.

38 Another good example of the uneven – and apparently *ad hoc* – development of welfare provision can be seen with the services and policy for the disabled in Japan during the 1980s which Nishida (1990: 115) summarizes as a battle between 'two basic momenta . . . one working toward "enrichment" of the services, and the other toward their fundamental "reassessment", namely their drastic cutback'.

39 Outside pressure, or *gaiatsu*, has long been significant in the development of Japanese social welfare policy. In the late 1960s and early 1970s, it was, to some extent, the International Labour Organization (ILO) which set the standards that Japanese pensions were expected to meet and which led to then Prime Minister Tanaka's plan for higher social welfare spending in general.

40 While this holds true in theory in Korea, it has to be said that at least through the 1970s and 1980s there was a tendency for government ministers – particularly in education – to try and 'leave their mark' by introducing radical, and often apparently contradictory, reforms.

41 This is to be distinguished from the '1.51 shock of 1983' when the Japanese divorce rate reached its post-war peak of 1.51 per 1000 population. This was widely interpreted in Japan as

a 'crisis' in family relationships. At this time, the divorce rates in England and Wales and the US were 3.20 and 4.80 respectively per 1000 population. The declining birth rate, however, has alarmed policy-makers to the extent that one of the major areas of growth in recent social welfare provision in the early 1990s has been in child allowances and maternity leave.

42 It should perhaps also be pointed out that all three societies hold essentially positive views of technology which can, and in the case of Japan increasingly are, drawn upon in order to make it physically possible for the elderly to continue to live by themselves or with their families in their own homes.

43 Japan was during the economic expansion of the past twenty years largely able to delay bringing in workers from outside by gradually redirecting, 'with government encouragement' (Hoshino, 1988: 267), labour-intensive industrial work to developing countries.

44 For more on Japan's current immigration 'problem', see Sellek (1994) and Shimada (1994).

45 The role of the media here, particularly during the 1970s, should perhaps not be underestimated. Through a content analysis of magazine articles, Takegawa (1988: 242) discovered that while up to 1975 all articles on welfare took either a positive or a neutral stance, from 1976 onwards the vast majority (around 95 per cent in his sample) took a negative position.

46 In the current recession, the government has invested very large sums to keep people in work through a total employment support programme. According to the *Japan Labour Bulletin* (1 May 1994) the 1994 government budget of Y331.1 billion is aimed at 'creating' one million jobs. A similarly clear indication of belief in 'full employment' as a welfare policy can be seen in Labour Ministry support for firms which retrain and keep on older workers.

47 The tradition for central government ministries to send able junior members overseas to learn about other models of administration – and for local as well as central government to reserve a substantial annual budget for overseas 'study tours' – is still very much alive in Japan today (despite occasional reports of the abuse of such funds) and is increasingly common in Korea and Taiwan.

References

Akamatsu, Tsutomu (1990) *Kindai Nihon ni Okeru Shakaijigyō no Tenkai Katei*. Tokyo: Ochanomizu Bunken.

Allen, G.C. (1981) *A Short Economic History of Modern Japan*. London: Macmillan.

Amsden, Alice H. (1985) 'The state and Taiwan's economic development', in Peter B. Evans, Dietrich R. Rueschemeyer and Theda Skocpol (eds), *Bringing the State Back In*. Cambridge: Cambridge University Press. pp. 78–106.

Anderson, Stephen (1987) 'The elitist origins of the Japanese welfare state before 1945: bureaucrats, military officers, social interests and politicians', *Transactions of the Asiatic Society of Japan*, 4th series, 2: 59–77.

Baba, Keinosuke (ed.) (1978) *Shakai Fukushi no Nihongata Tenkai*. Tokyo: Shakai Fukushi Hōjin.

Barrett, Richard E. and Chin, Soomi (1987) 'Export-oriented industrialising states in the capitalist world system: similarities and differences', in Frederic C. Deyo (ed.), *The Political Economy of the New Asian Industrialism*. Ithaca: Cornell University Press. pp. 23–43.

Ben-Ari, Eyal (1991) *Changing Japanese Suburbia: a Study of Two Present-Day Localities*. London and New York: Kegan Paul.

Bronfenbrenner, Martin and Yasuba, Yasukichi (1987) 'Economic welfare', in *The Political Economy of Japan. Volume 1: The Domestic Transformation*. Stanford: Stanford University Press.

Burks, Ardath W. (1985) 'Japan: the bellwether of East Asian human rights?', in James C. Hsiung (ed.), *Human Rights in East Asia: a Cultural Perspective*. New York: Paragon House. pp. 31–53.

Cameron, David (1978) 'The expansion of the public economy: a comparative analysis', *American Political Science Review*, 72: 1243–61.

Castles, Francis G. (1978) *The Social Democratic Image of Society*. London: Routledge and Kegan Paul.

Castles, Francis G. (1981) 'How does politics matter? Structure or agency in the determination of public policy outcomes', *European Journal of Political Research*, 9: 119–32.

Chang, In-Hyub (1985) 'Korea, South', in John Dixon and Hyung Shik Kim (eds), *Social Welfare in Asia*. London: Croom Helm. pp. 176–213.

Chao, W. (1988) 'Planned change in community development: its application in Taiwan', in P.C. Lee (ed.), *Dimensions of Social Welfare Transitions: Sino-British Perspectives*. Taipei: Chu Liu.

Chow, Nelson, W.S. (1985–6) 'Social security provision in Singapore, Hong Kong, Taiwan, and South Korea: a comparative analysis', *Journal of International and Comparative Social Welfare*, 2(1–2): 1–10.

Collick, Martin (1988) 'Social policy: pressures and responses', in J.A.A. Stockwin, A. Rix, A. George, J. Horne, D. Ito and M. Collick (eds), *Dynamic and Immobilist Politics in Japan*. Basingstoke: Macmillan.

Cumings, Bruce (1987) 'The origins and development of the Northeast Asian political economy: industrial sectors, product cycles, and political consequences', in Frederic C. Deyo (ed.), *The Political Economy of the New Asian Industrialism*. Ithaca: Cornell University Press. pp. 44–83.

Dale, Peter N. (1986) *The Myth of Japanese Uniqueness*. London: Croom Helm.

Dore, Ronald P. (1967) *Aspects of Social Change in Japan*. Princeton: Princeton University Press.

Esping-Andersen, Gøsta (1990) *The Three Worlds of Welfare Capitalism*. Cambridge: Polity.

Francks, Penelope (1992) *Japanese Economic Development: Theory and Practice*. London: Routledge.

Fujita, Yoshitaka (1984) *Employee Benefits and Industrial Relations*. Tokyo: Japan Institute of Labour.

Gluck, Carol (1985) *Japan's Modern Myths: Ideology in the Late Meiji Period*. Princeton: Princeton University Press.

Goodman, Roger (1990) *Japan's 'International Youth': the Emergence of a New Class of Schoolchildren*. Oxford: Oxford University Press.

Goodman, Roger (1992) 'Japan: pupil turned teacher?', *Oxford Studies in Comparative Education*, 1: 155–73.

Goodman, Roger (1993) 'Children's homes and children's rights in contemporary Japan', *Research Papers in East Asian Studies*, 1: 31–65.

Goodman, Roger and Neary, I.J. (eds) (1996) *Case Studies on Human Rights in Japan*. Kent: Japan Library.

Gould, Arthur (1993) *Capitalist Welfare Systems: a Comparison of Japan, Britain, and Sweden*. London: Longman.

Hall, Rachel (1988) 'Enterprise welfare in Japan: its development and role'. Welfare State Programme, Suntory-Toyota International Centre for Economics and Related Disciplines, London School of Economics, Discussion Paper WSP/31.

Heidenheimer, A., Heclo, H. and Adams, C. (1990) *Comparative Public Policy*. New York: St Martin's Press.

Hiraoka Kōichi (1984) 'Shakai hendō to tenkanki no shakai fukushi (Social change and social welfare in transition)', in *Keizai Shakai Gakkai Nenpō*, vol. 5. Tokyo: Jichōsha. pp. 127–52.

Hiwatari, Nobuhiro (1993) 'Sustaining the welfare state and international competitiveness in Japan: the welfare reforms of the 1980s and the political economy'. Institute of Social Science, Tokyo, Discussion Paper.

Ho, Samuel Ho (1978) *The Economic Development in Taiwan, 1860–1970*. New Haven: Yale University Press.

Horioka, Charles Yuji (1993) 'Consuming and saving', in Andrew Gordon (ed.), *Postwar Japan as History*. Berkeley: California University Press.

Hoshino, Shinya (1988) 'Perspective of the Japanese welfare state', in Robert Morris (ed.), *Testing the Limits of Social Welfare: International Perspectives on Policy Changes in Nine Countries*. Hanover: Brandeis University Press.

Ichikawa, Kazuhiro (1994) 'Trends of non-profit organisation in the Japanese welfare state'. Unpublished paper, London School of Economics.

Institute of Social Science, University of Tokyo (1985) *Annals of the Institute of Social Science*. University of Tokyo, Japan. No. 27.

Ishida, Hiroshi (1993) *Social Mobility in Contemporary Japan*. Stanford: Stanford University Press.

Japan (1993) *Heisei-4 Kōsei Hakusho*. Tokyo: Kōseisho.

JNC-ICSW (1988) *Law, Social Welfare, Social Development: National Report of the JNC-ICSW to the 24th International Conference on Social Welfare*. Tokyo: Japan National Committee of International Council of Social Welfare.

JNC-ICSW (1990) *Social Welfare Services in Japan*. Tokyo: Japan National Committee of International Council of Social Welfare.

Johansson, S. Ryan and Mosk, C. (1986) 'Income and mortality: evidence from modern Japan 1900–1960', *Population and Development Review*, 12: 415–40.

Jones, Catherine (1990) 'Hong Kong, Singapore, South Korea and Taiwan: oikonomic welfare states', *Government and Opposition*, 25(Autumn): 446–62.

Jones, Catherine (1993) 'The Pacific challenge: Confucian welfare states', in Catherine Jones (ed.), *New Perspectives on the Welfare State in Europe*. London: Routledge. pp. 198–217.

Kim, Kyong-dong (1991) 'Sociocultural developments in the Republic of Korea', in Thomas W. Robinson (ed.), *Democracy and Development in East Asia*. Washington, DC: AEI Press. pp. 137–55.

Kinoshita, A. (1991) *Shinken ni Tsuite*. Tokyo: Kodomo Gyakutai Bōshi Sentā.

Komatsu, Ryūji (1992) 'The state and social welfare in Japan: patterns and developments', in Paul Close (ed.), *The State and Caring*. London: Macmillan. pp. 128–47.

Korea (1994) *Report of the Ministry of Health and Social Affairs*. Seoul: Ministry of Health and Social Affairs.

Kwon, Huck-Ju (1995) 'The "welfare state" in Korea: the politics of legitimation'. DPhil thesis, University of Oxford.

Lin, Chao-yin (1994) 'The development of health insurance system in Taiwan, 1950–1990: a historical and political approach'. Unpublished paper, London School of Economics.

Lin, Wai-I (1991) 'Labour movement and Taiwan's belated welfare state', *Journal of International and Comparative Social Welfare*, 7(1–2): 31–44.

Lin, Wai-I (1993) 'State and social policy: comparative study in Taiwan and Sweden', *National Taiwan University Journal of Sociology*, 2: 95–147 (in Chinese).

Long, Simon (1991) *Taiwan: China's Last Frontier*. London: Macmillan.

Marmot, M.G. and Smith, George Davey (1989) 'Why are the Japanese living longer?', *British Medical Journal*, 299: 1547–51.

Maruo, Naomi (1994) 'The future of the social security system', *Economic Eye*, 15(2), 9–10. Tokyo: Keizai Kōhō Center.

Midgley, James (1986) 'Industrialisation and welfare: the case of the four little tigers', *Social Policy and Administration*, 20(3): 225–38.

Mishra, Ramesh (1990) *The Welfare State in Capitalist Society*. Toronto: University of Toronto Press.

Morishima, Michio (1982) *Why has Japan 'Succeeded'? Western Technology and Japanese Ethos*. Cambridge: Cambridge University Press.

Mouer, Ross and Sugimoto, Yoshio, (1986) *Images of Japanese Society: a Study in the Social Construction of Reality*. London and New York: Kegan Paul.

Nakagawa, Yatsuhiro (1979) 'Japan, the welfare super-power', *The Journal of Japanese Studies*, 5(1): 5–51.

Nenkin Seido Kenkyūkai (ed.) (1986) *Atarashii Nenkin Seido: Kokumin Nenkin, Kōsei Nenkin Hoken no subete*. Tokyo: Dai Ichi Shiryō Insatsu Kabushiki Kaisha.

Nish, Ian (1992) 'European images of Japan: some thoughts on modern European–Japanese relations', *Japan Foundation Newsletter*, 20: 3–15.

Nishida, Yoshiaki (1990) 'Reassessment of welfare services and the trend of welfare policy for the disabled', in *Annals of the Institute of Social Science*, no. 32. University of Tokyo, Japan.

OECD (1991) *Employment Outlook*, July 1991. Paris: OECD.

Pae, Sung Moon (1992) *Korea Leading Developing Nations: Economy, Democracy and Welfare*. Lanham, NY and London: University Press of America.

Panitch, Leo (1979) 'The development of corporatism in liberal democracies', in Philipe Schmitter and Gerhard Lehmbruch (eds), *Trends towards Capitalist Intermediation*. London: Sage. pp. 119–46.

Park, Byung Hyun (1990) 'The development of social welfare institutions in East Asia: case studies of Japan, Korea, and the People's Republic of China 1945–89'. PhD thesis, School of Social Work, University of Pennsylvania.

Pempel, T.J. (1982) *Policy and Politics in Japan*. Philadelphia: Temple University Press.

Pempel, T.J. (1989) 'Japan's creative conservatism: continuity under challenge', in Francis G. Castles (ed.), *The Comparative History of Public Policy*. London: Polity Press. pp. 149–91.

Peng, Ito (1992) 'Child and family services systems in Canada (Ontario), Britain, and Japan: a comparative review', in *Katei Shussan Mondai Sōgō Chōsa Kenkyū Suishin Jigyō Hōkokusho*. Special Research Commission on Issues Related to Family Functioning and Birth Rate, Ministry of Health and Welfare, Japan. Tokyo: Shakai Fukushi Hōjin. Discussion Paper no. 1, pp. 111–81.

Peng, Ito (1995) '*Boshi katei*: a theoretical and case analysis of Japanese lone mothers and their relationships to the state, the labour market, and the family, with reference to Britain and Canada'. PhD thesis, London School of Economics.

Peng, Ito, Iwakami, Mami and Takahashi, Shigehiro (1994) 'Kokusai Kazokunen o Kangaeru: EU no kazokuseisaku no ima, korekara (Thoughts on the International Year of Family: present and future of family policies in the EU countries)', *Mother and Child Well-being Around the World*, 37(10): 2–9.

Prybyla, Jan S. (1991) 'Economic developments in the Republic of China', in Thomas W. Robinson (ed.), *Democracy and Development in East Asia*. Washington, DC: AEI Press. pp. 49–74.

Rebick, Marcus E. (1993) 'The Japanese approach to finding jobs for older workers', in Olivia S. Mitchell (ed.), *As the Workforce Ages: Costs, Benefits and Policy Challenges*. Ithaca: ILR Press. pp. 103–24.

Rebick, Marcus (1994) 'Social security and older workers' labour market responsiveness: the United States, Japan, and Sweden', in Rebecca M. Blank (ed.), *Social Protection versus Economic Flexibility: Is There a Trade-Off?* Chicago and London: University of Chicago Press. pp. 189–221.

Rose, Richard (1989) 'Convergence and divergence in public policy: American Pacific versus Scandinavian Alternatives'. Centre for the Study of Public Policy, University of Strathclyde, Glasgow, Study Paper in Public Policy no. 178.

Rose, Richard and Shiratori, Rei (eds) (1986) *The Welfare States East and West*. Oxford: Oxford University Press.

Rozman, Gilbert (1991) *The East Asian Region: Confucian Heritage and its Modern Adaptation*. Princeton: Princeton University Press.

Rudd, Christopher (1994) 'Japan's welfare mix', *Japan Foundation Newsletter*, XXII(3): 14–17.

Sellek, Yoko (1994) 'Illegal foreign migrant workers in Japan: change and challenge in Japanese society', in Judith Brown and Rosemary Foot (eds), *Migration in Asia*. Basingstoke: Macmillan.

Shimada, Haruo (1994) *Japan's Guest Workers: Issues in Public Policies*, trans. R. Northridge. Tokyo: Tokyo University Press.

Shinkawa, Toshimitsu (1990) 'The political economy of social welfare in Japan'. PhD thesis, University of Toronto, Canada.

Skocpol, Theda (1985) 'Bringing the state back in: strategies of analysis in current research', in

Peter B. Evans, Dietrich R. Rueschemeyer and Theda Skocpol (eds), *Bringing the State Back In*. Cambridge: Cambridge University Press. pp. 3–43.

Soeda, Yoshiya (1990) 'The development of the public assistance in Japan, 1966–83', in *Annals of the Institute of Social Science*, no. 32. University of Tokyo, Japan. pp. 31–65.

Suh, Sang-Mok (1992) 'Korea's welfare policy: evolution of past policies and future direction', in *Welfare State: Present and Future*. Papers from International Conference on Social Welfare, Seoul, Korea.

Tabata, Hirokuni, (1990) 'The Japanese welfare state: its structure and transformation', in *Annals of the Institute of Social Science*, no. 32. The University of Tokyo, Japan. pp. 1–29.

Takahashi, Shigehiro and Peng, Ito (1992) 'Jidō to katei ni kansuru sabisu shisutemu no kokusai Hikaku', *Nihon Sōgō Aiiku Kenkyūjo Kiyo*, no. 28: 115–28.

Takegawa, Shōgo (1988) '"Fukushi kokka no kiki" sono ato ('"The crisis of the welfare state" and after)', in Shakai Hoshō Kenkyūjo (ed.), *Shakai Seisaku no Shakaigaku (The Sociology of Social Policy)*. Tokyo: Tokyo University Press.

Vogel, Ezra F. (1980) *Japan as Number One: Lessons for America*. Tokyo: Tuttle.

Whittaker, D.H. (1990) 'The end of Japanese-style employment?', *Work, Employment and Society*, 4(3): 321–47.

Woronoff, Jon (1982) *Japan's Wasted Workers*. Tokyo: Lotus Press.

Zenkoku Shakai Fukushi Kyōgikai (1989) *Fukushi Kaikaku (Social Reform)*. Tokyo: Shakai Fukushi Hojin.

8

Social Protection in Central and Eastern Europe: a Tale of Slipping Anchors and Torn Safety Nets

Guy Standing

In the countries ill-covered by the term 'Central and Eastern Europe', the notion of reform in the current upheavals has been subject to a disparate set of euphemisms and images, few of which have been quite so pervasive and misleading as the 'social safety net', a term widely used to convey a set of 'targeted' benefits designed to prevent the main victims of the social transformation falling into poverty. Ironically, levels of poverty and social deprivation have risen alarmingly and relentlessly, bringing falling life expectancy, falling fertility and social conflict.

In most countries, policy-makers have been encouraged to introduce what would amount to a 'residual welfare state', in the sense meant by Richard Titmuss, based on a mix of social insurance and social assistance, and a partial privatization of social policy. Yet the attempts to reform have come up against a legacy of what was essentially comprehensive social policy, such that recent social reform has accentuated the distortions of the past and contributed to a pattern of contradictions that make the future welfare 'system' hard to forecast.

That makes current debates extraordinarily intense, for it is an era of socio-economic experimentation in which *all* forms of 'welfare system' are being considered and to some extent tried, whether by design or as a consequence of a combination of *ad hoc* responses to specific crises and conflicting objectives.[1] Underlying the debates has been the most basic dilemma: how to provide greater social protection for the growing number of people in need, while cutting back on total social expenditure because of actual or perceived resource constraints.

This chapter will not try to do what is impracticable – summarize all the tendencies in social protection policies in countries that range from the affluent enclave of Slovenia to the impoverished nuclear military states of Ukraine, Belarus and the Russian Federation. In the early and mid 1990s, the countries of *Eastern* Europe, and in particular those of the Commonwealth of Independent States of the former Soviet Union, were in much worse structural crises than the main countries of *Central* Europe, led by the Czech Republic, which by 1995 had minimal open unemployment and considerable economic dynamism, and Hungary and Poland, which had experienced very high levels of open unemployment and considerable poverty, while having a dynamic private economy. In between are the large economies of Romania, Slovakia and Bulgaria, all of which have experienced chronic stagflation, and a few small countries that may find it impossible to develop or sustain any independent social policy, and may simply end up adopting those of their neighbours.

This internal differentiation should be borne in mind when contemplating the amorphous region of 'Central and Eastern Europe'. It is almost inappropriate to use the term for analytical purposes. One should also bear in mind that Russia and Ukraine are by far the biggest countries in the region, with over 200 million people.

So, rather than try to give a descriptive review or set of generalizations, this chapter will try to highlight crucial policy conflicts that have emerged, focusing on the spheres of social welfare policy that are unresolved and that may shape the emerging welfare 'system'. We take it as axiomatic that a welfare system has seven potential 'functions' – poverty relief, poverty prevention, provision of social *security*, income redistribution, preservation of 'social solidarity', promotion of (labour) mobility, and promotion of economic and labour market restructuring and productivity.

Put crudely, the former system performed some of those functions relatively well, notably the first four, and some very badly, notably the latter two. The current situation leaves doubt about improvement in all seven, although the reforms have probably marked improvements in the last two areas and deterioration in the first four.[2] Whether that pattern of changes is merely a short-term reflection of the upheavals or a long-term source of concern is the most basic question of all. In 1995, it was still too early to answer that question, although one should have expected more people to be asking the related question: are there policies that could be justified as short-term measures to ameliorate the immediate needs of the millions of people in acute poverty that would be distinctive from some long-term social protection system?

Another way of depicting the changes taking place is that the system that fell apart in the 1980s combined extensive low-level income *security*, coupled with limited inequality and system inflexibility, whereas in the post-war era, at their peak, Western European welfare states provided income security, limited inequality and adequate employment flexibility. Both systems depended crucially on the preservation of full employment, even though they tended to define that differently. While there were different factors disrupting the old systems, countries of both Central and Eastern Europe and Western Europe have been pushed into an era of growing insecurity, growing inequality and increasingly flexible labour markets. If there has been a convergence, it has been towards an era of social insecurity. Whether that is a transitional phase is an open question. If it is, it certainly is a very protracted one.

Distortions of bureaucratic statism

At risk of gross simplification, the predominant form of social protection in the 'Soviet' system was both universalistic and employment-related. It was what might be described as *serviced heavy, transfer light*. It is easily forgotten that the whole population gained from the systematic policy of consumer price subsidies that held down the cost of living to an extraordinary degree.[3] At the same time, only if a person was in employment was social protection guaranteed. Social policy operated primarily through the 'work collective', with general and individual social policy schemes being decided at the central level, by the Communist Party through branch ministries and state committees, which passed on resource allocations to enterprises to be dispersed by trade union officials, and to a certain extent enterprise managers, who were representatives of what were perceived as 'transmission belts'.

Guaranteed employment and wholesale consumer price subsidies were the means of legitimizing the social structure. The system was highly regulated at the formal level, in which benefit provision was elaborated in considerable detail in lengthy labour codes. To a greater degree than in Western Europe, the system operated on the basis of full employment, in which full-time wage employment for both men and women was the overwhelming norm, concentrated in large-scale stable enterprises and organizations, typically employing thousands, and often very many thousands, of workers. Unemployment existed in reality but its recognition was prevented because it was banned as a 'parasitic activity'. Everyone was in effect exploited by the state through the receipt of a very low wage. That wage was undoubtedly an 'individual wage', at best, rather than a 'family wage', and the irony was that the system actually required all workers to be individual units, paid enough to reproduce their own labour power.

Underlying the system's dynamic was the Leninist objective of achieving the 'decommodification of labour', by which the money wage would gradually 'wither away'. That is almost what happened. Thus, the ratio of social benefits to money wages rose steadily and the level of the money wage was low for almost everybody, with occupational wage differentials being modest, although not insignificant. The minimum wage was very close to the average wage, and neither were sufficient to provide an income that could provide adequate savings to cover a temporary period of interruption of earning power, the classic basic objective of social security in European welfare states.

There never was a 'Golden Age' of Soviet social policy, yet there is no doubting that it provided a very broad range of secure social benefits, and as long as the economy grew and was insulated from international economic forces, it was able to function reasonably adequately. The trouble was that it became increasingly inefficient along with the economic system in general.

The labour system entailed five major 'distortions' of direct relevance to the development of social protection after the late 1980s.[4]

First, the nature and degree of social protection and social services were not chosen on the basis of revealed preferences shown by those in need, but were determined by those who were not the recipients of benefits or the consumers of services, i.e. ministries and enterprises, which were mainly direct providers. This meant that there was no means of knowing the value of the benefits or of deciding on the equitable or efficient way of allocating resources to specific types of benefit or services. This contributed to the poor quality of services, because there was a tendency to undervalue what was a vast array of social services for workers and their families, from kindergartens to holiday homes. Principles of allocative efficiency were neglected, and 'discretionary' benefits predominated over distributional needs, since elites (party members, union leaders, etc.) were allowed to come to the front of queues, whether for subsidized goods and services, access to housing, holiday homes, health care or various other benefits.

Non-price rationing meant that the price distortion in the provision of such protection resulted in systematic 'bureaucratic inequity', even though in the interest of 'decommodifying labour' a wide range of low-quality services and benefits were provided at very low cost to the consumer, except when measured in terms of time to obtain access to them, through queues. Ultimately, the system was comprehensive at the basic or 'minimum income' level, and eligibility formally was determined by virtually compulsory employment of all adults in wage labour.

Second, there was an inherent distortion in that the distribution of benefits was heavily focused on enterprises, which in the main were huge industrial combines with many thousands of workers, around which were a network of authorities that existed to serve their perceived needs. What emerged were 'company towns', in which one or two giant enterprises dominated not just the industrial landscape but the range and level of social, cultural and educational services in the community. Entitlement was based on one's role and duration of employment in the enterprise. The enterprises were highly integrated vertically and horizontally, in that they were often involved in all stages of the production process of their main products and also produced a very wide range of products and services.

Thus, the monopolistic structure of production and distribution tended to be associated with monopolistic control over the generation and distribution of social services. Most crucially, the system was characterized by a high ratio of services to transfers, creating what was in effect a service-heavy, transfer-light welfare system. This is paradoxical, in that the image of Central and Eastern Europe was one in which 'services' were chronically underdeveloped. That image is not quite correct: it was the nature of the services, their rationale and distribution, that were undeveloped.

Third, a form of distortion was the pattern of labour mobility. The social norm may have been long-term, if not lifetime, employment in one enterprise, and there were severe impediments to geographical mobility, epitomized by the *propiska* (residence permit) system, which literally blocked legal movement without official sanction, and the lack of any housing market. Yet it would be a mistake to believe that immobility characterized the labour markets of the region. There was some considerable labour mobility, primarily due to 'job-hopping' between enterprises. This was regarded adversely by the authorities, and perceived as costly, yet it was quite extensive. What was absent was the sort of labour mobility that is needed in a dynamic economy. This had implications for the distribution and type of social benefits, since their level was often related to duration in the enterprise as well as party position and other status considerations. In the near absence of wage enticements, benefit provision was used to retain and attract workers.

Labour mobility was not favoured by the authorities in part because the level and structure of employment were so stable, as was the enterprise structure of production. However, in the context of very full employment, as long as there were other enterprises in the district in which a worker had a residence permit – or in which enterprise managements could obtain residence permits for potential workers – workers could shift from job to job quite easily because there was an inherent tendency for enterprises to experience 'labour shortage'. The enterprise's access to funds and the power and prestige of their managements were linked to the number of workers in their enterprise, so that there was always a tendency to create more vacancies than job applicants.

A fourth distortion was that although all socio-demographic groups were integrated into the labour force and employment, they were integrated in a stratified and segmented manner. Thus, women's labour force participation rates were almost as high as those of men, and their wages were probably close, by international standards. However, there was occupational and industrial segregation along gender lines, particularly the latter. Similarly, workers with disabilities had high employment rates, so that there was little need for the authorities to resort to the statutory 'quotas' that formally existed. Because enterprise managements tended to provide 'social employment' they tended to regard the employment of workers with physical or mental difficulties as part of their social obligations, although there was job stratification, as there was for ethnic minorities and for migrants. This pattern of stratified integration has had implications for the evolution of the social welfare system since the late 1980s.

Fifth, a basic distortion was that old-age and other pensioners, including those receiving a disability pension, normally worked in wage employment for many years after they started receiving a pension. Low pensions went with low wages, and few older workers had the savings to enable them to survive with any comfort on a basic pension. Moreover, in Central and Eastern European countries, the ages at which workers became entitled to an old-age pension were extremely low by international standards – 60 for men and 55 for women. But it was the expected norm that pensioners would work well beyond those ages *and* that the wage income would complement the low pensions. This caused increasing difficulties in the 1980s, since the fertility rate declined and an increasing proportion of the population were in the pension age brackets. This was to become one of the most awkward challenges for social policy reformers after 1989.

Besides these distortions, there are some important points to emphasize when looking back at the former systems in the region. While they had faults, in a sense they worked. There was widespread social security in terms of broad and secure access to basic services for those who complied with the obligation to remain in full-time employment, and there was a redistributive set of mechanisms that kept earnings differentials to moderate levels. The population was integrated through full employment, albeit artificially maintained.

Where it failed was in its inability to promote adjustment to changing demands and its lack of concern with 'dynamic efficiency'. The ultimately bureaucratic mechanisms for distributing social services and transfer payments were part of the system that broke down and contributed to that collapse. Yet its delivery of a broad range of minimum benefits for the whole population has not been forgotten.

Distortions of shock therapy

While the reform process in Central and Eastern Europe began with a legacy of deep distortions, the 'shock therapy' that various governments have attempted to various degrees introduced new distortions and compounded some of those that already existed. The countries of the region were suddenly plunged into the global economy, when their industries were chronically uncompetitive, suffering from antiquated technology, low and declining labour productivity and a pattern of integrated trading between themselves that became severed extraordinarily rapidly. Yet there was a traumatic rupture since, by design or by default, the reforms removed the three pillars on which the former system had been legitimized, and on which a majority of the population had come to rely and value, namely guaranteed employment, social protection via subsidized prices, and enterprise-based social benefits, mostly through the direct provision of goods and services.

As far as the reform of social and labour market policy is concerned, it is almost correct to state that the revolution that has been taking place in Central and Eastern Europe is the first in history in which social policy has been shaped and influenced by international financial agencies. This is not necessarily a criticism, merely a recognition of the realities and pressures under which numerous governments have had to operate.

What is a less contentious statement is that the reform of social policy has had considerable redistributional objectives and outcomes. There has been an enormous increase in inequalities, and the poor have lost benefits as well as wage incomes. In the process, there has also been a worrying undercurrent among policy-makers, politicians and national and foreign 'advisers', which is that under the previous regimes the populations were 'over-protected' so that they need a period of re-education to alter their consciousness.[5]

Essentially, the 'sequencing' of economic reform intensified the social policy difficulties that were certain to arise in any case with a transition to a more market-based economic system. Under 'shock therapy', the first step was price liberalization, accompanied to some extent by trade liberalization and moves to currency convertibility. This was followed by a tightening of monetary and fiscal stabilization policy, intended to squeeze inflationary pressure released by price liberalization. Then there was to be the introduction of a 'social safety net', because the tight monetary policy was required to depress domestic demand and lead to a curb on the public budget, leading to unemployment and declining incomes for many groups. Then there was to be mass privatization, by which 'hard budget constraints' would become the norm in firms, so that in the pursuit of profits they would indulge in the final stage of the reform process, namely enterprise restructuring of production, leading to mass layoffs, bankruptcies, and a revitalization of production through private enterprise, new companies and economic diversification.

Whatever the merits and demerits of this approach, this sequencing has had implications for social policy development. Price liberalization in a context of monopolistic enterprises led to a much greater inflationary pressure than if it had been preceded or accompanied by enterprise restructuring intended to create numerous smaller, self-managed units in place of the giant enterprises. Monopolistic enterprises merely raised prices and waited for further subsidies while building up huge debts. The actual process intensified the inflation-induced impoverishment directly, since prices rose much faster than money wages everywhere. By itself the sharp acceleration in inflation necessitated a tighter stabilization policy than if the enterprises had been forced by market pressures to hold down prices. The stabilization policies became so tight that many governments were unable or unwilling to sustain the approach, or could only go part of the way before recoiling in fear of the social suffering and protest that it generated.

The macro-economic policies, coupled with the collapse of the COMECON trading system and other disruptive processes, led to a huge contraction in output, and that led, albeit at a slower pace, to a massive decline in employment, with the decline in state employment being much greater than the rise in private sector employment. Mass unemployment in most countries – and the region overall – became as great as in Western Europe. But it did so in the absence of a social security system oriented to dealing with fluctuating employment and unemployment. The result has been widespread deprivation and impoverishment.

The tax-based incomes policy

The initial economic policies led to two types of incomes policy of relevance to the development of the welfare system. First, governments were pushed by foreign economic advisers and some international agencies to introduce what was a highly distortionary 'tax-based incomes policy' (TIP). Although there have been several variants, essentially this has involved imposing a punitive tax rate on increases in firms' average wages above a certain specified level. At a time of rising money wages, falling real wages and rapidly widening wage differentials, the TIP had a number of perverse effects. Among those, it contributed to the growth of a large body of working poor, since to keep average wages or the overall wage bill down while allowing wages of certain groups of privileged workers to rise to well above the norm, many unskilled workers were put on very low wages or – as has become extremely common in the two largest countries of the region, Russia and Ukraine – into the category of 'unpaid leave'.[6] This induced emergence of a growing category of very low-paid workers has meant a widespread and growing lack of entitlement to various forms of benefit, particularly some of the social insurance and social assistance schemes that have been set up since the late 1980s.

One irony of the TIP is that, while contributing to a more fragmented and inegalitarian wage process, it encouraged a perverse development in social welfare. In the context of the previous system's legacy of a concentration of social benefits in enterprises, a TIP encouraged enterprises to shift part of the money wage into the provision of non-taxed benefits. This meant that workers in such enterprises have tended to gain relative to those locked out of large enterprises, precisely at a time when more open labour markets and mass unemployment should have dictated a rapid transfer to such social benefits from enterprises to the national and local government – state provision in place of corporate provision.[7] This has been one factor in a major trend in much of the region, a process of fragmentation of benefit access, with certain groups having access to enterprise-based benefits and new or reformed state benefits, others having access to new social insurance benefits and private benefits, and a large minority having access to neither enterprise-based nor many of the newer forms of insurance-type benefits.

To give an example of the pervasive and continuing role of enterprise-based social benefits, Table 8.1 shows that, based on a representative survey of factories, most firms in Russian industry have continued to provide an extensive array of such benefits. What has been happening is that some firms have been giving them up under financial pressures or have been withdrawing them for more precarious categories of worker, while others have been strengthening their provision.

The tendency for enterprises to shift to non-wage benefits is paradoxical in other respects. It has tended to occur at a time when governments, pressured by international financial agencies, have been trying to cut social expenditure, primarily as a means of cutting the budget deficit as part of

Table 8.1 *Benefit entitlement, by worker category, Russian industry, 1994 (per cent)*

Benefit entitlement	Admin. workers	Regular workers	Non-regular workers
Paid vacation	99.6	99.6	53.3
Additional vacation	46.3	69.4	22.0
Rest houses	45.0	45.0	22.5
Sickness benefit	93.0	93.9	61.7
Paid health services	54.6	54.6	31.3
Subsidized rent	15.3	16.6	6.2
Subsidies for kindergartens	41.5	42.4	21.6
Bonuses	75.9	77.3	50.2
Profit sharing	69.9	69.9	32.2
Loans	84.3	84.3	41.9
Retiring assistance	78.2	78.6	29.5
Supplementary pension	7.9	7.9	2.2
Possibility for training	51.5	54.6	21.1
Subsidized food	19.7	19.7	13.3
Subsidy for canteen or benefit for meal	55.0	56.8	35.7
Subsidized consumer goods	9.6	9.6	9.3
Transport subsidies	31.4	33.2	18.5

Figures are based on a survey of 384 industrial enterprises, in five oblasts.

Source: Russian Labour Flexibility Survey, Fourth Round; G. Standing, *Reviving Dead Souls: Enterprise Restructuring and Russian Unemployment* (1995), Chapter 6

their stabilization and adjustment programmes. Had the sequencing of the shock therapy been different, with enterprise restructuring at the outset rather than at the end of the process, some of the social functions long practised by industrial enterprises could have been municipalized. As it is, even though there has been a relative shift from money wages to benefits in many state and privatizing enterprises to escape punitive wage taxes, firms have tended to underinvest in the social facilities they operated (e.g. health clinics, training institutes, housing, sanatoriums), so that they have been allowed to deteriorate or have been closed as enterprises have struggled to survive.

The peculiar role of the minimum wage

The second prong of incomes policy in the context of the stabilization policy pursued under the shock therapy adjustment strategy was to let the level of the statutory minimum wage drop to incredibly low levels. The minimum wage has played a much more important role in social policy in the region than elsewhere, so that the changing treatment of it by economic policy-makers has had a series of substantial effects. In every country for which we have data, the level of the minimum wage has fallen sharply relative to the average wage and has dropped to well below the official subsistence level of income, however that has been defined and measured.[8]

Although the number of workers contractually paid the minimum wage has been small, it has continued to determine the pay of many workers, because the wage 'tariff' structure has been based on multiples of the minimum wage. Even though that link has been withering, it has continued to have an influence. And in some countries, notably the biggest two, the number of workers paid only the minimum wage has been boosted by large numbers being placed on it as a result of administrative leave (layoff) or because of firms' inability to pay the full contractual wage. Moreover, some social transfer payments have been linked directly to the level of the minimum wage in almost all countries, most notably unemployment benefits and family benefits. In other words, certain social benefits have been calculated at some multiple of the minimum wage, or the minimum wage has been used as a floor or guaranteed level for the benefit. As a result, holding down the minimum wage soon became a means of holding down social expenditure, and was also perceived by some economic advisers to governments as a convenient means of reducing money wage inflation, since the old wage 'tariff' system has persisted in many of the countries, by which workers at different grade levels have received wages that were a multiple of the minimum wage base level.

For example, in Bulgaria, at the behest of the IMF and World Bank the minimum wage was held constant in monetary terms for over a year, in which time inflation exceeded 500 per cent, implying an enormous decline in its real value, when it was already inadequate to meet minimal living standards. A more recent example is the Russian Federation. In early 1995, the parliament wished to raise the minimum wage from a derisory 20,500 roubles a month (equivalent to about $8, or 20 per cent of the 'physiological survival income') to 54,000, which would still have meant that nobody could survive on the minimum wage. The IMF opposed this proposal and cited it as the reason for refusing to grant the government a loan. The justification was that by raising the minimum wage, family benefits and other transfers would have risen and the federal budget would have been pushed further into deficit. The policy answer seemed at hand. It was surely essential to sever the link between the minimum wage, which should be an instrument for protecting low-paid workers, and social transfers, which should be determined by need and social contributions. Yet it signalled the central importance of the minimum wage in social protection policy.

The shrinking social safety net

The shock therapy policies have undoubtedly contributed to the emergence of mass poverty and inequality, and have shaped the development of social policy more generally. Some might question the direct effects of the reform strategy, yet whatever the factors that have influenced them, the adverse socio-economic trends have been dramatic. The key stylized facts are worth stressing.

Throughout the region, poverty rates have soared, with the sharpest increases coming between 1990 and 1992.[9] And inequality has grown extraordinarily rapidly.[10] In the Russian Federation, for instance, the Gini coefficient for incomes increased from 0.256 in 1991 to 0.409 in 1994.[11] Since the late 1980s there has also been a massive haemorrhage of protected, full-time wage jobs, usually accompanied by extremely rapid growth of unemployment. In the latter trend, the region was led by Poland, which – despite a steady tightening of eligibility entitlements for unemployment benefits that discouraged registration of unemployment – still had an unemployment rate of over 17 per cent at the end of 1994. Some other countries suffered even more severely. For example, Bulgaria had an unemployment rate of over 20 per cent in 1994. By 1995, only the Czech Republic had escaped mass unemployment. This was due in part to its split with the Slovak Republic, which is where most of the heavy industry had been based, in part to its proximity with Germany, in part to its extensive use of labour market policies and in part, it has been claimed, to 'paternalism' practised by managers to protect their own position through maintaining what has been called 'social employment'.[12]

In Eastern European countries, most notably Russia, Belarus and Ukraine, recorded registered unemployment stayed even lower than in the Czech Republic.[13] But the appearance of low unemployment was due to statistical and arbitrary administrative rules. Employment there fell sharply, as it did throughout the region as a whole. And these developments created extreme pressure on social budgets, since the demands for transfers rose very sharply at a time when governments were being pressed to cut budget deficits and when new tax systems were neither established nor legitimized.

At the same time as open unemployment was rising, average real wages have fallen, in some countries by well over 50 per cent, and inflation rates have been upwards of 500 per cent in the past four years, with the worst case being Ukraine with over 10,000 per cent in 1993 alone. Poverty rates have risen to levels typically found in low-income developing countries, with 50 per cent or more of the population living below officially designated subsistence income levels, based on reasonable definitions – for instance, in Bulgaria, Romania, Russia and Ukraine, with over 40 per cent in Poland.

Life expectancy has dropped almost everywhere, and morbidity statistics are anything but encouraging. The worst recorded case is the Russian Federation, where in seven years the average male life expectancy at birth dropped by seven years, to just over 58, while the female life expectancy dropped to 68, incidentally making the gender difference the greatest in the world. Even in relatively dynamic countries such as Hungary, male life expectancy dropped, in Hungary's case from over 66 in 1970 to 65 in 1991. In Bulgaria, male life expectancy declined by over a year between 1988 and 1991, while female life expectancy stabilized.[14] Similar declines took place in other countries, such as Poland, Ukraine and Slovakia.

While the economic decline, coupled with the stabilization policy and incomes policy, were depressing living standards of a growing body of people, attempts to create a so-called social safety net have run into difficulties. Since the outset of the reform process, governments in most countries tried to reform their system of social protection by shifting from the patchwork of universalistic, mainly employment-related schemes to greater reliance on social *insurance* geared to cover market-related 'risks' or contingencies and to means-tested social assistance. They also resorted to greater 'targeting' of benefits, which meant adopting a new array of conditions for entitlement to old and to new forms of benefit. Here the story is far from complete, yet it opened with some tragicomic episodes. In some countries, there was a rush to introduce social protection schemes mirroring those found in certain 'Western' countries, and in some cases this created chaos and confusion, as well as inequity and social deprivation.

We can illustrate the changing character of social welfare policy by considering the main trends and forms of benefit, beginning with the main new form in the countries of the region.

Unemployment benefits

The introduction of unemployment benefits has been indicative of how the social protection system has been evolving – starting as a fairly generous system with an earnings-related component, and becoming increasingly a regulatory instrument with very restrictive entitlements, reaching only a small minority of those at risk.

The first country to introduce a form of unemployment benefits was Hungary, in 1986; this was reformulated as a more standard unemployment benefit system in 1989, when unemployment and entitlement criteria were specified. Other countries introduced similar schemes in 1990–1. Initially, these were fairly generous by international standards, with fairly long periods of entitlement to benefits and reasonably high income replacement rates for those who qualified for them. However, in some countries the number and complexity of entitlement conditions were considerable from the outset – for example, Russia, Belarus and Ukraine, under their respective variants of the 1991 USSR Employment Law – and in others they very soon became more complex, as in Poland. This trend accelerated, as the authorities modelled their schemes more closely on the more restrictive of 'Western' models, notably the Anglo-Saxon so-called 'liberal' systems.[15]

As registered unemployment rose, and as governments came under relentless pressure from the IMF, the World Bank and the Group of 24 (G24) 'donor' countries proferring their financial assistance for economic reform on their conditions, governments step-by-step pared back their unemployment benefits, making them harder to obtain, providing them for shorter periods, and ensuring lower replacement rates. The results have been predictable and dismal.

By 1994, across the region only a minority of the unemployed were receiving unemployment benefits. For example, only about a third were receiving them in Slovakia, probably less than 13 per cent in Russia, less than 10 per cent in Croatia and Ukraine, less than 25 per cent in Lithuania, less than 28 per cent in Bulgaria, about 35 per cent in Albania,[16] about 45 per cent in the Czech Republic and 48 per cent in Poland.[17] Of those who were receiving them, the average level of benefits has often been below any conventional notions of subsistence income. In Poland, by 1994 the unemployment benefit was a flat-rate 36 per cent of the average wage over the previous quarter of the year in employment, normally payable for up to 12 months.[18] The 'income replacement' ratios of unemployment benefits to average wages fell in all countries for which there were comparable data. For instance, in Bulgaria the ratio fell from 46 per cent in 1991 to 27 per cent in 1994, in Hungary from 41 per cent to 26 per cent, and in Romania from 43 per cent to 28 per cent.[19]

The most abysmal cases of low benefits are the countries of the former Soviet Union, where for the small minority of unemployed who receive benefits the average level of unemployment benefit has been equivalent to the minimum wage, even though the system of benefits is supposed to be earnings-related. What this has meant is that unemployment benefits have been about 10 per cent of subsistence income in Ukraine and about 20 per cent of the physiological survival income in Russia. Moreover, the conditions and levels of unemployment benefit have actually discouraged labour mobility, not only by creating conventional 'unemployment traps' (through precluding entitlement to benefits if any income was earned), but by discouraging the unemployed from taking part-time or low-income jobs and penalizing those who quit dead-end jobs (by banning entitlement to benefits for those who become unemployed 'voluntarily', as is often the case).

In Russia and Ukraine possession of a *propiska* (residence permit) has been one of the many conditions for entitlement to benefits, so that migrants between local labour markets are effectively blocked from receiving benefits.[20] Another criterion applied in those major countries has been that those receiving severance pay from firms making them redundant are automatically banned from receiving unemployment benefits for three months. Imagine what such a condition would do to registered unemployment rates in any other country.

In every country, there has been a gradual tightening of conditions for entitlement, and one result of most of the changes in unemployment benefits is that unemployment rates in *Eastern* Europe, in particular, have been chronically under-recorded.[21] The benefit system itself has contributed to the growth of labour-market related poverty and to the process of economic informalization that has become endemic in the region, with social policy implications that we will consider later.

In effect, unemployment benefits have drifted very rapidly from being a basically insurance-based transfer scheme to being a more tightly targeted and residual scheme for regulating the labour market, in which such political and economic objectives as keeping down the level of open unemployment and minimizing the financial demands on the state have predominated over provision for the unemployed.

The threat of active social policy

Underlying those objectives, one might wonder whether what could be called a *directional welfare state* has been emerging. In particular, the notion of active social policy has been growing stronger, influenced by trends in social policy in other parts of the world.

In Central and Eastern Europe, unemployment benefits have been subject to criticisms familiar to those who have witnessed the public debates on the welfare state in North America and Western Europe in the 1980s and 1990s, and so far there has been only muted defence from those who believe in a social democratic welfare state. It has been widely claimed that much of the unemployment in the region is 'voluntary' and that – if not actually encouraging such behaviour – at best unemployment benefits have been 'passive' policy. Although there is no statistical evidence to support the assertion that a large proportion of the huge number of registered – let alone unregistered – unemployed are 'voluntarily' unemployed, many observers and policy-makers have claimed that this is the case, typically citing anecdotes and correlations that could easily be spurious (such as that in some countries unemployment rates for those with more schooling have been higher than for those with less, which often arises for age and location reasons).

Even though unemployment benefits have been pitifully low and of increasingly short duration – shorter than in Western Europe, in the main – they are commonly presented as inducing unemployment and 'black economy' and 'informal economy' work. The presumption that they have these effects has been among the arguments for curtailing their duration and level and for tightening conditions for entitlement. To some extent, there is likely to have been self-fulfilling prophecy here, since the levels of benefit have been so low that to survive with any degree of human dignity a person must have some other source of income.

The tightening process can be illustrated by what has happened in Poland. In 1994, the period of entitlement to unemployment benefits was shortened to three months for those deemed to have lost their jobs through their own 'fault' and for those who refuse a job offer deemed by the authorities to be suitable.

There are perceived to be two villains: voluntary unemployment and black or informal economy work. To those, add the euphemism that un-employment benefits are *passive social policy* and you have a recipe for undermining their legitimacy. Increasingly, a contrast has been drawn with active social policy in the form of 'active labour market policies', to provide the unemployed and the potentially unemployed with training, public works, more training and much else to make them competitive employed workers. It has been easy to go the next step, which is to say that passive policies are 'crowding out' active policies, and that accordingly the former should be cut back to allow for an expansion of the latter.

Again, this has been an image that has come with the supply side economics that has been imported into the region. Why should social protection expenditure 'crowd out' an expansion in training? This is ultimately an ideological argument, for there is no *a priori* rationale for juxtaposing expenditure on these two types of policy. Of course, it is administratively the case that since the beginning of the reform process labour market policies and unemployment benefits have generally been paid from the same source, usually designated an employment fund, based largely on contributions from enterprises. Indeed, the creation of special funds has become one of the hallmarks of the social security reform since 1989. For instance, in Poland the Employment Fund has been expected to deal with both benefits and job creation, and training and career guidance activities.

Whatever the rationale, the policy language has been imported, so that euphemisms of passive versus active social policy have begun to influence thinking about the desirable development of the welfare state. The notion of 'passive' has a pejorative connotation, whereas 'active' sounds virile, dynamic and positive. So, little by little social policy has been tending to become directional, moving towards the notion of *workfare*, by which the unemployed or others receiving short-term social contingency benefits have been required to satisfy not just income-earning tests but behavioural tests, and have been required to act in certain ways to obtain some meagre income support, or in effect to avoid receiving that income support. These are early days, yet this trend has contributed to the widespread disentitlement to social transfers that has been occurring and is leading to a very regulatory approach, which in Central and Eastern Europe has worrying antecedents.

The example of unemployment benefits highlights two general strands of social policy development – the rhetoric of 'targeting' and 'active' policy. As in other parts of the world, these threaten to turn large numbers of people into passive clients given restrictive choices or pushed through the so-called social safety net into poverty. Four other trends are closely related: the nature of pension reform, the shift of the financing of social transfers from enterprises/employers to employees, the unresolved issues of *governance* and the partial *privatization of social policy*.

Pension reform

Pension reform has deserved the high priority it has received. The basic fact is that pensions of one kind or another have accounted for the largest component of cash transfers in all countries of the region. For instance, in Hungary they have accounted for about one-third of social expenditure, and in 1993 accounted for nearly 11 per cent of GDP.[22] Pensionable ages were low in the Soviet era and the level of pensions correspondingly low. A

Table 8.2   *Average and minimum pensions compared with the average wage, Russian Federation, 1985–1993*

	1985	1990	1991	1992	1993
Average pension as % of av. wage	37	34	52	27	35
Mininim pension as % of av. wage	25	24	31	18	19

Source: Ministry of Social Protection, Russian Federation, Moscow

very large proportion of the population have been receiving pensions of one kind or another, and this has persisted. In the Russian Federation, out of a population of 148 million about 36 million were receiving a pension in 1994, and that number had risen by about 10 per cent over the previous three years. In 1993, about 60 per cent of pension recipients were receiving the minimum amount.[23] As Table 8.2 shows, that was well below the average wage. It was also below the level of subsistence income on which bare survival could be assured.

In Poland, to give another example, the minimum pension was 26.3 per cent of the average wage at the end of 1993, and 8.5 million out of the population of 38.4 million were receiving a pension of some kind. What was most remarkable was that about 3.5 million, or 41 per cent, of the pensioners were receiving an invalidity pension.[24]

Because the pensionable ages were so low under the previous system, and because the pension funds were so underfunded, for reasons mentioned earlier, since 1989 there has been a general commitment among policy-makers to raise the normal pension age, coupled with a desire to raise the level of the basic state pension sufficiently to permit full retirement on receipt of it without penury. Many governments have moved in the direction of raising pension ages incrementally, and a few have moved to reduce the gender differential, which was traditionally five years.[25]

Actuarially, the dual challenge of raising the pension level and raising the pensionable age has created considerable difficulty. Some countries have begun to raise their pension ages, and in Poland by 1994 it was already 65 for men, 60 for women. Other countries, such as Bulgaria, have introduced a strategy of raising the pension age incrementally. In Hungary, the age of eligibility for women was scheduled to rise from 55 in 1995 to 60 in 2003, although the policy seems to have been postponed.

In most countries, old-age pensions have retained moderate income replacement rates (although at about 30–40 per cent of average wages, they have been low by Western European standards). In most cases, they have been subject to minimum and maximum levels; in some countries, the former link to the minimum wage has been cut, and as a result the minimum pension has exceeded the minimum wage. However, in most cases the minimum pension has remained well below the official subsistence income.

Invalidity (disability) pensions have generally moved in line with old-age pensions, although one of the most serious social trends in the countries of the region has been the impoverishment and social marginalization of people with disabilities. Often, the disability pension has been made conditional on non-receipt of unemployment benefit, and there has been a tendency to shift more people on to invalidity pensions as a response to unemployment, which seems to have been the case in Hungary, for instance.

In the context of persistently low pensionable age and low pensions, very few countries have introduced a full retirement condition for receipt of an old-age pension, although in some of them attempts have been made to discourage pensioner employment. For instance, for a while in 1991–2 the Bulgarian government imposed a punitive tax on enterprises employing pensioners, which resulted in many older workers being displaced. More generally, what has tended to happen is that high unemployment and the onset of mass redundancies have eased older workers out of the labour market, many into early retirement. In that respect, the countries are becoming more like those in Western and Northern Europe. It is ironic that while trying to raise the pensionable ages, governments have been resorting to early retirement as a labour supply reducing response to unemployment, as in Russia, Ukraine and elsewhere. In Romania, it has been estimated that but for a decree granting long-term paid leave for mothers of children under age one and a decree granting early retirement, unemployment would have been over 5 per cent higher than it was in 1993.[26]

Above all, pension reform cannot be divorced from the relentless external pressure to 'cut back the state', and it is in that context that variants of the 'Chilean model' of pensions have been advocated throughout the region, often through representatives of the World Bank.[27] Although it has not been adopted in its entirety, it has been very influential, and promises to become more so. In effect, a 'two-tier' or 'two-tier, two-pillar' approach has been emerging, in which there is expected to be a low state pension, topped by mandatory earnings-related components, coexisting with private and occupational pension schemes. This partial privatization of social policy may erode the principle of social solidarity that is crucial to a comprehensive social welfare system and may contribute to the growth of income differentiation.

The pressure to move towards a two-tier pension policy, based on a minimum flat-rate state pension and a mandatory private pension-fund pension, coupled with a third-tier voluntary pension, has been greatly increased by the publication of the World Bank's recent book advocating precisely this approach.[28] The World Bank suggested that the flat-rate minimum could be universal or means-tested, although it is clear it favoured the latter option. It argues against a social insurance approach, and unquestionably there have been pressures on governments in countries in Central and Eastern Europe to move in the direction of privatization of pensions. The World Bank claims that pay-as-you-go pension schemes in the context of ageing populations will necessitate excessive increases in contributions rates or diminishing benefits or, which amounts to much the same thing, a rising pension age. But it is not clear that funded pension schemes will be any better at dealing with ageing.[29]

Note one particular implication of the trend towards the privatization of pensions and other forms of social protection. This is that private commercial pension funds invest in capital markets, and thus could easily shift savings from countries with undeveloped stock markets to invest in oversea assets. This is exactly what the World Bank advocates, and it is consistent with the globalization of economies.[30] This could lead to a massive capital flight and impede national autonomy in monetary, fiscal and social policy.

Finally, the World Bank advocates that the base public pension should be similar to what it was in Chile, i.e. about 12 per cent of the average wage. Recognizing that this would be well below the subsistence income, it suggests that this could be topped up according to years of employment, such that the public basic pension would rise to 35 per cent of the average wage after 45 years of employment. Is this going to be the future?

The move to the partial privatization of pensions is consistent with the image of a residual social safety net in which the state is supposed to concentrate on targeting resources on the most needy, and is supposed to leave to 'the market' the provision of private pensions to raise people from subsistence to sufficiency and beyond. To reiterate the point: pension systems are likely to become a major source of socio-economic differentiation in the next few years. In that context, even in the Russian Federation, private pension funds have been multiplying at a remarkable rate,and look set to erode the legitimacy of the state system. Thus, in mid 1993 there were about 40 private pension funds operating in Russia, and by mid 1994 there were about 400.[31] Even enterprises have been setting up their own schemes. It seems that privatization of pensions and the fragmentation of the system will go hand in hand.

Financing social protection: social insurance's rocky road

As for the financing of social protection, reforms on various benefits in most of the countries have moved in parallel directions, essentially from employers to employee and from contributions to general tax revenue. The latter has come mainly because of the rising demands for transfers and the diminishing revenue from contributions, because of lower wages, less employment and non-receipt of contributions that should have been paid. For instance, in Poland up to 1988 contributions covered expenditure on social insurance. Since the second half of 1989, the state budget has been having to pay a growing proportion of the total. By 1991, contributions covered 84 per cent of expenditure; in 1994 it was estimated at less than 80 per cent.[32]

As policy-makers in many of the countries have seen it, a primary challenge has been to shift from direct funding by the government to financing through newly created specific contingency 'funds' – a pension fund, an employment/unemployment fund, a health care fund, and so on.[33] In Poland, a separate social insurance fund was set up as early as in 1987, after which three funds were set up under the Agency for Social Insurance (ZUS) – the main fund, one for agriculture and one for the clergy. The financing was clarified in a reform in October 1991, which removed priviliges for certain groups, a feature of the previous regime in most of the region.[34]

In all countries, the old fiction of the employer paying for the benefits has been preserved, although changes have been taking place to try to shift some of the burden transparently to employees. The actual outcomes have tended to be in sharp variance with the initial intentions, so that overall, as in much of Western Europe, the share of funding of social security coming from general tax revenue has increased relative to the insurance share.

In most cases, what the current situation involves is a substantial 'tax wedge' for employers, which has become onerous, since employer contributions have often become 50 per cent, if not more, of the money wage bill. Whether that manner of financing has had much effect on the level of employment is debatable, and it is an error to *presume* that this way of financing lowers employment. What is beyond reasonable doubt is that it has depressed the level of money wages, so that the cost has been passed on to workers. It has also led to widespread avoidance and evasion of contributions, so that (if economic rationale and the numerous anecdotes are to be believed) employers – private mainly, although there has been a tendency for state enterprises to do the same – have colluded with workers to report to the authorities that wages are much lower than in reality. And many employers have resorted to 'external labour flexibility', using casual labour, contract labour or 'self-employed' workers, although so far not much part-time employment.[35]

The most open case was in the Czech Republic (or the then Czechoslovakia), where in 1990–1 many employers opted to employ only those workers who possessed a self-employed business licence, thus avoiding social security contributions. This was forbidden at the end of 1991, but as it did not remove the incentive to the practice, one can be confident that many employers continued to find other ways of achieving the same result. In many cases throughout the region, enterprise managements have simply not paid the contributions and have, if necessary, bribed inspectors or refused to divulge 'commercial secrets' to the new authorities, who often have not had the authority to challenge the traditionally strong interests behind employers. Anecdotal evidence is not good enough, yet there is adequate cause and sufficient reason for this process to have become endemic. The growing informalization – with its roots in the widespread 'secondary employment' in the old system – is critical to a proper understanding of the development of social policy in most of Central and Eastern Europe.

The 'collectability' of contributions (insurance and other forms of levy) has been dismal; in some countries, estimates have suggested that less than one-third of the expected revenue has been collected. In Bulgaria, the non-receipt of contributions was estimated to be about 25 per cent, almost enough to finance a limited health insurance scheme.[36] In turn, social budget deficits have grown, leading to a tendency to raise contribution rates, which have encouraged a further erosion of collectability and a vicious circle of underfunding and low benefits, contributing to a further tightening of conditions for receipt of benefits. Moreover, the drift of employment and labour contracts into the non-contributing 'informal economy' has meant that increasing numbers of workers are not covered by the evolving contingency social insurance.[37] For many new types of employment relationships, workers on becoming unemployed do not have entitlement to unemployment benefits or to other forms of employment-related social transfers.

There is a trend to shift part of the contributions from employers to employees. In most countries, the employee contribution is still negligible. For example, in 1994, it was 1 per cent out of the 38 per cent contribution in Latvia, and it was even less in Bulgaria and Lithuania. In a few countries, the employee share is higher (e.g. 13.5 per cent out of the 49.5 per cent in the Czech Republic and 11 per cent out of the 60 per cent in Hungary). However, shifting more of the contribution directly onto the employees may not have the beneficial effects its advocates would like and expect. Since real wages are still low, it would lead to upward pressure on wages and would almost certainly lead to a greater resignation on the part of workers to accept precarious, flexible forms of employment by which they would be disentitled to social protection. However, at least a partial shift to employee contributions would increase the 'transparency' of the social insurance principle.

Another evolving issue relates to the peculiar circumstances that we could call *paternalistic individualism*. Under the former system, the wage was essentially an individual's wage, intended for the simple reproduction of a single worker's labour power. A family received services and transfers that reduced its costs to a minimum level, and all adult members were expected to be earning their individual wage. Because the state, through the enterprise employing the worker and through the transmission belts of the trade union and local authorities, provided a broad array of social services and transfers, all adults worked. This was far from the continental European welfare state of paternalistic social insurance, in which women were typically 'secondary workers' and expected to be mainly economically inactive, dependent on a male 'breadwinner' in stable full-time employment receiving a family wage.

In Central and Eastern Europe, the low individual wage encouraged the persistence of full employment in labour-intensive, low-productivity production, which contributed to the horrifying collapse of the economies of the region after 1989. Put crudely, low wages begat low productivity, which begat stagnant wages, which begat unmotivated lower-productivity workers, and so on. Since the reforms began in the late 1980s, money and real wages for some groups in some parts of the economies have risen dramatically, and as the number of relatively privileged wage earners grows, there will be pressure to increase the extent of earnings-related, insurance-type benefits. And if the state does not provide them, then the privatization of social policy will accelerate. So there has been a tension tending to generate inequality and to accentuate that inequality through the pattern of provision of social transfers.

Will the shift to earnings-related benefits induce more women to become 'secondary workers' or economically inactive, as 'home carers'? Will it lead to even stronger socio-economic differentiation than has been occurring? The latter seems likely. The former is much less likely. Although there is pressure in some spheres to encourage women to leave the labour force, one would have to be particularly pessimistic to expect it to succeed. So far, although women have suffered terribly from the economic decline since the late 1980s, there is no compelling evidence that they have suffered more than men or that with rising unemployment women have been marginalized as secondary workers.[38] Indeed, for complex reasons, women were in a better position to respond to the economic, social and psychological shocks of the collapse and are probably more adept at working in the informal, market-regulated activities that have been emerging. The continuing prominent economic role of women will be important in shaping the evolution of the social protection system.

Health care

As for health care, the old system was 'labour intensive', like everything else, in that there were high ratios of medical personnel to patients. In most countries, there was a comprehensive network of health services, financed mainly from the state budget, which meant that with restrictive monetary and fiscal policies under 'shock therapy', there has been an adverse effect on services, which some have described as 'devastating'.[39] Since 1989, there has been a tendency to convert health care into a social insurance-based system, most notably in the Czech Republic, Slovakia and Hungary. Yet politically it has been hard for new governments to curtail a well-entrenched universal health care system, even for those ideologically committed to doing so. The old pro-natalist policy of two years of paid maternity leave for all women having babies is hard to remove without a political backlash, especially at a time of very low and declining fertility. Similarly, making pensioners have to pay part of the costs of medicine and leaving them shivering in queues outside pharmacies, as was the case in Bulgaria in 1993–4, does not give a reforming government a popular democratic image.

Implicit and explicit privatization has been occurring here too, in that commercial private clinics and private access to better facilities have been spreading, while resources devoted to the public health care system have been curtailed and the private sector has been moving into the pharmaceuticals industry. In some countries, salaries and benefits for those working in the public health system have fallen relative to other groups, from an already low level by international standards. This trend has probably been strongest in Russia and Ukraine, where 'budgetary sector' salaries have been allowed to fall sharply relative to those in industry, let alone the emerging private sector. The induced 'internal brain drain' should be causing much more alarm than it has so far, since highly trained and experienced doctors and others are encouraged to leave their profession and take up some commercial activity to earn above-subsistence incomes.

The public social services sector is where the state has had most control over wages and earnings, so that it has been most 'successful' in holding down money wage inflation for such workers. Moreover, tightening social budgets has resulted in widespread and serious 'wage arrears' in the public health care system, in education and in social services generally, so that the wages actually paid have been even lower than they have appeared in official statistics, most notably in Russia.

Social assistance

Perhaps the most worrying tendency in all countries of Central and Eastern Europe is that there has been a strong drift to more widespread reliance on means-tested social assistance. This comes about through three routes: non-coverage because an insurance-type or universal transfer mechanism has not been introduced; *explicit disentitlement* through legislative changes tightening conditions for receipt of benefits; and *implicit disentitlement* through more people moving into statuses that do not entail entitlement to benefits.

As an example of explicit disentitlement, in Poland family allowances became income-tested in January 1995, whereby only those families in which their per capita income was less than 40 per cent of the average wage were entitled to the allowance. The income was to be determined over a six monthly period, so allowing for sudden unemployment. The point is that as a budget saving measure the change was likely to make it harder for those in need to obtain income support, if one accepts the view that income testing and any new condition tend to reduce the take-up of benefits.

The growth in numbers of people depending on social assistance has been remarkable. Thus, for example, in Bulgaria the number increased by 340 per cent between 1989 and 1992.[40] In Poland, the number increased from 1.645 million in 1990 to 3 million in 1993.[41] Such social assistance is often distributed on a discretionary basis at the local level. For the authorities to apply means tests and income tests equitably and objectively, local officials would need far more experience and training than they have had. There are ample reasons for believing that social assistance is not working, in the sense that numerous people needing financial help are being disentitled to it, whether through the arbitrary application of rules or through non-application through a sense of stigma or lack of knowledge.

'Take-up' rates of social assistance could be expected to be particularly low in countries where the capacity to operate the system has been so little developed, where the number of officials has been small and where the demand and need for transfers have been escalating at such rapid rates. Take-up rates of below 50 per cent are likely to be the norm. Moreover, the levels of social assistance benefits have been extremely low, and in some countries the level of subsistence income used to determine the level of benefits has been redefined downwards for budgetary reasons, notably in Russia and Ukraine, where in early 1994 it was about 20 per cent of the level of two years earlier.[42] In short, although reliance on social assistance has been growing, nobody should be under any illusion that they could operate fairly or efficiently to provide social protection to those most in need.

The Czech case: leader or exception?

The Czech Republic has been seen by many as distinctive and generally economically more successful than other countries undergoing an economic transformation. As noted earlier, for various reasons its unemployment rate has been lower than in most other countries – peaking at 4.4 per cent in early 1992 and being about 3 per cent in early 1995 – and its economic dynamism has been seen as greater than almost all other countries in Central and Eastern Europe. The development of the country's social policy has been controversial, since to a greater and more consistent degree than other countries in the region, its government has been openly committed to a liberal economic reform.

As in other countries in the region, after 1989 the Czech authorities moved in the direction of social insurance, strengthening a strong tradition in this respect, stemming from the nineteenth century. In 1990, it extended its insurance system to the self-employed, which was a rapidly growing category, and provided flat-rate family allowances. In the same year, the government transferred responsibility for social insurance to the government, removing participation of the trade unions. In 1991 a new unemployment benefit scheme was introduced.

Since the early phase of reform there have been substantial changes, including a reduction of unemployment benefit entitlement to six months. Separate insurance funds were proposed, covering basic pensions, supplementary pensions, sickness insurance, accident insurance and employment insurance, but as of early 1995 they were still in the process of being established. There has been a trend towards the privatization of health care, and a compulsory health insurance scheme was introduced in 1993. In principle, the governance of social protection is overseen by a tripartite Council of Economic and Social Agreement (RHSD), although the trade unions have complained that they have not been adequately consulted. The government has planned to reduce its own role in the council.[43]

Although state pensions have been financed from employee and employer contributions, there has been a trend towards revenue financing. In reforms proposed for 1995, the Czech government has indicated that the state pension should consist of a flat-rate component, indexed to the cost of living, coupled with an earnings-related part. It is proposed to reduce the income replacement rate over ten to fifteen years from 50 per cent of the average wage to 35 per cent of it, during which time citizens would be encouraged to participate in private insurance schemes, subsidized to a diminishing extent by the state. During the same period, the pensionable age would rise from 60 to 62 for men and from 52–55 to 54–57 for women.

The reform proposals also envisage a shift towards means-tested benefits, based on current incomes, for twelve or more forms of transfer, including child benefit, family allowances and housing benefit. Thus, child benefit is scheduled to be transformed from a universal insurance benefit to a targeted benefit, and a new housing benefit for the poor is planned. The level of all the means-tested benefits will be determined by the subsistence income, with a coefficient being set by the government. It is intended to avoid the acute poverty traps that would otherwise arise by setting different coefficients for the various transfers. However, not only are the administrative costs and arbitrary rules likely to bedevil such an approach, but the venture would promise to create a political risk for the group population, since they would be unable to estimate their likely benefit before the event.

In the country, there has been a growing role allocated to social assistance, which was established in the mid 1980s and reformulated by the Law on Subsistence Minimum of late 1990. Eligibility conditions have been tightened since 1990, although it is believed that take-up has increased among those eligible for assistance. The percentage of the population relying solely on social assistance has been quite low.

Progress in the proposed reforms will be keenly watched by policymakers and analysts in all countries of Central and Eastern Europe. The Czech authorities seemed intent not just on creating a residual welfare state but on privatizing social policy to a large extent, leaving the state to provide mainly low flat-rate benefits coupled with means-tested social assistance for the poor. Somehow, with its long traditions of social solidarity and social democracy, however disrupted by the Soviet era, the liberal reform agenda seems unlikely to be implemented.[44] But it could be.

Challenges of governance

One unresolved ongoing debate in Central and Eastern Europe concerns the appropriate mode of governance of social protection.[45] Whether the drift to targeting, active social policy, workfare and means-tested social assistance becomes overwhelming will depend very much on what form of governance emerges. By this is meant the institutional framework for formulating, implementing, administering, monitoring and evaluating social policy schemes.

In Central and Eastern Europe, the old mode of governance was essentially a 'command-transmission' system, with personalized discretion being restricted to the enterprise level, or via the party apparatus and to a certain limited extent at the local community level. Since the collapse of that system, various countries have experimented with some variant of 'tripartite board' governance and there has been a confused splitting of responsibilities between new ministries and government agencies. In some countries, the degree of decentralization to the regional or even sub-regional level of authority has been much greater than in others, in terms of control over income and expenditure and in the specifications of practical social protection policy. This is particularly the case in the largest countries, Russia and Ukraine.

The main issues in governance are fourfold:

1   Is independent social policy in one country feasible in the 1990s, especially given the pressure from the IMF and World Bank to adopt particular policies and the pressure from the European Union to have the emerging social protection systems 'converge' to patterns acceptable for potential members of an enlarged European Union?

2   What are the prospects of genuinely democratic 'tripartite' governance or some more broadly based representative system that gives a voice and decision-making role for groups of potential and actual beneficiaries?

3   Will the international trend towards social policy governance dominated by government bodies drawing on 'experts' and committees of specialists become the norm in Central and Eastern Europe? To what extent will such processes be democratically accountable?

4   What is the optimum degree of regional and institutional decentralization of social policy? Or to what extent should social policy have a geographically redistributive function?

The first question is sensitive, and there has been evidence that, for better or for worse, pressures amounting to social policy conditionality have been introduced into negotiations on loans from the World Bank and IMF, and financial assistance from other sources. This social conditionality is an important issue that needs to be brought into the open, since it seems to imply intervention in national policy-making.

The second question should be considered in the context of the growing informalization and flexibility of labour markets and the difficulty of identifying proper representatives of employers and workers. The most basic fact of all in assessing the reformulation of social policy in Central and Eastern Europe is that *all* institutions are weak, and as such the scope for negotiating binding agreements between contending interest groups is limited and fragile.

The third set of questions is no less important than the preceding two.

The likelihood is that public accountability and negotiations between interest groups will be eroded, although it is too early to be sure. There is plenty of scope for voice regulation of 'expertise' to become the guiding principle.

The fourth question deserves more attention than it has received, since in the most populous countries of the region, Russia, Ukraine and Poland – and particularly in the Russian Federation – the growing regionalization of social policy is building up a major fiscal crisis, especially as regional disparities in unemployment and poverty have become extreme.

The challenge in arriving at a balance between national and sub-national governance is to find ways of enabling sufficient national control to ensure that the redistributive function can operate and of enabling sufficient sub-national control to ensure that local needs and group interests are adequately taken into account.

Concluding points: in search of redistributive justice

For those living and working in the region, it is difficult not to be deflated by the course of events in the development of social protection policy in much of Central and Eastern Europe since the late 1980s. For all the talk of J-curves (a short dip in living standards that would be followed by a steep sustained improvement), the dip has already been long and very deep, even if some improvements in some countries were recorded in 1994.

One chilling statistic is worth reiterating and should give the reader a momentary concern: in Russia in 1995, male life expectancy at birth was a little over 58 years, having fallen about seven years in the past seven years. One might quibble with the data, yet nobody has questioned the enormity of the trend. Behind that statistic lies a host of puzzling others, such as the fact that the equivalent figure for women was 68 years, down from the past but by much less than for men, creating the widest gap in life expectancy between men and women in the world. In other countries, declines in life expectancy have also been sharp, although not as sharp as in Russia. These are not minor adjustments that can be relegated to footnotes in the euphoria of 'democratic reform'.

Another aspect of those figures is that morbidity and mortality rates have risen most for young and middle-aged men, and the causes of death that seem to have become much more prominent are *stress*-related illnesses. Much more research is required before definitive answers can be given, yet one very plausible hypothesis is that the economic, social and psychological shocks of the restructuring have precipitated a profound and widespread sense of *insecurity*, reflecting an inability to adjust to what are totally new and difficult circumstances. As a Russian cabinet minister said to me in conversation in 1993, when we were discussing why people were not protesting more about the evident deprivation, 'They are just going into their homes and dying.'

This conclusion began with those points to highlight the urgency and seriousness of social policy reform. Neither pessimism nor atavism would be appropriate at this stage. For the next few years, Central and Eastern Europe will be facing a *crisis* in the development of social protection, in the classic Greek sense of both a threat and an opportunity. The threat is that there will be persistently high levels of poverty, accompanied by widening inequality and socio-economic fragmentation; the opportunity is still there to create a new system that builds on the sense of social solidarity and desire for redistributive justice that are still prevalent in the region. One good point worth stressing is that social transfers have been able to reduce poverty rates substantially in countries such as Hungary and Poland, although they still have left a large residue of people in poverty.[46]

After the burst of euphoria around 1989, there was a widespread desire for market freedoms coupled with strong state guarantees of income security. This combination was never feasible or likely to be pursued by governments struggling for domestic and international legitimacy. External pressures to create a specific type of neo-liberal market economy were strong, and adverse distributional outcomes were presented as the short-term pain for long-term gain. Although welfare spending has remained high by international standards – for instance, in Hungary in 1993 it accounted for about a third of GDP, or nearly as much as in Sweden – systematic attempts to pare back spending have had their effects.

Growing concern about the severity of the social suffering and inequalities has forced the neo-liberal agenda onto the defensive in many parts of the region. There is widespread distaste for the grosser forms of inequality that have emerged, and for the ordinary person the archetypal villain has become 'the Mafia', a term that covers a very broad range of person indulging in opportunistic economic behaviour, from the *nomenklatura*, who have moved from their old perches as state functionaries to become commercial barons, to traders making monopoly profits, to successful participants in the mostly unrecorded informal economy and to criminals of almost every persuasion.

One problem with the fragmented social structure that is emerging is that the new wealthy have found it remarkably easy to opt out of the old *and* the new social security systems, and there is a very strong danger that a substantial minority or even a majority of the population will cease to feel they are direct stakeholders in the welfare system.

There is a sinister cynicism sometimes found among those influencing social policy reform in Central and Eastern Europe, which goes something like this. The countries of the region cannot afford a comprehensive social protection system, but it is essential to ensure that the 'middle classes' support the development of 'democracy' in the longer term. They must receive adequate social protection so that they do not become disaffected. This probably means that the poor cannot be provided with adequate benefits, because they could not be afforded. As this reasoning leads inexorably to the neglect of the poor, it was not surprising to hear one authority conclude, with ruthless logic, 'We must just write off this generation.' This chilling reasoning raises many questions. Above all, it highlights the urgency of an open, transparent debate about the direction of social protection reform in these societies.

The debate in Central and Eastern Europe is finely balanced. There are those who believe that, whatever the limitations identified by 'Western' critical analysts, Western European models of social insurance are the best option, so that a patchwork of contingencies should be covered by employment-related social security, with whatever risks that are unrelated to employment being covered by universal benefits and with poverty being prevented or remedied by social assistance. Others see this route as doomed, because of its applicability to a declining industrial employment model, because of dwindling resources coming from insurance-style contributions, because of the likelihood that more of the resources will have to come from general taxation and because of the growing proportion of the population contributing little and needing long-term transfers. Some of those who see the trends in this way have turned to targeting, and increasingly favour tighter conditionality and directional, active policy, coupled with partial privatization of social policy. The likelihood of this route being taken is strengthened by the fact that a social insurance system covering market risks has not been securely established, or in the case of countries such as the Czech Republic and Hungary has not been *re*-established, which takes time and experience of its value. This is in contrast with what Gøsta Esping-Andersen characterizes as the continental European welfare states, in that the entrenched legitimation of state-based welfare has checked the growth of a popular desire for private schemes.[47]

There is a third current, too radical and unorthodox to attract more than *sotto voce* discussion thus far. That is to reverse the dominant trends and to opt for building a system of social protection based on minimal universal income protection as a right of citizenship, topped up with needs-based social transfers and a richer array of social and community services, with a strongly democratic governance structure. In spite of the mafioso tendencies, there is surely enough social solidarity left in the region for this third option to be regarded seriously. Regrettably, other routes look more likely to be taken first.

Note

All views and conclusions are those of the writer, and should not be attributed to the International Labour Organization.

1 In that context, it is symptomatic that analysts have referred to 'post-totalitarian' or 'post-socialist' regimes, reminding the sceptic that use of the prefix 'post-' should be regarded as indicating a lack of knowledge about what we are identifying. Similarly, the notion of 'the transition' is problematical, since it is by no means clear that there is one type of transition or that it is a simple process of change 'from state socialism to market capitalism'.

2 Of course, poverty did exist in the countries of the region during the 1970s and 1980s.

See, for a review of studies, S.Marklund, 'Social policy and poverty in post-totalitarian Europe', *Scandinavian Journal of Social Welfare*, no. 2, 1993, pp. 104–14.

3 For example, in 1988 direct consumer subsidies in the USSR accounted for half as much as the total expenditure on the social consumption fund: S. Cazes and J. Le Cacheux, 'Inégalités de revenu, pauvreté et protection sociale en Union Sovietique', *Observations et diagnostics économiques*, no. 38, October 1994. In Poland, in 1988 price subsidies on consumer goods accounted for about 42 per cent of the public budget.

4 The notion of distortion is questionable. We use the term to refer to a pattern unlike that found in other types of economy and that operated with negative efficiency and equity effects.

5 For insightful critiques of this perspective, see S. Ferge, 'Human resource mobilisation and social integration: in search of new balances in the great transformation', Budapest, unpublished manuscript, 1992; and C. Offe, 'The politics of social policy in east European transitions: Antecedents, agents and agenda of reform', *Social Research*, vol. 60, no. 4, winter 1993, pp. 1–36.

6 For empirical assessments based on industrial surveys in 1994, see G. Standing, *Labour Market Dynamics in Ukrainian Industry in 1992–94: Results from the ULFS*, Budapest, ILO Central and Eastern European Team, International Labour Organization, 1994; *Enterprise Restructuring in Russian Industry and Mass Unemployment*, Geneva, Labour Market Papers, no. 1, February 1995.

7 For an analysis of this issue in the context of Russia, see G. Standing, 'Wages and work motivation in the Soviet labour market: Why a BIP, not a TIP is required', *International Labour Review*, vol. 130, no. 2, 1991, pp. 237–53. The shift from money wages to 'social consumption' and benefits was shown in the first three rounds of a survey of industrial enterprises in Russia, covering the period 1990–3.

8 D. Vaughan-Whitehead and G. Standing (eds), *From Protection to Destitution: the Minimum Wage in Central and Eastern Europe*, Budapest and Oxford, Central European University Press, 1995.

9 UNICEF, *Crisis in Mortality, Health and Nutrition*, Florence, UNICEF, Economies in Transition Studies, Regional Monitoring Report, no. 2, August 1994, Table 1.1, p. 2.

10 Even in the former East Germany, income inequality increased, although as of 1993 it had not reached the level of the former West Germany. The relative incomes of persons over 60 has grown much worse in Eastern Germany than in Western Germany. R. Hauser, J. Frick, K. Mueller and G.G. Wagner, 'Inequality in income: a comparison of east and west Germans before reunification and during transition', *Journal of European Social Policy*, vol. 4, no. 4, pp. 277–95.

11 The State Committee for Statistics of the Russian Federation, *Sotsialnoekonomicheskoe polozhenie Rossii, 1994 g*, Moscow, Goskomstat, January 1995, p. 147.

12 I. Mozny, 'An attempt at a non-economic explanation of the present full employment', *Czech Sociological Review*, vol. 1, no. 2, 1992, pp. 199–210.

13 Some foreign economists, eager to show the success of their 'advisory' role, claimed that this reflected the success of reform, or perversely that little 'shock therapy' was taking place. Thus, Richard Layard and Anders Aslund both persisted in claiming that unemployment in Russia was under 2 per cent in 1994, in the wake of an extraordinary collapse in output.

14 P. Kisseva, *Bulgaria: Social Protection and Social Security Country Profile*, Budapest, ILO Central and Eastern European Team, 1994.

15 The influence of foreign agencies from specific 'Western' countries on the evolution of social policy has yet to be analysed. Clearly, the large number of American, British and German consultants and agency representatives have helped shape its development, both directly and through the international financial agencies.

16 A. Cico, *Social Protection in Albania: a Country Profile*, Budapest, ILO Central and Eastern European Team, 1994, Table 13, p. 28. This referred to December 1993.

17 In the fourth quarter of 1990, 79 per cent of the registered unemployed in Poland were receiving unemployment benefits; in the fourth quarter of 1993 that was down to 48 per cent. I. Topinska, *Social Protection in Poland: a Country Profile*, Budapest, ILO Central and Eastern European Team, 1994, Table 12, p. 38.

18 There were some exceptions, notably in regions (*gminas*) designated as suffering from high 'structural unemployment'.

19 International Social Security Association, *Restructuring Social Security in Central and Eastern Europe: a Guide to Recent Developments*, Geneva, ISSA, 1994.

20 In 1994, in Russia this condition was removed formally by a presidential decree, but district employment exchanges continued to apply it.

21 The factors inducing this under-recording are discussed elsewhere: G. Standing, 'Why measured unemployment in Russia is so low: the net with many holes', *Journal of European Social Policy*, vol. 4, February 1994.

22 Hungarian Ministry of Finance. The share peaked at 11.6 per cent in 1992.

23 M.-A.Crosnier, 'Russie: la protection sociale entre deux systèmes', *Le Courrier des Pays de l'Est*, Paris, no. 383, October 1993.

24 L. Vinton, 'Poland's social safety net: an overview', *RFE/RL Research Report*, vol. 2, no. 17, 23 April 1993; M. Szczur, 'Main directions of public pension system reform in Poland: possibilities of their implementation', Warsaw, Institute of Labour and Social Studies, November 1994.

25 Life expectancy has been much higher for women, and the differential has been growing since the late 1980s, so that many women spend thirty years or more in pensioned retirement. This has contributed to the impression that female labour force participation rates in the region have been extremely high. They have been high, yet those rates are overestimated, since in the statistics a post-retirement age woman in employment is counted in the numerator, whereas the denominator only includes women aged 16–55, or 54.

26 Ministry of Labour and Social Protection, 'The social protection system in Romania', paper presented at the Cyprus Round Table on Design and Governance of Social Protection, organized by ILO-CEET and the Ministry of Labour of Cyprus, Larnaca, Cyprus, 23–25 March 1994.

27 Sometimes it has been promoted by consultants. See, for example, R. Holzmann, *Pension Reform Concept for Latvia*, paper prepared at request of World Bank, University of Saarland, Germany, May 1994.

28 The World Bank, *Averting the Old Age Crisis: Policies to Protect the Old and Promote Growth*, New York, Oxford University Press, 1994.

29 For a good critique of the World Bank's proposals, see R. Beattie, 'Reflections on the World Bank's pension policy', *International Social Security Review*, ISSA, Geneva, 3/4, 1995. For a critique of the Chilean pension scheme that is being advocated in Central and Eastern Europe, see C. Gillion and A. Bonilla, 'Analysis of a national private pension scheme: the case of Chile', *International Labour Review*, vol. 131, no. 2, 1992.

30 World Bank, *Averting the Old Age Crisis*, pp. 222–3.

31 I. Dyomina, 'Pension funds: a blessing or a new misfortune?', *Moscow News*, no. 33, 19 August 1994.

32 L. Nawacki, 'Polish experiences in tripartite negotiations on social policy transformation', paper presented at the Cyprus Round Table. Topinska estimated that the budgetary share of financing rose from 14.8 per cent in 1990 to 26.3 per cent in 1993: Topinska, *Social Protection in Poland*, Table 22a, p. 50.

33 In Latvia in 1994 the Minister of Social Protection, Janis Ritenis, was proposing to set up seven national funds. J. Ritenis, 'Driving forces behind the social protection reforms in Latvia', paper presented at the Cyprus Round Table.

34 Szczur, 'Main directions'.

35 For evidence based on a survey of 501 industrial enterprises in Bulgaria, see G. Standing, G. Sziracksi and J. Windell, 'The growth of external flexibility in Bulgarian industry', paper presented at Conference on Restructuring and Labour Market Policies in Bulgaria, Sofia, 18–20 May 1993.

36 ILO-CEET, *The Bulgarian Challenge: Reforming Labour and Social Policy*, Budapest, ILO Central and Eastern European Team, 1994.

37 At the end of 1994, in recognition of this tendency, the Polish government announced its intention to broaden the scope of income from which social insurance contributions should be

paid, to include 'civil law contracts' of employment. It will be interesting to see if this is achieved.

38 See, for instance, G. Standing, 'Implications for women of restructuring Russian industry', *World Development*, vol. 22, no. 2, February 1994, pp. 271–83; L. Paukert, 'Economic transition and women's position in four eastern European countries', paper presented at Technical Meeting on Enterprise Restructuring and Labour Markets, ILO Turin Centre, 31 May 31 to 2 June 1995.

39 M. Ksiezopolski, 'Social policy in Poland in the period of political and economic transition: challenges and dilemmas', Warsaw, Institute of Social Policy, Warsaw University, 1992, p. 11.

40 ILO-CEET, *The Bulgarian Challenge*, especially Chapter 6.

41 Topinska, *Social Protection in Poland*, Table 30, p. 55.

42 ILO-CEET, *The Ukrainian Challenge: Reforming Labour and Social Policy*, Budapest, ILO Central and Eastern European Team, 1994, Chapter 7.

43 J. Kral, 'Social protection governance: the case of the Czech Republic', paper presented at the Cyprus Round Table 1994.

44 For the latest in a series of studies of changing attitudes by the Czech population, see J. Vecernik, 'The emergent labour market and job prospects in the Czech Republic', *Prague Economic Papers*, forthcoming.

45 For a set of national reviews of attempts to come to grips with the issues raised in this section, see M. Cichon and L. Samuels (eds), *Making Social Protection Work: the Challenge of Social Governance in Countries in Transition*, Budapest, ILO Central and Eastern European Team, 1994.

46 P. Hausman, 'A comparative study of the effectiveness of social protection', unpublished paper, Walferdange, CEPS/Instead, November 1994. These data are for 1991–2. These countries are among the most favourable, and one should be wary of generalising about Eastern Europe.

47 G. Esping-Andersen, 'The continental European welfare states: the strategy of labour reduction and the impending overload of social insurance', unpublished paper, University of Trento, January 1995, p. 4.

CONCLUSION

9

Positive-Sum Solutions in a World of Trade-Offs?

Gøsta Esping-Andersen

One aim of this project was to identify future scenarios for the welfare state. Academics naturally shun futurology, which means that our work was concentrated on known facts and visible trends. The concluding chapter offers an opportunity to move beyond academic caution. Basically, I propose to revisit the major themes in this book in a more speculative vein, posing to myself the seemingly simple question: how do I now, after more than a year's work, understand the welfare state's problems and future? The answers I give to this question may be neither profound nor convincing, but they do suggest a less pessimistic scenario than when the project first began.

Three basic issues have occupied a prominent place in this study. The first could be called the global economy problem; the second has to do with the limits – and possibly adverse consequences – of a redistributive and egalitarian welfare state; and the third is essentially a political problem of consensus-building. Where we find trade-offs, are they genuine and, if so, can they be reconciled?

The global economy problem

The issues at stake here seem quite straightforward: a nation's growth today requires economic openness which, in turn, entails tougher competition and greater vulnerability to international trade, finance and capital movements. Governments' freedom to conduct fiscal and monetary policy 'at will' is therefore more constrained: profligate deficit spending to maintain employment or pursue redistributive ambitions will be punished; Keynesianism, let alone social democracy, in one country is accordingly no more an option. It may even be that governments' freedom to design discrete social policies has eroded, as contemporary pension reforms suggest. It is increasingly world finance which defines what is possible and desirable; not only in the ex-communist states or Latin America, but also recently in Italy and Sweden. There is the alarming prospect that globalization will eventually emasculate democratic choice.

Secondly, world-wide competition means that economies with high wage costs will lose jobs to those with cheaper labour. Hence, the spectacular industrial performance of the newly industrialized countries (NICs) went hand-in-hand with severe industrial job losses in the advanced nations. The Asian 'tigers' have, in fact, achieved a level of economic development within a few decades that it took Europe a century to attain. Global competition helps realize the goal of Third World development that has been so much prioritized by the advanced nations since World War II. As new NICs appear, Third World development will be given an additional boost, and next time around their success is likely to provoke 'deindustrialization' in Japan, Korea and Taiwan. But will such a chain reaction really entail that the First and Second World welfare states must suffer, and that welfare statism in the now developed NICs is precluded?

Let us re-examine these two facets of globalization from a welfare state perspective. As to the former, it may very well be true that Keynesianism in one country is no longer possible. Yet, was it ever? Or, put differently, what precisely are the conditions that have changed? In answering these questions, let us begin with a puzzle: throughout the postwar era the most advanced welfare states tended to develop in the most open economies such as Scandinavia and Germany; the more residualistic welfare states, in turn, cluster in countries with relatively protected domestic economies, such as the United States and Australia. The puzzle remains when we recognize that today's economic success stories, such as Japan and South Korea, occurred against the backdrop of substantial protectionism.

The answer to the puzzle lies, as a huge body of political science (and now also macro-economic) research has shown, in the way that domestic institutions facilitate, or not, broad consensual solutions. Thus, encompassing trade unions and employer organizations in Scandinavia negotiated themselves towards consensus and long-run relations of trust. Free-rider problems and unpleasant externality costs are minimized under such conditions since the principal economic actors are compelled to internalize possibly negative side-effects of their actions. Full employment and welfare became thus compatible. The Japanese practice of 'corporatism without labour' is an alternative version of the same practice. Vulnerability to the harsh world of international competition is, in contrast, much greater if the principal actors are incapable of mediating conflicting demands. In fact, it may be that Sweden's acute welfare state crisis in the 1990s has less to do with globalization than with the erosion of consensual social partnership. If interest intermediation is not possible, conflict more easily turns into zero-sum trade-offs. And, as we know, the outcome of such trade-offs is that one person's gain is another's loss. We shall return to this issue in the third section of this chapter.

As to the second issue of competitive labour costs, the pressure on the advanced economies is largely limited to low-skilled, labour intensive mass production. Here lies a main source of mass unemployment in Europe and low wages in North America. Rising labour costs in South Korea or Taiwan may provide a respite, but not for long since there is an abundance of even cheaper producers on the horizon. The most acute globalization problem that Europe and North America face may, indeed, be that the market for unskilled labour has become international.

Countries have responded very differently to the globalization of un-qualified labour, and it is here that welfare state differences matter. In the first wave of 'deindustrialization', many countries opted to subsidize their basically uncompetitive textile, steel or shipyard firms. As it became clear that the crisis was permanent rather than cyclical, governments turned to labour supply management. It is in this second wave that differences become marked with, as we have seen, Europe opting for an exit strategy, subsidizing workers to leave the labour market; North America and Britain favouring a wage deregulation strategy, thus bringing down relative wage costs; and Scandinavia stressing a retraining strategy and welfare state jobs, the latter mainly a source of women's employment.

Nowhere, of course, has the response to wage competition been uni-dimensional. North America and Scandinavia have also induced early retirement; Sweden has built up a rather large reservoir of sheltered jobs for redundant, mostly older, workers. And most continental European countries have launched an array of programmes designed to subsidize the employment of long-term unemployed. Our study shows quite clearly that each of these welfare state responses combines benefits and costs in a way which is hardly Pareto optimal.

An American type low-wage approach is positive because it minimizes unemployment and helps integrate youth and immigrants, but it is doubly negative: it implicitly subsidizes low-productivity firms, and it creates huge inequalities. Wage decline will easily exert a downward pressure on welfare state benefits owing to the poverty-trap problem. Hence, there develops a possible self-reinforcing negative spiral that locks a growing population into declining earnings and welfare benefits.

The labour-reduction strategy pursued *par excellence* in continental Europe is arguably positive from the point of view of raising productivity and restoring the competitive position of domestic industry. Generous compensation of the losers means also that growing inequalities are averted. But the downside is that the strategy blocks flexibility and fosters insider–outsider cleavages with mass exclusion. As we have seen, also this model has an inbuilt self-reinforcing negative spiral. In particular, it perpetuates family dependence on the traditional male earner, and prohibits female employment, thereby also wasting a tremendous reserve of human capital. Mass unemployment and exclusion are not a Pareto optimal solution to the dilemma.

At first glance the Nordic approach appears attractive and potentially a positive-sum solution. The problem of the unskilled is managed by a combination of public employment (subsidizing wages) and retraining schemes. Moreover, since public employment occurs in the sheltered, non-tradables sector, uncompetitively high wage costs should be of little consequence: basically, there is no international competition in the provision of day care. This is, however, not true since the financial requirements place a growing tax on the exposed sector and/or mounting public sector deficits.

Are we then unable to escape the trade-off between jobs and equality? There are several reasons why our assessment of the future need not be fatalistic. The first, and probably least convincing, reason is that the economies that so far have taken over unskilled mass production cannot in the long run maintain their low-wage advantage. Full employment in South Korea means also upward pressures on wages. This can be contained under dictatorships but only with great difficulty in a democracy. Also, because of both industrialization and democratization, such countries will be compelled to build more comprehensive social security systems. Hence, international differences in tax levels and wage costs should narrow. However, the problem here is that there is always another latent South Korea. Indeed, the older Asian 'tigers' are now severely threatened by the huge reservoirs of cheap labour in countries such as Thailand and Indonesia and, as in the West, pin their hopes for future growth on high-value-added production.

The second reason is more compelling. The surplus of low-qualified workers that shows up in the unemployment or poverty statistics of North America and Europe might simply be a transitional welfare problem. With the passage of time it might go away as the older unskilled cohorts die out. The burning questions are whether and if this will happen. A historical parallel may here be in order. In the postwar era, most of Europe and North America experienced a similar mass surplus of unskilled workers released from agriculture. Then, unlike now, they were easily absorbed on the (well-paid) industrial assembly lines. Some countries today face the unique problem that mass deruralization coincides with a decline in labour intensive mass production: Spain's extremely high levels of unemployment may very well be caused by such unfortunate timing. How, in other words, can we ensure that the unskilled will gradually disappear?

The obvious answer lies in education and training. As we know, the downward wage pressure is mainly directed at the unskilled and, indeed, the relative wage premium for qualified workers has risen considerably. It is for this reason that 'lifelong learning' and 'social investment' strategies offer a possibly positive-sum solution to the trade-off. Indeed, they do so for two reasons: firstly, because a universalization of training will eventually eliminate the surplus of unskilled workers; secondly, because even if postindustrial society is bound to offer a large amount of inferior low-paid jobs in consumer and social services, such jobs will not become life cycle traps if citizens are guaranteed the chance to acquire adequate skills. In brief, a Pareto optimal welfare state of the future might very well be one that shifts the accent of social citizenship from its present preoccupation with income maintenance towards a menu of rights to *lifelong* education and qualification.

A major problem with the design of postwar welfare states was that they pursued 'equal opportunity' more through income maintenance than through labour supply management. The reason is not difficult to identify: most countries suffered from labour shortages, some to the point of being compelled to import Third World labourers; the low-skilled had steady, well-paid jobs. Of course, all countries vastly expanded their education systems, but they did so without altering inherited inter-generational differentials. Thus, as is well known, schooling today – as before – replicates privilege and underprivilege from generation to generation. This means that children of unskilled parents or welfare mothers today are very likely to become yet another unemployment, low-wage or, especially in the United States, prison-inmate statistic. A 'social investment' type of welfare state might therefore opt for some degree of targeted human capital guarantees.

The philosophy behind a 'social investment' strategy is not revolutionary. It has been part and parcel of the Swedish social democratic model for decades; it is official rhetoric in the Clinton administration; and it constitutes the major strategy with which the Asian tigers today seek to respond to global competition. In fact, 'active labour market policies' have become a social policy buzzword just about everywhere. Nonetheless, even in Sweden active labour market policies appear shipwrecked. Why?

Some sceptics argue that training is meaningless when there are not enough jobs to go round. Their remedy is job-sharing (via reduced working hours) or a guaranteed minimum income. But this is not a particularly compelling argument if, as in the United States, a massive job expansion is possible via low wages. Hence, the question turns to *what* kind of training and for *whom*. The problem with the Swedish model is that additional job growth in the private and public sector is precluded owing to high labour costs, in some cases exceeding the marginal productivity of workers. Hence, greater wage differentiation is probably unavoidable. A second problem may be that Swedish active training programmes have assumed for too long a traditional industry-led economy demanding very specific, and quite limited, skill levels. An amazing fact that emerges from international statistics is that Sweden lags substantially behind its competitors in terms of average levels of schooling. The lack of significant monetary returns to additional education has probably been one cause; another can be attributed to the principles of active training programmes. In brief, even Sweden must learn to develop a 'social investment' strategy that addresses the needs of a postindustrial economy.

Because 'social investment' and 'lifelong learning' appear so attractive from a policy-making point of view, there is the great danger that they are allowed to become a substitute for traditional redistributive income maintenance. Clearly, many contemporary welfare states have pushed the income maintenance strategy to its upper limits; Southern Europe in particular. On one point both the new ultra-liberals and the old Swedish social democrats can agree: income maintenance should be 'productivistic' and linked to work, not a means to encourage passivity. The ultra-liberals, echoing a nineteenth century Manchester School ideology, pursue this aim by punishing the idle. The social democrats, at least in Scandinavia, pursue the same aim by aiding, with transfers and services, the idle to become active. Hence, in Sweden 90 per cent of single mothers work, although usually at reduced hours. Combined with Sweden's strong transfer system, the result is that these families command a level of resources that is hardly at variance with the population mean. Since we know that poverty and deprivation in childhood are good predictors of the same in adulthood, a generously subsidized workfare of the Swedish kind would seem cost-effective from the point of view of investing in the future.

Postindustrial society is characterized by declining marital stability and by women's desire to work. That they do work is also desirable for society at large. If this is so, we face a new set of challenges in terms of how to ensure higher fertility, family well-being, and adequate human capital resources within future generations. A positive-sum welfare state strategy for the future must include a network of strong guarantees that allows women to work and have children without being penalized.

In Europe it is feared that globalization and deregulation will lead to 'social dumping'. As capital moves to countries with a lower social wage and, hence, more competitive labour costs, the more generous welfare states will be forced to downgrade their standards. As we have already noted, a large number of traditional, labour intensive industries have already for decades moved out of the advanced economies, and there is no compelling argument for trying to keep them. In fact, if global development is a goal, there are good reasons to continue promoting this trend. In essence, once again, social dumping is a risk that is primarily addressed to low-skilled workers in the advanced economies. And if this is so, do we really desire a welfare state dedicated to maintaining an army of low-skilled workers? A positive-sum policy, it seems, would be one that proactively eliminates skill deficiencies, and thereby makes its workforce immune to cheaper competitors.

The equality problem

We should not confuse the welfare state with equality. Of course, it is not possible to imagine a welfare state that does not, in some way or another, redistribute incomes and resources. Whether it is a one-way redistribution from rich to poor is another matter. Social insurance is a mechanism of life-course or inter-cohort redistribution and, as is now well established, huge areas of welfare state activity – especially in education and the services – are probably of greatest benefit to the middle classes. We do know that comprehensive, universalistic and generous welfare states of the Scandinavian type are considerably more egalitarian in outcome than others, whether we measure this in terms of poverty rates or Gini coefficients. And, completely contrary to common wisdom, it is also well established that systems which target narrowly to the most needy perform rather badly in terms of redistribution or poverty eradication.

Welfare states, in fact, pursue different conceptions of equality. The social democratic model in Scandinavia is characteristic for its emphasis on universalistic egalitarianism – no one is special and no one should be excluded – and for its guarantee of adequate *resources* to all. In a way this means that income redistribution is the derivative of a much broader effort to ensure that all households have command over the bundle of resources deemed necessary in order to function in society the way everyone else does. This is a notion of equality that goes far beyond just money.

An inbuilt weakness of policies that pursue equality of result is that they may provoke perceptions of unfairness – of *inequity* ('why should someone who never worked get the same as I, who did?'). The Scandinavian model has, for long, been able to contain equity battles for two reasons: firstly, its universalism and favourable treatment of the middle classes; and secondly, its 'productivistic' emphasis (everybody in fact works).

The typical European (and South East Asian) social insurance model emphasizes equity over redistribution. Since the primary goal is status continuity, differentials in working life should ideally be carried over in income maintenance. Elite workers enjoy elite services (the civil service especially) while those strata with a weak labour force status tend to be treated as 'second-rate' social citizens; as a result, they have fairly high poverty risks. These welfare systems enjoy an enviable level of broad legitimacy because most programmes emphasize equity.

Residual welfare states, such as the American, also emphasize equity, but more an individualistic equity of earned rewards in the market-place, and equity in the sense of limiting non-contributory benefits to the deserving poor: hence, the prevalence of strictly targeting public resources to the really needy. Targeting scarce resources is an approach that enjoys enthusiastic support within the oddest coalition imaginable: it is often popular among traditionalist working class constituencies and within neo-liberal circles, the IMF included. It makes basic sense to the worker because it suggests taxing back the 'surplus value' from capitalists; it makes sense to IMF economists because in this way scarce resources seem most efficiently employed (the 'biggest bang for the buck').

We know that both are wrong. Narrow targeting is, generally speaking, inefficient because it is administratively costly, because it typically fails in its objective of securing adequate welfare to those in need, and because it nurtures poverty traps.

Ironically, targeted programmes are especially vulnerable to battles over equity since, almost by definition, redistribution goes exclusively to those who contribute very little and maybe nothing. Hence, as is very much the case in contemporary America, citizens and voters can easily be persuaded to support a radical erosion of social assistance programmes – but not a roll-back in more universal programmes, such as pensions or Medicare. There is a case to be made in favour of targeting. The Australian approach suggests that if the net is very wide and if eligibility is assessed via innocuous tax returns rather than stigmatizing means-tests, selectivity can be both efficient and legitimate.

The case for private welfare can be made on the grounds that it reduces public expenditure burdens, offers greater choice, and induces aggregate savings, but hardly on the grounds that it is egalitarian. It is also doubtful whether it can be genuinely equitable since it is typically discriminatory (workers in large strong enterprises are favoured while similar workers in small companies are not), and since it is vulnerable to information failure problems: people will never be equally capable of shopping for the best welfare deal.

Regardless of approach, a common characteristic of the contemporary welfare state is that its concept of equality is in a double crisis. The first, and possibly most severe, has to do with the historical transformation that the concept itself has undergone. Early social reform was closely tied to the 'working class question' – the poverty, insecurity, and misery that large sections of the working class found themselves in. During the postwar consolidation of what we, today, call the welfare state emerged the ideal of universal social citizenship and equalization of living conditions. Yet, everywhere, research in the 1950s and 1960s brought to public attention the astonishing fact that huge inequalities and heavy poverty remained, welfare state notwithstanding. New redistributive and egalitarian claims emerged now less from the working class and more from 'new' social groups. Some, such as pensioners, were the creations of the welfare state itself; others, like women and minorities, had simply been left out.

The new welfare state egalitarianism that emerged in the 1960s became increasingly fixated on equality 'for all, here and now'. This translated into privileged treatment of hitherto ignored, discriminated, or disadvantaged strata. The approach differed, as is evident in a simple contrast between the American combination of affirmative action and War on Poverty and the Scandinavian emphasis on equalizing resources and labour market chances. It is arguable that the Scandinavian welfare states avoided an 'equality backlash' because of their greater universalism and because their affirmative policies mainly addressed the broadly legitimate (and 'productivistic') claim for women's economic independence. Nonetheless, the welfare states' new conception of egalitarianism provoked an acceleration not only of social spending, but also of equity tensions.

The crisis that the advanced welfare states now face is almost certainly linked to their projection of a set of egalitarian principles that no longer command broad consensus. On the one hand, a traditionalist 'workerist' egalitarianism continues to dominate much social policy thinking. The reference for universalism, for example, is pretty much the blue collar mass worker. On the other hand, welfare states find themselves increasingly unable to manage an equality 'for all, here and now' as mass unemployment reduces revenues and raises costs and, as the United States demonstrates, because egalitarianism of the concerted affirmative action type provokes increasingly bitter equity battles while, at the same time, it induces a seemingly unstoppable rise of claims for preferential treatment.

Welfare states have to rethink their egalitarian principles in a radical way: firstly because societies may be becoming too differentiated and heterogeneous; secondly, because it is difficult to see how we can avoid growing inequalities of pay and final incomes (due to family change, for one). The most logical solution that presents itself is that we rethink the idea of redistribution and rights: accepting inequalities for some, here and now, but guaranteeing at the same time that those who fare less well 'here and now' will not always do so; that underprivilege will not be a permanent fixture of anyone's life course. This kind of dynamic, life-chances commitment to equality is arguably a positive-sum solution in that it stresses a social policy more explicitly designed to optimize the self-reliant capacities of the citizenry. Again, the core of such a model's social citizenship guarantees would combine education and proactive income maintenance.

There is another and somewhat less visible 'crisis' of equality that is especially acute in the two most diametrically opposite welfare state models: the hyper-egalitarian Swedish, and the narrowly targeted American. In both cases, the redistributive system is a fetter on the kind of comprehensive and universal human capital upgrading that post-industrial societies need. Sweden's welfare state combines egalitarianism with strong incentives to work. This appears at first glance optimal, but what counts is participation as such, not how much. From left to right, most analysts of the Swedish model now concur that the extremely egalitarian wage (and social wage) structure gives disincentives to work additional hours, or to augment skills and education: the marginal wage gain is simply too low. In fact, comparatively speaking Sweden suffers from an undersupply of skilled, educated workers. Hence, to repeat, if the major threat of globalization is concentrated within the less skilled population, and if this is where the 'social dumping' problem lies, the maximization of human capital must take priority to egalitarianism 'here and now'.

In the American model, the problem is surely not one of excessive across-the-board equality. Instead, it is the poverty-trap problem that targeting nurtures. The downward pressure on low-skilled workers' wages produces severe poverty traps unless also social transfers decline precipitously. In fact, both unemployment and social assistance benefits have eroded over the past two decades. But given that full-time minimum wage employment results in earnings below poverty level, the emasculation of the social safety net would have to be very harsh indeed. In brief, the American wage-setting and social transfer nexus easily produces a downward spiral of emiseration and disincentives to work or improve skills. The result is, as we know, a polarization of not only incomes but also of human capital.

Taking away the benefits (and even children) of welfare mothers is the preferred solution on the right. The left, in this case the Clinton administration, pursues a policy that combines guarantees of subsidized day care with induced training.

The political problem

The politics of the welfare state are, for obvious reasons, usually shunned in the reports and analyses that international organizations produce. Yet, the welfare state is the child of politics and so, also, will be its future. It is, indeed, when we bring in the political dimension that we are most inclined to conclude that the welfare state is here to stay.

Superficially, there are many factors which would suggest otherwise. Some of the principal forces that built the welfare state seem now to have lost ground – notably trade unions and social democratic parties, but to a degree also Christian democracy. As they have weakened so have neo-corporatist institutions and the capacity for broad, nation-wide social pacts. And, writing in the mid 1990s, it seems odd that ten or fifteen years ago most people believed that a 10 per cent rate of unemployment would surely unleash major revolts, perhaps even revolution. Yet, the citizens of Europe have come to accept the normalcy of chronic two-digit unemployment levels. Even the Swedes, with their almost religious adherence to full employment, seem resigned to a future with EC-level unemployment rates.

The fact of the matter, however, is that the alignment of political forces conspires just about everywhere to maintain the existing principles of the welfare state. This means that cutting occurs at the margin, that trimming is largely limited to the 'fat'. What is even more surprising is that this holds for rightist as well as leftist governments. Indeed, there is a case to be made that the right has been more loyal to the existing edifice than has the left.

The landscape of the advanced welfare states is composed of two great political failures. Firstly, even where the neo-liberal onslaught was strongest and most concerted, the result was surprisingly few victories. The solid majorities of the long Thatcher era may have tamed an expansion of the welfare state that otherwise might have occurred, but they dismantled very little. Some public housing was privatized, and public pensions became less generous. Similarly, the Reagan era brought about little change in the edifice of the American system; erosion occurred in the more residual programmes.[1] The second great failure is exemplified by the *non-emergence* of viable political coalitions capable of persuading, or willing to persuade, electorates and powerful interest groups to support an alternative, recast welfare state. Eschewing radical change, the politics of retrenchment can best be described as efforts to save the existing system by going on the least unpleasant diet on the menu. Let us examine more closely why this is so.

Public choice economists provide one very persuasive answer. They point to the mutual complicity in favour of the status quo that welfare state bureaucrats and clients foster. Even residual or service-lean welfare states employ a large proportion of the labour force; the Scandinavian public sector accounts for a third. These are also powerful, professionalized and highly organized lobbies. Ministers and governments come and go, the administrators remain. As a huge political science literature has shown, much of the really decisive policy-making occurs in bureaucracies, not in parliaments.

The welfare state clients may be equally, perhaps more, important. If the middle classes benefit from social security, it is difficult to imagine how they can be persuaded to support its abolition. It is exactly this which blocked the roll-back efforts of the Reagan and Thatcher administrations. In the former case, even the hint of weakening social security pensions provoked a storm of protest; in the latter case, the proposal to privatize national health care was shipwrecked. It is worth emphasizing that, in both cases, these radical measures occurred against the backdrop of a severely weakened trade union movement and a similarly emasculated left. Welfare states not only serve citizens, but also construct political alignments.

A second persuasive answer is that the mechanisms of broad neo-corporatist consensus-building are substantially more resilient than is widely believed. Unions may have weakened, and employer confederations may continue to prefer that they would vanish altogether. Yet, in most of Europe at least, comprehensive interest organizations can still insist that a bargained consensus is preferable to instability. At the micro-level, too, there is much evidence to suggest that employers are reluctant to sacrifice a stable environment of harmonious social partnership for the goal of maximum flexibilization. Hence, as our study has shown, the more success-ful welfare state cutback policies have almost invariably been implemented through broad, comprehensive deals with the main social partners. This is true for the quite successful liberalization strategy in Australia, for the German pension reform, and for the succession of increasingly severe cutbacks in the Swedish welfare state, including the most cherished pro-grammes such as pensions, sickness absence and parental leave.

The evolution of pension reform in Italy during 1994–5 provides perhaps the most telling evidence of why welfare state cutbacks may not only necessitate neo-corporatist deals, but may even revitalize neo-corporatism itself. Committed to act forcibly, the Berlusconi government's struggle to reduce the public deficit included a major overhaul of the pension system, disguised inside the annual budget proposal. While most would have agreed that Italy's pension system was out of control and in need of a radical overhaul, the attempt led to the government's fall – in main part because it was incapable of neo-corporatist consensus-building on the issue. The subsequent Dini caretaker government opted for the latter and succeeded (by and large) in producing a reform that will gradually bring Italy's pension system in line with mainstream practice. New Zealand is, as far as we can tell, a truly exceptional case that hardly warrants generalization.

In sum, within the advanced industrial democracies the contemporary politics of the welfare state is a politics of the status quo. This is less the case where welfare states are embryonic. The East Asian 'Confucian' familialistic welfare model appears to be under much more strain, and it is difficult to imagine how it will survive for long in its present shape. What alternative model will emerge is equally difficult to imagine. Latin America as a whole is now rapidly abandoning the traditional corporativistic principles that formed part and parcel of economic protectionism. But here there is not one, but two trends under way. The proto-social-democratic path taken by Costa Rica and Brazil hardly appears viable considering contemporary economic conditions, but neither is it particularly likely that a Chilean-style privatization approach will be able to stem a rise in public sector welfare in the longer run. East and Central Europe is clearly the most under-defined region, a virtual laboratory of experimentation. If it is at all possible to generalize, there is at least one clear trend: where neo-liberal welfare policies (often inspired by the Chilean model) were pursued most vigorously, they were punished in subsequent democratic elections. As in Western Europe, where cutback policies seem to revitalize neo-corporatism, so neo-liberal welfare policies in Eastern Europe seem to revitalize socialism.

As a way of concluding, one can therefore say that the cards are very much stacked in favour of the welfare state status quo. There are, accordingly, grounds for optimism for those who adhere to its principles. This is nonetheless quite problematic since, as our study indicates, a major overhaul of the existing welfare state edifice must occur if it is meant to produce a positive-sum kind of welfare for postindustrial society. The vast popular majorities in favour of the welfare state that opinion polls and election results regularly identify are essentially conservative ones because they rely on, and wish to perpetuate, a benefit structure that was put in place more than a generation ago. The political problem today is how to forge coalitions for an alternative, postindustrial model of social citizenship and egalitarianism.

Note

1 This discussion parallels and borrows much from Pierson's (1994; 1995) excellent work on the politics of cutbacks.

References

Pierson, P. (1994) *Dismantling the Welfare State?* Cambridge: Cambridge University Press.
Pierson, P. (1995) 'The new politics of the welfare state'. Zentrum fur Sozialpolitik Arbeitspapier, no. 3.

Index